BARBARA FOLEY

Spectres of 1919

CLASS AND NATION IN THE

MAKING OF THE NEW NEGRO

UNIVERSITY OF ILLINOIS PRESS

URBANA AND CHICAGO

Library of Congress Cataloging-in-Publication Data
Foley, Barbara, 1948–
Spectres of 1919 : class and nation in the making of the
new Negro / Barbara Foley.
p.   cm.
Includes bibliographical references and index.
ISBN 0-252-02846-5 (cloth : acid-free paper)
1. African Americans—Intellectual life—20th century.
2. African Americans—Politics and government—20th
century. 3. Right and left (Political science)—History—
20th century. 4. Radicalism—United States—History—
20th century. 5. Black nationalism—United States—
History—20th century. 6. New Negro. 7. American
literature—African American authors—History and
criticism. 8. African Americans—Social conditions—To
1964. 9. United States—Race relations—Political aspects.
10. Racism—Political aspects—United States—History—
20th century. I. Title.
E185.6.F65   2003
973'.0496073—dc21   2002155079

Contents

Preface

The year 1919 has for some time had a particular resonance for me. John Dos Passos, about whom I long ago wrote a Ph.D. dissertation, named the second volume of his extraordinary *U.S.A.* trilogy after this critical juncture. As both a leftist who came of age in the late 1960s and a scholar who increasingly focused on African American literature, I became aware that the so-called Red Summer of 1919—signifying at once the political repression of leftists and the bloody suppression of black rebellion—marked a moment in the struggle for human liberation in the United States when the issues of class and race were so closely linked that they could—and can—be separated only by a perverse act of will. It was when I began probing into the archive of wartime and postwar New Negro journalism, however, that I came to appreciate the full extent to which 1919 functioned as a revolutionary crucible, definitively shaping not just self-proclaimed radicals but many mainstream participants in and observers of history in the making. Although the radical movement subsided—and, as Dos Passos was to put it, the bankers "took a deep breath" while the "bediamonded old ladies of the leisure class went back to clipping their coupons in the refined quiet of their safe-deposit vaults"[1]—the spectre of revolution continued to haunt the United States for some time. Even Alain Locke's *New Negro* (1925), which is commonly held to have wrested leadership of the New Negro movement away from the radicals and placed it firmly in the hands of the culturalists, showed in its various drafts multiple efforts to efface the burrowings of the old mole of revolution. Hence my appropriation of Marx's rhetoric of 1849 for the conjuncture of some seventy years later: the warning issued in *The Com-*

munist Manifesto echoed loudly—as a challenge to some, a warning to others—in the wake of the World War I, the Bolshevik Revolution, and the Red Summer of 1919.

Spectres of 1919 aims to contribute to the growing body of revisionary scholarship testifying to the significant involvement of African Americans in leftist politics, which remains to this day one of the best-kept secrets of U.S. history. This study also takes a position in debates over race, class, and nation that, largely originating in the crucible of 1919, have continued to shape political activism and cultural production to this day. In particular, it queries the efficacy of nationalism—whether cultural pluralist nationalism, self-determinationist nationalism, or ethnic or race-based nationalism—as a means to emancipate those bearing the yoke of oppression and exploitation. I lend support to the argument that nationalism may well turn out to have been the Achilles heel of twentieth-century mass movements for liberation. Even as I highlight the importance of postwar African American radicalism in understanding the politics, activist and cultural, of the 1920s and beyond, I thus focus on the ways in which that radicalism at once opened up and delimited the potential for a fundamentally transformative politics.

While *Spectres of 1919* has been guided partly by political and historical concerns beyond the realm of the literary, it is centrally concerned with questions of discourse and trope. It bears mentioning here that this study was first conceived as a context-setting discussion of a study of Jean Toomer, whose masterwork *Cane* (1923) is often viewed as the first significant text of the Harlem Renaissance. As so often happens with projects of this kind, the "background" discussion mushroomed into an investigation and an argument in its own right; while I expect to follow up this volume with two additional volumes treating the life and work of Toomer, *Spectres of 1919* now has a being entirely apart from the author of *Cane*. The examination of the trope of roots and soil that will focus my discussion of Toomer is prepared for here, however, in my formulation of a strategy of representation, both political and discursive, that I am calling "metonymic nationalism," which I find useful in approaching the connection between ideology and image in much writing of the Harlem Renaissance.

Briefly, *metonymic nationalism* refers to a practice of establishing a claim to legitimacy and belonging through a series of linkages that posits the nation at one end, black folks at the other, and soil and region in between the two. In a society that was dominated by the nativist rhetoric of "100 percent Americanism" and the evolutionist rhetoric of eugenics and denied African Americans the most basic rights as citizens, the cultural pluralist assertion that African Americans might "stand for" the nation as ably as any other group—that they might figure metonymically to signify the whole—clearly was intended to combat disenfranchisement and bigotry. What I argue, however, is that this insistence on the "soilness" and "rootedness" of black folks did not entirely refute the arguments of the racists but instead ended up reproducing various features of the dominant ideology by reinforcing essentialist notions of racial difference. A purportedly antiracist nationalism thus conjoined with the nationalism of 100 percent Americanism. But there are also salient connections between metonymic nationalism and the doctrine of revolutionary self-determination embraced by many on the contemporaneous Left, of various races and nations. To the extent that not just cultural pluralist liberals but also leftists embraced the doctrine of progressive nationalism as a necessary stage in the movement toward internationalism and classlessness, the responsibility for this inability to negate and supersede current thinking about race must be broadly shared.

Spectres of 1919 combines archival investigation with political theory, literary criticism with intellectual history. While it is written from a leftist standpoint, it does not assume prior agreement on the part of its readers but instead aims to illuminate a period and offer a line of interpretation. Chapter 1 treats the potential for revolutionary change that was opened by the radical insurgencies of the postwar period, when a class—or at least "economic"—analysis of racism enjoyed currency among a broad range of liberals and progressives, white as well as African American. Although Locke's 1925 anthology would assert that the participants in the New Negro movement were "forced radicals," the record proves otherwise. Chapter 2 explores the limitations of the theory and practice of the Left—Socialists and fledgling Communists alike—regarding the linkages between and among race, class, and nation. Not just Socialist economism and racism but also an underestimation of the role of ideology and an insufficiently critical endorsement of nationalism by all leftist formations inhibited the development of a revolutionary analysis of racism and race.

In chapter 3, I shift my inquiry from contradictions within New Negro radicalism to outside constraints. The discourses of nativism and eugenics raced radicalism and radicalized race, with the goal of legitimating not only immigrant exclusion but also the extension of the one-drop rule. New Negro cultural nationalism was thus a defensive response not just to inherited U.S. racist doctrines but, more specifically, to the racist antiradicalism galvanized by the events of 1919. Chapter 4 examines the counterdiscourses by which leftists and progressives of the day sought to seize

the master's tools to dismantle the master's house—if only to end up, too
frequently, reoccupying the premises. My inquiry culminates in chapter
5 with a consideration of the metamorphosis of the New Negro radicalism of 1919 into the quietism of Locke's culturalist manifesto of 1925.

———————

I am grateful to the following friends, colleagues, academic associates, and family members for numerous insights, reactions, corrections,
and research leads: Patricia Carter, Martin Davis, Anthony Dawahare,
Peter Foley, Grover Furr, Marcial Gonzalez, Neil Larsen, James A. Mil-
ler, William Maxwell, Bill Mullen, Richard Ohmann, Leo Parascondola,
Adam Stevens, Houston Stevens, Margaret Stevens, and Alan Wald. I have
benefited from lecture and conference interchanges with Faith Berry,
Jamie Owen Daniel, Rich Daniels, Keith Danner, Madhu Dubey, Nathan
Grant, Patricia Keeton, Amitava Kumar, Jerry Phillips, the late Michael
Sprinker, Jonathan Sterne, Laura Sullivan, Hap Veeser, and Mary Helen
Washington. A number of my colleagues at Rutgers–Newark—especially Fran Bartkowski, H. Bruce Franklin, Charles Russell, S. Shankar, and
Virginia Tiger—have influenced my thinking about literature in general
and the New Negro movement in particular. I learned much from the
graduate and undergraduate students in my classes on the Harlem Renaissance, African American literature, Marxist theory, and the American
1920s. The library staff at Rutgers's Dana Library was most creative, persistent, and helpful; I especially thank Veronica Calderhead, Carolyn
Foote, Dorothy Grauer, and Natalie Borisovits. David Roediger provided
astute criticism and commentary, as did the other (anonymous) reader
for the University of Illinois Press. Willis Regier, the director of the press,
patiently oversaw the reorganization of this project into its present form;
Jane Mohraz approached the work of editing with extraordinary rigor and
care. Jake Kawatski produced a fine index.

I wish to dedicate *Spectres of 1919* to Gregory Myerson, my foremost
intellectual friend and coconspirator, whose encyclopedic knowledge and
unfailing political radicalism have continually challenged me to reexam-
ine my formulations and conclusions and reminded me that reality is
both complex and concrete.

SPECTRES OF 1919

1 The New Negro and the Left

> This is an era of war and revolution, of struggle and
> revision, of contest and change.
> —Masthead, *Modernist,* 1919

Writing in *The New Negro* in 1925, Alain Locke was purportedly describing a self-evident state of affairs when he proclaimed that the
"deep feeling of race" currently being manifested as the "mainspring of
Negro life" is "radical in tone, but not in purpose" and that "only the
most stupid forms of opposition, misunderstanding or persecution could
make it otherwise." Although, Locke conceded, "the thinking Negro has
shifted a little toward the left with the world-trend, and there is an increasing group who affiliate with radical and liberal movements," at
present "the Negro is radical on race matters, conservative on others, in
other words, a 'forced radical,' a social protestant rather than a genuine
radical." The "Negro mind"—a unitary phenomenon for which Locke
presumably felt privileged to speak—"reaches out as yet to nothing but
American wants, American ideas." Even the Negro's attempt to "build
his Americanism on race values," while a "unique social experiment,"
entailed "no limitation or reservation with respect to American life." It
actually constituted a realization of Americanism: "Democracy itself is
obstructed and stagnated to the extent that any of its channels are
closed. . . . So the choice is not between one way for the Negro and another way for the rest, but between American institutions frustrated on
the one hand and American ideals progressively fulfilled and realized on
the other." By "now becom[ing] a conscious contributor and lay[ing] aside
the status of a beneficiary and ward for that of a collaborator and partic-

ipant in American civilization," the New Negro accomplished, for Locke, two things: he or she moved beyond "the arid fields of controversy and debate"—presumably in large part over political and economic questions—and toward "the productive fields of creative expression." The zone of culture—where "race values" would be explored in the spirit of pluralism, not separatism—thus supplied an antidote to the radicalism that might otherwise move from "tone" to "purpose." The culturalist project embodied in *The New Negro* was indissolubly linked with both antiradicalism and American nationalism.[1]

Beneath its bravado, however, Locke's formulation of the New Negro movement rested on somewhat unsteady underpinnings. His admission that "an increasing group . . . affiliate with radical and liberal movements" hardly squared with his assertion that this affiliation was not to be taken seriously. Moreover, there was a veiled threat in Locke's assertion that "Harlem's quixotic radicalisms call for their ounce of democracy to-day lest to-morrow they be beyond cure." As Anthony Dawahare reads between Locke's lines, "U.S. political and economic rulers must legally recognize the rights of blacks to be offered what American capitalism has to offer, or else they may face some form of revolution." Nonetheless, Locke's normative definition of the New Negro movement as above all a cultural movement, simultaneously Negro nationalist and American nationalist, has been taken as not canon-forming but canonical by many of the literary critics and cultural historians commenting on the New Negro movement/Harlem Renaissance. From John Hope Franklin's 1947 assertion that "the writers of the Harlem Renaissance . . . gave little attention to the propaganda of the socialists and communists" to the more recent absence of New Negro leftism in accounts by Ann Douglas, Steven Watson, Mark Helbling, Michael North, and J. Martin Favor, most investigations of the movement have reduced its radical critique—when it is mentioned at all—to postwar militancy. After a brief nod to African American self-defense in the 1919 race riots and a perfunctory citation of Claude McKay's "If We Must Die," these accounts usually move rapidly from the assertion of a new selfhood in the zone of the streets to the articulation of a new discursive practice in the zone of representation. Chidi Ikonné and Robert Bone, who emphasize the movement's engagements with primitivism and pastoralism, relegate any consideration of radical politics to the margins. Even the canon-challenging studies of women Harlem Renaissance writers by Cheryl Wall, Gloria Hull, and Claudia Tate, which have reconfigured the gendered lineaments of the movement in significant ways, remain silent about the left-wing sympathies of the important African American women writers they treat.

Cary Wintz's recent volumes recovering many scattered and ignored texts of the Harlem Renaissance further codify the prevalent notion of the Harlem Renaissance as a purely aesthetic movement by occluding all radical voices from this—presumably exhaustive—archival project. Houston Baker, who views the progenitor of the New Negro modernists as none other than that most subversive of all tricksters, Booker T. Washington, limits the radicalism of African American modernism to cagey linguistic subversion: McKay's deployment of the sonnet form to oppositional ends, more than his call for class-conscious and anticolonial rebellion, constitutes the core of his politics. Walter Kalaidjian celebrates the supersession of class-based political radicalism by racial, gender, and sexual proto-identity politics. Robert Stepto and Carla Cappetti, while offering important critiques of the view that the New Negro movement should be unproblematically associated with Harlem or dubbed a "renaissance," do not regard exploration of its political origins as relevant to its reconfiguration. Even critics offering long-overdue revisionary views of the movement's interracialism—Douglas and North, Eric Sundquist, and, most signally, George Hutchinson—discern no significant connections between the unprecedented intermingling of whites and blacks in the early 1920s and the Left's call for class-based multiracial unity. As far as these accounts are concerned, the historical crucible of 1919 was important to the origins of the New Negro movement/Harlem Renaissance primarily for hastening African American migration to the North, with all the dramatic developments that this demographic shift entailed. The revolutionary politics shaping both discourse and practice during this era of global war and revolution would appear to have been, as Locke opined, largely irrelevant to the culturalist movement that, from its hesitant postwar beginnings, gained momentum after the 1923 publication of Jean Toomer's *Cane* and culminated in the publication of Locke's anthology two years later.[2]

The prevailing notion that the New Negro movement was from the start a cultural phenomenon, only peripherally influenced by leftist politics, has always been controversial. Some commentators have viewed the Harlem Renaissance's eventual culturalist emphasis as the product of a struggle that culminated in an outright betrayal of the movement's initial commitment to a Left-inflected political praxis. Nathan Huggins, targeting the corrupting influence of thrill-seeking white patrons, laments that the "militant and self-assertive" New Negro movement of the postwar years was doomed to be "shattered" because of its "naive assumptions about the centrality of culture, unrelated to economic and social realities." Theodore Kornweibel argues that the term *New Negro* originally designated "the attitude of militance that had been born in the war and nurtured in the 'Red Summer' of 1919"; he particularly associates it with such figures as the *Messenger* editors A. Philip Randolph and Chandler Owen, who, he argues, viewed the cultural issues that would preoccupy their successors as a distraction from the economic and political changes forming the core of the New Negro's historic task. Theodore Vincent declares that the New Negro movement was simply hijacked by conservatives. "The term 'New Negro' was originated by political radicals as a means of distinguishing themselves from traditional black leadership" but was "gradually co-opted by that very middle class which by radical definition was 'Old Negro,'" he writes. "Blacks who denounced radicals of all stripes commercialized the concept into a distinction between 'new' aggressive individualists who capitalized on the social changes that came with the move to the city, and the lethargic Negro of the Old South." David Levering Lewis, regarding the aesthetes of the post-1925 years as undeserving heirs to the legacy of the wartime and postwar New Negro rebels, adjudges the Harlem Renaissance "a somewhat forced phenomenon, a cultural nationalism of the parlor, institutionally encouraged and directed by leaders of the national civil rights establishment for the paramount purpose of improving race relations in a time of extreme national backlash." The Talented Tenth, in Lewis's view, reacted to the extreme violence and repression of the Red Summer of 1919 by "jump-start[ing]" a movement that "sublimated" African American revolutionary energies into textual—and therefore safe—channels of expression. Lewis's useful periodization of the Harlem Renaissance into the years 1919–23 and 1924–28 is premised on his estimate of the moment when this sublimation became definitive. For Huggins, Kornweibel, and Lewis, culturalism implies conservatism; the focus on aesthetic representation in the Harlem Renaissance of the mid- to late 1920s presupposed an overt rejection of the political radicalism informing the New Negro movement of the wartime and immediate postwar years.[3]

Some of the scholars who applaud the New Negro's mid-1920s emergence as culture hero acknowledge the movement's roots in postwar radicalism and emphasize Locke's formative role in its transmutation. Henry Louis Gates grants that the "mythological and primitivistic defense of the racial self that was the basis of the literary movement which we call the New Negro, or Harlem Renaissance" derived from the "aggressive self-defense" of the postwar period. "Locke's appropriation of the name in 1925 for his literary movement represents a measured cooptation of the term," he points out, from Randolph's earlier use of it to describe the "militant, card-carrying, gun-toting Socialist who refused to turn the other cheek."

Even though Gates's own focus on the vernacular tradition as central to African American letters draws, to some degree, on this same "mythological and primitivistic defense of the racial self," he grants that the debate over the identity of the New Negro initially went beyond the realm of letters. Arnold Rampersad, in his introduction to the 1992 reissue of Locke's text, observes that "[a] sense of the economic underpinnings of society" is largely absent from the anthology and that "[r]adical socialism is given short shrift." Locke's text "helped Harlem turn its back even more firmly on radical social movements," writes Rampersad. "[T]he unity suggested by *The New Negro* was mainly a front presented to the world." Gates and Rampersad remind us that Locke's anthology signifies less a recognition of the New Negro's arrival as interpreter of black modernity than an attempt—and a politically conservative one at that—to bring a certain version of that modernity into being. In their readings, Harlem Renaissance culturalism is the inverse of New Negro radicalism; the supersession of the latter by the former involves not a dialectic of transmutation but a process of takeover, eradication, and obliteration.[4]

Still another critical school argues that the New Negro's devolution into culture hero is itself largely a literary-historical myth, produced mainly by scholars who have ignored substantial evidence of a continuing radical strain in African American literature of the 1920s. Faith Berry has persuasively demonstrated that Langston Hughes's lifelong commitment to political radicalism, while peaking in the 1930s, began in the early 1920s and is continually visible in his work. Focusing on the central role played by McKay, James A. Miller has cautioned against viewing the Harlem Renaissance as, in Clyde Taylor's words, the "'happy hour of black literary and historical studies'"; McKay's political radicalism was, Miller argues, not anomalous but typical of a substantial segment of the movement's participants. William Maxwell proposes that Locke's 1925 manifesto be read not as coup de grace to a moribund New Negro radicalism but instead as a failed effort to displace a leftist politics that was influential throughout the decade. "It is only the immense rhetorical and institutional success of Locke's wrestling match with his predecessors that has permitted us to forget that the Harlem Renaissance outlined in *The New Negro* represents a stab at rearticulation," argues Maxwell. "The anthology is neither the originary moment nor the final truth of the postwar black renaissance, but—among many other things—a polemical attempt to reconfigure this renaissance according to a less radical design." Examining such hitherto neglected writers as the radical poet Andrea Razafkeriefo and reminding us of the persisting leftism of Hughes and McKay, Maxwell argues that anticapitalism and proletarian internation-

alism influenced African American writers throughout the 1920s. That
the literary proletarianism of the 1930s constituted a continuation of,
rather than a reaction to, the left-wing cultural production of the previous decade is a crucial corollary to these revisionary historians, for whom
culturalism exists in tension with a continuing "Red line" of radical literary and artistic practice that remained powerful throughout the decade.[5]

This study acknowledges its debt to those scholars who locate the
beginnings of the New Negro movement in wartime and postwar radicalism and envision the movement as part of the "Red line" of history,
both literary/artistic and political/economic. But that radicalism was
itself contradictory, and nationalism—both Negro and American—was
in many ways at the heart of this contradiction. In chapter 2, I examine
the ways in which the postwar radical movement's continuing emphasis on representation in the arena of politics helped lay the basis for the
movement's eventual emphasis on representation in the arena of aesthetics. In subsequent chapters, I explore the nature and extent of the postwar Thermidorian reaction and the role played by cultural pluralism in
further influencing the development of the nationalist culturalism of the
Harlem Renaissance. However, to the extent that the Harlem Renaissance
formed a bridge between the revolutionary moment of 1919 and the renewed radicalism of the 1930s, this occurred largely because, albeit in
varying degrees, all three moments were characterized by the notion, or
at least the hope, that a "good"—that is, democratic—nationalism could
be leveraged against the "bad" nationalism of 100 percent Americanism
and made to work for the working class, native and immigrant, white and
African American. The declaration of the Communist Party of the United States of America during the Popular Front era that "Communism is
twentieth-century Americanism" codified a "Left" patriotic—but essentially class-collaborationist—tendency that was inherent in the radical
movement from its very outset. The predilection of the postwar Left—
Second International and Third International alike—for linking emancipation from oppression with control over a given terrain, and identity
with a given soil, would end up critically weakening the New Negro
movement's structural critique of class inequality and hence racism. The
ease with which Locke's version of the New Negro became hegemonic
is attributable in no small measure to the Left's prior accession to Locke's
nationalist premise. Culturalism was thus not so much the inverse of
political radicalism as its loyal opposition, its dialectical counterpart. The
eventual substitution of the term *Harlem Renaissance* for *New Negro
movement* signals not simply the triumph of the poets over the protesters or the emergence of Harlem as a "race capital" through the massive

demographic shifts produced by the Great Migration but also the ascendance of a place-based nationalist politics in the discourse of the entire early-twentieth-century Left. The welding of place to race—Harlem, on the one hand, the South of the Negro "folk," on the other—was the distinctive contribution of the New Negro movement to this larger national and international trend. Although Locke's proclamation of the New Negro's nationalist identity was clearly an effort to bring this identity into being rather than a declaration of self-evident realities, his act involved not simply co-optation, hijacking, exclusion, or betrayal but also a refashioning of ideologies already integral to the outlook of many leftists and progressives, black and white. In short, to understand the process whereby Harlem Renaissance culturalism emerged from New Negro radicalism requires that the two poles of the contradiction be viewed as neither identical nor antipodal but as constituting a simultaneous unity and struggle of opposites. The concrete nature of this dialectic is the subject of *Spectres of 1919*.[6]

Before examining the contradictions internal to New Negro radicalism that would result in its eventual negation by culturalism, however, one must get a sense of the horizon of revolutionary possibility that was, however briefly, made visible by the massive class and antiracist struggles erupting in the wake of the Great War and the Bolshevik Revolution, because the emergence of the New Negro as warrior in the realms of both politics and culture is inseparable from the global postwar revolutionary upsurge. In 1919 and its aftermath, what the New Negroes were expressing was more than a vague hope for a better world coming out of the war; in the domain of U.S. race relations, they were reflecting the leftward shift of contemporaneous political discourse and praxis. I thus begin with an account of several events and situations that figure paradigmatically throughout this study. I next examine the radicalizing effect of the postwar upsurge on contemporaneous definitions of the New Negro offered by mainstream and liberal commentators, African American and white. I then demonstrate the pervasiveness of the conviction among leftists—again, African American and white—that it would take the abolition of capitalism to overcome racism. To an extent that many readers in the beginning of the twenty-first century may find difficult to imagine, left-wing ideas enjoyed a mass influence in the period following World War I, significantly affecting the ways in which radicals and nonradicals alike perceived historical developments and construed the relation between race and class. It was only because radical ideas were so pervasive that the contradictions within the postwar Left could exercise the influence that they would turn out to have.

"Are We to Have Scenes like This in America?": The Revolutionary Upsurge of 1919

Although Karl Marx had written in 1849 of the spectre of communism haunting Europe, by 1919 the ghost had been made flesh with the consolidation of the Russian Revolution of October 1917 and, by early 1919, the founding of the Third International. "The epoch of final, decisive struggle has come later than the apostles of socialist revolution had expected and hoped," declared the manifesto of the new Communist International. "But it has come." Insurrections for workers' power were briefly successful in Berlin, Munich, and Budapest. William Randolph Hearst's *New York American* warned of a "Nation-Wide Dynamite Conspiracy" by bomb-planting "Reds" and called for the deportation of aliens suspected in this "Reign of Terror." The success of the Japanese in securing their empire in the East, as well as the demands for colonial self-determination in many parts of the globe, suggested that another spectre—yellow, brown, or black—might join forces with its crimson Euro-American counterpart. As a horrified Lothrop Stoddard wrote in *The Rising Tide of Color* in 1920, the "phantom of internationalism" was haunting the Western world. The contradictions of the capitalist world order had been embodied in the recent devastating war, which, fought to safeguard bank loans, line the pockets of war profiteers, and carve up Africa and the Middle East, had degenerated into the haggling at Versailles. The proposed League of Nations offered an imperialist version of self-determination that parodied the cosmopolitan proletarian internationalism that, for many, held out the only possibility for a nonexploitative world order. That the world's first proletarian revolution had occurred where it was least expected, apparently bypassing the supposedly necessary stage of first consolidating bourgeois economic and political power, confounded the expectations of not just ruling classes but also evolutionary socialists. The lagging of theory behind practice would significantly impede the development and continuation of a mass radical movement, especially one that would contend effectively with racism as both ideology and practice. Nonetheless, in the aftermath of World War I, there was widespread anticipation, among both rulers and ruled, that the future—the near future—might look very different from the past and the present.[7]

In the United States, nothing resembling a workers' insurrection for state power occurred. But wartime strikes—such as the massive 1917–18 shipbuilders' strikes from Newark Bay, New York, to Newport News, Virginia, which involved white and black workers alike—had prepared the way for the labor upsurge of 1919. In 1919, approximately one in every seven workers went on strike in the United States; in New York City, it was one in four. As David Montgomery has noted, the 1919 strike wave showed that workers were deliberating their futures in terms that went far beyond the bounds of contracts over wages, hours, and working conditions. "The desire for a new way of living nurtured by the war," he writes, "had produced a fusion of immediate demands with grandiose social and political goals that simply confounded the union leadership." The Seattle general strike, which began as a gesture of sympathy with 35,000 shipyard workers refusing to accede to postwar wage cuts, resulted in a takeover of the city by the Central Labor Council. Workers' councils—self-dubbed "soviets"—organized soup kitchens and milk deliveries and maintained municipal order, giving a brief illustration of workers' self-government. A circular distributed to thousands of strikers read, "The Russians have shown you the way out. What are you going to do about it? You are doomed to wage slavery till you die unless you wake up, realize that you and the boss have not one thing in common, that the employing class must be overthrown, and that you, the workers, must take over the control of your jobs, and through them, the control of your lives instead of offering yourself up to the masters as a sacrifice six days a week, so that they can coin profits out of your sweat and toil." The right-wing commentator Boris Brasol viewed the Seattle general strike as "more than a strike, it was an actual revolt of the proletarians who aimed at the forcible overthrow of the duly elected municipal authorities and . . . established in their place . . . a proletarian Soviet which would rule its people on a Communist basis." In the wake of the Seattle strike, the *Literary Digest* featured a photograph of a Russian crowd with the caption "Are We to Have Scenes like This in America?: A murdering, pillaging Bolshevik mob taking possession of a Russian city." An observer in the "New United States" series in the *Nation,* by contrast, viewed the strike as "a revelation of industrial unrest and a demonstration of working-class power," showing that "a general strike, if it actually prevails, is a political as well as an economic revolution."[8]

That the Seattle general strike was succeeded by general strikes in several other U.S. cities heightened the threat of spiraling worker militancy. Job actions by coal miners, railroad workers, and Boston police paralyzed key industries and urban centers; the "great steel strike" of 1919 involved some 365,000 workers. Before the year ended, the most significant political strike in U.S. history occurred when Seattle longshoremen beat up scabs and refused to load materiel that was destined to help General Alexander Kolchak's White armies crush the incipient Soviet state.

Although in retrospect it is clear that in 1919 the U.S. working class was in no position to carry out a syndicalist seizure of the means of production, let alone a political seizure of state power, the conservative labor economist John Graham Brooks was hardly idiosyncratic in his 1920 perception that "the class which Burke called 'swinish' and Hamilton 'the beast' is now so far in control that it cannot be dislodged. It will retain its power and add to it. Very wastefully and with many rank abuses labor is now to try its hand in managing politics and industry. It has come to believe and upon the whole rightly believe, that the upper classes alone are at the end of their rope; that they are incompetent any longer to direct social forces without disaster to us all." Brooks's odium for the *profanum vulgus* was outstripped only by his fear that the insurgent masses "rightly believe[d]" that the rulers were no longer able to rule. Woodrow Wilson, cabling Congress from Versailles, worried that "the question which stands at the front of all others amidst the present awakening is the question of labor." The labor movement analyst Frank Tannenbaum, interpreting the phrase "dictatorship of the proletariat" to signify a situation in which "all men . . . participate in the functioning of the community on the basis of their personal contribution and not on the grounds of legal sanction or 'vested interest,'" adjudged that "the revolution is not to come. It is here."[9]

The upsurge in labor militancy was accompanied by a sharpening of debate—and conflict—within the labor movement and the Left. Although a number of the major strikes of 1919 went forth under the aegis of organized labor, it was clear that the leadership of the labor movement was confronting a crisis in credibility. In Seattle, the local affiliate of the American Federation of Labor (AFL) that organized the general strike endorsed a program far to the left of the class-collaborationist policy favored by the AFL president Samuel Gompers. The term *industrial democracy*, which originally signified a fairly tame program of worker-boss cooperation, took on increasingly radical meaning in the course of the war; the Communist leader Robert Minor—writing in a short-lived journal called the *Melting-Pot: An Exponent of International Communism*—even used the term in November 1919 to signify the dictatorship of the proletariat. At the same time, the Socialist Party of America (SPA) encountered challenges to its tradition of social democratic meliorism. Although in 1912 it had been torn between direct action and electoral strategies and had experienced significant defections to the more militant Industrial Workers of the World (IWW), the SPA was riven between pro-and anti-war factions in 1917 and moved inexorably toward a split in late 1919. The SPA garnered a significant number of votes in 1920 and briefly affiliated itself with the short-lived Labor Party, but it never regained its prewar standing as the leading force on the left. It was the fledgling Communist Party of the United States of America (CPUSA), formed primarily out of the merger of the Communist Party and the Communist Labor Party—themselves outgrowths of the SPA's former left wing—that would supplant the Socialists. Even though the labor movement and the SPA leadership remained mired in reformism and the new Communist-led formations took several years to gather a significant rank-and-file base, the Russian Revolution was widely hailed as the promise of a new world for the producing masses. Whether congratulating Lenin as a hard-nosed pragmatist, celebrating the Russian Revolution as the fulfillment of industrial democracy, or seeking the overthrow of capitalism in the United States, leftists and labor organizers of many stripes were, for a brief time, nearly unanimous in their sympathy with Soviet socialism and their desire to translate its lessons into terms relevant to the United States.[10]

The reaction of the U.S. ruling elite to the Bolshevik Revolution and the growing domestic labor insurgency was hardly passive. During the war, the editors of the *Masses,* a left-wing cultural journal, and several dozen members of the IWW went on trial under the Sedition Act. The *Call* and other SPA publications had their second-class mailing permits revoked; the Socialist press in the Midwest and West never recovered from the government assault; the radical *Messenger* and even the liberal *Crisis,* the official organ of the NAACP, were threatened with similar action. The SPA leaders Kate Richards O'Hare, Victor Berger, and Eugene Debs were imprisoned for their opposition to the war; Berger, a German Jew, was elected to Congress but could not take his seat. Even after the armistice, the wartime espionage and sedition acts remained in effect. New York State's Lusk Committee conducted surveillance of a wide range of institutions and worksites, from settlement houses to college campuses to publishing houses to shipyards; in 1920 it published *Revolutionary Radicalism: Its History, Purpose, and Tactics,* a four-volume, over 5,000-page report on radical activities in the state. Columbia University, City College, and New York University were cited as hotbeds of radicalism; the settlement houses on the Lower East Side were viewed as especially busy centers for dissemination of left-wing propaganda. The avant-garde publishing company Boni and Liveright was designated as dangerous because of its "special line of radical books." The SPA's Rand School— an adult education center that had some five thousand registered students in 1918—was raided by state agents during the Red Summer of 1919. Immigrant workers were targeted as carriers of the "Red virus," and clubs of Russian-born workers were singled out in the government antiradical raids of autumn 1919. Emma Goldman, the anarchist and *Mother Earth* editor who was deported on the so-called Soviet Ark in December 1919, was only the most famous among hundreds of such political deportees. The (in)famous immigration acts of 1921 and 1924, which would cut immigration by 85 percent (nearly completely from southern and eastern Europe), were preceded by the immigration acts of 1917 and 1918, which called for the formation of a special antiradical division. Gary Gerstle observes that the Bolshevik Revolution "forced a reframing of the immigration problem. Few events exerted as large an impact in the United States, in both the short and long terms, as the Bolsheviks' seizure of power in November 1917." The persecution of leftists, both immigrant and native-born, was accompanied by attacks on labor militants; spies were sent into worksites where strike activity was suspected. When strikes occurred, the repression was pronounced; Elbert Gary, head of the U.S. Steel Corporation who was known as Judge Gary, responded so violently to the great steel strike—where he thought "[t]he only outcome of the victory for unionism would be Sovietism in the United States and the forcible distribution of property"—that even his class allies called on him to cease and desist. The repression culminated in early January of 1920 when Attorney General A. Mitchell Palmer ordered nationwide raids on the headquarters of Communists that resulted in the arrests of thousands. By the early 1920s, there were over 450,000 "subversives" on the lists compiled by the young J. Edgar Hoover, head of the Bureau of Investigation (BI).[11]

If foreign-born workers were the principal targets of overt political repression, native-born African Americans were the principal targets of physical violence; the term *Red Summer* pertains not only to government antiradicalism campaigns but also to the blood spilled in the many lynchings and race riots of 1919. The lynchings were primarily a rural phenomenon, and many were not reported in the press. Within a fifty-mile radius of Sparta, Georgia—to be memorialized as Sempter in Jean Toomer's *Cane*—at least a dozen lynchings were recorded within three months alone in 1919. The Great Migration—beginning in the early 1910s, proceeding apace during the war, and involving some 900,000 migrants by 1919—produced increased anxiety on the part of white landowners and stiffening resistance among black tenants and sharecroppers. Growing rebellion against debt peonage provided the context of a spate of brutal rural killings—from the widely publicized 1918 lynching of the pregnant Mary Turner and ten other African Americans near Valdosta, Georgia; to the massacre of some sixty sharecropper organizers and their families in

Phillips County near Elaine, Arkansas, in 1919; to the 1921 murder of eleven debt peons in Monticello, Georgia. The famous soil of Georgia was reddened by more than clay; *rivering* entered the lexicon to describe the habitual practice of lynching by drowning.[12]

The riots were primarily urban. By the late 1910s, black workers fleeing rural lynch law and debt peonage crowded into urban centers farther north by the hundreds every day; it was a battle over insufficient housing that sparked the 1917 East St. Louis race riot. Often these newly proletarianized black workers were used as strikebreakers: the importation northward of some 30,000 to 40,000 African Americans broke the back of the great steel strike and, in the eyes of many labor historians, helped delay industrial unionization by a good two decades. Whether riots were precipitated by economic pressures or simply by the refusal of returning black soldiers to abide by what Richard Wright was to call the "ethics of living Jim Crow," African Americans demonstrated an increasing unwillingness to respond passively to abuse and violence. Wartime rebellions of black soldiers had occurred in Houston, Texas, in 1915—when over a dozen black soldiers were hanged—and Longview, Texas, in 1917. In several of the over forty urban race riots that occurred in the summer of 1919—most notably in Washington and Chicago—residents of black neighborhoods took up arms. President Wilson, already anxious about the loyalty of Jews on the East Side of New York and the nationwide labor upsurge, confided to his personal physician in 1919 on the way home from Versailles his fear that "[t]he American negro returning from abroad would be our greatest medium in conveying bolshevism to America." The Lusk Committee, worried at the warning by the black Socialist (and soon to be Communist) W. A. Domingo that Negroes might be "formed by the capitalists into a mercenary army for the suppression of social revolution," reprinted Domingo's entire text in *Revolutionary Radicalism. New York Times* headlines alerted the newspaper's readership of a "Planned Negro Uprising" and an "Increase in Mob Violence." Attorney General Palmer put the point most succinctly: "The Negro is 'seeing red.'"[13]

In this unstable situation, the usefulness of racism and ethnic division as mechanisms of social control was patent. NAACP investigators asserted that "by all accounts of eyewitnesses, both white and black, the East St. Louis outrage was deliberately planned and executed"; W. E. B. Du Bois concluded that the local trade unions, which systematically excluded blacks, had spread racist propaganda among whites. A labor detective firm hired to fight the great steel strike told its operatives, "Spread data among the Serbians that the Italians are going back to work.

Call up every question you can in reference to racial hatred between these two nationalities." In Chicago, the growing black-white labor unity in the packinghouse industry posed a serious threat to the owners; 6,000 of the nearly 18,000 Negro meatpackers—in a total force of 60,000—had joined the union by mid-1919. As Randolph observed in the *Messenger*, Chicago's business elite, alert to the danger posed by a multiracial union movement in the stockyards, did much to fan the flames of that summer's race riot. Even as racial division was the rule and was often openly fomented by those in power, certain instances of multiracial solidarity stood as possible symbols of the future development of the labor movement. In the summer of 1919, the AFL leadership, under pressure from an increasingly class-conscious rank and file, issued a proclamation—at least on paper—against discrimination, calling on all locals to desegregate. A more dramatic demonstration of rank-and-file unity, receiving widespread commentary in the black and liberal-to-Left white press, occurred when three white unionists in Bogalusa, Louisiana, lost their lives in December 1919 defending a black labor organizer from company vigilantes. The word *Bogalusa* would figure briefly as a metonymy for the better world that many envisioned. The continual slippage between *radical* and *black* in contemporaneous usage of the term *Red Summer* suggests that, despite the labor movement's long history of racial division, during the postwar upsurge the liberation of black people from bondage to "old Pharoah" was, in the minds of many, linked with the emancipation of the proletariat from wage slavery. It was of no small significance that John Brown's birthday was declared a national holiday by leftists of the time or that the term *reconstruction* was chosen by labor militants—later to be co-opted by experts in the emerging field of "industrial relations"—to describe the aspirations of labor in the postwar era.[14]

Not only did insurgent workers and union organizers take inspiration from the Bolshevik Revolution, but also a new spirit of internationalism was becoming manifest in a number of the class struggles in the United States in 1919. During the IWW-led Lawrence textile strike—which spread throughout the Northeast and involved some 120,000 workers—workers sang the "Internationale" in several dozen different languages. During the great steel strike, multilingual leaflets were distributed to the multinational striking work force; management's efforts to divide and conquer both spurred and were spurred by equally class-conscious activity by the strike's organizers. Internationalism pervaded much of the political discourse of 1919—on the organized left, in the labor movement, and among African American radicals. The political theorist Charles Conant Josey, who believed unabashedly that "[t]he maximum good of mankind as a whole may quite possibly be served by using certain races and groups of men as a means to support the rich and complex cultures of other races or groups," expressed concern that "[s]uggestions of this sort are violently opposed by the internationalist. Internationalism is opposed to all forms of exploitation of the weak by the strong. It is opposed to all restrictions on peoples based on race or nation." That the internationalist rhetoric of self-determination was being taken over by domestic labor militants was noted by Tannenbaum, who, remarking that "the growth of the labor movement is not compatible with the competitive and profit motive in industry," concluded that "all of the moral and ethical implications" of the movement were "bound up [with] the freedom of self-determination." The same discursive phenomenon worried Brooks, who commented that even sales clerks "have learned the troublesome liturgy about 'self-determination' and will have something of it for themselves." The use of the term *American Plan* to signify the open shop—first deployed by Seattle industrial relations experts in March 1919, a mere month after the end of the general strike—signaled employers' strategic identification of labor peace with patriotism. The antagonist to this peace was variously identified as "internationalism" or "cosmopolitanism"—the latter possessing a distinctly working-class character and leftist political connotation quite different from its present association with border-transgressing hybridity.[15]

Among African Americans, the rejection of 100 percent Americanism manifested itself in various blends of Pan-Africanism, black nationalism, and anticapitalist radicalism. As Wilson Moses has shown, a conservative black nationalism—civilizationist, genteel, mystical, acculturationist—had long been a staple of African American politics. Seizing on the rhetoric of self-determination infusing the entire spectrum of postwar politics, from Versailles to the Kremlin, advocates of Pan-Africanism moved this discourse to the left, not only proposing a global alliance of peoples in the African diaspora but also beginning to theorize African Americans as a colonized people. The conservative commentator Basil Mathews, remarking on the Pan-Africanist Congress of 1919, bemoaned the fact that "[i]n America, causes similar to those operating in Africa have been at work to create discontent and race feeling," with the result that American Negroes were making "common cause with every people in the world that is under white tutelage today in the cry for self-determination." The leftist offshoot of postwar black self-determinationism would eventuate in the Black Belt thesis endorsed by the CPUSA at the Sixth World Congress of the Comintern in 1928. More influential in the immediate postwar period, however, was the strain of pro-capitalist black nationalism espoused by Marcus Garvey's Universal Negro Improvement Association (UNIA), which, with its millions of members worldwide was, Winston James observes, "the largest black organization the world had ever known." The year 1919 marked not only the apex of class struggles but also the founding of Garvey's Black Star line. The term *Negro Renaissance* was first used by Garvey publicist William T. Ferris in describing the "rise and growth of the U.N.I.A." As James A. Miller points out, the role played by Garvey in the immediate postwar years cannot be underestimated; his was "a central and competing vision in the fierce debates about race, class, and the future of the black community." The preoccupation with African roots that would constitute a prominent trope in New Negro writing was thus inseparable from the emerging view of both Africa and the Caribbean as players to be reckoned with in the worldwide struggle of the ruled against the rulers.[16]

For participants and witnesses alike—whether Red-hunters on the Lusk Committee, rank-and-file workers caught up in the swirl of events, or leftists bent on revolutionary transformation—the immediate postwar era was rife with revolutionary potential. Social change could be imagined not as just reform—the flux between the antinomies of labor and capital—but as the negation of the old bipolar order, sublating many old elements in the new but radically altering social relationships through the abolition of classes and private property. For a brief period, the principal structural dynamic underpinning social reality—what Marx had called the "two great hostile camps" of "Bourgeoisie and Proletariat"— stood revealed in its transparent totality. Just as it was no accident that Marx and Engels had composed *The Communist Manifesto* in the crucible of the 1848 revolutions, it was no accident that Georg Lukacs—who had participated actively in the Budapest Soviet—would pen his monumental commentary on reification and the "standpoint of the proletariat," *History and Class Consciousness* (1923), in the wake of the class struggles of 1919. What was involved was not simply a change in weltanschauung but a recognition of the dialectical nature of historical process and the fundamental class antagonism at the heart of this process. Not only had the principal contradiction in the world shifted from the rivalry among competing imperialist elites to the contradiction between labor and capital, but also labor promised—or, depending on one's vantage point, threatened—to emerge as the principal aspect of that contradiction. John Dos Passos would later comment that what he and his peers thought at the time was "the beginning of the flood" would turn out to have been "the beginning of the ebb." Nonetheless, Brooks's conclusion that the rulers of the United States were "incompetent to direct the social forces" and "at the end of their rope" bespoke a very real fear; that it proved groundless does not diminish its reality.[17]

Whether on the left or the right, those commenting on contemporary events thus encountered, and at times contributed to, a discursive shift that was simultaneously political and epistemological. Which occurrences, even if resonant with inherited typicality, would be increasingly anomalous in the emerging configuration of the world? Conversely, which events, however apparently idiosyncratic, contained *in nuce* the shape of things to come? Was East St. Louis pointing the way to the future—or was Bogalusa? If current class struggles were heading the United States toward a second civil war, were those in search of historical precedents and political exemplars to turn to the polymorphously loving Walt Whitman or to the unremittingly combative John Brown? What kinds of metonymic operations could best describe the arc of historical development? Of concern to many actors following the script of current history, these considerations were of paramount importance to the participants in the debate over how best to define the New Negro, whose "newness" was being produced in the revolutionary crucible of 1919.

"The Spirit That Has Taken Hold of All the Submerged Classes of the World": Moderates, Liberals, and the New Negro

The *New Negro*, as the term suggests, historically occupied one pole in a binary opposition in which its counterpart was, of course, the *Old Negro*. As various scholars have pointed out, the term *New Negro* goes back to at least the 1890s. Even Booker T. Washington, who would come to epitomize Old Negro accommodationism, laid claim to the mantle of the New Negro in his 1900 call for self-help, *A New Negro for a New Century*. August Meier, finding the term first used "in the social and intellectual movements of the age of Washington," argues that it denoted both "an artistic movement and . . . a racial outlook." Gates discerns a "tension" from the outset between the term's reference to "strictly political concerns" and to "strictly artistic concerns." David Krasner, remarking on the usage of *New Negro* in the black theater in 1896, associates the term with the subversive caricature of racist stereotypes in the face of growing segregation and Jim Crow violence. In these formulations, the newness of the New Negro consisted in a capacity—at times straightforward, at times parodic—to transcend a denigrating typology and assert a selfhood not wholly contingent on the goodwill of whites. Yet, inextricably tied as it was to the discourse of uplift, the prewar New Negro was of necessity a defensive figure—part cultural, part political, part sociological—bearing multiple traces of the social inequality she/he was invented to combat.[18]

In the wartime and postwar movement to the left, discursive and political, the signifier *New Negro* came to posit a different referent and to provoke a different debate. To appreciate the full dimensions and impact of the radical trend, one needs to consider not just the emergence of a self-conscious black radicalism but also the process of osmosis by which left-wing ideas seeped into almost all the discursive spaces of the day. When in 1919 Washington's successor as president of Tuskegee, Robert Russa Moton, counseled African American troops in France to go back to the rural South after the war, warning them of the dangers and poverty-stricken conditions they would face in such northern centers as New York, his conservatism was met with near-universal jeers. The *Amsterdam News* remarked sardonically that Moton "would have us all return across the Red Sea of the Mason-Dixon Line into the land of Egypt to help fill the Jim-Crow cars and work the convict farms." Noteworthy about Moton's situation was his isolation from mainstream African American opinion; Locke's decision to include a piece by him in *The New Negro* signaled his desire to include under the big tent of his anthology a figure almost universally maligned by progressives of the day. Other traditional black leaders, however, were hedging their bets and developing a range of political contacts and alliances. Emmett Scott, a Howard University administrator who had been a secretary to Booker T. Washington and a special assistant to Woodrow Wilson's secretary of war, spoke at Marcus Garvey's 1918 Free Africa conference. His Carnegie Hall speech was reported on favorably in an article entitled "Negroes of the World Unite in Demanding a Free Africa" in the *Crusader*, an organ of the radical African Blood Brotherhood (ABB). Kelly Miller, a Howard University dean, while decrying the "destructive radicalism" of "riotous 'Reds'" and proclaiming the Negro a "natural conservative," predicted that the Bolshevik Revolution would alter the Negro's future and enable a "moral revolution" to emerge from the postwar "reconstruction." "Revolutions always lessen the domain of oppression and increase the area of liberty," he wrote, adding, "Democracy for the world, and the world of democracy, has become the beyond of the convulsive struggle in which the nations and races of mankind are involved." Moreover, the postwar violence had pushed the Negro past the limits of patience: "It is too much to hope that [the black man] will forever requite cruelty with kindness and hatred with love and mercy." In 1923, Miller met with Richard B. Moore, an ABB leader and a Communist, to help organize the 1924 "Negro Sanhedrin" united front conference for Negro leaders. Lambasted as "Old

Negroes"—or "Old Crowd Negroes"—by such firebrands as Randolph and Owen, as well as Moore and his *Crusader* coeditor Cyril V. Briggs, Scott and Miller hardly hoisted up the Red flag. Nonetheless, they cultivated acquaintances with anticapitalist radicals that would have been unthinkable for Howard University administrators a decade earlier.[19]

Mainstream Negro newspapers registered the postwar leftward shift. Exemplary are the contradictory representations and editorial assessments of the political scene in the *Washington Bee,* which was edited by William Chace, an ardent supporter of Booker T. Washington up to the educator's death in 1915. The 20 December 1919 issue, for instance, included a news story about a planned memorial for Negro soldiers at the capital city's Liberty Hut that quoted at length Supreme Court associate justice Wendell Phillips Stafford's declaration, "Cite me a Negro traitor. . . . Show me a Negro anarchist. . . . Let me see a Negro Bolshevist. . . . The only red flag the Negro ever carried was when his shirt was stained crimson by the sacrificial blood he gave to America." (The *Bee* refrained from mentioning that the Liberty Hut had been the gathering-spot for the white returned soldiers who had gone on a rampage against the city's black population the previous summer.) The *Bee* also upheld the traditional two-party system, advocating that its readers vote Republican against the segregationist Wilson administration in the coming election. But there were limits to the *Bee*'s loyal Americanism. In a commentary on the "unrest prevalent among the twelve million colored people of this country," the editors denied that "Bolsheviks are at work" and declared, "We heard nothing of this so-called 'Bolshevism' until the unrest in Russia had inflamed and aroused the persecuted common people during the world war. It is not Bolsheviks, but just AMERICAN INJUSTICE, that is responsible." They also effectively undercut their own editorial endorsement of the Republicans when they remarked indirectly on Bogalusa, "The fact that white members of white organized labor in lynch-encrusted Louisiana dared to make the supreme sacrifice in defense of a Colored member of their organization must necessarily give weight and reason to the Labor party's bid for the Colored vote." The repeated references to "sacrifice" in this single day's issue of the *Bee,* if coincidental, questioned whether the paper's readers were to identify with a sacrificial patriotism defined by antiradicalism or with a sacrificial class-consciousness defined by antiracism. Combining Old Negro calls for movement upward within the current socioeconomic system with opposition to Red-baiting and occasionally sympathetic portrayal of socialists, the *Bee* exemplified the leftward shift in postwar African American political debates.[20]

Although in 1915 the *Bee* had dismissed the NAACP as "a sham and a mockery"—"All this rot about the advancement of Colored People could be poured into a two-ounce bottle," an editorial declared—after Washington's death the newspaper became a solid supporter of the civil rights organization, whose D.C. chapter had expanded to a membership of 1,164 by 1916. The NAACP personified Old Negro temporizing to the radicals of the *Crusader* and the *Messenger;* nonetheless, the conflicting views and affiliations of key figures in the association further illustrate the leftward pressures of the postwar period. In 1916, William Pickens, an NAACP field secretary and Morgan State dean, maintained that "the colored soldier and the masses of the race are still loyal. There is no hyphen in the short word 'Negro': he is every inch American; he is not even Afro-American." In 1920, by contrast, Pickens threatened that "[the Negro] was human long before he was American—and human beings do not remain loyal to anything which is never loyal to them. But if the call ever goes forth for volunteers for clean up the backward civilization of Georgia and Mississippi, we can stake our reputation on the prediction that every Colored American from sixteen to sixty would join the army in a week." The following year, Pickens wrote a hard-hitting analysis of the relationship between debt peonage and lynching in a pamphlet entitled "The American Congo." Excerpted in both the *Nation* and the *Bee,* this commentary on the recent burning alive of Henry Lowery before an audience of thousands of Georgians presupposed various elements of an anticapitalist class analysis. "Most of the lynching evil is traceable to economic wrong," wrote Pickens. "There is a conviction that the colored American as a class is to be kept under in human society: that when a black man works and sweats, it is not primarily for his own good, but for the good of the dominant race in America. This is class feeling." Pickens did not extend his analysis of class here to take in differences within the "dominant race"; on the contrary, he asserted that when "a black man works and sweats," all members of the "dominant race" benefit. Nonetheless, he traced the "lynching evil" not to some inborn hatred that whites bear for blacks but to the conviction ("class feeling") that "the colored American as a class is to be kept under." This association of racial violence with the profit motive was underlined by Pickens's designation of the South as the "American Congo," where "the quest . . . is not for rubber and ivory, but for cotton and sugar. Here labor is forced, and the laborer is a slave . . . [in] a cunningly contrived debt-slavery to give the appearance of civilization and the sanction of law." In contemporaneous radical discourse, the term *Congo* signified the worst ravages of the European conquest of Africa; Vachel Lindsay's representation of the

Congo as a site of "mumbo-jumbo," in need of missionary salvation, was being challenged by an alternative paradigm that stressed the barbarism of white colonizers. That Pickens should declare a limit to the Negro's patriotism and compare a region of the United States with the Congo signals an implicit theorization of the South as a U.S. colony as well as a fissure in his earlier postulation of a metonymic relation between the Negro and the nation. This NAACP field secretary evidently viewed racial violence, both domestic and international, as the consequence of, and accompaniment to, economic exploitation; some mediations are lacking, but the lineaments of a base-superstructure analysis are apparent.[21]

Other prominent African Americans in the supposedly moderate NAACP exhibited sympathy with left-wing politics and organizations. Its executive secretary, James Weldon Johnson—poet, novelist, essayist, lynching investigator, and former U.S. diplomat in the Caribbean—published frequently in the radical press during the late teens and early twenties. In a 1918 article appearing in one of the first issues of the *Liberator*—sequel to the *Masses* and precursor to the *New Masses*—he wrote that "[the Negro] has been seized by the spirit that has taken hold of all the submerged classes of the world. He has seen the breaking up and melting down of old ideas and conventions. . . . He is to-day realizing the truth that no submerged or oppressed class ever got a right that was worth having or that it didn't have to fight to get, and also that no submerged or oppressed class ever kept a right that it didn't have to fight to keep." Although Johnson was probably alluding to Frederick Douglass's famous statement—made, notably, in the context of a speech about abolitionism in the Caribbean—that "power cedes nothing without a demand"— Johnson's near-identification of "the Negro" with a "submerged or oppressed class" is significant, if only because the casual slippage in his formulation indicates his premise that, for *Liberator* readers at least, no further clarification is required. Johnson also appears to take as given the internationalist connection between Negro liberation in the United States and contemporaneous upsurges elsewhere on the globe. His declaration that the Negro has seen "the breaking up and melting down of old ideas and conventions" may even echo Marx's statement in *The Communist Manifesto* that, as capitalism follows its course of development, "all that is solid melts into air." In the late 1910s, Johnson urged Florida cigar workers to strike for unionization and higher pay, and he supported the IWW, which brought him to the attention of the Lusk Committee. He praised the emerging evidence of black-white labor solidarity, writing in *New York Age* that the white workers' defense of their black comrade in the Bogalusa episode "gives promise that the day will come when the

white working men of the South will see and understand that their interests and the interests of the black working men of the South are identical. .... When white and black working men get together in the South
for their common economic advantage, there are going to be some mighty
changes." Johnson's prediction of "mighty changes" suggests that he, like
other observers of class struggles in 1919, was anticipating more than a
trade-union level of alliance and was thinking in internationalist terms:
the "spirit that has seized hold of the submerged classes of the world"
might also bring down the system of Jim Crow. Johnson's speaking at a
conference of the African Blood Brotherhood in 1923 indicates his will-
ingness to ally with the black radicals of the *Crusader.* The subject of a
Bureau of Investigation inquiry in the early 1920s, Johnson was clearly
affected by the postwar political ferment. That this composer of the
"Negro National Anthem"—"Lift Every Voice and Sing"—also had
friendly personal ties with whites on the left is shown by his hosting an
interracial fund-raising and seeing-off party in his apartment at 507 Edge-
combe Avenue for Claude McKay when the poet departed for the USSR
in 1922. While much of the received lore about the Harlem Renaissance
tars its multiracialism with the brush of patronage provided by the likes
of Charlotte Mason and other revisionary accounts strip this multiracialism of its radical political content, it bears noting that, at least at its
beginnings, the legendary mixing of races at parties in "507" occurred
within an explicitly leftist, pro-Soviet, ambience.[22]

Even Walter White, an NAACP assistant field secretary who in later years was a staunch anticommunist, evinced sympathetic identification with various aspects of a leftist analysis in the postwar period. Investigating some thirty-five lynchings and nine race riots in the late 1910s
and early 1920s, White concentrated on the horrific particulars of the
racial violence he was documenting. A white man in physical appearance,
the aptly named investigator frequently risked his life and "passed" in
order to report on lynchings for the *Crisis;* when investigating the Elaine,
Arkansas, sharecropper massacre he was himself almost caught and
killed. Based on this firsthand experience, White's commentaries on
lynching and debt peonage located racist repression in economic moti-
vation. "Lynching protects money," he bluntly stated in 1922 and reas-
serted several years later in *Rope and Faggot.* White also pointed out that
the South's lynch culture controlled white as well as black labor. As the
narrator in White's 1924 novel, *The Fire in the Flint,* remarks of poor
whites, "They had been duped so long by demagogues, deluded generation after generation into believing their sole hope of existence depended on oppression and suppression of the Negro, that the chains of the

ignorance and suppression they sought to fasten on their Negro neighbors had subtly bound them in unbreakable fashion." The NAACP official who had the closest contact with whites guilty of perpetrating racial
violence registered the fullest comprehension of the class purposes served
by their participation in that violence.[23]

This tracing of racial violence to elites' need to maintain social control was not confined to NAACP members living in the political fast
track of Harlem. The Washington, D.C., clubwoman, poet, and NAACP
activist Carrie Clifford in November 1919 organized support for unionization efforts on the part of domestic workers so that "they may have
a share in bringing about industrial democracy and social order in the
world." Clifford's coupling of "industrial democracy" with "social order" hardly signals an endorsement of the term's more radical usage by
Socialists, Wobblies, and Communists. But her support for unionization
reveals her involvement with a kind of activity and advocacy not traditionally associated with the racial uplift efforts undertaken by clubwom-
en of the Negro Four Hundred. Clifford's 1922 volume of poetry, *The
Widening Light,* displays not only untrammeled anger at racist violence
but also the influence of a class-based analysis of its causes. Her tribute
to Mary Turner is an outcry against the *"ruthless . . . human beasts"* who
left *"two bodies—and an unborn babe . . . there upon the ground."* In
"Race-Hate (On the East St. Louis Riot, July 28, 1917)," she apostrophizes
her subject, "Thou has no one deceived, not e'en thyself, / *Thy bloody
hands are raised for power and pelf!"* "Silent Protest Parade (On Fifth
Avenue, New York, Saturday, July 28, 1917, Protesting against the St.
Louis Riots)" describes the protesters as "[p]oor black workers, who'd
fled in distress from the South / To find themselves murdered and
mobbed in the North." The marchers

> . . . carried our banner,
> On which had been boldly inscribed every manner
> Of sentiment—all, to be sure, within reason—
> But no flag—not that we meant any treason—
> Only who'd have the heart to carry Old Glory,
> After hearing all of the horrible story,
> Of East St. Louis? and never a word,
> From the nation's head.

An "Old Crowd Negro" by her generational and class ties, Clifford was
moved by the militant rank-and-file resistance of 1919 to heighten her
outrage, broaden her sympathetic identification with "poor black workers," and question her patriotism.[24]

Archibald Grimké, an NAACP local chapter president who was also a member of the capital city's Negro aristocracy, went through a dramatic transformation during the war years. Brother to the activist clergyman Francis Grimké and father to the poet and teacher Angelina Grimké, Archibald Grimké was something of a thorn in the side of the Old Negro aristocracy. Outraged by the 1915 legal lynchings of black soldiers in Houston, Texas, Grimké authored an angry elegy, "Her Thirteen Black Soldiers." When the *Crisis*, pleading fears of government repression, declined to print the poem, Grimké found a publishing venue in the fearless *Messenger* and began an association with Randolph and Owen that resulted in a 1919 invitation to Randolph to address the Washington NAACP chapter. But when Jesse Moorland, a local NAACP official, threatened to resign, Grimké was pressured to step down from the presidency. In his final chapter address, "The Shame of America," Grimké declared his admiration for the "new Negro" of the "new generation," who was prepared to "challenge injustice in his own land and to fight wrong with a courage that will not fail him in the bitter and perhaps bloody years to come." Grimké praised the *Messenger* for daring, like the *Liberator*, to "speak out now when others grow silent and submit to be muffled."[25]

Various prominent white members of the NAACP were Socialists who shared their black colleagues' class-based (or at least "economic") view of U.S. race relations. The social worker, novelist, and essayist Mary White Ovington demonstrated the profitability to capital of black super-exploitation in her 1911 sociological study, *Half a Man*, for which the pioneering antiracist cultural anthropologist Franz Boas wrote an introduction. In her 1920 novel, *The Shadow*, Ovington pointed up the psychological brutality of the "one-drop rule," linked immigrant women workers' struggles on the job with the African American fight against Jim Crow, and criticized racism in the SPA. The author of a review column, "Book Chat," which was regularly featured in African American newspapers (including the UNIA's *Negro World*), Ovington kept readers informed about current books addressing racial issues and criticized those pandering to stereotypes. Ovington was above all a strong partisan of black-white, working-class solidarity, commenting of Bogalusa that "[l]awlessness and cruelty will continue in the South as long as this carefully stimulated race hatred keeps the working class apart." Like Grimké, Ovington wrote a letter of support to the *Messenger*, praising its editors— a little oddly—as "two good Socialists of college training who are giving up their life to the spread of Socialist thought."[26]

Herbert Seligmann, a white NAACP member, poet, and literary critic whose publishing venues ranged from the *Nation* to the *Dial* to the *So-*

cialist Review, singled out the *Messenger* for praise in his 1920 study, *The Negro Faces America.* "Never before particularly concerned in the doctrine of class struggle, [the Negro] is having it preached to him by his own newspapers and magazines which are quick to seize upon the economic motives of his detractors and exploiters," wrote Seligmann. Bogalusa, he proclaimed, "indicated the beginning of the end of the exploitation of both white and colored workers which had been accomplished by pitting these groups against one another and by fanning the animosities that left them hostile." Seligmann's use of the phrase "beginning of the end of exploitation" is, to be sure, ambiguous. If he meant by "exploitation" the added surplus value extracted from labor through racist strategies of divide and conquer, then this practice could presumably be ended without ending capitalism as such. If he signified the sale of labor power for wages, however, then the "beginning of the end" he heralded in Bogalusa was the political unification of the workers as a revolutionary force bent on eradicating capitalist social relations. Naming his chapter on lynching "The American Congo," Seligmann expanded on the theme of Pickens's pamphlet by that name, relating the "terrorism" of the state in the Arkansas peonage cases to the violence of colonialism. Investigated by J. Edgar Hoover for what the BI called his "Bolshevik activity amongst Negroes" during a 1919 trip to the South, Seligmann exemplified the trajectory of the antiracist white liberal drawn into the Left's orbit.[27]

The NAACP's *Crisis* oscillated between establishment and radical politics. In some respects, the *Crisis* was entirely conventional. Its reportage on the activities of successful Negro professionals and businesspeople, as well as leisured clubwomen, spoke to the interests of an upwardly mobile middle class. Its habitual featuring on its cover of a demure, domesticated black woman, often light-skinned, countered racist and sexist stereotypes by appropriating the iconography of bourgeois culture. Accompanying its regular publication of statistics and narrative accounts of lynchings, the magazine urged a reformist legal and legislative strategy as the principal route to social change; the struggle to pass the Dyer antilynching bill constituted the NAACP's major activity during the postwar years. In response to the 1919 Washington riot, the *Crisis* called for investigations into the *Post's* role in inciting white ex-servicemen to racist violence. When a Georgia jury found John S. Williams guilty of murdering eleven debt peons on his Monticello "death farm," a *Crisis* editorial declared that although "Negroes are held today in as complete and awful a soul destroying slavery as they were in 1860 . . . there comes a ray of hope. Georgia is to be congratulated on the conviction of Williams for murder." In response to Georgia governor George Dorsey's April

1921 publication of *The Negro in Georgia*—a pamphlet that detailed scores of instances of debt peonage, murder, and abuse—the *Crisis* warmly congratulated Dorsey for the "shrill cry of [his] revelations, [which] corroborates every word *The Crisis* ever wrote." It would appear that the NAACP magazine wished to "speak truth to power" by cultivating its ties with prominent liberals and maintaining its image as the voice of reason and moderation. The *Crisis* unambiguously supported the war effort and featured the participation of African American soldiers in the conflict (see figure 1). The *Crisis's* angry but restrained response to the spate of postwar lynchings was epitomized in a 1919 drawing depicting a black male migrant preparing to leave the South in response to a lynching (see figure 2). His face contorted in anger, his muscular body barely contained within the suit he has apparently bought for the trip north, the migrant projects a determination to channel his outrage into creating a better life for himself, away from the shadow of the lynching tree. As a New Negro, he will adhere to the rules, as the lynchers have not; even though a proletarian, he will adopt the dress—and presumably the outlook—of the American middle class.[28]

Yet the *Crisis* also gave more than sporadic voice to radical perspectives. In 1919, the magazine castigated Moton for expressing mystification about the causes of the recent Negro rebellions in Arkansas and Nebraska. The "real causes of the race riots" lay, the *Crisis* claimed, in economic exploitation. Despite the lack of spine in its decision not to publish Grimké's "Her Thirteen Black Soldiers," the NAACP organ published some fairly radical literary texts. The November 1918 issue, for example, contained Alfred Kreymborg's "Red Chant"—dedicated to the African American poet Fenton Johnson—which premised multiracial friendship on a common class position:

> Let a master prick me with his pin—
>   the bubble of blood shows red.
> Let a master prick you with his pin—
>   the bubble of blood shows red.

Declaring that there is no "Negro" or "white" blood, only red blood, the poem displays the link between communism and antiracism: the "Red" who opposes the "master's" violation of the worker's body also recognizes no differences based on race. In January 1921, the *Crisis* reported on the prominent Communist organizer John Reed's call for multiracial proletarian solidarity at the Moscow meeting of the Communist International, where Reed "urged the union of American Negroes with the radicals of all nations to further world sovietism." Three months later, the magazine

Figure 1. "At Bay," by William Edward Scott, *Crisis*, November 1918

Figure 2.
"The Reason," by
Albert A. Smith,
Crisis, May 1921

published Claude McKay's anticolonial poem "Exhortation," which urges its readers to look to the USSR for the future: "Wake from sleeping; to the East, turn, turn your eyes!" During the war, the *Crisis* may have managed to escape the political repression visited on more left-wing organs that had their mailing permits revoked or their editors jailed, but the New Negro lurking in its pages was by no means entirely safe for democracy. In 1919, the Lusk Committee included the NAACP magazine among the revolutionary periodicals that it regularly monitored, pronouncing that the *Crisis* took a "decidedly radical stand" and that "[c]ertain of the board of directors of [the NAACP] have extended their sympathy and support to the Socialistic group headed by Randolph and Owen."[29]

The *Crisis* exercised influence beyond its own articles and editorials by offering monthly lists of recommended readings on race issues; these selections reveal that contemporaneous commentators of various political stripes also saw themselves on the brink of world historical change. For example, Carter G. Woodson's *Negro in Our History* (1922), primarily an account of black achievement written in the Old Negro spirit of race uplift, ended with a chapter entitled "The Negro and Social Justice" in which the author sounded a different kind of prophetic note. "The laboring man is no longer a servile employee of serf-like tendencies," Woodson wrote, "but a radical member of a dissatisfied group, demanding a proper division of the returns of his labor." Woodson concluded, somewhat regretfully, that the United States had developed "from progressivism almost to socialism"; in this context, the Negroes, while "constitut[ing] the most conservative and most constructive stock in America," were being "forced into the ranks of the Socialists and Radicals." A similarly reluctant admission of growing Negro radicalism was voiced in Benjamin Brawley's *Social History of the American Negro* (1921), also recommended by the *Crisis*. Discerning in Bogalusa the same metonymic relation to a possible future perceived by Johnson, Ovington, Seligmann, and the *Bee* editors, Brawley cautiously remarked, "The significance of this incident remain[s] . . . to be seen; but it is quite possible that in the final history of the Negro problem the skirmish at Bogalusa will mark the beginning of the end of the exploiting of Negro labor and the first recognition of the identity of interest between white and black workmen in the south." Brawley's use of the term *exploiting* to describe racist superexploitation indicates that he, like Seligmann, viewed an end to exploitation as attainable under capitalism. Nonetheless, Brawley's speculation about the potential significance of "the skirmish at Bogalusa" shows him trying to separate the wheat from the chaff, the typical from the anomalous. That Brawley, like Seligmann, saw in Bogalusa the possible "beginning of the end" of the old order suggests the prevalence of the search for a new trope adequate to the epistemological as well as political shifts emerging from the class struggles of 1919.[30]

The *Crisis* also recommended *The Soul of John Brown* (1920), a fascinating meditation on U.S. race relations in which the popular British journalist Stephen Graham conveyed an apocalyptic sense of historical possibility. Expanding on his 1919 series of *Atlantic Monthly* articles entitled "Marching through Georgia," Graham situated the coming defeat of Jim Crow in the context of international revolutionary upheaval. Since "Bolshevism is eminently a slave movement," Graham declared, "Russian serfs and military slaves and wage slaves and Negroes are finding an accord, and here we have the foundation for a grand proletarian revolutionary movement throughout the world." Despite the current antipathy between white and black workers, Graham prophesied:

[i]t is not the lynching crowd on whom vengeance will ultimately be taken. The Negro mob, when it rises, may easily join with the lynchers and make common cause against those who should have administered the law, and against those who have stood idly by. In those days we may see the ugly crowd making its way to the Pilate governors, who so often wash their hands, and beating them to death and burning their wives. That is the real movement. There is nothing very reasonable in it, but the risen mob is not guided by logic.

The multiracial "risen mob" of the future may be irrational and incendiary, but its "common cause" against the "Pilate governors" of the ruling class puts a new twist on the biblical trope. In Graham's insurrectionary scenario, rank-and-file lynchers will supersede the illusory bond of color that has aligned them with the white elite and will unite with black Christs; the trope of Christ as lynchee—a tragic convention in African American poetry from McKay to Gwendolyn Brooks—here takes on a distinctly class-conscious cast. Although Graham's somewhat utopian notion that southern blacks would "easily" close ranks with white working-class lynchers manifests a superficial acquaintance with the dynamics of Jim Crow, the British journalist's enthusiasm for a leftist analysis of racial antagonism is evident. For the liberal *Nation* editor Oswald Garrison Villard, writing about Brown in 1911, it had been "the man on the scaffold, sacrificing, not taking life," who had inspired those who fought for the North. For Graham, writing less than a decade later, the figure of John Brown takes shape as a proto-Bolshevik; as his soul "marches on," "Georgia" is transformed from a metonymy for lynch violence into a site of proletarian revolution.[31]

The gravitation toward leftist analysis in texts both published and recommended by the NAACP also surfaced in the white liberal press of the time, where expressions of pro-Soviet sympathy mingled intermittently with class-based analyses of black-white relations. This overlap occurred partly because prominent NAACP officials—Pickens, Seligmann, Johnson, White, Ovington—frequently wrote for the *Freeman*, the *New Republic*, and especially the *Nation*. But other articles and editorials in these organs stressed the economic underpinnings of racial violence and treated rebellion as a justified response to unbearable social conditions. Geroid Robinson's article "The New Negro" in an early issue of the *Freeman* linked race with class oppression and praised the *Messenger* for its militant eloquence, sardonically citing Attorney General Palmer's view of Randolph and Owen's paper as "'the most able and most dangerous of all the Negro publications.'" The *New Republic* reported regularly on lynchings. An April 1918 editorial queried—in a grim echo of H. L. Mencken—whether lynching was "an American Kultur," and during the summer of 1919 the magazine cited case after case of racist murder and called for federal legislation against lynching. The *New Republic* also denounced the roles of the press and the police in the 1919 race riots and commented that "[had instances of this brutal beating] occurred, let us say, in Moscow, we should unfailingly have hailed them as evidence of a nation's inability to govern itself." Seeing in Bogalusa a wave of the future, the magazine connected lynching with economics and, in its subsequent coverage of the "death farm" in Jasper County, Georgia, pointed out the basis of racial terrorism in the system of forced labor that was "essentially a continuation of the system of slavery."[32]

The *Nation*, the most left-leaning of the prominent liberal magazines, embraced various essentials of the socialist analysis of racial antagonism. Commenting on the bloody 1921 race riot in Omaha, the editors noted, "The Negro is economically a competitor and when to a man who is a labor competitor there is added a dark color of the skin you have one of the despised." Referring to the burning alive of John Henry Williams and to the "wholesale murders in Jasper County," they further warned, "If [the South] does not begin to put its house in order and . . . give economic justice and freedom to its colored citizens it will some day pay a terrible price. The white Czars once thought the Russian serfs would never rise. Twice now have the serfs set themselves free." Like Graham, the *Nation* editors framed a prophetic analogy between the situations of pre-revolutionary Russian peasants and African American sharecroppers: if Russian peasants could throw off the yoke of serfdom through proletarian revolution, so might Negro sharecroppers and tenant farmers. At times the *Nation* editors were at least as frightened as they were energized by the prospect of proletarian insurrection, depicted as a "terrible price" to pay for past abuses. As in its reportage on the Seattle general strike, the *Nation* was warning the elite to forestall revolution as much as it was encouraging the prospect. John Spargo, a fulminating ex-Socialist, overstated the case somewhat when in 1919 he described the *Nation* as "a journal exceedingly generous in its treatment of Bolshevism and the Bolsheviki." Nonetheless, the Lusk Committee had some basis for its claim that the *Nation* was—along with the *New Republic*—an "exponen[t] of revolutionary social ideas."[33]

"Coming Unities" and "Ethnic Fictions": Du Bois and Locke

In the revolutionary crucible of 1919, the term *New Negro* signified a fighter against both racism and capitalism; to be a political moderate did not preclude endorsement of at least some aspects of a class analysis of racism or sympathy with at least some goals of the Bolshevik Revolution. It is widely known that Du Bois, even if labeled an "Old Crowd Negro," had socialist leanings early on; it is less often recognized that Locke, before becoming the guiding spirit of Harlem Renaissance culturalism, had significant affinities with a leftist and anti-imperialist program. Du Bois, fifty-one years old in 1919, was both generationally and politically alienated from the radical young New Negroes of the *Messenger* and the *Crusader;* he also kept his distance from the SPA, having joined it in 1911 but dropped out to support Wilson in 1912. Du Bois displayed continuing skepticism whether the Socialists had the ability—or the courage—to confront the issue of racism within the working class, declaring in the *Intercollegiate Socialist* in 1917 that "[t]he Negro problem is the great test of the American Socialist." Du Bois also recurrently expressed doubt whether U.S. white workers would overcome their racism sufficiently to act in revolutionary fashion. Writing in his 1915 *Atlantic Monthly* series, "The African Roots of War," that "[t]he white working-man has been asked to share the spoil of exploiting 'chinks and niggers,'" Du Bois supported U.S. entry into the war on the grounds that African Americans should "close ranks" so that after the war they would be in a position to demand recompense for their service to the nation. When in 1921 he considered the slim possibilities for class-based revolution in the industrialized nations, Du Bois once again charged that white workers "may not be as conscious of all they are doing as their more educated masters, called Nationalists and Imperialists, but they are consciously submitting themselves to the leadership of these men"; the "individual white employee" is thus a "co-worker in the miserable modern subjugation of over half the world."[34]

But—decades before his late-in-life decision to become a Communist—Du Bois evinced a strong anticapitalist streak. Even in his prewar Darwinian phase, when he hoped—like many other socialist sympathizers of the time—that evolution would naturally tend toward equality, he insisted that Darwinism taught "the abolition of hard and fast lines between races, just as it called for the breaking down of barriers between classes." In his weirdly resonant poem "The Song of the Smoke" (1907), the personified smoke moves from an Afrocentric stance ("blackness was ancient ere whiteness began") to a near-Marxist one: "I whiten my black men—I blacken my white! / What's the hue of a hide to a man in his might"? As early as 1909, Du Bois also expressed a passionate respect for John Brown, whom he treated as an honorary black man, an example of "the inspiration which America owes to Africa." In *Darkwater* (1920),

Du Bois proclaimed that "the Will to Human Brotherhood of all Colors, Races, and Creeds[,] the Wanting of the Wants of All," was "the finest contribution of current Socialism to the world" and the "idea back of its one mighty word—Comrade!" In 1924, he noted that the "Negro working-man," as opposed to the European, "came out of an organization of industry which was communistic and did not call for unlimited toil on the part of the workers." African heritage was inseparable from a collectivist ethos having much in common with modern socialism.[35]

The Du Bois of the wartime and postwar years was riddled with contradictions about race and class. Although he had encouraged Negro participation in the war, his famous postwar *Crisis* editorial "Returning Soldiers" contained a veiled threat:

> [B]y the God of Heaven, we are cowards and jackasses if now that war is over, we do not marshal every ounce of our brain and brawn to fight a sterner, longer, more unbending battle against the forces of hell in our own land.
> *We return.*
> *We return from fighting.*
> *We return fighting.*
> Make way for Democracy! We saved it in France, and by the Great Jehovah, we will save it in the United States of America, or know the reason why.

"Or know the reason why": in an ironic echo of Tennyson's charging light brigadiers, Du Bois promised to explore the root cause of continuing inequality; it is not coincidental that this editorial appeared in May 1919, the month of maximum international class struggle in the postwar period. Du Bois expressed increasing enthusiasm for the Bolshevik Revolution, remarking in 1921 that "time may prove . . . that the Russian Revolution is the greatest event of the nineteenth and twentieth centuries, and its leaders the most unselfish prophets." He also at times contradicted the position that white workers "share the spoils" of the superexploitation of workers of color. While he argued that, even if materially disadvantaged by their own racism, white workers enjoyed the "psychological wages" of their whiteness, as early as 1915 he also held that "there can be no permanent uplift of American or European labor as long as African laborers are slaves." "The more far-seeing Negroes sense the coming unities," he wrote in *The Negro*, "a unity of the working classes everywhere, a unity of the colored races, a new unity of men." Moreover, he noted in *Darkwater* that the whiteness of the white worker was itself a historical construct accompanying Jim Crow and imperialism: "The discovery of personal whiteness among the world's peoples is a very

modern thing." That "whiteness" operated as a social control mechanism, disciplining not only the black victims of Jim Crow but also the
working-class whites recruited to enforce this discipline, was implied if
not explicit in Du Bois's formulation. Reiterating this point in relation
to the Jim Crow–riven Georgia of 1925, he mused, "[White and black] hate
and despise each other today. They lynch and murder body and soul. They
are separated by the width of a world. And yet—and yet stranger things
have happened under the sun than understanding between those who are
born blind." Although some commentators relegate Du Bois's embrace
of a class-based radicalism to the final years of his long life, in fact, as
Du Bois's biographer David Levering Lewis points out, a provisional endorsement of the aims and values of socialism runs throughout much of
his work. Du Bois was stirred by the possibilities opened up by the revolutionary upsurge of 1919, even as he held out for more definitive proof
than he had yet received of the class-conscious potential of the U.S. proletariat. Although the radicals at the *Messenger* and the *Crusader* insistently designated Du Bois an "Old Crowd Negro," it was not without
justification that the Military Intelligence Division referred to Du Bois
in 1919 as the "Karl Marx of Negroes."[36]

Less commonly acknowledged than the fissures running through Du
Bois's thought are the contradictory tendencies in the writings of Locke,
whose political trajectory before 1925 is routinely oversimplified and
viewed in a narrowly American context. As a student in prewar Europe,
first in Oxford and then on the Continent, Locke had come under the influence of Indian, African, and German revolutionaries and socialists conversant in Marxist doctrine. This to-be-famous anthologist's first editorial act was to coedit in 1908 the *Oxford Cosmopolitan*, a short-lived journal
voicing the views of Locke's fellow students from the colonized world.
Addressing the Yonkers Negro Society for Historical Research in September 1914 about the outbreak of the Great War, he declaimed against the
"foolish[ness . . . [of] regard[ing] the rivalries as merely political, involving merely the personal ambitions of rulers, or the designs of contending
bureaucracies." Two years before the publication of Lenin's *Imperialism:
The Highest Stage of Capitalism*, Locke was asserting that the war was
"a race war" fought "for the utopia of empire and the dream of an unlimited and permanent overlordship." Moreover, in a series of lectures delivered at Howard in 1916—originally conceived as a course called "Race
Contacts and Interracial Relations: A Study in the Theory and Practice
of Race," Locke sounded a distinctly Marxist note when he critiqued the
biologically based theories of race enjoying near universal currency at the
time as "ethnic fictions." "[Race antipathy] is cultivated, very often de-

liberately cultivated," he wrote, "and much is not only cultivated but controlled and modified." Exploring the role of "indoctrination" in stirring up "racist antipathies" even between "divergent sects or divisions of the same race or the same ethnic strain," he concluded that "[r]ace issues are only very virulent forms of class issues, because as they can be broken up into class issues they become possible of solution in society." In his notes for the course syllabus, Locke was even more forthright. Arguing that "false race theory" functions as an "apologia for prevailing practice," he maintained that the essential "practice of race" is based in the "competitive and industrial basis of modern imperialism." Because "race feeling" is rooted in "social practice," however, it is "eradicable and to be eradicated." In declaring that there is validity to the notion of race not "in the ethnological or biological sense" but only in the "sociological" sense, Locke proposed that race is not just a social construct but also an ideological one, serving the imperatives of capital. His deconstruction of race was inseparable from his conviction that "false conceptions of race" were "an obstacle to progress and a menace to civilization."[37]

As is discussed at greater length in chapter 5, in the last of the 1916 lectures, "Racial Progress and Race Adjustment," Locke backed away from the potentially revolutionary implications of this argument and went through a number of logical contortions to propose that, to contest the hold of supremacist ideology on whites and to combat internalized racism among blacks, some kind of positive conception of race—which he dubbed alternatively "race pride" and, more obscurely, "secondary race consciousness" and which might be called strategic essentialism today— was requisite. The connection between "secondary race consciousness" and the pragmatist notion of race guiding *The New Negro*—as well as the distance between both concepts and his earlier designation of the very notion of race as "indoctrination"—should be apparent. Locke's biographer Jeffrey Stewart has suggested that governmental investigations into Negro radicalism (resulting in the removal of literature perceived as incendiary from the library at Howard University) may have played a determining role in Locke's retreat from leftism. "Locke had gotten the message by 1919," Stewart concludes. "So completely did he drop his critique of American racism that he did not publish anything of significance between 1919 and 1922." Stewart speculates that Locke's opportunity to edit the landmark issue of the *Survey Graphic* that eventually become *The New Negro* came when he was still casting about for a paradigm that would replace his earlier attraction to a more leftist—and materially grounded—politics. Although it is evident that, by 1925, Locke had quite successfully distanced himself from his earlier radicalism, it would appear that his path toward founding fatherhood of the Harlem Renaissance was by no means a linear one. When Locke banned the Left from *The New Negro*, he was repudiating a paradigm with which he had once been intimately familiar. That the terms in which he would frame this repudiation would be partly derived from the categories of the contemporaneous Left itself is, as will be seen, a deep historical and political irony.[38]

"The Negro Is Seeing Red": Radicals and the New Negro

Although the wartime and postwar years witnessed a decisive shift toward the left among moderates and liberals, African American and white, the expanded political horizon was most fully limned forth in the leftist press—not just the organs of the Socialists and Communists but also the magazines edited by those New Negroes for whom blackness was necessarily colored by Redness.

The *Call*, the most widely read socialist daily in the United States, hailed the New Negro in 1917: "The New Negro is here; and there will be more of them to enrich the Socialist movement in the United States." Although the SPA did not routinely advocate "social equality," that bugbear to Jim Crow racists, the *Call* consistently urged multiracial proletarian unity on the job. Moreover, the *Call* regularly reproduced statistics about lynchings and covered lynchings and other instances of racial violence. When a choreographed 1919 lynching in Ellisville, Mississippi, was brazenly advertised in advance in a Jackson newspaper, the *Call* reprinted the notice—first reproduced in the *Crisis*—in all its horror (see figure 3). Upon the outbreak of race riots in Washington and Chicago during the summer of 1919, the *Call* covered the events in close detail and editorialized:

> American capitalism is about as foul as will be found anywhere in the world. Of pogroms we have the most atrocious in the world. These things are the more disgusting when it is remembered that swarms of patriotic fakirs continually yawp the praises of American "democracy." Not until our black brothers are free to walk the streets of American cities unmolested, not until they have free access to all callings and professions, not until they are free to organize politically in the South and to vote without being clubbed and shot, will this country be anything else than an autocracy to them.

Associating the race riots with pogroms, the *Call* analogized anti-Negro racism with anti-Semitism; opposing "brother[hood]" with the cant of "patriotic fakirs," it ironized the democratic pretensions of the "100

THE CRISIS

(Reprinted from the NEW ORLEANS STATES)

3,000 WILL BURN NEGRO

Kaiser Under Stronger Guard Following Escape Of Crown Prince

| Frank Simonds Writes For States | NEW ORLEANS STATES |

VOL 39   NO 177   NEW ORLEANS, LA. THURSDAY, JUNE 26, 1919

(Reprinted from the JACKSON DAILY NEWS)

JOHN HARTFIELD WILL BE LYNCHED BY ELLISVILLE MOB AT 5 O'CLOCK THIS AFTERNOON

Governor Bilbo Says He Is Powerless to Prevent It— Thousands of People Are Flocking Into Ellisville to Attend the Event—Sheriff and Authorities Are Powerless to Prevent It.

HATTIESBURG, June 26.—John Hartfield, the negro alleged to have assaulted an Ellisville, young woman, has been taken to Ellisville and is guarded by officers in the office of Dr. Carter in that city. He is wounded in the shoulder but not seriously. The officers have agreed to turn him over to the people of the city at 4 o'clock this afternoon when it is expected he will be burned. The negro is said to have made a partial confession.

GOV. BILBO SAYS HE IS POWERLESS.

When Gov. Bilbo was shown the above dispatch and asked what action, if any, he intended to take to prevent the affair, he said: "I am powerless to prevent it. We have guns for state militia, but no men. It is impossible to send troops to the scene for the obvious reason that we have no troops.

"Several days ago, anticipating
for the lynching has now been fixed for five p. m.

A committee of Ellisville citizens has been appointed to make the necessary arrangements for the event, and the mob is pledged to act in conformity with these arrangements.

Rev. L. G. Gates, pastor of the First Baptist church of Laurel, left here at one o'clock for Ellisville to entreat the mob to use discretion.

THOUSANDS GOING

Figure 3. *Call*, 14 July 1919, reprinted from the *Crisis*

percent Americans" and proposed a higher allegiance based on the recognition of universal humanity.[39]

Not just in its news coverage and editorials but also in its cultural commentaries, reviews, and poems, the *Call* promoted a class-conscious internationalism and antiracism. An untitled serial fable about the wanderings of a seeker for Truth, penned by "the Dreamer," portrayed the Great War—in which the Dreamer's neighbors "flew at each other's throats" and "killed their best friends"—as the impetus to his abandonment of "Dogmatic Theory." It would be only by exploring the "Mountains of Experience," where presumably he would learn the true identities of friends and enemies, that the Dreamer—clearly a critic of the Second International's abandonment of proletarian internationalism during the war—would find the Truth that had been "lost in the blood-red mire of the great human sacrifice." Pointing at a more particular truth lodged in U.S. history, a negative review of Hill Peebles Wilson's *John Brown: Soldier of Fortune*—tellingly entitled "Spattering Mud on John Brown's Halo"—faulted Wilson for portraying the abolitionist as an opportunist and a religious fanatic. A fuller understanding of Brown's martyrdom, urged the *Call* editor David Karsner, was available in Eugene Debs's writings about Brown, as well as in the real-life parallel between the two men. Reviews of Brawley's *Your Negro Neighbor* and of Johnson's latest book of poetry were among several such efforts to acquaint the *Call*'s mostly white readership with what it meant to be a Negro in the United States.[40]

The *Call*'s attempt at class-conscious antiracist education is exemplified in "The Negro Worker," a poem reprinted from the *Seattle Union Record* by one "Anise" (Anna Louise Strong). The poem examines the employment situation facing an African American returning veteran:

> [H]e went out hunting
>
> * * *
>
> A JOB
>
> * * *
>
> In the shipyards
>
> * * *
>
> From some of these patriots
>
> * * *
>
> Who made a lot of money
>
> * * *
>
> From the war.
>
> * * *
>
> But the employment managers
>
> * * *

And the men

* * *

Were very UNWILLING

* * *

To take on a NEGRO.

* * *

They said to him

* * *

"We are afraid

* * *

You will get a RIVET

* * *

Or a MONKEY WRENCH

* * *

Dropped on you." . . .

* * *

And he said to me . . .

* * *

"I DO KNOW

* * *

That I can't get into

* * *

The UNION I belong to. . . .

* * *

I wonder why

* * *

They are so short-sighted

* * *

As not to realize

* * *

That every time

* * *

They keep ANY WORKER

* * *

Man or woman

* * *

White, yellow, or black

* * *

OUT of a UNION

* * *

They are forcing a worker

* * *

To be a SCAB

* * *

To be used AGAINST THEM."

In this "ragged-verse" poem—a style frequently found in newspaper poetry of the period—Strong portrays the white workers' lack of class-consciousness as "short-sightedness" and stresses the division of interest between the "employment managers" and the "men," even as they commonly embrace the doctrine of white supremacy. Written in the wake of the AFL's hypocritical 1919 desegregation pledge, the poem emphasizes that fighting discrimination is beneficial to white and black workers alike; its three points of view—the white workers', the black worker's, and the narrator's—portray the fight against racism as a struggle within the consciousness of the working class. Although the *Call* was not entirely typical of SPA organs in its antiracism—the New York branch of the party was, Philip Foner points out, more advanced in this regard than most others—its editors clearly considered overcoming racial antagonism to be crucial to consolidating the working class in its struggles against exploitation. On the *Call*'s fifteenth anniversary in 1923, the *Messenger* praised the paper for having "always stood four square . . . on the Negro question, . . . evincing a sympathetic and scientific understanding of its most subtle ramifications. . . . All workers, black and white should read [the *Call*] and contribute to its maintenance. May its readers soon number in the millions."[41]

The cultural Left clustered around the *Liberator* also viewed the struggle against Jim Crow as intimately related to the fight for a better world. Its editors, Crystal Eastman and Max Eastman, announced in the first issue that the magazine would "assert the social and political equality of the black and white races, oppose every kind of racial discrimination, and conduct a remorseless publicity campaign against lynch law." The crucial words "social and political equality" clearly indicated that the *Liberator*, unlike the *Call*, did not plan to equivocate over interracial marriage or voting rights. Moreover, the editors' choice of a title echoing the name of the most famous abolitionist newspaper of the previous century patently linked the Left's ultimate goal—the abolition of wage slavery—with emancipation from chattel slavery. The *Liberator* published trenchant commentaries on lynching and racial violence; it was here that Ovington's account of the Bogalusa incident first appeared. Where the *Crisis* and the *Nation* congratulated the judge and jury for convicting the Jasper County "death farm" owner John S. Williams of murder and sentencing him to life in prison, the *Liberator* commentator Esau Jones argued that Williams had been scapegoated by a ruling elite desirous of keeping intact its lucrative practice of debt peonage:

> In a Northern court Williams would probably have been found guilty of murder and paid the death penalty, but a life sentence was all any jury

would be courageous enough to impose in the Black Belt, and already the good news has gone forth that the next Governor will pardon him. Willie went too far. (Not because the muddy yellow rivers and red hills of Georgia gave up eleven mutilated bodies, for what's a niggah more or less?) But Williams ought to have shown better judgement in the time and quantity of the killings. To clear the good name of Georgia he must be sent up.

At stake for the powers-that-be in the public representation of the Williams case, Jones realized, was not so much whether "justice" had been served—a patent impossibility in a state where "one niggah more or less" was beneath notice—but whether "Georgia" had managed to evade being metonymically identified with the neoslavery of debt peonage.[42]

Lynch violence was a persistent theme in pieces published in the *Liberator*, as evidenced in Lucy Maverick's "Out of Texas"; E. Merrill Root's "Southern Holiday"; Jeannette Pearl's "Negro Bodies"; Daytie Randle's "Lament," a poem featuring a black woman whose son has been lynched and whose daughter is prey to rapists; and Ralph Chaplin's "Wesley Everest," a sonnet describing the lynching of the white Wobbly leader later to be memorialized in Dos Passos's *1919*. Mary Burrill's "Aftermath" portrays a returning black soldier who, learning of the recent lynching of his father, storms out to kill the murderers; most probably he will meet his own death, but—as a "New Negro" of the war's "aftermath"—he is unwilling to abide by the old rules of Jim Crow. Robert Minor's drawing "The Exodus from Dixie" (see figure 4) portrays the northward migration not as the flight of determined, upwardly mobile individuals—as did the *Crisis*—but as the departure of outraged masses threatening reprisal.[43]

That the *Liberator*'s antiracist commitment extended beyond explicitly leftist political declaration was signaled by its publication of graphics, imaginative texts, and essays, by African American and white artists alike, that depicted blacks in nonstereotypical stances, surveyed the black cultural scene, and voiced generally progressive—though not necessarily socialist or communist—political commentary. Drawings by Hugo Gellert—"Negro Boy"—and Boardman Robinson—"In a Street Car"—showed African Americans in everyday lives with which any reader could readily identify. Stuart Davis's "Return of the Soldier" suggested the black soldier's longing for the harmonies created by white and black piano keys. Georgia Douglas Johnson's "Octoroon" explored the paradoxes of the one-drop rule. James Weldon Johnson publicized the activities and goals of the NAACP in "What the Negro Is Doing for Himself." Walter White contributed a scathing commentary on a 1921

Figure 4. "The Exodus from Dixie," by Robert Minor, *Liberator*, June 1923

white supremacist speech in Birmingham, Alabama, by the newly elected Warren G. Harding, as well as a laudatory review of James Weldon Johnson's 1922 anthology of Negro poetry. The *Liberator* also published favorable reviews of Woodson's *Negro in Our History* and White's *Fire in the Flint*. Although Angelina Grimké in a 1921 letter faulted the magazine for "forgetting about us," the charge was not entirely fair: the *Liberator* devoted considerably greater attention to African American life and art than did any other periodical edited primarily by whites and, with new subscriptions, included a copy of Claude McKay's *Harlem Shadows*.[44]

Part of the reason for the *Liberator*'s antiracist editorial policy was doubtless the role played by McKay, who coedited the magazine for six months in 1922 with the literary Marxist Mike Gold. It was in the *Liberator* that McKay first published his famous (and oft-to-be-reprinted) sonnet "If We Must Die"—prompted by blacks' militant resistance during the 1919 race riots—when McKay's usual publishing venue, *Pearson's Magazine*, would not touch the defiant poem. As William Maxwell has pointed out, during the period of McKay's coeditorship the *Liberator* published ten poems, five essays, and a short story by the Caribbean-born writer; during its duration the magazine was "the first home of over one-third of the seventy-four poems gathered in *Harlem Shadows*; of the five poems by McKay included in *The New Negro*, three were first published by Eastman, Gold and company." Ranging from personal memories of Jamaica to such anticolonial pronouncements as "To Ethiopia," McKay's *Liberator* poetry cut a broad swath of topics.[45]

It has frequently been pointed out that McKay's tenure as coeditor was problematic. When he took the position that the pages of the *Liberator* should be devoted to African Americans according to their percentage in the U.S. population (about 10 percent), some members of the editorial board objected that this policy might turn away potential subscribers. In his last review for the magazine before resigning in July 1922, McKay wrote—reviewing T. S. Stribling's *Birthright*—that "the problem of the darker races is a rigid test of Radicalism" and "may be eventually the monkey wrench thrown into the machinery of the American revolutionary struggle." Harold Cruse, in his influential *Crisis of the Negro Intellectual* (1967), has argued that the purportedly stormy McKay-Gold relationship epitomizes the deleterious effects of white radical—specifically Jewish—paternalism on African Americans. As will be seen in chapter 2, the reformist economism—and at times the uninterrogated racism—of the SPA (the place where, for better or worse, most of the *Liberator* editors and contributors had shaped their politics) no doubt influenced McKay's conclusion that too many of his white fellow radicals thought his writing should be "more broadly socialistic and less chauvinistically racialist." But McKay's biographer Wayne Cooper documents a largely amicable relationship between the two *Liberator* editors; James A. Miller notes that McKay's "ideological disputes" with the *Liberator* staff did not "dete[r] him from traveling to the Soviet Union later that year to witness the results of the revolution with his own eyes"; and Maxwell points out that, in his "Negroes in America," McKay especially recommended to New Negro writers that they link themselves with "the new school of critics, chiefly Jews." Mark Solomon demonstrates that by the time McKay went to the USSR he was no mere fellow traveler, having been a full-fledged underground party member since the first months of the Communist Party's formation and having helped recruit the ABB leader Cyril Briggs. McKay's principal point of disagreement with the party line at this point, Solomon contends, centered not on racial matters but on the strategy—embraced by the so-called Goose Caucus—of having an underground, instead of an openly communist, organization. Even in his largely jaundiced autobiography of nearly two decades later,

McKay commented fondly on the "free and easy intercourse between people of different classes and races" in the *Liberator* group. While hardly a utopian space free from the almost overwhelming pressures of U.S. racism, the *Liberator* provided a site where interracial radicalism could be articulated and, to a degree, lived.[46]

The New Negro continued to be identified as a class-conscious radical in the *Workers Monthly*, which served as a bridge to the *New Masses* between 1924 and 1926. Primarily a theoretical supplement to the Communist daily, the *Toiler*, the *Workers Monthly* focused on revolutionary working-class organizing on a range of fronts but regularly treated racial issues, stressing the key role of black workers in U.S. industry, calling for black-white labor unity, and increasingly attacking Garveyism as retrograde. The "New Negro," opined the *Workers Monthly*, was "a healthy working class left wing in the [UNIA]," one that "refuses any longer to submit to the servile anti-Negro program that Garvey has been attempting to thrust down their throats." Although the Communist Party would fully codify its view of African Americans as an oppressed nation within a nation only in 1928, the *Workers Monthly* anticipated several aspects of the position, noting in 1925 that Negroes were an "oppressed people" in need of alliance with both the white U.S. working class and, internationally, their "African kindred"—a formulation clearly influenced by both contemporaneous Pan-Africanism and the Leninist principle of self-determination. That these doctrines were not viewed as incompatible with a "left" patriotism was signaled by the *Workers Monthly* cover for July 1926, which featured a flag picturing a coiled rattlesnake, a pine tree, and the slogan "Don't Tread on Me," along with the caption, "One of the First American Revolutionary Flags." While the pine tree—a symbol for the nation dating back to colonial times—had been the icon of choice for the Ash Can artists of the 1910s, clearly the *Workers Monthly* editors had a more radical message in mind. Moreover, many readers familiar with postwar revolutionary culture would have known that "Don't Tread on Me" was also the title—and refrain—of a frequently reprinted militant poem first published during the spring of 1919 by the *Crusader* contributor Andrea Razafkeriefo. Although the U.S. Communist movement would not make its breakthrough in organizing among African Americans until the 1930s, the analyses of class struggle promoted in the *Workers Monthly* during the mid-1920s gave more than passing attention to the necessity of fighting racism in the ranks of the working class.[47]

If less fully than the *Liberator* that preceded it and the *New Masses* that succeeded it, the *Workers Monthly* promoted revolutionary culture through its graphics and its poetry. Jay Lovestone's article "The Great

Negro Migration," for example, was accompanied by Lydia Gibson's litho-graphs featuring families fleeing from the land of Jim Crow. Some half-dozen poems by Langston Hughes—containing some of his most left-wing declarations of the decade—appeared in the *Workers Monthly* between November 1924 and February 1927. "God to Hungry Child" presages the theme of Hughes's more famous 1932 attack on Christianity, "Goodbye Christ," in its characterization of God as apologist for the capitalist class and a capitalist himself:

> Hungry child,
> I didn't make this world for you.
> You didn't buy any stock in my railroad.
> You didn't invest in my corporation.
> Where are your shares in standard oil?
> I made the world for the rich
> And the will-be rich
> And the have-always-been rich.
> Not for you, hungry child.

Through its metaphor of an ocean heaving up foam, "Rising Waters" suggests both the parasitical nature of the ruling class and the limited span of its reign:

> To you
> Who are the
> Foam on the sea
> And not the sea—
> What of the jagged rocks,
> And the waves themselves,
> And the force of the mounting waters?
> You are
> But the foam on the sea,
> You rich ones—
> Not the sea.

In Hughes's *Workers Monthly* poems, the voice of the New Negro was virtually indistinguishable from that of the class-conscious proletarian of any race or nation. Clearly the figure usually seen as the first folk trou-badour of the Harlem Renaissance did not need to wait for the Great Depression to write pro-communist poetry foregrounding the class con-tradiction.[48]

Before examining the formulation of the New Negro in the *Messen-ger* and the *Crusader*, both published by unabashedly Red black editors, one should take a brief look at the *Negro World*, organ of the UNIA, which exhibited marked contradictions in the late 1910s and early 1920s. On the one hand, the *Negro World* took reactionary positions on a range of issues. It advocated not just black capitalism but black nonparticipation in labor movements of any kind. It established a "friendly and faithful correspondence" with the *The Rising Tide of Color* author Stoddard. It praised Warren G. Harding's segregationist Birmingham speech and dubbed him "a friend of the Negro people." The *Negro World* joined in the efforts of the mainstream press to blame the ABB for the 1921 Tulsa riot, in which scores, possibly hundreds, perished. In the same year, the newspaper announced Garvey's friendly meeting with the KKK's Grand Wizard, a stance that severed once and for all the UNIA's always tenuous ties with the Left.[49]

On the other hand, in its early phases the UNIA aligned itself, however sporadically, with radical class-based and anticolonial movements. The SPA member Randolph was invited to attend the 1919 Pan-Africanist conference in Paris as a UNIA delegate; the *Emancipator* editor Domingo, who in the early 1920s would leave the UNIA for the Communist-aligned ABB, served as editor of the *Negro World* in the immediate postwar period; and Hubert Harrison edited the newspaper from 1920 to 1922, functioning as "a principal radical influence on the Garvey movement during its radical high point in the 1920s." Editorials in the *Negro World* occasionally expressed solidarity with not just oppressed peoples but also political groups opposed to repressive regimes. One 1920 issue declared that the red in the UNIA flag showed the members' "sympathy with the 'Reds' of the world, and the Green their sympathy for the Irish in their fight for freedom." In 1921, Garvey happily predicted that Lenin and Trotsky would join Indian, Japanese, and Chinese nationalists in fighting for "Africa for the Africans." A BI agent assigned to spy on the UNIA reported in March 1921 that, at a recent Russian Club picnic, UNIA members "sang the Internationale as lustily as did the Ruskys." Even though Garvey publicly professed his love for America at a mass rally in New York's Liberty Hall in July 1921, Harrison in the same year wrote—in a piece tellingly titled "Wanted—A Colored International"— that "we have no faith in American democracy." In 1922, the Garveyite paper published Harrison's review of Frederick Palmer's *Folly of Nations*, in which Harrison chided the author for failing to grasp that the war's "deep underlying causes" could be found in "[i]mperialism, which puts the war-making powers of the modern state in the hands of those who own the earth and its products, and sends its millions of men to die abroad for markets when they lack meat at home." Until Garvey made his pact with the KKK, the contradictory politics of the UNIA held significant appeal for many African Americans tending toward the left—an appeal no doubt enhanced by the fact that, with its peak weekly circulation of 200,000, the *Negro World* reached more readers than did the *Crisis*, the *Crusader*, and the *Messenger* combined. As late as 1 May 1926, Richard Moore, now a member of the CPUSA, ran an advertisement for the May Day activities of the Communist-sponsored American Negro Labor Congress in the pages of the *Negro World*. When the Lusk Committee charged that in the *Negro World* "the Soviet rule is upheld and there is open advocation of Bolshevism," it was not entirely off target.[50]

Although primarily an organ of news and commentary, the *Negro World* had a regular poetry column and debated the role of politics in literature—"almost always," the Garvey scholar Tony Martin writes, "[coming] down on the side of 'propaganda' in the great debate of the 1920s on the place of propaganda in art." The *Negro World* literary editor Eric Walrond in 1922 praised René Maran's Goncourt Prize–winning anticolonial novel *Batouala* for its portrayal of "the underdog in revolt," fighting "straight from the shoulder slashing, murdering, disemboweling!" The verse published in the *Negro World* reflected the UNIA's contradictory politics on nation, class, and race. On the one hand, "Back to Africa" themes dominated many of the poems. Fred J. Edwards's "African Chief" typifies the *Negro World*'s heroization of African heritage:

> Chained in the market-place he stood,
>   A man of giant frame,
> Amid the gathering multitude
>   That shrunk to hear his name;
>
> All stern of look and strong of limb,
>   His dark eye on the ground;
> And silently they gazed on him,
>   As on a lion bound.[51]

Ethel Trew Dunlap, a regular contributor, frequently wrote in celebration of black nationalism in general and Garvey and the Black Star line in particular. "In Respect to Marcus Garvey" states:

> He saw a flag eyes could not see—
>   A nation yet unborn—
> A land where black men might be free,
>   The dawn of freedom's morn.
>
> He did not deem the price too dear
>   (Whatever it might be)
> For black men to regain their soil
>   And set their country free.

Most of Dunlap's poems exhibit a startling sameness; even one of her partisans on the *Negro World* editorial staff diplomatically noted that "she seems to lack the power of conveying in her poems a large amount of intricately arranged rhyme without apparent difficulty." But the very banality of much of Dunlap's verse, with its obsessively reiterated rhymes—"free," "sea," "see," "flee," "me," and "be"—openly reveals the politics guiding her aesthetic practice.[52]

On the other hand, some of the poetry published in the *Negro World* could without difficulty have appeared in the *Crusader* or the *Messenger*. Razafkeriefo's "Rising Tide" (1920)—its title echoing that of Stoddard's best-seller—warns the "Anglo-Saxon" that his "dikes of race-subjection" can no longer "[s]top a long imprisoned sea," since the "rising tide of color" / Is the menace of today." Carita Owens Collins, writing in the spirit of "If We Must Die," proclaims in "This Must Not Be!" (1919):

> Your toil enriched the Southern lands,
> Your anguish has made sweet the sugar cane,
> Your sweat has moistened the growing corn,
> And drops of blood from the cruel master's whip
> Have caused the white cotton to burst forth in mute protest.

According to Tony Martin, the Lusk Committee, turning literary critic in pursuit of incendiary radicalism, "was scandalized" by "This Must Not Be!" "prefer[ring] to see in such sentiments a cause rather than an effect of the violence" of 1919. The frequent *Negro World* contributor Leonard Brathwaite, outraged by the Jasper County peonage murders, addresses in "Georgia" the same questions Esau Jones raised in the *Liberator:*

> I wonder
> * * *
> If
> * * *
> "The pillars"
> * * *
> Of Georgia
> * * *
> Are aware
> * * *
> They are making
> * * *
> History.

Georgia, Brathwaite sardonically concludes, is both the product and the symbol of its rulers' social practices:

> If they are
> * * *
> So much
> * * *
> The worse
> * * *
> As
> * * *
> The future history
> * * *
> Of Georgia
> * * *
> Will be
> * * *
> What
> * * *
> Past and present
> * * *
> Georgians
> * * *
> Have made it.

For Brathwaite, the word *Georgia* served metonymically to signify the brutality and exploitation transpiring on its soil.[53]

Finally, the *Negro World* even printed the occasional poem that was explicitly anticapitalist. Dunlap was moved in 1920 to pen "The Toiler," where she mused:

> Like a prisoner serves his term
>   For the crime that his hand has done,
> So the toiler serves capital
>   From the rise to the set of the sun.
>
> What has capital taught?
>   Only how greed may thrive,
> What has the ballot done?
>   Aided the rich to connive.
>
> Brain must battle with brain
>   The masses must rise and rule
> The industrial world, if man
>   Would cease to be labor's tool.

In a poem that could easily have been published in the *Call* or the *Liberator*, Dunlap condemns wage slavery, dismisses electoral politics as a tool of the wealthy, and proposes that the workers end their alienation by seizing control of the means of production. That the *Negro World* would publish such a poem indicates the indeterminate, or at least fluid, nature of the UNIA's political outlook in the wake of 1919. Even as Garvey's organization was engaging in increasing Red-baiting and nearing its rapprochement with the Klan, it was publishing a poem that took as its title the name of the Workers (Communist) Party's newspaper.[54]

Randolph and Owen's *Messenger*—self-described when first published as the "Only Magazine of Scientific Radicalism in the World Published by Negroes"—offered the most influential left-wing representation of the New Negro in the wartime and immediate postwar period, achieving a monthly circulation of 150,000 by 1919. The most prominent black Socialists of their generation, Randolph and Owen directed their magazine to a general audience but particularly addressed African Americans, urging them to oppose the war, defend themselves when attacked, vote Socialist, and align themselves with the labor movement, especially the IWW. They hailed the Bolshevik Revolution as "the Banquo's ghost to the Macbeth capitalists of the world whether they inhabit Germany, England, America or Japan. It is a foreword of a true world democracy. The Soviets represent the needs and aims of the masses." *Messenger* editorials unceasingly argued that "[o]rganized labor must harness the discontent of Negroes and direct it into working-class channels for working-class emancipation." In the realm of politics, the *Messenger* declared, the New Negro demands "political equality" and "universal suffrage." In the realm of economics, the New Negro, "as a worker, demands the full product of his toil." The social aim of the New Negro— "decidedly different from [that] of the Old Negro"—was "absolute and unequivocal *social equality.*" Although Randolph and Owen adhered to the Second International's bedrock position that—in the early words of Debs—socialism "had nothing special to offer to the Negro," they pressed wherever possible for fuller and more serious attention to the "Negro question," in both its international and national dimensions, calling for Pan-Africanist self-determination, on the one hand, and the need for black-white labor unity, on the other. Visible in political life both uptown in Harlem and downtown in Greenwich Village, Randolph and Owen taught a class called "The Economics and Sociology of the Race Problem" at the Rand School in the spring of 1919. In response to Bogalusa, they exclaimed, "All hail to the white workers of Bogalusa! You are learning! . . . Only class-conscious, militant labor can change the

South. And when it is sufficiently educated, labor will change the South from a place of autocracy and lynching to a place of democracy and freedom." Where the *Liberator* radicals looked more frequently to Whitman for a usable past, the *Messenger* editors held up John Brown as revolutionary exemplar and announced in March 1920 the formation of an interracial organization called the Friends of Negro Freedom that would, among other things, propose that a national holiday be celebrated on the abolitionist's birthday. That the call for socialism would invoke an international perspective was guaranteed by the contributions of Domingo, who continually linked the antiracist class struggle in the United States with movements against colonialism around the globe. That "[American Negroes] and all oppressed dark peoples will be the greatest beneficiaries in a socialist world," he pointed out, "has not been sufficiently emphasized by Socialist propaganda among Negroes."[55]

The editorials and reportage in the *Messenger* were highly charged, combining vivid imagery with hard-hitting political analysis. In a January 1918 article entitled "War Shouters and War Contracts," the Socialist economist and Rand School teacher Scott Nearing fulminated, "Profiteers! Profiteers! digging gold out of ground that is soaked with the blood of other men—Profiteers!" Turning against Jim Crow racists the anti-German rhetoric of wartime propaganda, Randolph and Owen denounced the lynchers of Mary Turner and her unborn child. "In Georgia," they declared, "the abdomen of a woman, upon the eve of bearing a child, was ripped open, the form emptied upon the ground, while American HUNS buried their heels in its brains." The regular columnist and former army lieutenant William Colson, pursuing the equation of Huns with lynchers, described the training and outlook of African American soldiers during the recent war: "When black officers taught black men bayonet practice they usually substituted a picture of the rabid white Southerner for that of the Hun. . . . The sentiment was that with the Huns of America over there the incitement necessary to the proper dash and courage would be forthcoming. They would then be fighting to make America safe for all classes. . . . [The] next war for 'democracy' would be in the land of the 'THE STAR-SPANGLED BANNER.'" Colson came close to calling for civil war; it is small wonder that the Lusk Committee cited this article in its effort to suspend the *Messenger*'s mailing permit. Randolph and Owen insistently analyzed lynching in the context of class division and exploitation, arguing that lynching "is used to foster and to engender race prejudice to prevent the lynchers and the lynched, the white and black workers from organizing on the industrial and voting on the political fields, to protect their labor-power." Offering a class analysis of debt peonage, the journal noted that the "howl of disgust [that] went up . . . when the bodies of eleven Negroes were found in the Alcovy River or buried in shallow graves on John S. Williams's 'death farm'" evaded the economic causality of the murders in the drive to exploit. Interpreting the largely northern race riots in the context of shifting capitalist imperatives to employ more blacks in industry, they predicted that, despite the spate of postwar rural lynchings, urban racial violence was the wave of the future. Although the *Messenger* reiterated the SPA position that capital is color-blind, its emphasis on the tragic consequences of black-white divisions in the working class suggested a competing—if not fully theorized—view of racism as essential to class formation and social control in the United States.[56]

The *Messenger*'s graphics powerfully reinforced its political message. Although, like the *Crisis*, the magazine customarily showcased on its cover a decidedly unproletarian icon of modest Negro womanhood, the *Messenger*'s visual politics were in other respects radical and hard-hitting. Its trademark emblem—which featured the clasped hands of black and white labor—conveyed the magazine's commitment to interracial labor unity (see figure 5). A cartoon lampooning Du Bois, Moton, and Kelly Miller portrayed "Old Crowd" Negroes as complacently watching while African Americans are beaten by policemen in the shadow of the Statue of Liberty (see figure 6). A drawing accompanying the commentary on the 1919 Washington race riots depicted an armored car of African American men blazing machine-gun fire at fleeing politicians (see figure 7). Another cartoon, offering a satiric commentary on capitalist techniques of racial divide and conquer, pictured two large dogs labeled "Negro Labor" and "White Labor" fighting over a meatless bone, while a smaller white dog labeled "Capital" feeds greedily off a large ham and an "Agitator Dog" warns, "Drop that bone, and get the ham! You are just *working dogs!*" (see figure 8). Another drawing showed a black worker and a white worker, each dragging a ball and chain and carrying on his shoulders an enormous boss who goads him on by uttering racist epithets against his presumed antagonist (see figure 9). More than mere illustrations of points being made in the magazine's analytical articles, such sharp visual images effectively distilled the *Messenger*'s Red politics and at times conveyed fairly complex arguments. A drawing with the caption "Congressman Byrnes of South Carolina Alarmed at Banquo's Ghost of the New Crowd Negro" showed the reactionary politician, a copy of the *Messenger* in hand, at once calling to mind the *Messenger*'s own image of the New Negro as gun-blazing motorist and recoiling at the vision of "Progress," presented as an African warrior who bears the spear of "Agitation" and the shield of "Education" and "Organization" (see figure 10). The spectre haunting the U.S.

bourgeoisie, the *Messenger* suggested, was at once national and international and would use force as well as reason in its warfare against the
capitalist state; that the journal quoted itself—both in the allusion to
"Banquo's Ghost" and in the reproduction of the gun-wielding New Negro—indicated the editors' awareness of the crucial role played by its own
Marxist analysis in sharpening the class contradiction. It was no accident
that the Lusk Committee would choose as the frontispiece to volume 2
of *Revolutionary Radicalism* a July 1919 *Messenger* graphic entitled "The
Mob Victim," which linked lynching and Americanism through the image of a black man being roasted alive in the flames of a burning U.S. flag
(see figure 11). Would the dead rise from the grave in revenge?[57]

The poems published in *Messenger* also underlined its condemnation
of capitalism and its promotion of multiracial revolutionary class consciousness. In the September 1919 issue, which was devoted largely to
an analysis of the recent Chicago race riot, McKay's sonnet "Labor's Day"
proclaimed:

> Once poets in their safe and calm retreat
> Essayed the singing of the fertile soil,
> The workman, bare-armed in the noonday heat,
> Happy and grateful at his peaceful toil;
> But now their voices hollow sound and cold,
> Like imitated music, false and strange,
> Or half truths of a day that could not hold
> Its own against the eternal tide of change.

Predicting that "Labor" would "sing modern songs of hope and vision,"
McKay's sonnet at once aligned itself with the movement to produce "a
new world under labor's law" and critiqued the aesthetic that conjoined
pastoralism ("singing of the fertile soil") with the obfuscation of exploitation ("[the] workman . . . [h]appy and grateful at his peaceful toil").
McKay's December 1919 sonnet "Birds of Prey" concretely embodied a
counteraesthetic to the "false and strange" poetry naturalizing the violence of capitalist rule. Comparing the capitalist class with "greed-
impelled" vultures that "[watch] the toilers with malignant eye," the sonnet turns the discourse of Darwinian "survival of the fittest" to the end
of multiracial Red critique:

> They swoop down upon us in merciless might,
> They fasten in our bleeding flesh their claws
> (We may be black or yellow, brown or white)
> And, tugging and tearing without rest or pause,
> They flap their hideous wings with wild delight
> And stuff our gory hearts into their maws.

Figure 5. *Messenger,*
September 1919

Figure 6. "Following the Advice of the 'Old Crowd' Negro,"
Messenger, June 1919

Figure 7. "The 'New Crowd' Negro Making America Safe for Himself,"
Messenger, July 1919

Figure 8. *Messenger,* December 1919

Figure 9. "Workers of the World, Unite!" by W. B. Williams, *Messenger*, August 1919

Figure 10. "Congressman Byrnes of South Carolina Alarmed at Banquo's Ghost of the New Crowd Negro," *Messenger*, August 1919

The Mob Victim

And it was in a Christian land,
With freedom's towers on every hand,
Where shafts to civic pride arise
To lift America to the skies.
And it was on a Sabbath day,
While men and women went to pray,
I passed the crowd in humble mode
In going to my meek abode.
From out the crowd arose a cry,
And epithets began to fly;
And thus like hounds they took my
track—
My only crime—my face was black.
And so this Christian mob did turn
From prayer to rob, to rack and
burn.
A victim helplessly I fell
To tortures truly kin to hell;
They bound me fast and strung me
high,
Then cut me down lest I should die
Before their savage zeal was spent
In torturing to their hearts' content.
They tore my flesh and broke my
bones,
And laughed in triumph at my
groans;

They chopped my fingers, clipped
my ears
And passed them round for souv-
enirs.
And then around my quivering
frame
They piled the wood, the oil and
flame;
And thus their Sabbath sacrifice
Was wafted upward to the skies.
A little boy stepped out of the crowd,
His face was pale, his voice was loud:
"My ma could not get to the fun,
And so I came, her youngest son,
To get the news of what went on."
He stirred the ashes, found a bone—
(A bit of flesh was hanging on)
He bore it off a cherished prize,
A remnant of the sacrifice.
Alas! no doubt, the heathen reads
Of Christian lands of noble deeds
By men with Christian hardihood
To shield their race's womanhood;
And yet around my burning frame,
Quivering by the scorching flame,
Their women danced around the
scene,

And each was christened "heroine."
They took my flesh as souvenirs,
And showed their pride with yells
and cheers.
And this where men are civilized,
And idol worship is despised;
Where nations boast that God hath
sent
The angel of enlightenment.
But while you sing America's pride,
Where men for liberty have died,
Compare the strain with double
stress
To her reward for harmlessness,
When burning flesh makes sporty
time,
And innocence is greatest crime.
O heathen minds on heathen strand,
What think you of a Christian land,
Where men and boys and women
turn
From prayer, to lynch, to rob and
burn,
And oft their drowsy minds refresh
Thru sport in burning human flesh?
Yet none dare tell who led the
band;
And this was in a Christian land.

Figure 11. "The Mob Victim," by W. B. Williams, *Messenger*, July 1919

McKay was evidently aware that his imagery here pressed against the limits of poetic respectability, for when "Birds of Prey" was reprinted in *Harlem Shadows*, it was substantially revised, with a sestet that reads:

> From their exclusive haven—birds of prey
> They swoop down from the spoil in certain might,
> And fasten in our bleeding flesh their claws.
> They beat us to surrender weak with fright,
> Without let or pause.

While in the later version the speaking "we" voices the terror of a worker of any racial designation, in the earlier text the speaker explicitly notes that proletarians of all races yield up their hearts to the capitalist class. The difference between the two versions carries palpable political significance.[58]

Although Langston Hughes's production of radical poetry would drop off dramatically between 1926 and 1932, several of his contributions to the *Messenger* in 1924 and 1925 articulated a radical class consciousness and underlined the centrality of racism to capitalism. "Johannesburg Mines" reminds the reader that the seductive, tom-tom-beating Africa of "Danse Africaine"—published three years earlier in the *Crisis*—is also the site of a superexploitation that defies artistic representation, let alone celebration:

> In the Johannesburg mines
> There are 240,000
> Native Africans working.
> What kind of poem
> Would you
> Make out of that?
> 240,000 natives
> Working in the
> Johannesburg mines.

Insistently anti-imagistic, the poem queries the social bases of both capitalism and lyric poetry. In "To Certain Intellectuals," Hughes's speaker, describing himself as "poor, / Black, / Ignorant and slow," declares that those he addresses—of unspecified race—are "no friend of mine." He is, it seems, not so "ignorant and slow" as not to know a friend from an enemy. In "Steel Mills," Hughes simmers with a class-conscious anger reminiscent of the young Carl Sandburg:

> The mills
> That grind and grind,
> That grind out new steel
> And grind away the lives

Of men,—
In the sunset
Their stacks
Are great black silhouettes
Against the sky.
In the dawn
They belch red fire.
The mills,—
Grinding out new steel,
Old men.

According to his autobiography, Hughes had written this poem—a tribute to his steelworker stepfather—many years earlier, when he was in high school. That he chose to publish it in the *Messenger* indicates his positive estimate of the magazine's commitment to a leftist practice that was simultaneously political and cultural.[59]

While it has been argued that the *Messenger* did not take seriously the project of developing a leftist culture, these examples suggest otherwise: from the outset Randolph and Owen were clearly cognizant of the role that art and literature could play in generating, concretizing, and reinforcing revolutionary ideas and attitudes. Moreover, they recognized the potential of mass culture to act as a solvent of racial divisions in the working class. In "The Cabaret—A Useful Social Institution," published in August 1922, Owen observed that, even as the city of Chicago was being torn apart during the race riots of 1919, the cabaret acted as a "dynamic agent of social equality," "breaking down the color line" and "destroying the psychology of caste." Although it "disseminat[ed] joy to the most humble and the most high," the cabaret was above all creating unity among the "so-called common people, white and black," who alone held "the basic solution of the race problem"—as opposed to the "wealthy classes," who "seldom take active part in mobs" but sit in "ice-cooled and steam-heated offices" from which they "produce opinions which create in turn the desires by which the 'common people' are 'egged on.'" In Owen's formulation, the cabaret was a "useful institution" not because it provided a utopian space free from the contradictions of the class struggle but because it supplied a ground on which the working class could strengthen itself to participate more effectively in that struggle. Even his allusions to Greek mythology and Shakespeare recruited "culture" into class warfare. That the cabaret was "destroying the hyra-headed monster of race-prejudice" was, he declared, "a 'consummation devoutly to be wished!'"[60]

Unequivocal in their call for an integrated labor movement and in their support for the SPA, the *Messenger* editors drew sharp distinctions between friends and enemies. They were severely critical of the AFL leadership, condemning the hypocrisy of its belated 1919 announcement of its intent to desegregate its locals and urging blacks instead to affiliate with the IWW. But Randolph and Owen were at least as hard on "Old Crowd Negroes," lambasting Moton and calling Tuskegee "a factory for producing scab labor." Such figures as Kelly Miller and Du Bois, who wavered between accommodation and opposition, were dismissed as at best transitional figures who would yield leadership to the New Negroes, whose object "is to destroy all [Old Crowd Negro leaders] and build up new ones." Du Bois "fails as a theorist," they declared, because he "is the only alleged leader of an oppressed group of people in the world today who condemns revolution." Randolph and Owen increasingly denounced Garveyism as a reactionary movement favored by the ruling class on the grounds that "it broadens the chasm between the black and white workers and can only result in the creation of more race hatred which will periodically flare up into race riots." When it was revealed in the summer of 1922 that Garvey had met with the Klan, they dubbed the UNIA leader a "black imperial wizard" and "messenger boy of the white Ku Klux Kleagle" for having "proclaimed to all of the fifteen million Negroes of the United States of America that they should cease fighting the Ku Klux Klan." "[I]n all its sinister viciousness," they vowed, "Garvey and Garveyism" had to be "driven . . . from the American soil." The *Messenger*'s attacks on Garvey became so sharp that Randolph received a number of death threats, including in September 1922 a package containing a severed hand and a message—signed "K.K.K."—warning him to "remain in your nigger improvement association" and "unite with your own race" if he wanted to live. This gesture only led Randolph and Owen to emphasize the links between the UNIA and the Klan and to speculate that the hand might have been sent by the UNIA.[61]

It was a significant indicator of the temper of the times that the *Messenger*'s rhetorical fervor and clearly drawn class politics garnered it considerable respect instead of driving away potential supporters. Angelina Grimké praised the magazine for its "utter fearlessness and courage." Seligmann was referring to Randolph and Owen when he wrote approvingly of the rising generation of leaders bringing left-wing politics to the attention of the average Negro. Charles Chesnutt wrote an appreciative letter in response to the May 1923 special educational number, and even F. Scott Fitzgerald—writing from Great Neck, Long Island, in May 1923— praised the same issue: "I read *The Messenger* from cover to cover and thoroughly enjoyed its intelligent editing and its liberal point of view." Randolph and Owen's enemies paid them the supreme compliment of taking them seriously: Palmer targeted the *Messenger* as the "most able and most dangerous of all the negro publications," while Hoover adjudged it the "headquarters of revolutionary thought." A secret British government report discussing the possibility that African American political radicalism might affect the empire's Caribbean colonies singled out the *Messenger* as particularly threatening: because of their "extreme radicalism and excellent diction," the analysts wrote in some consternation, Randolph and Owen's editorials were being quoted not just in the radical press but also in "the daily press of the large cities." James Weldon Johnson, looking back on the *Messenger* of 1919, adjudged that it had been the "most influential black organ in the country." Philip Foner, although severely critical of Randolph and Owen's refusal to confront SPA racism and their alliance with the party's right wing in the 1919 split, concedes that "[i]n its militancy, the *Messenger* was far in advance of anything up to that point in the history of black radicalism."[62]

The *Crusader*, the second most influential of the "Red black" journals in the postwar period, cast its representation of the New Negro in a decidedly more Afrocentric mold. Appearing first in late 1918 and attaining a circulation of 33,000 per month by 1921, the *Crusader* was edited by the ABB members Briggs and Moore; in its short life (lasting only until early 1922) the magazine moved from advocating African self-determination and African American nationalism to issuing increasingly confident calls for multiracial working-class revolution. Where the *Messenger* stood for SPA-style electoral politics, the *Crusader* largely eschewed chasing after the vote; by the time it ceased production, it had become unequivocal in its call for working-class revolution, and its editors were either members of or aligned with the Communist Party.[63]

In its early cultural nationalist phase, when, Winston James observes, it was "politically almost indistinguishable from the *Negro World*," the *Crusader* invoked inverted—and at times essentialist—notions of racial difference to defeat claims of Negro inferiority. The women showcased on its cover as mothers of the race were generally darker-skinned than those featured in the *Crisis* or the *Messenger* (see figure 12). The *Crusader* advertised such Afrocentric works as W. L. Hunter's *Jesus Christ Was Part Negro* and published such essays as George W. Parker's "Children of the Sun," where it was argued that "every great nation of the past was not white, but black." In 1919, Briggs and Moore declared, "Whether the caucasian reads the news dispatches from Egypt or from West Africa, from the Capital of the United States or from the West Indies, from Chicago or from Panama, it must be now dawning upon his junker mind that his self-constituted lordship of the world is at an end." In 1921, they opined

THE
CRUSADER

JUNE, 1921

15 Cents a Copy $1.50 a Year

Figure 12. *Crusader,* June 1921

that Jews and Africans had a similar "race genius" for collectivity and that "the oppressive capitalist system was . . . inconceivable to our communist African forefathers." Briggs and Moore effaced distinctions of class among Jews and Africans and between working-class and ruling-class whites; their use of the racial category "caucasian," devoid of class content, implied that biology underlies the drive toward a "self-constituted lordship of the world" or at least that whites form a united phalanx in this enterprise. Briggs and Moore prefaced their reprinting of Boas's review of Stoddard's *Rising Tide of Color* (retitled as "Rising Tide of Color Sets White World A-Trembling") with the observation that it was high time that peoples of color gained global hegemony. Like the *Negro World*, the *Crusader* was enthusiastic about Stoddard's tract because, in spite of its egregious white supremacism, it acknowledged the threat posed to Euro-American imperialism by the postwar upsurge of peoples of color.[64]

Yet the *Crusader* was also resolutely internationalist in a Leninist— as opposed to racialist—mode. The ABB journal denounced Du Bois for abandoning the demand for African self-determination at the 1919 Pan-African Conference and served as the publicity organ for the Hamitic League of the World, a group dedicated to pressing the Paris Peace Conference to extend the right of self-determination to all colonized peoples. The ABB's attraction to the USSR was premised largely on its admiration for the Soviets' strong support of anticolonial struggles. "Soviet Russia is the only Power in the world," the *Crusader* editors wrote, "which puts into execution the principle of 'self-determination' in its dealings with weaker peoples, and . . . does this regardless of the color of the people with whom she is dealing." The *Crusader* was also militantly antipatriotic. A 1920 ABB recruitment advertisement modeled itself on an army recruitment poster, castigating as "yellow" and a "slacker" anyone who would not "go the limit" for "African Liberation and Redemption." Where the Socialist *Messenger* was beginning to cool its antigovernment heels by 1921, the *Crusader* evinced a growing disrespect for the U.S. flag, prompting the BI agent Herbert Boulin to write in a report on a rally speech by Moore that he had "never heard anyone who spoke so defiantly and disrespectfully of the U.S.A. and the flag." Moore had become, Boulin concluded, "the most outspoken, daring and radical among all the other negro 'Reds' in Harlem."[65]

The *Crusader*'s oscillating positions on the relationship between race and nation reflected its changing assessment of the possibility for black-white working-class unity in the United States. In a 1919 editorial entitled "The Negro's Place Is with Labor," Briggs argued that "the Negro is essentially a worker" and that "[t]he interest of the workers is then the interest of Negroes and vice versa. . . . [P]roviding white labor does its share toward erasing the resentments raised by its unwise attitude in the past there is no power on earth that can keep permanently apart these two important sections of the world proletariat." The *Crusader* analogized the deportation of striking black workers from Coatesville, Pennsylvania, with the government's banishment of radical European immigrants: "The capitalists who would bring the Negro North during a crisis and then shuffle him back willy nilly to the old hateful conditions and to Lynch Law—all of which were cited in the argument to make him leave the South—are the same capitalists who would send out of the country all workers who dare to talk against the system." Abandoning an earlier advocacy of Negro "outmigration" as the solution to U.S. racism, in 1920 Moore explicitly compared the white workers' laying down their lives to defend their black fellow unionist in Bogalusa with John Brown's raid. "[W]e dare hope," he exulted, "that the sacrifice of Bogalusa holds as great significance for the 15,000,000 black freedmen (?) and for their white follow-citizens (?) as held the sacrifice of Harper's Ferry for the chattel slaves of the South and the free laborers of the North." By the end of 1921, the *Crusader* had lost all sympathy for Garveyism, ruthlessly lampooning the black nationalist for his discovery of pro-captialist common ground with President Harding (see figure 13). By 1922, the ABB, unambiguously aligned with the Communists, fulminated against the "socialist surrender" to an "emasculated, diluted" electoral strategy that amounted to making peace with capitalism. Despite the *Messenger's* greater notoriety in 1919 with Hoover, Palmer, and the Lusk Committee, by the time the Tulsa uprising occurred two years later, it was the *Crusader*, not the *Messenger*, that the government accused of having fomented the riot. While the charge was probably unwarranted, it was true that the ABB had expanded considerably beyond its original base in Harlem. "At its peak in 1921," writes Foner, "the ABB claimed 2,500 members in fifty-six posts throughout the nation, including areas of strength among the black coal miners in West Virginia."[66]

The *Crusader's* poetry column published militant verse voicing the magazine's shifting positions on race and class. Three times it printed Razafkeriefo's "Don't Tread on Me"—a celebration of the "Harlem Hell-Fighters," the famous all-black Fifteenth Infantry—where the poet proclaims:

> There is a wondrous symbol
> Which has come from 'cross the sea
> It's worn by every member
> Of the Fifteenth Infantry:

A snake, curled up, prepared to strike—
  And one can plainly see
That by its threat'ning attitude
  It says, "DON'T TREAD ON ME!"

O! race! make this your battle-cry—
  Engrave it on your heart
It's time for us to 'do or die,'
  To play a bolder part.

For by the blood you've spilled in France
  You must—and will—be free
So, from now on, let us advance
  With this, "DON'T TREAD ON ME!"

Echoing Tennyson—as does Du Bois in "Returning Soldiers," published
in the *Crisis* in the same month and year—Razafkeriefo's speaker portrays
France as the site where he has taken on the power, like the snake, to
kill. Where the rhyming of "sea" with "free" in *Negro World* poetry customarily evoked a spiritual return to Africa as the path to liberty, the poet

Figure 13. "The Moses That Was To Have Been. The Judas That Is," by Argee,
Crusader, December 1921

deploys these rhymes to declare that it is the black soldier's journey overseas, where he has learned how to take up the gun, that enables him to return to fight for freedom from Jim Crow.[67]

As the ABB joined forces with the Communists, *Crusader* poetry increasingly coupled its militancy with the call for multiracial working-class unity. In early 1922, the magazine reprinted from the *Seattle Union Record* Anise's "To Stir up Race Hatred," where a radical voice declares:

> "You know the Chicago riots!
> * * *
> We are collecting evidence
> * * *
> That the PACKERS
> * * *
> Had men employed
> * * *
> Among the Negroes
> * * *
> To tell the nasty things
> * * *
> White workers said about them,
> * * *
> And among the white workers
> * * *
> To stir THEM UP
> * * *
> Against the Negroes."

Where previously the *Crusader* had implied that every "caucasian," regardless of class, enjoys "lordship of the world," here racism among workers is formulated as false consciousness and traced to the imperatives of capitalist rule.[68]

By 1922, many of the lines of differentiation among the various organizations and magazines discussed here would harden into divisions; contradictions that appeared nonantagonistic—between Socialists and Communists, liberals and radicals, reformers and revolutionaries, advocates of the ballot and proponents of insurrection—would be revealed as irreconcilable in theory and in practice. For a brief time, however, there existed an ecumenical radicalism that arose from and contributed to a widespread sense of revolutionary possibility. In November 1919, the *Messenger* praised the fledgling *Crusader* as "a real addition to the field of radical journalism," noting that "with a few notable exceptions we agree on the whole with [its] policy"; with the arrival of the ABB organ, the *Messenger* relinquished the claim to being "the only magazine of scientific radicalism in the world published by Negroes." The *Crusader*—which would soon launch virulent attacks against groups that it accused of black nationalism or reformism—at first eagerly promoted other magazines taking militant and class-conscious stands against Jim Crow, calling on its readers to buy and read the *Negro World* and the *Messenger* and to vote for Randolph and Owen in the November 1918 elections. The *Crusader* also published a regular column entitled "From the Radical Press" and recommended the *Liberator*, the *Call*, the *Nation*, the *Freeman*, and the *New Republic* to "every Negro with sufficient intelligence to be interested in the fight for equal rights and opportunities and freedom from mob law." In 1921, the *Messenger*, the *Crusader*, and the *Emancipator* even considered a joint publication scheme; Domingo for a short while occupied editorial positions at both the *Negro World* and the *Messenger*. The *Negro World*, for all its stated distrust of white radicals, expressed concern at the threatened banning of the *Liberator*. The *Crisis*, despite being regularly criticized as an organ of "Old Negroes," defended the *Messenger* and the *Negro World* when they were threatened with revocation of their mailing permits. Moreover, the *Crisis* regularly published a survey of "periodical literature on the Negro" in which it called attention to white-edited journals—the *New Republic*, the *Literary Digest*, the *Nation*, the *Survey*, the *Independent*—containing commentary on racial issues. Such manifestations of solidarity were, to the government, grounds for considerable concern. The *Call* and the *Liberator* were being perused by a sizable Negro readership, warned the Lusk Committee; the *Crisis* was too closely tied to Randolph and Owen; even the *Negro World* had suspicious links with both the SPA and the NAACP. Four years after the 1919 split in the SPA, the *Call* continued to function as a publishing venue for the broad cultural Left, carrying poems, essays, and graphics by artists and writers by then associated principally with the Communists.[69]

Just as significant as these explicit expressions of mutual support were the multiple reprintings, borrowings, and citations in the liberal-to-Left press, black and white, from 1918 to 1922. Given the meticulous documenting of lynchings and riots in the *Crisis*, it is perhaps to be expected that the NAACP's press organ would be copiously cited even in magazines that disagreed with the association's moderate editorial stance. Walter White's gruesome account of the Mary Turner lynching was quoted in both the *Crusader* and the *Messenger*. The *Crisis*, for all Du Bois's skepticism about socialism as a cure for the U.S. race problem, reprinted the *Call*'s anticapitalist analyses of a range of issues—from women's oppression to labor unrest. The *Call* regularly reissued articles from black press organs—not just the Socialist-affiliated *Messenger* but also the *Crusader* and the *Negro World*. The *Nation* often excerpted sections of longer books and pamphlets by NAACP journalists, thus effectively advertising the association's activities. In 1919, the *Messenger*—which was to tear into Garveyism two years later—reproduced a commentary by Domingo, who was then the editor of *Negro World*, about the importance of using the upper-case spelling of *Negro*. McKay's "If We Must Die," which originally appeared in the *Liberator*, was reproduced several times in the *Crusader*, the *Messenger*, and the *Crisis*. Anise's poem "The Negro Worker," originally published in the *Seattle Union Record*, reappeared in both the *Call* and the *Messenger*. Ovington's coverage of the Bogalusa incident, first published in the *Liberator*, was later cited in the *Freeman*. Esau Jones's *Liberator* article on the Williams "death farm" trial was reprinted in the *Crusader*. Pickens's *Nation* piece "The American Congo" was quoted extensively in the *Bee*. Franz Boas's *Nation* review of Stoddard's *Rising Tide of Color* reappeared in the *Crusader*. The *Call's* coverage of the Coatesville deportations was reprinted in the *Crusader* and the *Crisis*. While loose copyright laws may have facilitated these borrowings, it is evident that the impetus behind this extensive pooling of information and opinion was substantial political agreement. Engaged in vigorous internal debate, the postwar U.S. Left was nonetheless broad and, for a time, motivated by a shared revolutionary vision. It was well-nigh impossible for anyone aware of the militant upsurge of the day not to be aware of the bright-red politics by which it was largely animated.[70]

This brief survey of the moderate, liberal, and leftist press, African American and white, as well as of several prominent writers and activists, suggests that in the immediate postwar period there existed in the United States a discourse about the relationship between racial oppression and capitalist exploitation that drew on a common fund of left-wing premises. Certain contemporaneous events—for example, the 1919 race riots, the lynching of Mary Turner, the Elaine massacre, the "death farm" murders, the Bogalusa incident—figured metonymically to signify the racist horror systemically grounded in capital's need to exploit—and, in the case of the Bogalusa incident, the potential for class-conscious multiracial resistance to that horror. Moreover, these incidents were processed through an interpretational paradigm based on certain interlocked assumptions: racial division in the working class was caused by economic factors, especially job competition; racial violence did not represent an upwelling of natural antipathy but was instead fostered by elites bent on maintaining dominance; and racial antagonism was against the objective interests of white and black workers alike. Left-wing ideas were, in short, part and parcel of mass consciousness. It is no coincidence that a figure frequently invoked as an insurgent ancestor—by African Americans and whites alike—was John Brown. For those who espoused revolution, the inevitable corollary of these propositions was that only in an egalitarian society run by the producers would the material basis for racial antagonism be removed; capitalism, therefore, had to be supplanted, by either the ballot or the bullet, if racism were to be ended. But even moderates and liberals unwilling to go this far embraced various features of a class analysis of U.S. race relations and viewed with sympathy the growth of not just militancy but also political leftism among Negroes during the Red Summer of 1919. The postwar New Negro was, in the eyes of many, an anticapitalist radical who envisioned African American emancipation as inseparable from—if not identical with—the project of a class-conscious, multiracial alliance.

It is also evident that, especially in the leftist press, there was general agreement that "culture"—particularly as embodied in graphics and poetry—could and should function in fairly straightforward fashion to underline conceptually and expand experientially the radical political message conveyed in accompanying analytical articles. While Locke would in 1925 proclaim in relief that the New Negro had abandoned the "arid fields of controversy and debate" for the "productive fields of creative expression," the leftist New Negroes of the immediate postwar period—as well as such class-conscious, antiracist white radicals as Anise—clearly had a different notion of the function of art within a more general theory and praxis aimed at profoundly transforming existing social relations. Contrary to Locke's assertion, not only was these radicals' radicalism un-"forced" but also their conception of the role and nature of "creative expression" was a far cry from the culturalist doctrine that would weld liberation to artistic creativity, artistic creativity to folk roots, folk roots to race, race to soil, and soil to nation. Yet that cultural nationalist doctrine would also spring, if indirectly and through multiple mediations, from the postwar radicals' theory and praxis. It is to a consideration of this process and this irony that we now turn.

2 Nation, Class, and the Limits of the Left

> International Socialism, while not opposed to true
> nationality, is antagonistic to that anarchistic national-
> ism struggling to find markets and necessitating armed
> camps and war. True nationalism, based in the main
> upon language [and the natural characteristics and
> genius peculiar to the people of a particular locality],
> demands the right of a people to control its destiny . . .
> and is today the aspiration of millions.
>
> —*Call*, 27 March 1919

In the crucible of 1919, a class-based analysis of racism enjoyed widespread currency among liberals, progressives, and leftists; the struggle against racial inequality was frequently linked with the necessity to transform or abolish capitalist social relations. But if this was the case, why was this trend reversed? How did the New Negro devolve into *The New Negro*, with apparently little opposition? Theodor Adorno would have it that, with the failure of the bid for working-class power, politics flees to the realm of the aesthetic—that when the "time for political art" recedes, "politics . . . migrate[s] into autonomous art." Adorno usefully reminds us that radical artistic movements, if they are to survive and develop, need to be underpinned by radical political movements; as Marx remarked in *The German Ideology*, "The existence of revolutionary ideas in a particular period presupposes the existence of a revolutionary class." Adorno's general insight begs the particular question, however, of why, when the U.S. proletariat failed to develop into a "revolutionary class," culturalism—the programmatic notion that the zone of culture should supply not merely support for but also the *site* of African American liberation—won the day among antiracists in the postwar United States.[1]

The causality here is more complex than may first appear, for an analysis of not only what happened but also what did not happen is necessary. To understand fully how the New Negro class struggle warrior of 1919 could reemerge as the culture hero of the Harlem Renaissance, the inquiry needs to be broken down into its component parts. In chapters 3 and 4, two principal developments of dominant ideology in the wake of 1919 are examined: the rise of racist antiradicalism and, simultaneously, the emergence of cultural pluralism. First, however, what is, in a sense, a nonevent must be investigated. Why did the revolutionary postwar upsurge fail to produce, if not a U.S. equivalent to the Bolshevik Revolution, at least a radical antiracist movement that would continue, after the early 1920s, to appeal to a broad range of leftists and progressives? Why did Bogalusa, hailed by many in 1919 as the harbinger of days to come, so rapidly recede from the contemporaneous imagination? Can the causality behind the waning influence of a class analysis of race and racism be attributed wholly to government repression, the crushing of the labor movement, the zealousness of anti-immigrant xenophobes, and the revived Ku Klux Klan? Or did various features of the Left's own formulation of the relation of race to class and of class to nation contribute to the substitution of culturalism for class struggle?

The Sombartian Query

To pose questions of this kind involves, first, re-posing that irksome but never quite banishable question first formulated by Werner Sombart in 1906: "Why is there no socialism in America?" Most of the standard responses offered over the past century—influenced by the very terms in which the question is framed—entail one or another version of the thesis of American exceptionalism, according to which 1919 was an anomaly, a blip on the screen of history: instead of signaling fundamental and irresolvable contradictions in the U.S. body politic, the year's intense class struggles constituted a rupture with traits and trends that have always differentiated the United States from other industrial nations. In one variant, as the doctrine of consensus, American exceptionalism proposes that the Left never exercised a significant influence on the U.S. working class, which, being "born free" in a nation lacking genuine revolutionary traditions, experienced what Louis Hartz has called "civic integration." Frederick Jackson Turner, in a formulation of the consensus thesis even predating Sombart, held that the frontier operated as a safety valve for worker insurgency, posing an ideal of agrarian independence that defused class consciousness. The cold war–era historian Seymour Martin Lipset stressed the role of expanding enfranchisement in siphoning off the potential alienation of white male workers, whom he viewed as irrevocably wedded to capitalism. For these historians, the absence of a feudal past precluded—and would always preclude—a radical proletarian challenge to the bourgeois state.[2]

More recent variations on the consensus paradigm have followed Warren Susman's lead in *Culture as History* (1984), proposing that it was the movement of post–World War I U.S. society into consumerism that rendered moot the rhetoric of class warfare. Newly positioned to act in the capitalist economy as not only producers but, increasingly, buyers and enjoyers of the commodities they made, the U.S. working class underwent a process of what Lizbeth Cohen calls "embourgeoisement," succumbing to the blandishments of a reifying mass culture and moving into that hazy region of middle-classness that it supposedly inhabits to this day. While elites benefited from the social control accompanying the preoccupation with consumption, argues T. J. Jackson Lears, this process was more than merely ideological in that it supplied the ordinary American with a therapeutic identity and "a vision of transcendence, however fleeting." According to the various versions of American exceptionalism, the fact that African Americans, other people of color, and women were largely excluded from the feast only underlines the racist, sexist, and fundamentally conservative impulses presumably at the core of the identity formation of the (then) largely white and largely male American working class. Moreover, proponents of the doctrine of "embourgeoisement" do not envision working-class participation in consumerism as false consciousness; the U.S. proletariat—encoded as white and male—is held not just to have been treated differentially but also objectively to have benefited from its position in both the national and the global economies.[3]

Some historians, less inclined to blame the victim for the disease, seek the causes of the U.S. working class's failure to develop revolutionary class consciousness in its hobbling by various "internal constraints." Where consensus theorists view labor as the "'sweetheart' of capital," the labor historian Patricia Cayo Sexton remarks, adherents to the doctrine of internal constraints view labor as a "'crippled' combatant." Racial and ethnic division within the working class often figures centrally in internal constraints analyses. Mike Hill stresses the inability of the native-born proletariat to ally with the immigrant proletariat in the class struggles of 1919. David Roediger, Michael Reich, Alexander Saxton, and

Theodore Allen, while construing the nature of white working-class "interest" in significantly different ways, all propose that the division between black and white labor has been the fatal flaw. Other internal constraints scholars—David Montgomery, Jeremy Brecher, and Michael Goldfield—target the trade union leadership, particularly the AFL, which historically split the work force into more and less privileged sectors, thereby creating a labor aristocracy won to the belief that workers' welfare is bound to the health of the capitalist system.[4]

Other scholars contemplating the Sombartian query have emphasized the determining role played by state repression—that is, *external* constraints—in preventing the growth of a class-conscious revolutionary movement in the United States. Robert Goldstein, documenting the significant presence of radicals in the wartime and immediate postwar labor movement, traces the impact of government repression of the Left and corporate assaults on strikers. "By December, 1919," he points out, "the number of monthly strikes had dropped to a six-year low, and the union movement had been sapped of much of its strength and vigor." David Bennett and Howard Abramowitz demonstrate that post–World War I nativist movements differed from their predecessors both in the extent of direct elite involvement and in the insistent targeting of radicals. Sexton concludes that those historians who represent the U.S. working class as passive and lacking class consciousness have consistently overlooked the "war on the labor-left," which has been waged without surcease, she shows, from the late nineteenth century onward.[5]

Different paradigms for understanding the nonemergence of the U.S. working class as a class-conscious agent have yielded different interpretations of U.S. cultural history. Applying the external constraints hypothesis to the origins of U.S. modernism in the 1920s, some scholars have argued that the revolutionary energies manifested in the upheavals of 1919 underwent a classic process of repression, displacement, and sublimation. Marianne DeKoven proposes that the threat (or promise) of revolution haunts all of U.S. modernism; its characteristic aesthetic of *sous rature* entails an "unsynthesized dialectic" that exhibits "ambivalence toward the twentieth-century revolutionary horizon." Specifically focusing on the Harlem Renaissance, Nathan Huggins and David Levering Lewis conclude that overt state repression played a determining role in directing African American modernism into culturalist channels. In Lewis's analytical model, Freud is writ large: the Red Summer of 1919, followed by "conservative backlash," produced "the trauma that led to the cultural sublimation of civil rights." In these accounts, culture functions as a site not for transmuting social antagonisms but for defusing them.[6]

Other students of U.S. modernism have responded to Sombart's challenge by denying its premise: 1920s culturalism is not a symptom of the
failure of revolution but instead is the form that revolution took. Reframing in contemporary terms Locke's claim that the New Negro turned from
the "arid fields of controversy and debate" to "creative expression,"
Walter Kalaidjian and Ann Douglas propose that there *was* a continuing
postwar leftist movement—in the zone of cultural subversion. One can
argue that potentially insurgent energies were siphoned off into "merely" cultural activity after 1919, they warn, only if one assumes that culture is less material than other modes of praxis. Kalaidjian proposes that
the "emergent aesthetic ideology" of the Harlem Renaissance constituted
a Gramscian war of position that challenged bourgeois hegemony more
effectively than had the class-based radical activism of 1919. Douglas
argues that the cultural diversity, formal experimentalism, and appropriation of mass culture embodied in a broadly reconceived U.S. modernism—especially among African Americans recognizing that "[t]o be black
in modern America was a command to strategize"—superseded the revolutionary energies of 1919 in productive and important ways. "Barred
from most meaningful direct political activity," she argues, African
Americans "were not abandoning politics so much as translating politics
into cultural terms." Although she concedes that black modernism did
not defeat Jim Crow and debt peonage, Douglas views it as a significant
refocusing of what radicalism could mean in a country where working-
class revolution had never been—and indeed could never be—on the agenda. For Douglas, the cultural supersession argument thus takes American exceptionalism as its premise.[7]

Still another school of cultural historians grants that the possibility
for revolutionary upheaval rapidly receded in the postwar era but insists
that there nonetheless persisted a vital revolutionary culture positing continued potentialities for insurgent agency in the working class and envi-
sioning radical cultural activity as reinforcing that agency. Left-wing politics continued to exercise significant influence in the art and literature
of the 1920s, the argument goes, supplying a link between the leftist culture of 1919 and the cultural radicalism that would achieve maturity in
the next decade as self-consciously "proletarian" literature and art. Joining the growing group of revisionist commentators seeking to end the
blackout on left-wing cultural movements in the United States, proponents of what might be called the "persistence" view argue that 1930s proletarianism could rapidly develop precisely because of its continuity with
the cultural production of the preceding decade. Cary Nelson, in his aptly titled *Repression and Recovery: Modern American Poetry and the*

Politics of Cultural Memory, 1910–1945 (1989), proposes that radicalism remained alive and well in 1920s poetry: the asterisk-laden leftist labor poems of Anise are, he claims, as integral to U.S. modernism as the works of Wallace Stevens or T. S. Eliot. Douglas Wixson, in his biography of the Midwest proletarian writer Jack Conroy, argues that this "worker-writer" was able to compose *The Disinherited* (1933) because of his experiences both as a proletarian—his 1920s was not the Jazz Age but the anti-labor Thermidor—and as a bearer of a working-class, socialist cultural tradition carried forward from his parents. Chip Rhodes has polemicized against the canonical view of the 1920s as a time when writers wallowed in anomie and retreated from history. Faith Berry, James A. Miller, William Maxwell, and Anthony Dawahare all stress the abiding Marxist presence specifically in African American literary production of the 1920s. For these scholars, political radicalism, an integral element of U.S. modernism in general and the New Negro movement in particular, extended into and through the Harlem Renaissance for the entire decade. They argue it is the ideological dominance of anticommunists and ex-radicals among cold war–era constructors of U.S. literary history—frequently in combination with the more covert but no less embedded anticommunism premised in the postmodernist antipathy to totalization—that has continued to promote the myth of the typical 1920s writer, white or black, as an alienated recluse from historical process and political praxis.[8]

Spectres of 1919 situates itself squarely in these debates. The quiescent American proletariat posited in the consensus and co-optation theories is belied by the history of U.S. labor struggles, which, as Montgomery and others have abundantly demonstrated, in their violence have often surpassed workers' struggles in other industrialized countries. That there has never been a large social-democratic party in the U.S.—which has proven of dubious value in any case to working classes elsewhere in the world—hardly means that this country has not had its share of class struggles. To propose that class struggles were successfully transmuted into culture wars, however, as do the proponents of the supersession argument, trivializes the very real setbacks experienced by the U.S. producing masses—rural and urban, African American and white, immigrant and native-born—in the 1920s. As Langston Hughes would comment ironically in *The Big Sea*, "The ordinary Negroes hadn't heard of the Negro Renaissance. And if they had, it hadn't raised their wages any." The theories of constraint, external and internal, offer greater possibilities for historical materialist analysis. But the repression-displacement paradigm runs the risk of positing a view of culture as merely epiphenomenal, thereby offering an inversion of the supersession paradigm—in which class struggle is effectively collapsed into textuality—and affording little insight into the political origins of culturalism. Various versions of the external constraints model stressing government and business repression cannot be ignored. Taken as primary causes, however, they tend to direct the beam of analysis away from the weaknesses within the working-class movement that enabled the repressive apparatus to be as effective as it was. The doctrine of internal constraints is more promising; as theorists from Hegel to Marx to Mao to Bertell Ollman have pointed out, analyzing the contradictions internal to any entity or process is central to dialectical historiography and political analysis. But many accounts of U.S. labor history that subscribe to the notion of internal constraints do not adequately examine the reasons for the vulnerability of the U.S. working class to racial and ethnic division or to misleadership by pro-capitalist trade unions. The question still remains: *why* did the U.S. proletariat, in the aftermath of 1919, so rapidly lose the gains it had made during the war, such that the mass proletarian movement of resistance to capital would have to be built largely from the ground up in the next decade?[9]

This last question suggests the inadequacy of the persistence view, which holds that the spirit of revolutionary radicalism remained alive and well throughout the 1920s, needing only to be revived in the capitalist crisis of the following decade. It is vitally important to recover any and all evidence of the "Red line" of cultural history; the recent wresting of modernism away from the legacy of the New Critics and the New York Intellectuals has occurred in no small part through the efforts of cultural and literary historians insisting on the nonerasure of the Left. One of my goals in *Spectres of 1919* is to demonstrate the necessity of understanding leftist politics if one is to understand U.S. modernism. From the hordes stumbling across the cracked plains in Eliot's waste land to the club-waving strikers on the margins of Babbitt's consciousness in Sinclair Lewis's novel of that name, many a text composed in the wake of 1919 is haunted by the phantom of proletarian revolt. Moreover, as is shown by the uninterrupted transmutation of the *Liberator* into the *Workers Monthly* and then into *New Masses*, a continuous connection between the organized Left and literary radicalism remained throughout the decade.

Examining the continuing influence of the Left in the 1920s entails not just celebration of its persistence but, as crucially, critical scrutiny of those defects that prohibited this influence from being more powerful. One seriously underestimates the nature and extent of the postwar reaction and the inability of the Left to counter that reaction if one fails to acknowledge that the production of literature inflected with revolutionary politics had slowed to a near-trickle by the last half of the decade. This was particularly true of radical African American literary production. By the late 1920s, McKay had ceased penning class-conscious poetry and had taken to writing novels bathed in primitivist premises; Andrea Razafkeriefo had been transformed into the popular songwriter Andy Razaf well before the decade's end; Hughes wrote few revolutionary poems between 1926 and kept radical social analysis under careful wraps in *Not without Laughter* (1930). Critics who insist on the continuity of 1919 to 1932 thus run the risk of mistaking the residual for the dominant and the dominant for the emergent. Scholars legitimately wishing to contest the blackout on leftist cultural production can be so energized at glimpsing a continuing radical presence that they inflate its significance and fail to grasp the extent to which contradictions informing not just the historical moment taken as a whole but also the leftist discourses and practices helping to shape that moment may have contributed to its relative quiescence. If one sees a ghost, one needs to ask why it *is* a ghost, not pretend it is real.[10]

This chapter, which explores the contradictions internal to the postwar Left, is thus the skeptical sibling of chapter 1: limitation is the dialectical counterpart to potentiality. To make the claim that the fate of the working-class movement in the United States cannot be understood apart from the fate of the Left is of course nothing new; most of the labor historians adhering to internal constraints paradigms at least touch on the sins of the Socialists. Nor is there anything novel in the proposition that the early-twentieth-century radicals were especially crippled, in theory and practice, by their shortcomings with regard to what came to be known as the "Negro question." Featuring the early Socialists' racism has become a staple of the historiography of U.S. leftist movements at least since the 1960s. Moreover, most criticisms of the SPA trace its weaknesses on race and racism to its "economist" privileging of class over any other form of oppression. Critical commentaries coming out of the intellectual legacy of American communism—a legacy that remains more widely influential, in my view, than is often realized—routinely trace the Socialists' weakness to their failure to appreciate the need for African American self-determination. A more recent line of critique, influenced mainly by poststructuralism and neo-Marxism, charges that not just the historical SPA but all "orthodox" Marxisms to this day impose a class reductionist "scientism" on the multivalent experience of subaltern social groups—including African Americans—better defined by identity or performativity than by relation to production. But whether critics of the Socialist legacy envision African American nationalism as a necessary theoretical corrective to class analysis or launch a broadside assault on class analysis as such, they generally concur that the early-twentieth-century Left was fatally hampered by a mechanistic overemphasis on class as the primary category to guide antiracist theory and practice.[11]

I propose a different line of political critique: the Left of the early twentieth century should be faulted not for imposing *too rigid* a class analysis but for subscribing to, and acting on, an *insufficiently comprehensive and materialist* conception of class. I develop a series of five interrelated propositions, summarized briefly here.

1. The SPA's reformism consisted not simply in scrambling to elect Socialists to public office—and catering to a lowest-common-denominator racism among their constituency in the process—but in endorsing a view of the state as an arena open to contestation and control by any and all classes, rather than, as Marx and Lenin had both maintained, an instrument of class rule. The Left's failure fully to query the nature of political representation in the democratic capitalist state thus contributed to the postwar ascendancy of a politics of cultural representation. Reformism and culturalism, while operating in different discursive registers, were intimately interrelated in their mutual commitment to representation as praxis.

2. Rather than pursue the thread in the Marxist tradition that analyzes the proletariat as a potentially revolutionary political agent, early-twentieth-century Socialists generally bypassed this aspect of the Marxist legacy and concentrated on that aspect that theorizes the worker structurally in relation to production as "labor." By designating the collectivity of workers solely as "labor," the Left largely confined class struggle to the struggle over wages and did not consistently call the wage relation itself into question. "Economism" involved not overstressing class to the exclusion of other categories of identity but taking as given the commodification of labor power. Socialism was thus theorized as the altered distribution of wealth rather than transformed relations of production; the proletariat was the beneficiary of this transformation rather than the collective subject that would effect its self-emancipation through revolution.

3. Because it routinely substituted economics for class analysis, economic determinism for historical materialism, the SPA was hamstrung in its attempts to theorize the ways in which racism is necessary—not just convenient but necessary—to U.S. capitalism. Where an expansive understanding of the role played by racism as a mechanism of both capital accumulation and social control was needed, the best that the Left could come up with was the narrow doctrine of Negro versus white labor competition. This doctrine reified accepted notions of race, ignored

African American superexploitation, and failed to specify the deleterious effects of this superexploitation on the white working class as well. It failed to analyze the ways in which capitalism, to maintain class rule, requires racism and does not simply take opportunistic advantage of it.

4. A crucial link between its economism and its reification of race was the SPA's near-complete inattention to the category of ideology. Instead of systematically analyzing and contesting the attitudes and beliefs invisibly binding workers to the system that oppressed them, the Socialists formulated the relation of consciousness to power in terms of ruling-class "propaganda," on the one hand, and working-class "psychology" or "instinct," on the other. The Socialists thus failed to appreciate the full significance of the simultaneously anti-immigrant, anti-Negro, anti-Semitic, antiradical, and pro-Americanist discourse interfused throughout the declarations of eugenicists and nativists during the wartime and postwar repression.

5. Indissolubly linked with its racist, economist, and reformist weaknesses, as well as its limited grasp of the nature and role of ideology, was the Socialists' largely uncritical accession to nationalism. Despite its antiwar stance and its railing against 100 percent Americanism, the SPA never articulated a critique of nationalism as such. The right wing of the party, after the 1919 split, attempted to co-opt the discourse of U.S. patriotism, proposing the "co-operative commonwealth" as the logical fulfillment of U.S. representative democracy. But even the left wing, which metamorphosed into the CPUSA, endorsed a theory of revolutionary self-determination that, if more cosmopolitan and anticolonial than the patriotism of the right wing, nonetheless preserved nationalism as the prerequisite for internationalism. The Left's attempts to articulate a genuine alternative to 100 percent Americanism were from the outset hobbled by their accession to many of its premises. The Left's embrace of self-determination would constitute a counterdiscourse to the dominant nationalist ideology, not a means to its negation.

Since the critique of nationalism figures prominently throughout *Spectres of 1919*, a clarification of this last point is in order. The "left" nationalism of the Bolsheviks, calling for colonial emancipation from imperialism, was qualitatively different from the "right" nationalism of the Second International, which not only had recently called on the workers of most industrialized nations to join in the interimperialist slaughter of the Great War but also construed colonialism as a positive good, to be retained even under socialism. Nonetheless, I argue—with the great advantage of hindsight gained over the course of the past eight decades—that *all* nationalisms have proven to be essentialist and class-col-laborationist, insofar as they assume that one or another kind of nonclass-based unity—articulated as identification with a "people," a "folk," or a "nation"—is necessary, even if only temporarily, to the emancipation of the producing masses. The view of self-determination as a "moment"—temporal and epistemological—in the movement toward a nationless and classless world would be, in practice, enacted as the valorization of a "people's" belonging to and on a geographically defined "soil." The "good" nationalism of Leninism would thus set the limit to the Left's ability to combat the "bad" nationalism" of 100 percent Americanism, insofar as it linked the emancipation of peoples of color not to the aboli-tion of structurally defined relations of production—at least not as the immediate demand—but to the possession and control of terrain, of place. The contradictions in many Harlem Renaissance writers' near-obsessive preoccupation with roots and soil, as well as their characteristic inabili-ty to move beyond the aporias created by the discourses of folkishness, region, and nation, cannot be understood apart from the conjunction of nationalisms—both "good" and "bad"—in the political discourse of the contemporaneous Left. The linking of soilness with culturalism in the discourse of the Harlem Renaissance would inescapably fuse racial iden-tity with nation, insofar as culture would invoke a notion of cultivation that was premised on a relationship of a folk to mother earth that was, at the same time, a relationship of a citizenry to the fatherland. Alain Locke's success in deploying the notion of the folk to proclaim the New Negro as culture hero and Harlem as both a black Mecca and a crucible of American democracy cannot be grasped apart from the discourses of nationalism guiding the theory and practice of the Left emerging from the conjuncture of 1919.[12]

A methodological proviso: I am not making the argument that all the developments I analyze in this chapter—much less the multiply me-diated cultural forces and movements discussed in future chapters—can be traced back to decisions made in the smoke-filled rooms of the Social-ist, and later Communist, leadership. My claim is for a "softer" kind of determination in the realm of the political—namely, that the strengths and weaknesses of the movement to "change the world" established the limits, both theoretical and practical, within which participants in the po-litical and cultural movements of the day might define their projects. The conception of causality involved here entails not proclaiming inevitabil-ity but delineating the parameters within which agency could occur. How-ever, this notion of determination is equivalent neither to the pluralist notion that causality consists in a congeries of "factors" nor to its putative Marxist cousin, overdetermination, which emphasizes the relatively autonomous and conjunctural nature of historical causality, thereby often inviting methodological pluralism in through the back door. Those features of mid- to late-1920s culturalism that ended up superseding and displacing postwar African American modernism's genesis in political radicalism realized tendencies that had been present in this radicalism from the outset. But by stressing the determining role played by the Left's line during and following the revolutionary upsurge of 1919, I am insisting—against the current of much contemporary analysis of discourses and social practices—that what Socialists and Communists were saying and doing (as well as not saying and not doing) had a significant impact even on the thought and activity of those not immediately in their orbit.[13]

"American Radicals . . . Share the Typical White Psychology towards Negroes": Socialist Racism

It was difficult for white Socialists in the early twentieth century not to imbibe and to some degree reproduce the racism saturating the atmosphere of the early-twentieth-century United States. That the SPA contained—in both leadership and rank and file—significant numbers of racists is undeniable. In 1905, the *Appeal to Reason* proposed as a selling-point that socialism would "separate the races." The SPA leader Victor Berger, reflecting the influence of Social Darwinism on the socialist movement, confidently declared that "there can be no doubt that the Negroes and mulattoes constitute a lower race." The SPA leader Kate Richards O'Hare—who was to be imprisoned along with Debs during the war—some years earlier proclaimed, "We Socialists don't love the 'nigger' any better than he loves us. We don't admire the shape of his nose or the color of his skin any more than he likes our insolence and intolerable attitude, but we have sense enough to know that capitalism chains us to the negro with iron chains of economic servitude and we would rather have the negro free from the chains. Because if the black man is chained it spells slavery for the white man and woman and girl—we must share it." In O'Hare's view, racial segregation did not mean black super-exploitation; rather, landowners gave "rich and fertile soil" to black tenants and "poor land up in the hills" to whites. White bigotry—"our insolence and intolerable attitude"—was thus justified and was "intolerable" only from the point of view of blacks; it hurt whites only insofar as it prevented them from freeing themselves from the chains binding them to both wage slavery and black people. Socialism thus required segregation as part of utopia. "Let us give the blacks one section in the country where every condition is best fitted to them," O'Hare wrote. "Free them from capitalist exploitation; give them access to the soil, the ownership of their machines and let them work out their salvation." Her exclusionary formulation of the "we" in "we Socialists" and her miscegenationist fantasies about black men chained to white women and girls suggest an imagination not far removed from that informing Thomas Dixon's *Leopard's Spots* or *Clansmen*.[14]

Such visceral expressions of white supremacy faded from official party rhetoric after 1913, when the SPA began to recognize more fully the urgency of the "Negro problem" in dividing the working class. Subsequent SPA theory and practice, however, revealed at best an uneven commitment to confronting, much less opposing, racism. In James Oneal's important pamphlet *The Next Emancipation* (1922)—which was to define party policy on the "Negro Question" for many years—the prominent Socialist theorist opined that "social equality" was not a goal of socialism, which guaranteed the freedom to choose one's associates. "If a man is opposed to forced equality in human relationships," wrote Oneal, "he should be opposed to the wage system of robbery which often imposes an equality that is personally distasteful." By a disturbing logic, racism is mobilized in the service of anticapitalism; the coercive nature of the exploitation experienced by the white worker is associated with the right of African Americans to work, live, and marry as they choose. That segregationism was embraced not just by leading SPA theorists but also by thousands of rank-and-file white Socialists is demonstrated by the SPA's custom—routine throughout the South and not infrequent elsewhere—of barring blacks from its meetings. Theresa Malkiel, a New York textile organizer, caused a stir when, in a series of *Call* articles detailing her 1911 tour through the South, she exposed the party's Jim Crow practices. "'SOCIALISTS' DESPISE NEGROES IN SOUTH,'" read the headline; "'Comrades' Refuse to Allow Colored Men in Meeting Halls or Party." The anarchist Emma Goldman, berating the SPA for its opportunist electoral strategies, characterized its leadership as "racial philistines" and "moral eunuchs" whose "propaganda [was] limited to vote baiting." In 1919, the *Emancipator* editor W. A. Domingo concluded that "American radicals . . . share the typical white psychology towards negroes." Warning that strike-breaking Negroes might emerge as the "Cossacks" of the United States, Domingo scored the SPA for its failure to welcome blacks into its ranks. "The failure to make negroes class-conscious is the greatest potential menace to the establishment of Socialism in America, whether by means of the ballot or through the dictatorship of the proletariat," he declared.[15]

Denigrating racial stereotypes were at times uncontested or reproduced in the Socialist press. A noteworthy blindness is displayed in the *Call*'s 1923 review of S. J. Holmes's *Studies in Evolution and Eugenics.* Although the reviewer, one Dr. John A. Glassburg, chastised Holmes for "shed[ding] no light on the subjects [of the benefit or detriment of racial crossing and intermarriage]," he failed to contest Holmes's view that "the Negro with his strong passions, weak inhibitions and his habit of living only in the present" has been "[p]hysically . . . running down hill since the Civil War." In this review, to be sure, it was the reviewer, not the *Call* editors, who overlooked this expression of racism in the book being evaluated. But the editors can hardly be let off the hook for publishing Zelda Stewart Charters's "Is the Rapist in the Mulatto the Black Man or the White Man?" an article whose title alone indicates the author's premises. That the *Call* could spot academic racism in its most apologetic form is shown in its 1923 review of Lothrop Stoddard's *Revolt against Civilization,* which it dismissed as "an ill-balanced, opinionated work, that easily becomes an apology for the most sordid features that characterize the present epoch." Even here, however, Stoddard was criticized as much for his antienvironmental premises and his lack of "balance" as for his reactionary notions about people of darker hue. That these kinds of slippages went unscrutinized even in the most forward-looking press organ of the SPA—even as that organ praised African American militancy and chided white workers for their prejudices—indicates the extent to which racist assumptions permeated the discourse of early-twentieth-century socialism.[16]

Unlike the *Call,* the *Liberator* called for social equality, promoted works by Claude McKay and other writers of African heritage, and regularly published texts and graphics by antiracist whites. Yet, in a generally laudatory 1918 review of James Weldon Johnson's *Fifty Years and Other Poems,* Floyd Dell, the *Liberator*'s editor, declared, "I believe there is a Negro way of looking at a sunset. And I believe it is a more splendid way. . . . The Negro—again I fall back upon dogmatic assertion—is an instinctive poet. His words do have a natural grace and order of a peculiar kind." In an early version of the primitivist inversion of stereotypes that would become a staple of the Harlem Renaissance, Dell saw in the loveliness of Johnson's words not skill but instinct and nature. Amanda Hall's "Coon Town" incorporates similar premises in its description of a Negro neighborhood as "crazy cabins huddle[d] in the gap . . . Too lazy to combat the grown town," where a "nucleus of hot smells . . . blister[s]" and one hears the "honey-drawl of voices making love." Fenton Johnson's "Sunset," from a 1918 poem cluster entitled "Negro Free Verse," reveals that black as well as white writers could reproduce the rhetoric of a highly sexualized primitivism: "A young girl, golden brown, whose litheness would pluck the Angel Gabriel from the skies, lies on her bed in the cabin of the heavens, awaiting her brawny lover, whose breast is darker than a shadow and whose eyes are moons of passion." Fenton Johnson's central metaphor supplies some rationale for Dell's faux pas about Negroes and sunsets. The *Liberator*'s successor, the *Workers Monthly*, exhibited a comparable blend of racism and antiracism, publishing alongside Langston Hughes's militant class-conscious poems and Robert Minor's calls for black-white labor unity such plantation tradition poems as Keene Wallis's "Harvest Stiff Comes Back to Town." Detailing the experiences of an itinerant Wobbly returning home for a respite from the class struggle, the poem rhapsodizes over the "weather-beaten shanties / [That] swarm with dogs and bucks and aunties, / Howling, laughing, making eyes" and celebrates "[o]ne black mammy [who] ups and carols: / Goan to hebbem, yass my Lawd." As in the *Liberator* poems by Amanda Hall and Fenton Johnson, home, region, and earthy black folk conjoin in a highly racialized discourse of "belonging." To come home is to rediscover a site rendered familiar by its association with simple, spontaneous, and natural Negroes.[17]

Even those white Socialists who struggled vigorously against the dominant discourse on race sometimes absorbed and reproduced various of its aspects. The SPA member and NAACP official Herbert Seligmann, a champion of black advancement and social equality, in 1920 expressed hesitancy about whether blacks and whites possessed equal intellectual capabilities. "In the existing state of industrial organization," he noted in the *Socialist Review*, "the Negro's capabilities as they may be limited or determined by racial inheritance, play a small part. With few exceptions industries are not so thoroughly organized that slight individual and psychological differences make themselves felt in large-scale production." The *Liberator* coeditor Max Eastman, in an introduction to McKay's *Harlem Shadows*, revealed lurking doubts about racial equality even as he honored the poet's brilliance. "If any defined quantitative difference is ever established between the average abilities of races," he declared, "it will be a relatively slight one. The difficulty in establishing it, is a proof of that. And a slight difference in the general average would have no application whatever as between individuals, or any minor groups of individuals." Reacting to the barrage of IQ-based, bell-curve statistics currently being offered by scientific racists, Seligmann and Eastman revealed their inability to controvert the logic of the bell curve even as they proclaimed its irrelevance to the individual case.[18]

Eugenics, not yet tarred with the brush of Nazism, appealed to a range of early-twentieth-century leftists, from Jack London to George Bernard Shaw. In 1912, the U.S. Socialist theoretician and Rand School teacher Scott Nearing wrote enthusiastically about "America's distinctive opportunity" to develop a "Super Race." A materialist, Nearing stipulated the importance of nurture: "Modern society may well be compared to a garden [in which] [s]owing, weeding [and] cultivating" are "carried forward through social institutions." When a youth goes astray, the problem may be that "the seed has been neither prepared, watered, nor tended, and the young shoot has grown wild." Yet Nearing also held that the United States was favorably positioned to develop the "Super Race" because of its "admirable blending of Western European peoples." The gardener "turns his attention to the seed bed" only after he has "produced his seed," wrote Nearing, thereby "guaranteeing a good heredity by breeding together those individual plants which possess in the highest degree the qualities he desires to secure." Utilizing the organic trope that pervaded eugenicist discourse, Nearing naturalized the developmental process in which he purported to reserve a determining role for environment.[19]

"The Negro Is My Brother": Socialist Antiracism

It would be a serious oversimplification, however, to conclude that the shortcomings in the SPA's theory and practice on race and racism can be traced exclusively or even primarily to white Socialists' reproducing the racism of the larger society, for many white Socialists took principled stands against racism. Seligmann untiringly condemned racist exploitation and violence in the liberal-to-Left press; his *Negro Faces America* was one of the books McKay would take to the USSR and use as a source for the monograph he wrote and published there about the Jim Crow practices of his native land. The Eastmans created in the *Liberator* the first leftist cultural magazine in the United States that would give substantial airing to race-related themes and be coedited by an African American. William English Walling, an NAACP founding member and SPA leader, explicitly rejected evolutionist doctrines on race and battled against Asian exclusionism, denouncing the view of his fellow SPA member Berger that Asians were "'unassimilable'" as a "hackneyed appeal to ancient history, familiar in all reactionary reasoning." The NAACP founding member, writer, and Socialist activist Mary White Ovington was a lifelong breaker of color barriers, living as the sole white resident in an otherwise all-Negro building in New York and inviting Negro artists to attend previously segregated social and literary events.[20]

Eugene Debs, the SPA chairman and perennial presidential candidate, spoke out with increasing force against racial discrimination, in both the society at large and the party's own ranks. Debs's most frequently quoted statement regarding race and class is his 1903 assertion that "[t]he class struggle is colorless. . . . We have nothing special to offer the Negro, and we cannot make separate appeals to all the races." Yet Debs refused to address segregated audiences and, after 1912, moved from a sometimes equivocal stance on social equality to a more aggressive stance against prejudice. In 1915, he urged SPA members to join the NAACP in picketing D. W. Griffith's pro-KKK *Birth of a Nation*; in his 1918 *Intercollegiate Socialist Review* exchange with Du Bois, he threw down the gauntlet to his party. Any Socialist who would not boldly defend "the Negro's right to work, live and develop his manhood, educate his children, and fulfill his destiny equally with whites," Debs declared, "misconstrues the movement he pretends to serve or lacks the courage to live up to its [cardinal] principles [of freedom and equality]." In a declaration contrasting vividly with O'Hare's, Debs declared, "[T]he negro is my brother. . . . The color of his skin is no more to me than the color of his hair or eyes. He is human and that is enough." Even if Debs here assumes that "the Negro" is "he" and that "Socialist" and "Negro" are distinct categories, his statement strongly testifies to egalitarian principle. Randolph and Owen repeatedly praised Debs's antiracism in the *Messenger*, calling "the great 'Gene'" the "harbinger and prophet of the noblest philosophy ever conceived in the mind of man" and declaring that "we, the most crushed of peoples, loved thee since thy first struggles for economic justice began."[21]

It was not simply a few enlightened members of the national SPA leadership—or of the relatively advanced New York City branches—who contested prejudice and segregation. In some regions, entire branches of the SPA adhered to Debs's cardinal principles. In St. Louis, in the wake of the 1917 riot, the SPA pursued a vigorous campaign in opposition to an AFL-sponsored move to segregate neighborhoods; the Oklahoma SPA was also known for its antisegregationist activity. There is ample anecdotal evidence that even where the SPA organizationally practiced segregation, individual rank-and-file Socialists bucked the tide. White depression-era radicals from Socialist backgrounds, such as the novelist and *Anvil* editor Jack Conroy and the journalist and fiction writer Meridel Le Sueur, would later record memories of their parents' often courageous acts of antiracism. Ovington, recalling her travels in the prewar South, wrote of a white Alabama party member who, because of his principled espousal of racial equality, had lost both his family and his job. "This was part of the meaning of revolution," Ovington meditated. "What did we in New York know of party loyalty? Our locals talked revolution. This man lived it." Yet the "talk" about "revolution" in New York was apparently carried on in a sufficiently egalitarian manner to induce the radical New Negroes Randolph and Owen to hitch their wagon to the star of the SPA.[22]

Instead of hastily dismissing the SPA as hopelessly mired in racist thinking or, equally perversely, congratulating it for doing all it could within the existing historical limits, one should recognize that the early-twentieth-century Left contained within its white ranks unreconstructed racists, principled antiracists, and would-be antiracists struggling against a pervasive dominant ideology. To understand the inability of U.S. Socialists to encounter and combat the racism crippling the working-class movement, one must examine not just the racism quotient of the SPA, taken individually and en masse, but the theoretical paradigms that shaped Socialist practice.

"Irresistible Economic Forces Lead with the Certainty of Doom to the Shipwreck of Capitalist Production": Socialist Evolutionism

The Socialists' embrace of evolutionism carried implications that were racist and class-collaborationist. The notion that societies evolve inexorably through a fixed series of stages, from lower to higher, readily overlaps with the racist notion that "primitive" societies are made up of people of lesser intelligence and capability. Although the anthropological work that the Socialists routinely cited—such as Henry Lewis Morgan's research on Native American societies, which so strongly influenced Engels—did not necessarily stipulate racial superiority and inferiority, it was easy to draw this conclusion. Berger's view that "Negroes and mulattoes" constitute a "lower race" echoed this assumption. Even Randolph and Owen subscribed to a hierarchical classification of civilizations. In their 1917 pamphlet *Terms of Peace and the Darker Races,* the two black Socialists declared that "only incidentally are the darker peoples exploited. It is not because of their color per se, but because colonial peoples happen to assume such a low place in the scale of civilization just now, as to make such exploitation attractive, easy, and possible." While understandably eager to distinguish their Marxist analysis of colonialism from the official Garveyite position, which occluded the issue of class, Randolph and Owen evidently embraced the same "scale of civilization" premise used by the colonialists to justify their racial dominance. The black Socialists' implied modes of production narrative—which insisted that all peoples and nations must go through full capitalist development, thereby creating a proletariat exclusively empowered to carry for-

ward the torch of history—was readily compatible with the evolutionist
doctrine preaching the inherent inferiority of those nations and peoples
that had not yet risen to the capitalist mode of production. The Socialist
theorization of Negro sharecroppers and tenant farmers as "peasants" and
therefore "non-historical peoples" had its bourgeois counterpart in biological racism of the crudest kind.[23]

The Socialists' endorsement of an evolutionist modes of production
narrative also led, by another route, to a reformism that was intricately
interwoven with the SPA's failure to demand full "social equality" for
African Americans, for evolutionism (as understood at the time) involved
the proposition that change—in society as in nature—would come not
by leaps and bounds but gradually, through a succession of inexorable
stages. The Second International theorist Karl Kautsky voiced the orthodox theory when he declared in 1892, "Irresistible economic forces lead
with the certainty of doom to the shipwreck of capitalist production. . . .
The substitution of a new social order for the existing one is no longer
simply desirable, it has become inevitable." That this "substitution" is
"inevitable" implies that transition to socialism can be both peaceful and
agentless and that the existing state need not be "smashed"—as Lenin
would insist—but can instead be taken over through the electoral process. Articulating the merging of Marx and Herbert Spencer that would
characterize the outlook of most early-twentieth-century Socialists, the
Danish-born Laurence Gronlund—known by British Socialists of the time
as the "spiritual father" of Fabianism—wrote in his *Cooperative Commonwealth* (1884) that socialism was "INEVITABLY . . . the . . . next stage
in our development." Gradualism was essential to the process. "[We] are
not here concerned about how to institute that New Order," he wrote.
"[W]hen the time is ready, when we reach that brink, a bridge will grow
before our way, *somehow.*" The SPA's espousal of electoral reformism had
been the key issue in its 1912 split with the IWW, which advocated direct action at the point of production. When, in the context of the 1919
split, the *Liberator* coeditor Crystal Eastman remarked that the recent
history of political repression should have disabused Socialists of the illusion that "human liberty ca[n] be secured or maintained through the
institutions of political democracy," she was, as a member of the SPA's
left wing, contesting not just electoral politics but also the doctrine of
peaceful evolution toward socialism that underpinned those politics.[24]

By 1919, the anti-Bolshevist implications of evolutionary socialism
had become patent. As Eastman's comment suggests, evolution and substitution involved not just gradualism but also a formalistic view of the
state as a neutral site; although currently under the domination of the

bourgeoisie, the state might, through patient pressure by the working class, evolve into an institution serving all the people. John Spargo, who would become a prominent right-winger in the party even before the split, made the point in his and George Louis Arner's *Elements of Socialism* (1912): "To meet and overcome the capitalist use of the agencies of the State, . . . [c]lass-conscious working people are everywhere organizing into Socialist or Labor parties for the express purpose of gaining control of the machinery of the state. The capture of the State by the proletariat, through political education and organization of the workers, is the primary aim of all Socialist parties. With the conquest of the powers of the State by the proletariat class ownership of the means of production and exchange will be abolished." The Socialists' reliance on electoral politics as the principal strategy for attaining the "cooperative commonwealth" had distinctly negative consequences for African Americans. Not only did this program frequently result in opportunist appeals to racist white voters, but also the commitment to a politics of electoral representation meant that its strategy for organizing among Negroes—insofar as it had one at all—was shaped around, and delimited by, a politics of inclusion. Given the SPA's persistent failure to acknowledge the special oppression of blacks, it was, as Philip Foner points out, a victory for Socialist antiracists that, at its 1918 national convention, the party declared African Americans to be an especially exploited minority. Yet this recognition was linked with the demand that states abrogating Negro voting rights be deprived of congressional representation. Inclusion or exclusion from the arena of electoral politics thus framed the entire discussion of African Americans' "special oppression." Similarly, the *Call*'s angry denunciation of the 1919 race riots was accompanied by a dismissal of the "patriotic fakirs [who] continually yawp the praises of American 'democracy'" and the declaration that "[n]ot until our black brothers are free to walk the streets of American cities unmolested, not until they have free access to all callings and professions, not until they are free to organize politically in the South and to vote without being clubbed and shot, will this country be anything else than an autocracy to them." The United States was far from granting Negroes the democratic rights that the *Call* stipulated. Yet, in the *Call* editorial, equality for African Americans was limited to equality before the law; representation of the Negro as a fully enfranchised American, one who could metonymically stand for the body politic as fully as any other citizen, appears to have been both the goal and the limit of SPA antiracist strategy. This fundamentally bourgeois notion of political representation would affect the notions of cultural representation shaping the Harlem Renaissance.[25]

"Capitalism Knows No Color Line": Socialist Economism

Closely linked to the Socialists' classless theorization of the state was their economist conception of "labor." Amidst the class struggles of 1919, it remained impossible to compartmentalize politics and economics. In the Seattle general strike, for instance, the shipbuilders' wage demands quickly escalated into an exhibition of citywide proletarian solidarity that in turn raised larger questions about worker self-management and self-government. In the great steel strike of 1919, the demand for higher wages and union recognition raised the prospect of nationalization. Yet SPA doctrine continued to posit a separation between the Socialists' electoral strategy, on the one hand, and the "labor movement," on the other. This dualism, as Montgomery points out, effectively abandoned labor to an AFL leadership that, having little interest in working-class emancipation from exploitation, simply adopted a more militant rhetoric to placate the insurgent proletariat. In the wake of the Seattle general strike, however, the AFL leadership backpedaled furiously to dissociate itself from the rhetoric of the "Seattle Soviet" and reassure the capitalists that nationalization—much less revolution—was not on the horizon. Having confined its strategy for labor organizing to the "labor movement," the SPA was—as the Thermidor of the early 1920s set in and its own left wing split away—less equipped than ever to confront, let alone contest, the continuing Jim Crow practices of organized labor.[26]

The Socialists' relegation of "labor" to the "labor movement" was linked with its conflation of "labor" with "wage labor," a slippage that tacitly legitimated the exchange of labor power for wages. Randolph, tailoring *The Communist Manifesto* to distinctly American ends, declared that "lynching will not stop until Socialism comes. You can strike a death blow of lynching by voting for Socialism. Black and white workers unite. You have nothing to lose but your chains; you have the world to gain." Yet he theorized lynching as "a practice which is used to foster and to engender race prejudice to prevent the lynchers and the lynched, the white and black workers from organizing on the industrial and voting on the political fields, to protect their labor-power." While he targeted the divide-and-conquer function of lynching, he also implied that the pursuit of higher wages, rather than the overthrow of the wages system, was the goal of Socialist activity, at least in the "industrial . . . field." The significance of Bogalusa, then, was not that the proletariat was overcoming those internal divisions that foreclosed the possibility of revolution and disabled its self-constitution as subject of history but, instead, that black and white workers were uniting to demand a greater share of surplus value from the capitalist. The SPA's separation of the labor movement from the political arena, in both theory and practice, thus further stripped workers of revolutionary agency. Evolutionist doctrine precluded the necessity for the proletariat to act purposively to bring into being the "collective commonwealth"; the economistic reduction of labor to wage labor theorized away the necessity for abolishing the class relations that turn labor into the commodity of labor power to begin with.[27]

Oneal's discussion of race and class in "The Next Emancipation" is worth quoting at some length, for it displays the contradictory implications of SPA economism and reformism for the working class in general and black workers in particular:

> Human labor power is the source of all values produced. The labor power of a Negro worker embodied in a bar of steel a car or coal or the basement of a building is just as essential as the labor power of a white worker. The color line is not seen in the bar of steel, the car of coal or the basement. . . .
>
> Human labor is human labor, whether it is the labor of the Negro or the white, the American or the German, the Italian or the Englishman. To labor one must get the consent of others. We have seen that the factories, mines, shops, railroads and industries in general are owned by the capitalist class. . . .
>
> The other way is to transfer the natural resources, mills, mines, railroads and industries in general to the whole people to be the public property of all. *Social ownership instead of private ownership. Common ownership instead of capitalist ownership. Mastery of industry by useful labor instead of mastery by a few powerful owners. . . .*
>
> The future belongs to the workers of all countries. They are called upon to reorganize the world on another and more human basis. The color line must go. National prejudices must go. Religious hatreds must be wiped out. The ranks must be closed up. Workers must not divide their power between two parties owned by their masters. They must unite in a party of their class.

Oneal speaks as an egalitarian Socialist, pointing up the centrality of human labor to the goods enjoyed by all, condemning the capitalists' concentrated ownership of the means of production and domination of the political process, and calling for an end to the religious, national, and racial categories that divide workers. Moreover, his decision to title his pamphlet "The Next Emancipation" locates the fight against wage slavery in the history of the fight against chattel slavery and draws on the parallel between the postwar radical insurgency and Reconstruction animating the Left's discourse of the day.[28]

Yet Oneal's formulation of labor, labor power, and value subtly reifies exploitation and ratifies the sale of labor power for wages. Marx asserted in *Critique of the Gotha Programme*—one of the foundational theoretical texts of the Second International—that the Lassalleans were wrong in positing "labour" as "the source of all wealth." This proposition, Marx argued, overlooks the role of nature in supplying humanity with use values and adopts the perspective of capital, assigning "value" only to products that can be bought and sold for profit. "[A] socialist programme cannot allow such bourgeois phrases to pass over in silence the *conditions* that alone give them meaning," cautioned Marx. Ignoring Marx's warning, however, Oneal compounds the Lassalleans' error by proposing that "[h]uman labor *power* is the source of all values produced." By further stipulating labor power rather than labor as the source of value—and then paralleling *"useful labor"* with *"a few powerful owners,"* as if these are ontologically equivalent entities—Oneal presupposes the commodification of wage labor and reduces workers to their function under capitalism. In his formulation, insofar as workers produce, they are not agents; insofar as they are agents—that is, engaged in *"social ownership"* as the "whole people"—they are citizens, not workers. This dualism, which suggestively connects with the Socialist separation of political action from the labor movement, is compounded by Oneal's misconstrual of the significance of labor power in the theory of exploitation set forth in *Capital*, for the revolutionary essence of the notion of labor power, and what separates this concept from the more inclusive category of labor from which Marx himself had struggled to free himself for years, is precisely that labor power is a commodity, *not* an activity. The extent to which labor power is a "source of values" depends on its capacity to expand value—to produce a value greater than that measured by the wage for which it is purchased. The entity "labor power," in short, is meaningless without the informing context of exploitation, which in fact Marx theorized the concept to explain. To note Oneal's misuse of the term *labor power* is thus not to engage in Marxological quibbling but to designate a core aspect of SPA reformism, for Oneal's corollary advocacy of "[s]ocial ownership instead of private ownership" and "[c]ommon ownership instead of capitalist ownership" involves a redistribution of the wealth created by "[h]uman labor power," not the negation of the wage system itself.[29]

Oneal's failure consistently to link the fight against exploitation with the abolition of classes is reflected throughout "The Next Emancipation." Although the terms *Negro worker, white worker, workingman,* and *workingwoman* frequently appear in the text, as do the terms *capitalist class* and *owning class,* only once in twenty-nine pages does the term *work-*

ing class appear—and then it is as an adjective ("working class voters"), not as a noun. Oneal's reference to the workers' "party of their class" in the passage quoted here is the closest approximation. The reluctance of this leading SPA theorist to use *working class* as a noun to describe the principal agent of historical change may help illuminate the confused definitions of *class* offered by the activists and commentators in the Socialists' orbit of influence. If the SPA itself did not offer a clear definition of the relation of class to labor to exploitation, it is no wonder that such progressives as Stephen Graham, William Pickens, and James Weldon Johnson used the term *class* in the contradictory ways noted in the previous chapter. After the 1919 split, the emergent Communist and Communist Labor parties spoke more frequently of "the working class," as both a producer of value and the subject of history. The SPA left-winger Nearing, who prefaced his *Labor and the League of Nations* (1919) with the note that 1 May 1919 had been "the first day of the Workers' New Year," repeatedly used the noun *working class* to describe the collective agent that would bring into being a true internationalism, as opposed to the "Organization of Capitalist Empires" contained in Woodrow Wilson's "League of Robber Nations." In an April 1920 *Liberator* review of Harold Stearns's *Liberalism in America,* Mike Gold (still writing under his given name, Irwin Granich) scoffed at the pretensions of would-be progressive intellectuals and asserted, "[T]he working class, which suffers most under capitalism, alone can develop the desire and strength to destroy this system." W. A. Domingo used the terms *working class* and *proletariat* throughout his analysis of the danger posed by the Socialists' inattention to the issue of race. In the rhetoric of the SPA, however—particularly after the split, when it rallied around the line of its right wing—the working class figured less prominently as revolutionary historical actor.[30]

In some respects, the SPA's clouded theorizations of *labor* and *class* emerge from a radical tradition always uncertain about its relation to the revolutionary agency of the proletariat as proposed by Marx. In his highly influential *Mass and Class: A Survey of Social Divisions* (1906), the U.S. Socialist W. J. Ghent—although citing *The Communist Manifesto* in defense of the "economic interpretation of history"—discerned six different classes in contemporary capitalist society: proletarians, self-employed producers, social servants, traders, idle capitalists, and retainers. Ghent's schema—following Marx's practice in *The Eighteenth Brumaire*—had the virtue of differentiating among various class sectors. Unlike Marx, however, Ghent did not see these as configuring between the two poles of proletariat and bourgeoisie. As Mike Hill points out, when the early American Socialists like Ghent theorized class conflict in bipolar terms, they were more likely to oppose "producers" to the "parasitic money powers," using language closer to Thorstein Veblen's counterposition of "industrial" to "pecuniary" interests than to the Marxist portrayal of "two great hostile camps, . . . two great classes facing each other: Bourgeoisie and Proletariat."[31]

But the problem here is not simply that the SPA failed to stick to the Marxist script, for Marx himself at times was somewhat ambiguous on the relation of classes to masses, of masses to proletariat, and of labor to all three. As Étienne Balibar has pointed out, Marx uses the term *proletariat* to designate the working class in its self-conscious (that is, class-conscious) moment, as a class not just "in" but "for" itself. By contrast, the term *masses* is used to describe the working class in its spontaneous moment. *Mass conflicts* are thus to be contradistinguished from *class struggles* according to the degree of working-class self-consciousness they contain and project. *Labor* is used to denote the working class in the moment of its relation to production: hence the omnipresence of the term in *Capital*, where *proletariat* and *masses* alike rarely appear. For Marx, the terms *working class, masses, labor*, and *proletariat* thus possess multiple significations—sometimes overlapping, sometimes not. It is hardly surprising that, freighted by reformism and evolutionism, early-twentieth-century U.S. radicals fell back on *labor* as a catchall term to designate the working class in its various moments, leaving the causality for change in inevitable historical processes and agency—when needed—to the Socialist politicians.[32]

This failure to view the proletariat as revolutionary—or potentially revolutionary—bore particular implications for SPA doctrine on the role of African American workers in producing—or, alternatively, preventing—revolution. The SPA has frequently been faulted for embracing the category of class so rigorously that it failed to recognize in theory—and combat in practice—the special nature of black oppression. It is certainly true that some SPA theorists almost entirely overlooked the questions of race and racism: Spargo and Arner's *Elements of Socialism*, a basic primer of the prewar years, devotes only one sentence to the disempowering consequences of working-class division along the lines of race, ethnicity, and religion. But even when the SPA came to address the "Negro question," as Oneal did in "The Next Emancipation," it still minimized the effects of racism on African Americans. Thus Oneal maintained that African Americans constitute only one more sector of the working class, argued that "the Negro question . . . is at bottom a LABOR question," and pointed out that "*[t]he Mass of Negro wage workers . . . cannot escape from the servitude of wage labor until the white wage workers also es-*

cape. Both must escape together or neither will escape." Avoiding such
matters as race riots and lynchings, Oneal claimed that capital knows "no
color line": in the past, white indentured servants endured the same ag-
onies as black slaves, just as "the anti-Irish prejudice was once as deep-
seated as the anti-Negro prejudice is today." Nor, Oneal argued, had
whites been differentially affected as a consequence of racism. "Ignorance
and prejudice" might lead the white worker to direct hostility to black
fellow workers rather than against the "white masters," Oneal opined,
but "[i]f every Negro's place in the South was filled by a white man conditions of the white workers would be what they are now." Defying the
evident reality that white workers in the South—in the fields, the mines,
the lumber and textile mills—themselves experienced extra exploitation
because of Jim Crow, Oneal determined that "[t]he only function served
by color prejudice" was "to keep the workers divided." Black superexploitation—as well as its concomitant depression of the living standards
of white workers—was invisible to Oneal.[33]

No doubt this insistence on capital's color-blindness could serve,
Mark Pittenger suggests, as a "convenient mask for racism." But Negro
and white Socialists alike endorsed this theoretical model. Randolph and
Owen sought to heighten the SPA's awareness of racial issues and pushed
for the party to declare African Americans "the most oppressed portion
of the population of the United States, . . . especially discriminated against
in economic opportunity." The *Messenger's* analyses of debt peonage,
lynching, and race riots show that its editors well understood the connections between violence and superexploitation. But they, too, embraced
the doctrine of capital's imperviousness to color—as evidenced in their
1917 comment that "only incidentally are the darker peoples exploited"
as well as in their 1919 assertion, echoing Debs, that "capitalism knows
no color line. It will coin the blood, sweat and suffering of white women
and white children and black women and black children into dollars and
dividends." Moreover, while praising Debs for his antiracism, Randolph
and Owen very rarely themselves criticized manifestations of racial prejudice within the SPA. When in 1918 Du Bois published his withering
commentary on Socialist racism and Debs responded, the exchange was
published in the *Intercollegiate Socialist;* Randolph and Owen reproduced
no part of this exchange in the *Messenger,* nor did they seize this opportunity to press for the organization to increase its recruitment efforts
among African Americans. Even Domingo, who sharply chastised the SPA
for not contesting the racism in its own ranks and not recognizing the
threat to the working-class movement posed by scabbing black workers,
failed to offer an alternative paradigm for explaining the relationship

between the persistence of racial antagonism, on the one hand, and the imperatives of capitalist social control, on the other. That capitalism needs racism, foments it, and does not simply opportunistically make use of preexisting racial antagonisms was at the time beyond the full theoretical comprehension of black and white Marxists alike.[34]

"To Increase Their Bargaining Power": The Limits to Labor Competition

The widely accepted view that a virtually all-white Socialist Party crudely ground the particularity of black oppression under the wheels of a reductive class analysis does not quite mesh with reality. What bears further examination is the model for understanding racial antagonism that white and African American radicals commonly *did* embrace—namely, the thesis of labor competition. This doctrine is ably articulated in the dog cartoon from the December 1919 *Messenger* in which, it will be recalled, dogs representing Negro labor and white labor are shown fighting each other over a paltry bone; racial prejudices are fanned by the dog of Capital, which runs off with the ham of profits, while the Socialist Agitator dog pleads with the worker dogs to cease quarreling and unite against their common foe. That this explanation for racial antagonism possessed analytical power is undeniable—especially in an era when recently migrated and newly proletarianized blacks, emerging from the lynch-crazed South, were being used to defeat the postwar labor insurgency. But the model has various flaws. First, it does not reveal why one group rather than another should continually end up as the loser in the struggle for survival. In the *Messenger* cartoon, the body of the black dog is at least as large and healthy as that of the white dog. By proposing a Darwinian labor jungle, the jobs competition thesis leaves open the possibility that whites, not blacks, will lose out in the struggle for survival—as O'Hare had implied when she fantastically asserted that landowners routinely treated black tenants better than whites. In its more modern variant as split labor market theory, the jobs competition thesis proposes that white workers benefit from race-based divisions and, from the standpoint of crude self-interest, would be quite reasonable in excluding African Americans and other minorities from the workplace. The SPA, to its credit, never embraced the notion that the differential treatment accorded white workers amounted to an objective good; Randolph and Owen repeatedly sent out the message that "labor must be shown that it suffers from race prejudice and that it will benefit from the abolition of race prejudice, which keeps black and white workers divided." Nonetheless, the pragmatism undergirding the jobs

competition thesis did not permit antiracism to be articulated as a crucial component of a class-based morality; indeed, as Alexander Saxton has
argued, the jobs competition argument "tends to exonerate members of
the excluding group from charges of bias or bigotry, since the existence
of job competition is clearly not their fault and they can hardly be blamed
for protecting their economic interests."[35]

By confining the class struggle to the realm of the economic, the jobs
competition thesis made the need for black-white labor unity a matter
of pragmatic immediacy. Socialist discussions of capitalist-based racial
antagonism often ended with the observation that only under socialism
would all workers be emancipated from wage slavery. It was usually made
clear, however, that the co-operative commonwealth was a long-term goal
and that eradication of race consciousness should be seen as a byprod-
uct, rather than a precondition, of attaining that goal. In the short run,
the struggle around wages and hours was all. Egalitarianism was thus for
all practical purposes conflated with equal opportunity under capitalism
and had little or nothing to do with the eradication of racial inequality.
Oneal strongly implied that the call for social equality might impede the
struggle for a better world; O'Hare more bluntly proposed segregation as
a vital aspect of utopia. Racism and economism were thus mutually reinforcing: notions of racial difference contributed to and were reinforced
by the doctrine that jobs competition, and jobs competition alone, supplied the material base of such notions. As Randolph and Owen declared
in a July 1918 editorial entitled "Reasons Why White and Black Workers Should Combine in Labor Unions," "Black and white workers should
combine for no other reason than that for which individual workers
should combine, viz., to increase their bargaining power, which will enable them to get their demands."[36]

Finally, the jobs competition thesis applied only to the situation of
the newly proletarianized blacks who had journeyed North to establish
new homes in the cities. It had nothing to say about the position of African Americans in the South, trapped in sharecropping, tenant farming,
or debt peonage and subject to lynch terror. Because the Negroes of the
South were theorized as a peasantry, not yet evolved into the history-
bearing status of wage earners, their fates were largely irrelevant to the
project of transforming society. The special oppression to which southern blacks were subjected was, in Socialist eyes, a great tragedy, but it
was essentially viewed as the residue of a vanishing mode of production
rather than as a coercive mechanism vital to the continuing expropria-
tion of surplus value in the modern capitalist agricultural economy. Even
Randolph, in his otherwise penetrating analysis of lynching's basis in

capitalist rule, underrated the importance of the interpellation of the poor white as "white" in the South of modernity. He noted that, on the one hand, "out of the 3337 persons lynched between 1882 and 1903, there were 1192 white persons," and, on the other, that "[t]he press is owned and controlled by the employing class and . . . is used to . . foment race hatred" and "give wide circulation to that insidious doctrine of the Negroes being the hewers of wood and the drawers of water for white men." He did not, however, link the two propositions or demonstrate that the participation of poor whites in the terrorization of Negroes was instrumental in their own oppression and exploitation, indeed terrorization. Given their great prestige among progressives and leftists—from Seligmann to Ovington, Angelina Grimké to Georgia Douglas Johnson—the *Messenger* editors' shortcomings with regard to theorizing racism as a mechanism for social control would play a significant role in limiting the horizon of contemporaneous debate over the relation of race to class.[37]

The "Psychological Wage" of Whiteness: Psychology and Propaganda versus Ideology

Integral to the U.S. Socialists' economism was their limited grasp of ideology as a means of social control operating through the naturalization of capitalist social relations. If evolutionary development would bring the cooperative commonwealth into being, and class-conscious activity, while hastening the process, was of secondary importance, then presumably there was no urgent need for the Left to attend to the proletariat's possession of a revolutionary, egalitarian, and therefore antiracist consciousness. The Socialists were cognizant that the ruling class promoted its interests and controlled the means of articulating these—and that the working class needed to respond in kind. Owen and Randolph's discussions of race riots and lynching were very clear on the role played by the press, the church, and the educational process in winning white workers to participate in, or at least accept, racist brutality; "propaganda," they declared, "is employed by all classes and races to mobilize and crystallize public opinion in the interest of their cause." But the Socialists' categories for describing the consciousness shaped by workers' everyday experience under capitalism were inconsistent and sketchy, relying primarily on such empiricist concepts as "instinct" and "psychology" derived from contemporaneous social science. Ghent attributed to his different class sectors different species of "class instinct," directly reflective of the different groupings' material life circumstances. Veblen's designation of an "instinct of workmanship" that is suppressed under capitalism directed attention away from exploitation—even as it targeted alienation—and formed the basis of his technocratic view of socialism. Ordway Tead proposed a broadened anatomy of working-class consciousness by means of categories of "instinct" ranging from "sex," "the herd," and "play" to "workmanship" and "pugnacity." In an approving *Liberator* commentary on Tead's *Instincts in Industry* (1918), the reviewer, one B. Harrow, displayed an interesting set of assumptions:

> A discussion of instincts in industry can not be complete unless we try to understand what instincts motivate the employer, and where these instincts come into conflict with those of the employé. The key to such an understanding is the workingman's instinct—which seems to me his strongest—of submissiveness; strongest chiefly because he has accepted altogether too naively and literally the philosophy of Christianity—a philosophy of meekness. The employer has taken advantage of this by developing a kingship idea, permitting him to assume the dominating role, while giving to the employé the part of the meek who shall inherit the earth—in heaven.

Presumably the Christian ideal of meekness is embraced by workers *prior to* their insertion into class relations; employers need only "take advantage" of this preexisting instinct to secure their hegemony. That the foremost journal of the cultural Left could produce no more searching a commentary on the epistemological and political limitations of Tead's paradigm reveals a deficit in the Left's comprehension of the class forces shaping consciousness.[38]

As deployed by early-twentieth-century leftists and progressives, the term *psychology* was only slightly more useful than *instinct* in filling the gap left by an operative conception of ideology. Tead, in a 1921 *Dial* review of a series of books on "the new psychology," noted the relevance of this emerging academic field to the current historical situation:

> We are, as a civilization, coming out of a period of warfare of unprecedented magnitude where the co-operative effort called into play was likewise on an unprecedented scale. The machinery of "persuasion," of propaganda, of crowd influence was developed and used with a precision heretofore unthought of. Inter-allied administrative agencies operated successfully on a scale formerly impossible. The forces of destruction invented and made manifest were hideous; the forces of constructive human power, of moral devotion and fortitude displayed were grand. Prophecy concerning reconstruction after an era of such deep-seated contradictions is of little avail. But if civilization is becoming too heavy to carry itself, we shall at least be warned; we shall see human nature for what it is and we shall continue to overtax it at our peril.

Tead was evidently aware of the power of the "new psychology" to illuminate the uses to which the "machinery of 'persuasion'" had been put by governments bent on "crowd influence." Nonetheless, he viewed some of these uses as "constructive" and opined that the subject matter of the new field was, finally, "human nature." "It is because the new psychology can without becoming sentimental or too conjectural consider these problems of social control, 'heritage,' and 'reconstruction,'" he concluded, "that we have a right to be cautiously hopeful about it." Randolph was less inclined to grant beneficent motives to the ruling class in his commentary on lynching, where he emphasized the role of the press in "foment[ing] race hatred." "[B]old headlines [featuring] such titles as 'lynch the black brute,' 'young white girls raped by black burly fiend,'" he pointed out, "produc[e] a psychology which expresses itself through the mob." Randolph argued that racism requires constant reinforcement through "propaganda" controlled by the ruling class and does not simply reproduce itself in some relatively autonomous sphere—or, as Barbara Fields has sardonically put it, "'have a life of its own.'" Yet Randolph relied on a mechanistic stimulus-response conception of the material basis of mob psychology and underplayed the ideological functioning of racism in the everyday lives of southern white sharecroppers and poor farmers. Even when Domingo blasted the SPA as "American radicals . . . shar[ing] the typical white psychology towards negroes," his formulation failed to locate sufficiently the source of this "psychology" in capitalist social relations, thereby understating the role of the ruling class in shaping consciousness and implying the immutable nature of white racism. While Randolph and Domingo had views of postwar "reconstruction" quite different from Tead's, the use of the term *psychology* by all three blurred the relation between ideology and consciousness. Alternating between a conspiratorial view of ruling-class "propaganda" and an empiricist notion of working-class "instinct" or "psychology," early-twentieth-century socialists of various stripes were insufficiently equipped to analyze the complex and mediated role played by racism in class formation. For Randolph and Domingo, the source of this shortcoming was not too rigid an adherence to class analysis but a failure to appreciate the centrality of racism, as both ideology and practice, to what even Tead described as "social control"; Socialist economism shrank rather than expanded the domain of historical materialist inquiry.[39]

In the context of the Socialists' weaknesses in theorizing ideology, Marx's famous statement on race—"Labor in the white skin cannot be emancipated as long as in the black skin it is branded"—is more useful than may first appear, for although Marx was, in this passing comment, addressing specifically the "branding" produced by slavery, his trope encompasses Jim Crow racism as well. The notion that labor is something that can assume different colors of skin implies that race differences are only skin-deep: the appearance of difference belies an essence of similarity. Yet the proposition that "black skin" is "branded" not only acknowledges the special oppression endured by those seared with a hot iron and thus marked for superexploitation but also suggests that the blackness of the human chattel's skin may both *cause* and *derive from* the placing of the mark. Although it might be overstating matters to make Marx into a social constructionist of race *avant la lettre*, he seems here to view enslavement as a process requiring consensus around categories of representation in order to naturalize and legitimate itself. Skin color is, for Marx, a matter of consciousness—of signifying practices—as well as of biology. Furthermore, he proposes that white workers will achieve emancipation only when the branding is stopped. For Marx—who cannot be faulted for giving short shrift to class analysis—the liberation of the entire proletariat is therefore contingent on the abolition of not just divisive economic practices but also wage slavery and the ideological categories by which it is naturalized.[40]

U.S. Socialist discourse did not pursue any of the more far-reaching implications of Marx's formulation. In the *Messenger* dog cartoon, "Negro Labor" and "White Labor" signify self-evident realities rather than epistemological categories themselves produced by capitalist "branding." Even as the *Crusader* and the *Crisis* were routinely featuring cover girls displaying the range of complexions encompassed by the term *Negro* in a country obsessed with the "single-drop" doctrine, the *Messenger* cartoon makes the black worker-dog very black, the white one very white. Moreover, that "racial antagonism" was theorized in two ways—as "propaganda" and as "psychology"—offered explanations in two quite different registers. In its mode as "propaganda," racism was viewed as a plot devised by bosses to divide and conquer—hence the dog cartoon or the August 1919 cartoon depicting bosses plotting to safeguard their profits by using the word *nigger* to divide white from black workers. In its mode as "psychology," however, racism was viewed as experientially based in the structure of capitalist social relations. The Socialists' acceptance of race as a founding category—biological, epistemological, political—precluded an appreciation of the centrality of "race-ism," as ideology, to ruling-class hegemony. The problem was thus not simply or even primarily that white Socialists projected their inherited prejudices onto the screen of history, for even such African American Socialists as Randolph and Owen took as given the "fact" of race and, as Pittenger notes, "never directly engaged the issue of scientific racism." Where the African Blood Brotherhood editors of the *Crusader* alternated between embracing an Afrocentric essentialism and interrogating the reality of race, the SPA-allied black Socialists—and antiracist white Socialists—tended to ignore this debate during the key years 1918–22, appreciating its significance only when the energies of the mass movement were substantially depleted.[41]

To note the limitations of class-based antiracist discourse in the late 1910s and early 1920s is not to assert that there were no important attempts to theorize racial antagonism—or race itself—in ideological terms. Du Bois, in his continuing project of analyzing the social forces that shape the "souls of white folks," echoed Marx's formulation in *The Negro* (1915) when he declared that "so long as black laborers are slaves, white laborers cannot be free." In a discussion of the significance of the 1917 East St. Louis race riot, Du Bois argued that white workers' antagonism toward black migrants facilitated their employers' accumulation of capital and reinforced their own entrapment in racial categories produced by colonialism and capitalism. "The discovery of personal 'whiteness,'" he wrote, is "a very modern thing,—a nineteenth and twentieth century matter, indeed." Harrison, asking in *The Negro and the Nation* (1917) whether the United States would live its future under "Socialism or Southernism," observed that "[w]henever a certain social arrangement is beneficial to any class in a society, that class soon develops the psychology of its own advantage and creates insensibly the ethics that will justify that social arrangement." Since "every ruling class has always controlled the public instruments for the diffusion of ideas," Harrison argued, these "ethics" will be "diffused . . . throughout the society . . . [and] will be, if need arise, imposed upon the other classes." Harrison's formulation—which anticipates Richard Wright's brilliant satiric portrayal of Jim Crow "ethics" two decades later—shows him synthesizing the "psychology" of the masses with the rulers' hegemonic imperatives. McKay, in "The Negroes in America," theorized the material basis of the eager participation in "that great American sport, lynching" by a significant sector of the white working class. McKay instructed his Soviet readers about the relation of race to sexuality in the United States. "The Negro question is inseparably connected with the question of woman's liberation," he declared. "[The American bourgeoisie] artificially maintains a war between the races over sex. Every crime—be it class inequality, lynch law, or the exploitation of labor—is concealed by the fetish of sex as behind a smoke screen." The unwillingness of the American Left to examine the operation of this fetish, McKay concluded in frustration, meant that the debate over the politics of racial antagonism was put "in the hands of the reformist bourgeoisie," where it was sure to be divested of its class character.[42]

Yet even these probing theoretical statements were constrained by the limitations of contemporaneous leftist thinking about race and class. Du Bois did not explicitly link fallacious "scientific" theories of "race" with the maintenance of wage slavery and vacillated over the crucial issue of whether white workers could be said to benefit from what he would call, in *Black Reconstruction in America* (1935), the "public and psychological wage" of whiteness. This often-repeated phrase may adequately describe the white worker's sense of advantage, but it obscures the reality (which Du Bois, conversant with socialist doctrine, well knew) that the term *wage* inevitably implies an unequal exchange: workers who receive a wage have surplus value extracted from their labor, regardless of their state of consciousness. In deploying the term *psychology* to describe the outlooks of white and black workers alike, Du Bois further depoliticized the genesis of racially coded consciousness. Harrison's formulation was hamstrung by his stipulation that the rulers' "psychology of its own advantage" is, in the form of "ethics," "imposed upon the other classes" as "the need arise[s]," rather than "diffused" through everyday consciousness. The lack of a single analytical term to conjoin *psychology* and *ethics* left Harrison oscillating between a narrowly conspiratorial view of "imposition" and an undertheorized notion of "diffusion." Harrison also wavered in his analysis of the causality of racism, at times posting that "[c]lass consciousness must be learned, but race consciousness is inborn and cannot be wholly unlearned": "It [race feeling] does not change essentially with changes of economic systems. It is deeper than any class feeling and will outlast the capitalist system. It persists even after race prejudice has been outgrown. It exists not because the capitalists nurse it for economic reasons, but the capitalists rather have the opportunity to nurse it for economic reasons because it exists as a product of biology." Although Winston James views such statements as evidence of despair rather than conviction—Harrison's black nationalism was, in his view, "the last resort of a black socialist in a racist land"— such notions surely impeded Harrison's ability to theorize the means by which capitalists would "nurse" racism "for economic reasons."[43]

McKay came perhaps the closest to framing racial antagonism in ideological terms in his deployment of the concept of the "fetish" to explain procedures of obfuscation and displacement that are simultaneously psychological and political. While he used the term in accordance with current anthropological discourse, he may also have had in mind Marx's notion of commodity fetishism—the only concept through which

Marx presented anything resembling a theory of ideology in *Capital*. Yet McKay left undeveloped the linkage of race with sex; moreover, his conclusion that the principal "screen" behind which racial violence operated was sex contradicted the reality that—as the NAACP's recent *Thirty Years of Lynching in the United States* had just demonstrated—the preponderance of lynchings were precipitated not by allegations of black male sexual aggression toward white women but by disputes over "economic" issues. It was above all the "fetish" of "race"—that is, its reification and naturalization—that, even more than the fetish of sex, "maintain[ed] a war between the races." Even the most advanced theoretical formulations of the wartime and postwar years thus reacted against and were constrained by the inadequate theorizing of both race and racism ("race-ism") as ideology. Socialist economism entailed not the usurpation of the relatively autonomous domain of race by a reductive class analysis but an insufficiently expansive notion of what class analysis should entail.[44]

"[The People] Must Write a New Declaration of Independence": Socialism and Nationalism

The limitations in the early-twentieth-century Socialists' theoretical paradigms—their reformism, economism, evolutionism, and inattention to ideology—both shored up and were shored up by their commitment to nationalism, of one kind or another. Whether American exceptionalist or self-determinationist, nationalism—in even its most apparently revolutionary forms—would end up further hobbling the ability of the Left to oppose racism and organize an effective postwar "reconstruction."

It may appear perverse to fault the U.S. Socialists for having an insufficiently internationalist outlook. The "countrylessness" of the proletariat was, after all, a fundamental tenet of Marxist theory as outlined by the Second International. As Kautsky declared in 1892, "The capitalist system, by expropriating the worker, has freed him from the soil. He has now no settled home, and therefore no country. . . . [T]he modern proletarian journeys with his wife and family in order to settle wherever he finds conditions most favorable. He is not a tourist, but a nomad." Proletarian migrancy is here portrayed not as deracination but as the need to follow where capital leads; insofar as the proletarian "belongs," it is to a class, not to a soil. Even though most of the European Socialist parties abandoned this stance during the war, the SPA was one of very few branches of the Second International that called on its members to refuse to participate in the conflict, declaring at the 1917 St. Louis convention that "[t]he Socialist Party of the United States is unalterably opposed to the system of exploitation and class rule which is upheld and strengthened by military power and sham national patriotism. We, therefore, call upon the workers of all the countries to refuse support to their governments in their wars. . . . As against the false doctrine of national patriotism, we uphold the ideal of international working-class solidarity." For the Lusk Committee, this declaration signaled that "the social revolution, not political office, is the end and aim of the Socialist Party." At a 1917 SPA Boston antiwar rally, according to the *Call*, "[h]undreds of Socialists were beaten and forced to kiss the flag on their knees." Socialists elected to public office—including Berger—were not allowed to take their seats because of their antiwar stance; the Socialist press was banned from the mails. O'Hare and Debs were imprisoned for their antiwar views, the latter sentenced to ten years for declaring that corporate leaders "are today wrapped in the American flag and shout their claim from the housetops that they are the only patriots . . . [with magnifying glasses in hand . . . scanning] the country for evidence of disloyalty, eager to apply the brand of treason to the men who dare to even whisper their opposition." In the discourse of wartime and postwar racist antiradicalism, *cosmopolitan* was equivalent to *seditious* and *alien; socialist* was coterminous with *un-American*.[45]

African American leftists were among the most outspoken advocates of internationalism. When Pan-Africanists of various stripes were expressing admiration for Japan's growing status as a world power, Randolph insistently dubbed Japan as "imperialistic, . . . autocratic . . . and reactionary," arguing that Japan's ascendancy in the "rising tide of color" did nothing for the Japanese working class or the Asian peoples subjugated by the Japanese Empire. Owen wrote that the industrial nations' success in undermining workers' strikes by importing wares from abroad amounted to a system of imposed "international scabbing." The BI agent assigned to follow the African Blood Brotherhood leader Richard B. Moore reported, it will be recalled, that he had "never heard anyone speak so disrespectfully of the U.S.A. and the flag." Accompanying all issues of William Bridges's *Challenge*, a black radical newspaper appearing briefly in 1919, was "An Oath," which read in part, "By ETERNAL HEAVEN—I swear never to love any flag simply for its color, . . . I am a Patriot. I am not merely of a Race and a Country, but of the World. I am BROTHERHOOD." In its August 1919 issue, the paper expanded, "We demand . . . that instead of being re-Americanized into accepting sterner patriotic obligations we be thoroughly informed why we should be loyal to any government that does not protect our lives and property the same as it protects those of other people with less claim to protection." In the same month, William Colson's *Messenger* article prophesied that the "next war for 'democracy'" would be directed against the "Huns of America" "in the land of 'THE STAR-SPANGLED BANNER.'" The July 1919 *Messenger* drawing of "The Mob Victim"—depicting a black man being lynched in a bonfire created by a burning American flag—implied that patriotism was fueling the fires of racial violence. The antipatriotic theme was followed up by the cover of the September 1920 issue devoted to "Americanism of Today," which featured a bas-relief sculpture of a black man, bound to a tree and writhing in pain, being torn from the embrace of a black woman while a crowd of laughing lynchers presses forward, ready for the kill (see figure 14).[46]

Despite their antipathy to 100 percent Americanism and enthusiasm for internationalism, however, most U.S. leftists, black and white, never fully broke with nationalism. The IWW's wartime free speech fights often involved Wobblies' chaining themselves to lampposts and reciting the Declaration of Independence—a symbolic gesture that at once signaled governmental hypocrisy and encoded governmental repression as a violation of American democratic values. The labor movement's wartime discourse of "industrial democracy," while raising the spectre of worker control for anxious owners of the means of production, rarely went beyond advocating a program for nationalization in which workers would share power with, rather than wrest power from, corporate magnates. That the captains of industry could so readily transpose the rhetoric of "industrial democracy" in their postwar institution of "industrial relations" as part of the virulently antilabor American Plan indicates the term's limited utility as a counterdiscourse to 100 percent Americanism. Spargo, in *Americanism and Social Democracy* (1918), proclaimed that "the ideals of democratic Socialism are identical with Americanism" and that "[l]oyalty to America is consistent with the utmost devotion to internationalism." Nationalism, he contended, had a "natural" hold on the human psyche: "[W]hen the issue is drawn between nations, national feelings, which have their roots much deeper in the life of the race than class feelings, soon demonstrate their supremacy." The steel strike leader William Z. Foster, himself attacked as un-American, protested that the meetings where strikers translated their demands into multiple languages were "schools in practical Americanization," to be counterposed with the false Americanism promoted by the likes of Judge Gary. In March 1919, the *Call* contrasted "[t]rue nationalism, based in the main upon language [and the natural characteristics and genius peculiar to the people of a particular locality]," which "demands the right of a people to control its

Figure 14. "Americanism of Today," by C. L. Kelley, *Messenger*, September 1920

destiny," with the "anarchistic nationalism struggling to find markets for commodities and necessitating armed camps and war." Americanism, the *Call* concluded—without irony—is the "true democratic ideal."[47]

The sympathy for nationalism was especially pronounced among the right-wing Socialists: Spargo voted against the St. Louis Resolution and subsequently quit the party over its support of the Bolshevik Revolution. But Debs's statement that corporate magnates "claim . . . that they are the only patriots" implied that the SPA leader—who had gone to prison for protesting against the war—considered himself a truer patriot than the "Wall Street Junkers," whom he termed "the real traitors of this nation." The left-winger Nearing, railing against the League of Nations as a "League of Robber Nations," couched his critique in the terms of a disappointed patriotism. "Again tyranny has raised its ugly head in the guise of capitalist imperialism," he declared. "The day of the people has come. They must write a new Declaration of Independence—independence of plutocracy and all of its works." Nearing's indignation was patent, but his use of the term *the people* lacked class content; furthermore, "independence of plutocracy" implied a goal of detaching from, rather than destroying, the class system and its state. In Robert Minor's powerful graphic representing angry black migrants leaving the lynch-ridden South, one of the women clutches to her breast a picture of Abraham Lincoln; American democracy, it seems, supplies a tradition to which these potential revolutionaries may cling (see figure 4 in chapter 1). Nor did most of the black Socialists, for all their denunciation of the "Huns of America," altogether reject the discourse of American nationalism. Bridges's play on the theme of world patriotism did not expunge the concept but appropriated it for alternative ends—as, for example, when he counseled black Americans to refuse to sing "The Star-Spangled Banner" so long as "Southern hillsides are spangled with the blood of many [an] innocent negro." The New Negro, he urged, should "raise [a] . . . determined, unafraid voice," crying "'Give Me Liberty or Give Me Death.'" Presumably the New Negro—authentic inheritor of the mantle of Patrick Henry—would sing the anthem once lynching had ceased. Colson's angry denunciation of "the treachery of the white American" was similarly double-edged: Jim Crow racists were traitors to the promise of American democracy, a promise that fell to the New Negroes to uphold. Even the title of Harrison's compiled writings about African Americans and socialism was, tellingly, *The Negro and the Nation*— hardly a choice emphasizing the Negro's relation to the world proletariat.[48]

Randolph and Owen, moreover, even at their most fiery, did not entirely break with the doctrine of American exceptionalism. In a manifesto published in the *Messenger* in March 1919, the prefatory graphic of the

American flag coexisted with the text's stated desire to legalize "the red flag which represents the brotherhood of man." Their "welcome" to "a Bolshevism which overthrows Kaisers, Czars and Kings" did not stipulate the need for a U.S. Bolshevism that would overthrow presidents and members of Congress, much less the capitalist class. In an editorial three months later, Randolph and Owen expanded on this implied endorsement of exceptionalist doctrine, proclaiming, "We want more Bolshevik patriotism in this country. . . . We need more patriotism which loves the country, because the country accords to all a chance—the humble and the high, the lowly and the lordly, . . . the strong and the weak, the rich and the poor." Although they also asserted that they wanted "a patriotism which is proclaimed by the teeming millions and not by the scheming few who make millions of dollars," they were clearly signaling that, in their projected ideal nation, "the humble and the high" and "the rich and the poor" would continue to exist, if under conditions that would "accor[d] to all a chance"—as some would now say, level the playing field. Like other members of the SPA, Randolph and Owen appear to have embraced the notion that the United States did not, finally, need a revolution against the capitalist state to bring into being the "cooperative commonwealth." When in 1922 Owen declared the intention to keep attacking Garvey until he was "removed from American soil"—and, in a strange unity of bedfellows, aided and abetted the efforts of the BI to get rid of Garvey— the *Messenger*'s borrowing from the wartime discourse of the nativists did not constitute a complete divergence from the magazine's earlier practice. Denouncing Garvey as not just a "Black Kluxer" but an "anarchist," Owen expressed outrage at the "unmitigated effrontery" that "a group of foreigners should come into our country and fight, *not for free speech for themselves—but to deny free speech to the citizens of this country.*" Hardly a denunciation of Garvey as a black capitalist, much less a tool of the capitalist class, this statement played to the very patriotism and xenophobia that they had earlier criticized.[49]

The rhetorical appeal to conventional U.S. patriotism in the *Messenger* editors' attack on Garvey would be expressed with increasing frequency and force as they moved to the right after their open break with the Communists in the summer of 1923. "Negro Communists," charged Randolph and Owen, "are a menace . . . to the workers, themselves, and the race" because of their "unsound, unscientific, dangerous and ridiculous . . . policies and tactics"; their "preachments and antics" were "tragically disastrous to the aggressive, independent and rationally radical manhood efforts of the Negro." Changing the subtitle of the *Messenger* to *New Opinion of the New Negro*, the editors gradually dissociated themselves from radical causes, aligning with the previously scorned AFL and—anticipating *Ebony* magazine of some decades later—filling the magazine's pages with portraits of Negro socialites and praise for the acumen and drive of exemplary Negro businesspeople. The November 1923 issue, called the "Negro Business Achievement Issue," even contained an article entitled "The Future of Negro Business" by the editors' former *bete noire* Robert Russa Moton. By early 1924—when the journal was renamed the *World's Greatest Negro Monthly*—the editorial doctrine explicitly guiding the *Messenger* was the open embrace of America as the land of opportunity, with each issue containing a two-page pictorial narrative of a rags-to-riches Negro role model who was explicitly held up as a "pioneer."[50]

While the altered character of the *Messenger* signified important shifts in Randolph and Owen's outlook and practice—not least their serious engagement in union organizing among Negro Pullman workers—most germane to our purposes here is how the *Messenger* editors' increasing conservatism relates to their explicit U.S. nationalism and their approach to culture—and culturalism. Where previously the function of the *Messenger*'s poems and graphics had been to reinforce the magazine's leftist political analyses, the revised identification of the New Negro as successful entrepreneur entailed a splitting off of cultural and literary from explicit political commentary. The May 1923 special educational issue—appearing one month before the open break with the Communists—signaled this trend with the graphic on its cover depicting the New Negro as The Thinker (see figure 15). Displacing the image of the New Negro as gun-blazing motorist roving the streets of the nation's capital, this New Negro had time for the arts. At this juncture, Theophilus Lewis began to contribute his regular column on the Negro theater, and he and George Schuyler initiated "Shafts and Darts," a regular "Page of Calumny and Satire" commenting on the cultural and political scene. This change in the magazine's editorial policy did not occur overnight; through 1925, Langston Hughes would contribute to the *Messenger* such radical poems as "Johannesburg Mines" and "Grant Park," even though their themes and rhetoric would be substantially compromised by their juxtaposition with photographs of wealthy, well-coifed Negro women exemplifying the new policy of "Exalting Negro Womanhood." But the view of culture increasingly emerging from the pages of the *Messenger* was one that eschewed anticapitalist critique while promoting racial pride, on the one hand, and American nationalism, on the other.[51]

When the special Harlem issue of the *Survey Graphic* appeared in March 1925, the former firebrands greeted it with a bland commentary on the value of multiracial intellectualism:

Far more significant than the articles in the Harlem Number of the *Survey Graphic* is the spirit which gave it birth. It marks an interesting turn in the attitude of intellectual white America toward the Negroes. It was planned by white and black intellectuals. This is as it should be. Such contact is creative and constructive even though the product may not always meet with the whole hearted approval of either white or black

Figure 15. "The New Negro," *Messenger*, May 1923

peoples. At least a larger section of serious minded white America is brought up to view the Negro problem from the point of view of black and white thinkers. That they should vary in conclusion and presentation is to be expected. It is also to be expected that Negroes will condemn that which they deem as adverse criticism though the adverse criticism be sound. This is true of all races and peoples. Criticism is what everybody needs but nobody wants. Contrary to a number of Negroes we don't consider the Harlem issue of the *Survey Graphic* as hostile criticism. Much of it is very flattering; some of it is quite indifferent.

Devoid of class content, the review praised the special Harlem issue for drawing together the efforts of "black and white thinkers"; proletarian multiracial unity had devolved into the pairing of Rodinesque figures drawn from among "intellectual white America" and "the Negroes." Taking as given the nationalist discourse that would posit both "white America" and "the Negro problem" as foundational categories of analysis, Randolph and Owen took as the limit of equality the "creative and constructive . . . contact" of the "intellectuals" of both races; as the limit of critique, they took the representational adequacy of the images that the special Harlem issue conveyed. Moreover, where previously they had continually addressed the "propaganda" effect of discourses engaged in racial representation, evaluating the extent to which texts either reinforced or refuted anti-Negro "instincts" in the "psychology" of the white working class, here ideological critique was abandoned in favor of an aesthetic gauged by "adverse criticism," on the one hand, and "flatter[y]," on the other.[52]

Owen's February 1925 article "The Black and Tan Cabaret: America's Most Democratic Institution" epitomized the *Messenger*'s revised message and mission. Beginning with a near-replication of the discussion of the cabaret as a solvent of racial tensions that had appeared in his article on the same subject in August 1922, Owen shifted his terrain. Where previously he had valorized the mixing of races and classes in the cabaret because it created the basis for the multiracial proletarian unity needed to solve the "race problem" and strengthen the "common people" in their struggle with capital, here the principal benefit was that it defused tensions of all kinds:

> The white man of affluence and prestige says, "If I can meet, mix and mingle with colored people then I can afford to be tolerant with poor whites." The poor white says (the lower ever aping the higher): "If rich white people of influence and prominence can associate with Negroes, I too, can certainly afford to." And the Negro who invariably hates the poor whites (his chief competitors) says (also aping his superior rich whites):

"If rich white people can accord to associate with these poor whites, then, I, a Negro, will condescend to do likewise."

The result is a trend toward the norm, toward common understanding through general contact. All learn with Shakespeare:

If you tickle us we laugh; if you prick us we bleed.

Does anyone know a more democratic institution in America than the "black and tan cabaret"?

Although Owen nodded toward the doctrine of labor competition, his repeated assertion that the different cabaret-goers learn to "afford to be tolerant" revealed that his intention was to paper over the class contradiction that made the "white man of affluence and prestige" not the co-reveler but the enemy of both the black worker and the white. Where Owen had previously alluded to *Hamlet* to drive home the point that the unifying of Negro and white workers was a "consummation devoutly to be wished," here the Shakespeare of *The Merchant of Venice* was invoked to reinforce the notion of art as the purveyor of a universal humanism. *Macbeth* was irrelevant; the Banquo's Ghost of the revolutionary upsurge of 1919 had been laid to rest in a celebration of culture—Negro and Euro-American alike—as the solvent of class antagonisms in the most "democratic institution in America."[53]

"Classed as an Oppressed Nation": Communism and Nationalism

It could be objected that the U.S. Socialists' descent down the slippery slope of U.S. nationalism was predictable, especially after the 1919 split, but what of the fledgling Communist movement? After all, American communism, emerging from the left wing of the SPA, was from the outset linked with the Third International, which sprang into being largely in response to the Second International's abandonment of proletarian internationalism during World War I. The Third International expressed unequivocal support for uprisings of colonized peoples of color against the imperialist world system—and the accompanying great nation chauvinism—that held them in thrall. In a series of writings undertaken between 1913 and 1916, Lenin argued that, for colonized peoples, nationalism was the necessary precondition to internationalism. While only worldwide revolution, proletarian internationalism, and the destruction of the bourgeois state would usher in the era of the dictatorship of the proletariat and, ultimately, classless society, peoples who had been subjected to colonial rule must, constituting themselves as nations, have the right either to secede from or to federate with any

more "advanced" industrial power. Drawing an analogy between secession and marital divorce, Lenin wryly noted that "the recognition of the
right of women to leave their husbands is not an *invitation* to all women
to do so." Lenin had no fondness for nationalism, pointing out that
"Marxism is incompatible with nationalism, even the most 'just,' 'pure,'
refined, and civilized nationalism." The reason he welcomed the growth
of such industrial metropoles as New York was that they would, he felt,
serve as solvents of the nationalist particularisms accompanying their
newly proletarianized migrant inhabitants; the Communist conception
of the melting-pot was quite different from that of the prewar assimi-
lationist liberals.[54]

But Lenin hoped that, as Walker Connor puts it, "rather than acting
as stimulant," the Communists' taking a position in favor of national self-
determination would "prove to be an anaesthetic." In Lenin's formulation, self-determination, while taking geographical form, was in its essence a historical process, stemming from the uneven development on
which imperialism thrived. Nationalism was a moment—a phase in a
process at once temporal and epistemological—in the larger movement
by which nations—and nationalism itself—would be negated altogether. As a moment in the totality of the global class struggle, national self-
determination was a crucial but not determining distinction within a
larger unity, a necessary but transitory phase in a larger historical process. Just as the proletariat in the "advanced" countries must become
class-conscious to abolish itself as a class, Lenin theorized, oppressed
peoples in the colonized parts of the globe must become nation-conscious
to abolish nationalism. Nationalism and internationalism were thus to
be understood dialectically, not as the antinomic poles of a binary opposition but as mutually determining aspects of a contradiction marked,
like all contradictions, by both unity and conflict. Since conflict is the
principal aspect, in the long run, of any contradiction—as Lenin, an avid
Hegelian, well knew—negation of one pole by another (in this case, of
nationalism by internationalism) would win out over oscillation between
the two within a framing stasis.[55]

It would be difficult to overstate the appeal that the Leninist doctrine
of self-determination had for African American leftists and progressives
in the wake of World War I, particularly since Lenin drew attention to
parallels between Russian peasants and U.S. sharecroppers and declared
that Negroes should be "classed as an oppressed nation." Although the
view of African Americans as an oppressed "nation within a nation"
would be codified only at the 1928 World Congress of the Comintern—
and the Communists would until then at least officially adhere to the

position of capital as color-blind that they inherited from the SPA—the understanding that oppressed peoples of color should have the right of secession engendered great enthusiasm among black American radicals. The *Crusader* in early 1922 ran an ad for the friends of Soviet Russia stressing the role of the USSR in aiding the "liberation struggles" of the "darker peoples." During the year that the Afro-Caribbean Otto Huiswood and the Japanese Sen Katayama—both to be formulators of the 1928 position—spent studying in New York City at the Rand School (1919–20), Harlem leftists frequently discussed the question of Negro self-determination. At the Fourth World Congress of the Communist International in 1922, U.S. blacks were described as "nationally oppressed." In contrast to the Wilsonian cant about self-determination, which meant simply that colonies would be redescribed as "protectorates" under Allied rule in a redivided globe, the Soviets' unequivocal support for colonial self-determination spoke not only to the Pan-Africanist aspirations emerging reinvigorated and radicalized from the war but also to the anger of an African American population that had sent its sons and husbands to fight to make the world safe for democracy, only to see them return to the race riots and lynchings of the Red Summer of 1919. Moreover, the summons to the oppressed peoples of colonized lands to shape their own destinies—coupled with the fact that the Russian Revolution itself had occurred in a largely peasant country, confounding the evolutionism of the Second International—rescued rural people of color from the fate of being "non-historical peoples." The peasants—including the soulful black folk of the rural South—were, at least potentially, as much agents of history as anyone else was.[56]

Despite its evident superiority to the Second International's evolutionism, economism, and racism, the self-determination thesis contained several ambiguities, both theoretical and practical. For one thing, the Marxist legacy was hardly consistent in its designation of what was meant by "nation." In *The Question of Nationalities and Social Democracy* (1907), the Austrian Socialist Otto Bauer had defined a nation as "a set of human beings linked by a common fate and common character"—a formulation that Lenin himself criticized as "psychological" but would nonetheless shape the official Bolshevik position on national self-determination as encoded by Joseph Stalin in 1913, which Lenin himself approved. The "common fate and common character" criterion was also unclear regarding the question of terrain, especially in relation to diasporic peoples: even if the people constituting a given nation were not designated a priori as inhabitants of a given geographically defined space, did their diasporic character require a "homeland" to give concrete embodiment to what would otherwise remain a dispersed identity? The "common fate and common character" criterion of nationhood was also ambiguous regarding the question of class: at what analytical point did the "common fate" of all the members of a nation give way to their dif- ferential—and antagonistic—positioning in the social relations of produc- tion? Was the goal of encouraging a nationalism that would "break the links in the imperialist chain," thereby emancipating the colonies from European rule and hastening the collapse of capitalism in the industrial nations, at odds with the goal of sharpening the struggle against exploit- ative ruling classes, of whatever location and hue? The "common fate and common character" criterion was, finally, indeterminate regarding his- torical process. What constituted a temporary stage in the movement toward revolution? How long was "temporary"?[57]

Starting in *The National Question and Autonomy* (1908–9), Rosa Luxemburg pondered these issues and reached conclusions quite differ- ent from Bauer's. The concept of "rights," she argued, was non-Marxist: "A 'right of nations' which is valid for all countries and all times is noth- ing more than a metaphysical cliché of the type of 'rights of man' and 'rights of the citizen.' Dialectic materialism, which is the basis of scien- tific socialism, has broken once and for all with this type of 'eternal' for- mula. . . . The 'right' of a nation to freedom as well as the 'right' of the worker to economic independence are, under existing social conditions, only worth as much as the 'right' of each man to eat off gold plates." Moreover, she argued, the "formula of the 'right of nations' . . . ignores completely the fundamental theory of modern socialism—the theory of social classes." For her, the "concept of the 'nation' is one of those cate- gories of bourgeois ideology which Marxist theory submitted to a radi- cal revision." In a class society, Luxemburg pointed out, "'the nation' as a homogeneous sociopolitical entity does not exist. Rather there exist within each nation, classes with antagonistic interests and 'rights.'" There was, furthermore, no unified self that could engage in national self- determination, Luxemburg declared: "Who is [the] 'nation' and who has the authority and the 'right' to speak for [it] and express its will?" Given existing class relations, it would be always the exploiting class that would seize the right to represent the presumably unsutured body politic that was the nation. Revolutionaries, she therefore urged, should fight to re- alize "not the right of nations to self-determination but only the right of the working class, which is exploited and oppressed, to self-determina- tion." Pursuing this critique into the next decade, Luxemburg only deep- ened her conviction that national self-determination was at best an illu- sion and at worst a ruse, declaring in her 1916 "Junius Pamphlet"—

written in the midst of the Great War—that "[s]o long as capitalist states exist, i.e., so long as imperialistic world policies determine and regulate the inner and the outer life of a nation, there can be no 'national self-determination' either in war or in peace." Where Bauer saw the nation as a natural phenomenon, meeting deep psychological and cultural needs even for those peoples dispersed in time and space, Luxemburg viewed the nation as an ideological construct of the bourgeoisie, serving only to legitimate inequality in the name of unity.[58]

While Lenin is generally credited with having found a viable middle course between the opposed positions of Bauer and Luxemburg, a long backward glance over twentieth-century attempts to graft a leftist politics onto movements for national liberation suggests that Luxemburg's skepticism may well have been justified. In her debates with Lenin, Luxemburg may not have been right about "super-imperialism" or the inevitable collapse of global capitalism through its own internal contradictions; Lenin had a superior grasp of the dialectics of uneven development and the necessity for capitalism to lead to interimperialist war. But Lenin's famous pragmatism had its downside: it was logically inconsistent—and in the long run would turn out to be politically disastrous—to assert, on the one hand, that "Marxism is incompatible with nationalism" and, on the other, to call for national self-determination. Clearly a significant divide separates the nationalism of anticolonial liberation movements from the nationalism of great power chauvinism; the one cannot be collapsed into the other. Nonetheless, as it would be played out in real time and place over the rest of the century and around the globe—from Egypt to Indonesia to South Africa—the Communists' support for national liberation as a moment—both epistemological and temporal—in the movement toward proletarian internationalism resulted in an assertion of self-determination that would be, of necessity, either a region-based nationalism articulated as the need for control over terrain or a pan-nationalism built on essentialist notions of race, folk, or people. Moreover, it would involve the strategic—that is, stagist—support for hierarchical regimes that would simply replace one exploiting class by another, albeit of different language and hue.[59]

It is even questionable whether the original pragmatic move on the part of the Bolsheviks in January 1919—that is, calling for self-determination to beat Woodrow Wilson to the punch—was dictated by historical necessity. Although the *Call* proclaimed in 1919 that "true nationalism" was the "aspiration of millions," W. A. Domingo, for one, saw things quite differently, writing in July 1919 that "millions of oppressed peoples are flocking to the banner of international Socialism":

The 384,000,000 natives of India groaning under the exploitation of the handful of English manufacturers, merchants and officials who profit out of their labor are turning from Lloyd George and the capitalistic Liberal Party to Robert Smillie, the Socialist and the Independent Labor Party. The 4,000,000 Irish who suffer national strangulation at the hands of British industrialists and militarists have turned to the Socialists of England for relief besides becoming Socialists themselves. The Egyptians who are of Negro admixture being convinced that their only hope for freedom from British exploitation is in international Socialism are uniting forces with British Socialists and organized labor. In fact, every oppressed group of the world is today turning from Clemenceau, Lloyd George and Wilson to the citadel of Socialism, Moscow.

Eric Hobsbawm supports Domingo's contention, arguing that, in the era of the Great War, "what looked like mobilizing the masses . . . was social revolution rather than national self-determination." The national self-determination slogan gained ascendancy only when the Allies "play[ed] the Wilsonian card against the Bolshevik card." But while the Bolsheviks may have successfully "overtrumped" the Allies, as E. H. Carr suggests, the result was an upsurge in what Hobsbawm calls "territory-oriented movements for liberation" that displaced class struggles as struggles over the control of land. The notion that, in the aftermath of the war, all oppressed peoples were clamoring for national self-determination may be itself a retrospective historical construct, shaped to no small extent by the Left's attempt to co-opt the rhetoric of the imperialist bourgeoisie.[60]

I offer this speculative and critical commentary on the postwar Left's embrace of self-determinationist nationalism with all the humility of hindsight; there was no way that the deleterious effects of this strategic move could have been foreseen in the crucible of 1919. I bring in this internationalist perspective, however, as both historical narrative and theoretical critique, because the contradictions informing the U.S. Left as a whole and the New Negro movement in particular cannot otherwise be fully understood. From its inception, U.S. communism reflected the conflicting tendencies in the Bolshevik legacy regarding nationalism. The Workers Party lambasted the post-split SPA for its increasingly class-collaborationist patriotism. Crystal Eastman scored the right wingers for "abandon[ing] their former economic view-point, ceas[ing] to criticize the political forms of democracy, and tak[ing] refuge in pre-Marxian documents like the Constitution and the Declaration of Independence." The SPA was, she concluded, "the party of old-fashioned Americanism." A principal reason for the disunity of the Communist Party (CP) and the Communist Labor Party (CLP) in the aftermath of the 1919 split was that the former consisted primarily of Russian and other immigrant workers, the latter of U.S.-born workers. The CP—which believed that "the problems of the American workers are identical with the problems of the workers of the world"—blasted the CLP for "not hav[ing] yet severed the umbilical cord binding it to the Socialist Party [and its] treacherous ideology of 'Americanism.'" Yet when the CP and CLP joined forces, the fledgling party's advocacy of self-determination was not incompatible with the notion that there could be a "left," or "good," nationalism; indeed, the move toward unification by the two groups was facilitated by the identification of internationalism with a left patriotism. It is significant that one of the pro-Communist revolutionary journals appearing briefly in the United States in 1919 called itself *The Melting-Pot*, with the subtitle *An Exponent of International Communism*. Even as its name appropriated the symbol of prewar American progressivist assimilationism for proletarian internationalist ends, the journal came trailing the clouds of its nationalist origins. It is also telling that, when a group of Communists were arrested in New York on the first evening of the Palmer raids, they were carried off to jail singing both the "Internationale" and "The Star-Spangled Banner." Despite the fears of the Lusk Committee, the internationalist revolutionary of the future—the "cosmopolitan," the "rootless proletarian"—did not consistently haunt the iconography and discourse of the Left. Although students of U.S. radicalism ordinarily posit that the coupling of leftist politics with U.S. nationalism was a creature of Popular Front–era "twentieth-century Americanism," a careful scrutiny of what was being said and done by the World War I–era Socialists and Communists alike reveals that it was they who actually laid the basis. for the contradistinction between regressive and progressive nationalisms that would, between the mid-1930s and mid-1940s, be recodified as the opposition of fascism to antifascism.[61]

In the struggle against racism in the United States, the role played by the discourse of nationalism in 1919 is particularly rife with irony. Political self-determination was embraced by Communist and Communist-affiliated forces largely in antiracist response to the evolutionist Socialist doctrine that portrayed the colonized masses living in precapitalist modes of production as "non-historical" and, therefore, inferior. The inhabitants of Ireland, Asia, and Africa, as well as such diasporic homeless populations as the Jews, asserted the Communists, had as much right to define their destinies, assert themselves as historical actors, and, if need be, lay claim to homelands as did all other populations. But, crucially, self-determination recapitulated in politics the stagism that it was repudiating in culture and biology: now it was necessary, or at least not to be contested, that a racially oppressed and economically superexploited people ignore its internal class stratification and constitute itself as a nation before confronting the imperialist class contradiction that had caused its oppression and superexploitation in the first place. As postwar class conflict in the United States encountered ruling-class repression, on the one hand, and internal demoralization, on the other, however, it was easy for the demand for colonial self-determination to be rearticulated as the demand that democratic inclusion be extended to peoples—specifically, African Americans—constituting themselves as a "nation within a nation." In the absence of a consistent leftist critique of nationalism in all its forms, the revolutionary doctrine of anticolonial self-determination could be transposed into the metonymic nationalist—and profoundly reformist—project of claiming that one group had as much right to stand for, and belong in, the nation as any other. As the postwar Thermidor set in, African American self-determination came to imply that Negroes should be identified not just with the primordial soil of Mother Earth—or of the continent that Du Bois musingly called "Mother Africa"—but also with the nation—that is, the Fatherland—into whose regions and states they had been diasporically dispersed. As the New Negro movement devolved into the Harlem Renaissance, with Harlem as its "race capital," its "Mecca," the struggle would increasingly become one over the Negro's right to represent, and be represented in, the Fatherland—not in the political sphere (a battle that would be deferred for some forty more years) but in the realm of culture. The emergence of culturalism was hardly a purely cultural phenomenon, for the cultural pluralists' struggle to define African Americans as an *American* folk—whose "natural characteristics and genius" could be construed as "peculiar to . . . a particular locality," in the *Call*'s formulation—was linked, logically, historically, and politically, to the Left's accession to nationalism as a necessary stage in social transformation. Alain Locke's celebration of Harlem as a "laboratory of great race-welding" for a people "fus[ed] [in] sentiment and experience," although articulated in the liberal discourse of cultural pluralist Americanism, cannot be separated from the contemporaneous leftist debate over self-determinationist nationalism.[62]

I conclude this extended response to the Sombartian query with an emphasis on nationalism because, as I next demonstrate, nationalism above all else provided the paradigm, both epistemological and political, enabling artists and writers identified with the Left to participate in the transition from class struggle to culture wars in the course of the 1920s. If the nation constituted an organic unit wherein contradictions could be resolved through an unflagging pursuit of genuine democracy, clearly the task at hand, particularly in an era of coercively diminished radical activity, was to challenge the nation's current claim to popular representation with a new and more genuinely representative model, one proposing that every inhabitant had an equal right to signify, and be signified by, the nation. In practice, it would prove simple enough to negotiate between the self-determinationist (and presumably radical) notion that African Americans constituted a nation within a nation and the inclusionist (and unabashedly liberal) notion that black folk were one more element contributing to the richness of the nation's soil. Hobsbawm correctly notes that the postwar "resurgence of nationalism . . . was plainly something that filled the void left by failure, impotence, and the apparent inability of other ideologies, political projects, and programmes to realize men's hopes." But he neglects to mention that it was largely because the "ideologies, political projects, and programmes" of the Left had failed to supersede nationalism that—reconfigured as both self-determination and inclusion—it so easily rushed in to fill the void. Contrary to Adorno's comparable view that aesthetics is what migrates to fill the vacancy, one must look from general theories to particular historical conjunctures, examining the epistemological and political overlap between a given politics and the specific aesthetic by which it is accompanied. Culturalism— as not just a practice of representation but an *ideology* of representation— is the product of the aftermath of 1919. When one contemplates the process whereby the postwar gun-brandishing New Negro became *The New Negro*, what at first appears to be a matter of transformation—the supersession of internationalism by nationalism, the supplanting of politics by aesthetics—turns out to be a matter of repetition or oscillation produced by the failure of negation. That this failure of negation would generate multiple contradictions, material and discursive, grounds in politics and history the project of the New Negroes who, in the aftermath of 1919, aspired to cultivate the cultural soil of the United States.[63]

3   The Rhetoric of
Racist Antiradicalism

Do we desire a mongrel population in America such as
that which gave birth to Sovietism in Russia?
—Clinton Stoddard Burr, *America's Race Heritage* (1922)

Thus far the derivation of the New Negro movement in the political radicalism of the wartime and immediate postwar years and various contradictions internal to the theory and practice of the Left that would contribute to the supersession of class struggle by culturalism have been analyzed. In future chapters of *Spectres of 1919*, the attempts by radicals and progressives to fashion counterdiscourses to the rhetoric of 100 percent Americanism are examined and linked to Alain Locke's culturalist manifesto in *The New Negro*. At this point, however, the nature and extent of the ruling-class ideological offensive in the wake of the class struggles of 1919 must be taken into account. Even if contradictions internal to the Left set the limits of its ability to contest the dominant discourse and made it vulnerable to the culturalist offensive, the overwhelming force of the assault, both material and discursive, that occurred during the postwar Thermidor must be not be underestimated. External constraints, after all, shape the conditions of possibility under which internal contradictions can work themselves out.

While intellectual historians and historians of science have long acknowledged the links between racism and antiradicalism, I hope to contribute to the discussion of this issue in two ways. First, I trace the connections between, on the one hand, existing discourses associating biology with political radicalism—discourses that, before the war, were directed primarily against Europeans of non-"Nordic" descent—and, on the other hand, the emerging concern among ruling elites about so-called disgruntled agitators among the nation's mulatto population. Although the post-1920 reclassification that obliterated the category of mulatto from the U.S. census was in some respects the logical consequence of several decades of Jim Crow, it cannot be isolated from the fears aroused among ruling elites by the revolutionary upsurge of 1919. Second, I analyze the central role played in reactionary rhetoric by a heavily racialized organic trope linking soil with nation, root with its past, fruit-bearing tree with its present, and seed with its future. This trope would be central in the rhetoric of cultural pluralism, which occupied a parasitic—or at least dependent—relation to the discourse of the nativists and eugenicists. Third, I consider the achievements and limitations of the opposition to racist antiradicalism offered by the emerging school of cultural anthropology associated with Franz Boas, whose work, it is widely acknowledged, would eventually drive the racists from the field and provide indispensable scientific and methodological grounding to the program of the Harlem Renaissance. Whereas critical discussions of the Boasian project routinely focus on the cultural anthropologists' inability fully to break with the dominant discourse regarding race, I stress the extent to which the Boasians were constrained by the limitations of contemporaneous socialist politics, with which they were, individually and as a group, openly sympathetic.

"Democracy Has No More Virtue Than Mumbo-Jumbo or a West African Ju-Ju": Nativism and Eugenics in the Era of 1919

The discourse of racist antiradicalism that reached flood level in the wake of 1919 had its origins in a long history of pseudoscience invoking "nature" in defense of social inequality. As early as the 1830s, biological doctrines bearing scientific-sounding names—for example, ethnology and craniology—had been trotted out to rationalize slavery. In the wake of the European revolutions of 1848, the French count Arthur de Gobineau, whose theories vaulted the ocean with little difficulty, decried the excesses of democracy, celebrated the achievements of the "Teutonic race"—which alone among the races, he opined, was motivated by "honor"—and proposed a categorization of human types, with Africans at the very bottom. Although "the intellect [of the negroid variety of humanity] will always move within a very narrow circle," he cautioned, "he often has an intensity of desire, and so of will, which may be called terrible." Francis Galton, Charles Darwin's cousin, launched the eugenics movement, calling for "race improvement" on both the individual and group level. He targeted as inferior to Britons not only Negroes—whose "average intellectual standard . . . is some two grades below our own"—but also the French, among whose "abler races . . . the guillotine [had] made sad havoc." Noteworthy in the rhetoric of these early proponents of race theory was a tendency to equate race with nationality, on the one hand, but to insist on biologically based class distinctions, on the other. For Gobineau, who granted that a certain amount of racial admixture was necessary for the development of a hardy nation, a tragic decline toward inferior hybridization was inevitable, leaving racially pure elites at the mercy of the insurgent mongrel masses. For Galton, the French, it appears, comprised several "races," evidently closely linked with classes. The ideologically saturated categories that would rationalize Jim Crow by codifying whiteness and blackness as essences, needing no further explicit identification with either nation or class, were still in the making. But both theorists of racial hierarchy would exercise influence well into the next century, Gobineau through the translation and U.S. publication of his magnum opus in 1915 (the same year as the appearance of *Birth of a Nation* and the revival of the Ku Klux Klan) and Galton (who had been knighted in 1909) through the founding of the National Eugenics Society.[1]

Updating the antebellum pseudosciences, late-nineteenth-century racial theorizing increasingly drew on Darwinism to assert the deterioration of the Negro population after Emancipation. Frederick L. Hoffman wrote in 1896 that African Americans were headed toward extinction because of their inherited "race traits and tendencies." Even mulattoes were on the way out, since "the mixture of the African with the white race has been shown to have seriously affected the longevity of the former and left as a heritage to future generations the poison of scrofula, tuberculosis, and most of all, syphilis." The ethnologist William Ripley preferred to work with craniological measurements, proposing that the brains of African Americans were demonstrably smaller than those of other "races"; the so-called cephalic index would be a crucial term in the scientific racism based on Ripley's work. An opponent of environmentalist explanations of race-coded differentials, Ripley contended that higher Negro "predisposition to consumption" in northern cities should be traced not to such social factors as poverty and segregation but to the problems posed by skin thickness and nose shape. Ripley's main project, however, was not to demonstrate Negro inferiority, which he took as given, but to argue that "there was no single European or white race of men." At least three distinct "racial" strains, he theorized, had migrated from Europe to the United States—hierarchically ordered as the Nordic, the Alpine, and the Mediterranean; admixture among any such groups might result in biological regression, that is, reversion to the more primitive type. The prominent University of Wisconsin sociologist Edward Alsworth Ross, using Ripley's categories to urge early restrictions on immigration, remarked on the predominance of what he called the "Caliban type'" among newly arrived immigrants: "hirsute, low-browed, big-faced persons of obviously low mentality." "Unmistakable" signs of "inferiority of type," proclaimed Ross, are "sugar-loaf heads, moon-faces, slit mouths, lantern-jaws, and goose-bill noses." Driving down the wages, the standard of living, and hence the birthrate of the rest of the population, the new immigrants, he warned, threatened "race suicide." Thomas Bailey Aldrich, an early advocate of immigration restriction, captured an antipathy both racial and political in his 1895 *Atlantic* poem "Unguarded Gates," in which he exclaimed:

> Wide open and unguarded stand our gates,
> And through them presses a wild motley throng—
> Men from the Volga and the Tartar steppes,
> Featureless figures of the Hoana-Ho,
> Malayan, Scythian, Teuton, Kelt, and Slav,
> Flying the Old World's poverty and scorn;
> These bringing with them unknown gods and rites,
> Those, tiger passions, here to stretch their claws.

For Aldrich, however, the association of race with radicalism was not absolute, for even Teutons might be among those "stretch[ing] their claws" in his lurid extrapolation from the theory of natural selection.[2]

The combination of pseudoscientific jargon with flights of metaphorical fancy characterizing much prewar racist discourse was epitomized in Madison Grant's 1916 *Passing of the Great Race*. Long on opinion if short on evidence, Grant unabashedly converted the hypothesis of biological regression into a certainty. "The cross between a white man and an Indian is an Indian," he declared. "The cross between a white man and a Negro is a Negro . . . and between any of the three European races and a Jew is a Jew." Moreover, like Gobineau and Galton, Grant premised racism on elitism, celebrating the nation's founding by a superior "Teutonic" genetic strain and scolding that "those engaged in social uplift and in revolutionary movements are . . . usually very intolerant of the limitations imposed by heredity." In a feudalistic metaphor uncannily at odds with the modern weaponry being deployed in the Great War, Grant asserted a holistic view of the body politic. "In an aristocratic as distinguished from a plutocratic or democratic organization," he declared, "the intellectual and talented classes form the point of the lance while the main shaft represents the body of the population and adds by its bulk and weight to the penetrative impact of the tip." Conflating nationalism, militarism, and male sexual prowess, Grant "completed the transformation of race into an explicit and eloquent expression of elitist attitudes," as the eugenics historian Mark Haller points out: "[R]ace was identified with class and class with biological fitness." Grant's distinction between "aristocratic" and "plutocratic or democratic" forms of society and his clear preference for the former indicated his kinship with the unabashed elitism of Gobineau. Whiteness made its appearance here in contradistinction to blackness, but split into its component parts ("the three European races") in contradistinction to Jewishness. Racism was beginning to assume its modern form.[3]

Well established in a variety of inherited American discourses of racial hierarchy, biological determinist doctrine burst forth in its full glory with the arrival of the Bolshevik Revolution and the events of 1919. *The Passing of the Great Race* was not a best-seller when it first appeared; as the nativism scholar John Higham points out, it was published when the United States was at war with Germany, and Grant's enthusiasm for things Germanic was out of tune with the temper of the times. Grant's polemic was rediscovered and reissued in 1921 and 1923, receiving favorable notice in the mainstream press and widely cited as an authoritative source. But Grant's aura of patrician superiority was comparatively mild in the lurid atmosphere of the postwar "Red scare." In *The Rising Tide of Color against White World-Supremacy*—which, accompanied by a laudatory preface by Grant, rapidly went through several editions in the first few years after its publication in 1920—Lothrop Stoddard delineated the threat posed to white civilization by the colored races of the world. The "white flood" of European colonialism was experiencing "the beginning of the ebb"; unless it repaired both its "outer dikes" and "inner dikes," European civilization would be overwhelmed by "the rising tide of color." Alluding to the ascending status of Japan, on the one hand, and the restiveness of Europe's African colonies, on the other, Stoddard, no longer principally concerned with distinguishing among different European strains, was evidently forming his notion of embattled whiteness in a global context. "The Nordic race," he cautioned, "must gather itself together in time, shake off the shackles of an inveterate altruism, discard the various phantoms of internationalism, and reassert the pride of race and the right of merit to rule."[4]

Stoddard struck the specifically anticommunist note that would be repeatedly sounded in postwar racist doctrine, warning that "the menace of Bolshevism is simply incalculable" and dubbing Bolshevism "a war of the hand against the brain." The threat posed by Bolshevism is "antiracial as well as anti-social," Stoddard warned. "Lenine, surrounded by his Chinese executioners, sits behind the Kremlin wall, a modern Jenghiz Khan plotting the plunder of a world." The Bolshevik of European origin, in particular, was "the arch-enemy of civilization and the race," the "renegade, the traitor within the gates, who would betray the citadel, degrade the very fibre of our being, and ultimately hurl a rebarbarized, racially impoverished world into the most debased and hopeless of mongrelizations." Both Grant's and Stoddard's warfare metaphors posited a sexualized nostalgia for feudalism. But where Grant's chosen trope—the tipped lance—depicted a militarized phallus, with elites directing the force of the masses, Stoddard's chosen trope—the besieged citadel—posited a feminized space in danger of betrayal, rape, and impregnation by those entrusted to guard it. The threat posed by Lenin—advocate of colonial self-determination as much as of proletarian internationalism—was as racial as it was political. Bolshevism entailed the threat of mongrelization; those persons of European heritage who joined the Reds were traitors to both race *and* nation. It is impossible not to hear in Stoddard's raced and gendered antiradicalism a fear of insurgent New Negroes, on the one hand, and, on the other, Bolshevism, rising anticolonialism, and Pan-Africanism. The "phantoms of internationalism" were the key opponents of the "Nordic race" in a rape fantasy—with American whiteness as victim—gone global in the aftermath of 1919.[5]

In his 1922 *Revolt against Civilization*, Stoddard enlarged on his antiradical theme, proposing that Bolshevism was a "primitive . . . incarnation of the atavistic past." He opined, "Hatred of civilization is mainly a matter of heredity. . . . Bolsheviks are mostly born and not made." Unlike the "proletarian biology" that asserted the equal intelligence of all human beings, eugenics was "the hope of a progressive future." Until enforced sterilization could screen out the undesirable elements—largely recent immigrants who "breed like mice"—political repression was necessary. "As a *fetich*," Stoddard pronounced, "democracy has no more virtue than Mumbo-Jumbo or a West African ju-ju"; even the liberal political institutions presumably safeguarding civil liberties were racially stigmatized. Radical European immigrants were thus tarred with the brush of African primitivism and vice versa; no longer was it sufficient to "other" them as non-Nordics. Synthesizing inherited racist categories with an antiradicalism raised to fever pitch, Stoddard—who had written his 1914 doctoral thesis on the Santo Domingo slave revolt—demonstrat-

ed that the mission to "get people thinking racially" was inseparable from
that of defusing class struggle and curtailing democracy. The doctrine set
forth in *The Revolt against Civilization* might have particular appeal to
ruling-class males, as F. Scott Fitzgerald would show in his 1925 portrait
in *The Great Gatsby* of Tom Buchanan, ranting over the warning by "this
man Goddard" in "'The Rise of the Colored Empires'" that "the white
race will be . . . utterly submerged. It's all scientific stuff; its been proved."
Stoddard had clearly been bent on reaching a broader audience, however, publishing in the *Saturday Evening Post* in 1920 a twelve-part series
of articles on the persistence of racial types. That his message was taken
up by political theorists of the day is evidenced by Charles Conant Josey's extensive citation of Stoddard in *Race and National Solidarity*
(1923), in which Josey argued that "class hatred . . . becomes greatly intensified when loyalty to race and nation becomes impaired." "The "bril-
liancy" of European culture rested on the "exploitation" of the rest of the
world, Josey forthrightly declared. The European nations and the United
States must "avoid the broad humanitarianism which, in placing all men
on the same footing, removes the possibility of using pride in race and
culture as levers in creating the social solidarity that is necessary if we
are to maintain our position of dominance."[6]

Many of the postwar proponents of racist antiradicalism quickly
learned the value of invoking genetics to supply more "scientific" grounds
for asserting racial hierarchy. As the eugenicist Charles Davenport remarked in his address to the 1921 International Congress of Eugenics,
"People do not have heated discussions on the multiplication table; they
will not dispute quantitative findings in any science." Eugenics, which
bolstered its claims about genetically based racial hierarchy with charts
and bell curves, largely supplanted the craniological discourse of skull
shape and the Darwinian discourse of warfare that had enlivened the
metaphorical language of Ripley and Grant, respectively. Davenport wrote
in 1914 to his fellow eugenicist Charles Gould that "[t]he idea of a 'melting-pot' belongs to the pre-Mendelian age. Now we recognize that characters are inherited as units and do not readily 'break up.'" Davenport
sent extensive case histories through the grid of Mendelian genetics to
prove the existence of genes for such phenomena as "nomadism": apparently the huge influx of immigrant labor into the country, as well as the
massive demographic shifts taking place within its borders, could best
be accounted for as manifestations of the absence, among workers hard-
wired for migrancy, of a "simple sex-linked gene that 'determines' domes-
ticity." Rejecting such morally loaded terms as *vagabondage, vagrancy,*
and *wanderlust,* he chose *nomadism* to describe the "tastes and impulses

of the restless man" precisely because of its anthropological overtones. While it is generally supposed "Bushmen" and other wandering peoples "are nomadic because they hunt," wrote Davenport, it is "more probable that their nomadic instincts force them to hunting rather than agriculture for a livelihood." Nomads from all walks of life, he concluded, are "members of the *nomadic race.*"[7]

Paul Popenoe and Roswell Hill Johnson, in their *Applied Eugenics* (1918), cited the results of Louis Terman's 1916 military I.Q. testing as proof of genetic differentials in intelligence among races and classes. Specifically targeting the "socialist belief in substantial equality of natural ability, where opportunity is equal," they concluded that the Negro-white "color line" was a natural response to genetically based inequality. Stoddard also extensively cited Terman and Popenoe and Johnson in his 1922 defense of the "iron law of inequality." Recent developments in "psychology" as well as "biological discoveries," he declared, bore out his argument that "the basic attitude of the Under-Man is an instinctual and natural *revolt against civilization.*" William McDougall—at the time "the nation's best-known psychologist," according to Carl Degler—filled his 1921 *Is America Safe for Democracy?* with bell-curve graphs and grids of I.Q. data, rejecting the view of the liberals—whom he called "race-slumpers"—that "all men are born with the same mental endowments." "*[T]he great condition of the decline of any civilization*" he warned, "*is the inadequacy of the qualities of the people who are the bearers of it.*" The Princeton psychologist Carl Brigham, in *A Study of American Intelligence* (1923), argued that Terman's data not only gave irrefutable proof of the "marked intellectual inferiority of the negro" but also cast doubt on the "popular belief that the Jew is highly intelligent." In the wake of 1919, the refutation of egalitarian doctrine invoked eugenic notions of racial health as well as nativist notions of alienness.[8]

Stoddard was hardly alone in his assertion that inherent racial inequality refuted the viability of not just socialism but even capitalist democracy. McDougall's very title—*Is the World Safe for Democracy?*—answers the question it asks: the recent Allied victory was incomplete so long as the threat of mob rule by an inferior race remained. Alleyne Ireland, in *Democracy and the Human Equation* (1921), cited at length the findings of Popenoe and Johnson to conclude that "[if] good government . . . depends ultimately upon good human qualities" rather than upon "good political machinery," then "all discussions of government must be founded in biology." While they purported simply to be reporting discoveries based on "quantitative findings," the racist ideologists of the postwar Thermidor were well aware of the political valence of their writings. In correspondence with Grant about the formation of the eugenicist Galton Society, Davenport wrote that the association was to be "very limited in members and also confined to native Americans, who are anthropologically, socially, and politically sound, no Bolsheviki need apply." Discussing recruitment to the Eugenics Society in 1924, Davenport drew attention to the necessity of verifying the potential members' politics, remarking that it must not become like the Rand School, that wartime "hotbed of radicalism." Moreover, a number of the eugenicists and nativists sought actively to link their doctrines with government policy; Grant and Stoddard both played important roles in urging the passage of the immigration restriction bills of 1921 and 1924. Although essentialist notions of both race and nation clearly predate the crisis of 1919, the conjunction of nativism and eugenics in the essentialized discourse of 100 percent Americanism was a pure product of racist antiradicalism, produced in the moment referred to on the masthead of the *Modernist* as the "era of War and Revolution, of struggle and revision, of context and change."[9]

"Alien Filth," "International Jews," and "Militant Mulattoes": Enemies of the Nation

The principal targets of racist antiradicalism were three. One was the European immigrant—especially of southern or eastern European origin—suspected of carrying the incubus of political radicalism. Occasionally the polemicists would restrict themselves—if not always with complete metaphorical coherence—to matters of doctrine. The sociologist Peter Roberts, who had served as leader of the YMCA's wartime Americanization campaign, believed that "race consciousness is in the blood" and opined that the nation was beset by "radicals whose souls are lashed by breezes of doctrines, emanating from continental Europe, writhing in the hands of doctrinaires who treat a starving and bankrupt patient." Attorney General A. Mitchell Palmer, who held that "[f]ully 90 percent of Communist and anarchist agitation is traceable to aliens," referred to the "alien filth" captured in the January 1920 raids in terms borrowed freely from the nativist discourse melding politics with physiognomy. Echoing Ripley, the Red-hunter Palmer observed that the radical immigrants possessed "sly and crafty eyes . . . lopsided faces, sloping brows and misshapen features," sheltering "cupidity, cruelty, insanity and crime." Where Ripley had stressed the migrants' dull animality, however, Palmer saw moral depravity and incendiary threat. The raids on radicals were necessary, he asserted, because "the blaze of revolution" had been "eating its

way into the homes of the American workingman, [and] its sharp tongues
of heat were licking the altars of churches, leaping into the belfry of the
school bell, crawling into the sacred corners of American homes, seeking
to replace marriage vows with libertine laws, burning up the foundations
of society." As in Stoddard's dystopian fantasy, the nation's patriarchal
stability was being threatened by the fiery—and, again, sexualized—threat
of alien European radicalism.[10]

Among the various immigrant populations designated as both biologically unassimilable and politically dangerous in the postwar Red scare,
Jews were singled out most frequently. Like the doctrine of Negro inferiority, anti-Semitism was nothing new to the United States; the lynching
of Leo Frank in Atlanta during the early months of the war in Europe was
but one reminder of anti-Semitism's continuing vitality. In the wake of
the Bolshevik Revolution, however, anti-Semitism took on new meaning
and direction. *The Jewish Peril: The Protocols of the Learned Elders of
Zion*—a spurious set of documents claiming to expose a Jewish conspiracy to take over the world, composed early in the century and disseminat-
ed after the Bolshevik Revolution by czarist sympathizers hoping to re-
instate the old order—was first published in the United States in 1920. In
the American edition of *The Cause of World Unrest* (1920)—issued by the
conservative publisher G. P. Putnam with "chilling anonymity," a *Nation*
editorial commented—*The Protocols* was extensively cited in support of
the charge that worldwide dissent was being stirred up by a "secret revolutionary movement . . . mainly engineered by Jews." In postwar congressional discussions of the need for close surveillance of radicals, Representative John Raker, a Democrat from California, asserted that Jews
constituted 75 percent of the Bolsheviks in the USSR. The KKK accused
Jews of masterminding the League of Nations and contended that "having no national government of their own they seek to attain them all."
The Grand Dragon of Georgia stipulated "American Nationalism" as the
only antidote to the "Cosmopolitanism advocated by International Jew-
ry." Stoddard argued in 1922 that the incendiary danger posed by Marxism was inseparable from its author's Jewish origins. The labor historian
J. R. Commons, in the 1920 edition of his *Races and Immigrants in
America*, noted that one of the fruits of past anti-Semitism was that now
"the oppressed Jews are the dictators of the proletariat." Palmer, preoccupied as ever with the trope of fire, wrote in a memo of May 1919 that
the current "communistic outbreaks" and "plague of social arson" were
"the penalty that the Gentile is paying for his injustice of the past"; as
with Commons, however, his principal regret about the nation's past practice of anti-Semitism was not ethics but consequences.[11]

In a series of highly influential 1921 *Saturday Evening Post* articles calling for immigration restriction, Kenneth L. Roberts—who had served as a captain in the Intelligence Section of the Siberian Expeditionary Force of the U.S. Army that invaded the Soviet Union in 1919—anticipated Nazi rhetoric in his proclamation that "the Jews of Poland are human parasites, living on one another and on their neighbors of other races by means which too often are underhanded." Ascribing the cramped quarters inhabited by impoverished Jewish immigrants to their biological proclivities, he complained that Polish Jews "continue to exist in the same way after coming to America and . . . are therefore highly undesirable as immigrants." All immigration from Europe should not be restricted, however; the formerly aristocratic "waifs of an Empire" fleeing from the Bolshevik terror should be welcomed, Roberts urged, since their values were compatible with those embraced by the "Nordic" ancestors of America's true founders. Impoverished Jewish immigrants were homeless parasites opportunistically nesting in the body politic; dispossessed Russian owners of the means of production, however, were orphans needing shelter in a racially compatible homeland. Whether the nation would be a host to aliens or a nurturing mother depended on its immigration policy. Roberts's trope worked on two levels, not only associating Jews metaphorically with parasites but also labeling them a different species, thereby biologizing the notion of the nation itself. The rhetoric of 100 percent Americanism—in which anti-Semitism figured centrally—was simultaneously racial and national, racist and nationalist.[12]

The third group singled out for racist invective in the wake of 1919 was the mulatto. The discourse of specifically anti-Negro racism underwent a notable sea change in response to the revolutionary upsurge. Familiar doctrines of Negro inferiority were repeated and reframed, since the continuing subordinate position of African Americans in the most exploited sectors of the U.S. work force—and the abiding presence of blacks in the rural South—necessitated perpetuation of the view that they were by nature suited only for hewing wood and drawing water. Emery S. Bogardus, editor of the *Journal of Applied Sociology,* held in his *Essentials of Americanism* (1919) that the easy conditions of life in tropical Africa had allowed inferior racial stock to survive. In the Darwinian struggle produced by the slave trade and then slavery, he asserted, the best had rebelled, leaving "the unambitious and mediocre" as survivors. The sociologist Samuel J. Holmes flatly remarked in 1921 that "the doctrine of the mental equality of black and white does not commend itself to most of those who have had much experience with the colored race."[13]

Some of the ideologists bent on refuting "the doctrine of the mental equality of black and white" were, however, less blithely arrogant; the wartime and postwar militancy of the nation's black population, accompanied by the massive demographic changes produced by the Great Migration, called for some revision of plantation stereotypes. If the president of the United States was confessing to his private physician in 1919 his nightmarish fear that "[t]he American negro returning from abroad would be our greatest medium in conveying bolshevism to America," evidently the spectre of the New Negro was haunting the nation's ruling elite. Of particular concern was the prevalence of light-skinned mulattoes among the New Negro activists, who included not just the familiar figure of W. E. B. Du Bois but also Walter White, A. Philip Randolph, Cyril Briggs, and Richard B. Moore. Some commentators accounted for the growing radicalism and unrest by updating inherited discourses about mulatto instability. Seth K. Humphrey, in his 1917 *Mankind: Racial Values and the Racial Prospect*, rejected the notion of melting-pot assimilationism not so much because people of different races would conflict with one another but because assimilation meant amalgamation; racial mixture *within* individuals, he opined, violated the laws of nature. "[The mulatto's protest] is not the protest of a Negro—no Negro protests his race," asserted Humphrey. "It is the cry of a forceful Aryan in soul-entanglement with an utterly strange being." Progressive-era assimilationism had been a cover for "mongrelization": "[O]ur 'Melting-Pot' would not give us in a thousand years what enthusiasts expect of it—a fusing of all our various racial elements into a new type which shall be the true American." Humphreys's fears would be allayed after 1920, when the Bureau of the Census would, Joel Williamson remarks, "add its strength to the effort to create a simply biracial America" by eliminating the category of "mulatto" from the U.S. census.[14]

The more sophisticated theorists of race and ethnicity associated with the emerging Chicago school of sociology rejected overtly biologistic racial doctrines but embraced psychologically based notions of race that were scarcely less essentialist. Robert Park opined that where the Anglo-Saxon is "a pioneer and frontiersman," the Negro "is primarily an artist, loving life for its own sake"—whence his famous conclusion that the Negro is "the lady of the races." The conjunction of inherited fears of biological admixture with presumably forward-looking notions of race and nation is epitomized in the work of Park's student Edward Byron Reuter, who established his credentials as an expert on the mulatto question in his 1918 *Mulatto in the United States: Including a Study of the Role of Mixed-Blood Races throughout the World*. Although he continually referred to Negroes as a "backward" or "lower" race, he insisted

that "[f]or the purpose in hand we are not concerned with race as a physical concept but with race as a social unity which arises by and through
social development." This concession to social constructionism did little to detract from the viciousness of his analysis, however. By nature
"unstable . . . dissatisfied and unhappy" because of "the stigma which
attaches to a tainted ancestry," mulattoes, Reuter wrote, were the "disgruntled agitators" behind the current radical movements, which had
little base of support among "the real Negroes." Indeed, "[t]he exclusion
policy of the whites is in line with the natural tendency of the blacks,"
of whom "an overwhelming majority . . . accept racial separation as a
simple and natural matter of fact." While the "bitter" demands of the
mulatto minority amounted to "a plea for special privilege," their strategy was currently "defeat[ing] its own object," for, opined Reuter, "the
effect is to identify the complaining individuals more closely with the
masses of the race" and to "solidify the race and, in the thinking of the
white man, to class the agitators with it."[15]

The "complaining individuals" were not able to see the silver lining
in the segregationist cloud, Reuter lamented. Increased segregation—the
"stricter and . . . more conscious and purposeful drawing of the color
line . . . where it had previously not been drawn"—would prove "an advantage both to the black and to the yellow man." "[T]he black Negroes
are the gainers by having their natural leaders thrust, even though it be
against their will, back upon the race," wrote Reuter, while "[t]he mulattoes are gainers in that they are thus forced to see and to embrace the
great opportunity which the presence of the people of their own race af-
fords them for a useful and a valuable life of real leadership." The "present
tendency . . . toward an increased application intensively and extensively of this segregation policy"—presumably Reuter had in mind such practices as the Wilson administration's recent institution of racial segregation in federal office buildings, strongly protested by the NAACP and
welcomed, among African Americans, only by Tuskegee's Robert Russa
Moton—was thus beneficial to the "real Negroes" and therapeutic for the
distressed minority of "mixed blood." "Agitation gives place to work; self-
reliance replaces self-pity," concluded Reuter. The mulatto "no longer
lives 'behind the veil'; he is dealing with objective reality." The harden-
ing of the color line, accompanied by hard work, would remove the veil;
Reuter played Washington against Du Bois, and Du Bois against Du Bois,
in a distinctly modern rationale for a distinctly modern practice. Segregation was the wave of the future.[16]

Reuter further stressed the freshness of his theoretical model by comparing the current rise in "nationalistic spirit" among Negroes with the

"Irish National movement," applauding "the effort being made by the Negroes themselves to create a Negro history," and remarking that "[t]he gift which so many Negroes have for effective public speaking is another thing of which the race is exceedingly proud." (He could not resist adding, "The point here is that regardless of the slender basis of fact upon which many of these things rest, they have an immense effect upon the thinking of the race," since "[i]t is the opinion that a race has of itself that counts in the growth of a nationalistic spirit.") Self-determination was thus welcomed as the flip side of segregation: "The further the Negroes develop a sense of nationality, the further do they voluntarily separate themselves from the white world." Reacting to the wartime fulminations of the "disgruntled agitators," Reuter warned that "[s]ome of the opponents of the segregation policy even predict race wars and revolutions." No doubt a year later, during the Red Summer, he would have less confidence in his prediction that "the placid disposition and the native common sense" of African Americans, alien to "the anarchistic teachings of . . . malcontents," would prevent "rioting and the growth of a spirit of racial ill-will." But Reuter evidently envisioned the increasing segregation in all aspects of U.S. life as a necessary and progressive response to the "objective reality" dispassionately set forth in modern psychology, sociology, and political science. That his rationale deployed some of the same terms Locke would use to celebrate the emergence of Harlem as culture capital based on "race-welding" and the ascendance of the New Negro as culture hero should perhaps give us pause.[17]

"A Fundamental, Eternal, Inescapable Difference": The Cultural Thermidor

The discourse of racist antiradicalism went into the cultural groundwater, to reemerge as a dominant ideological paradigm shaping many aspects of intellectual and political life. Wars over the literary canon did not originate in the 1980s; contention about what properly constituted "American" culture was heated in the aftermath of 1919. Contemporary scholars accustomed to associating experimental modernism with political quiescence may be interested in knowing that the postwar opponents of modernism often linked formal rupture in the arts with social revolution. Stoddard asserted that such experimental movements as futurism, cubism, and vorticism, as well as the interest in West African art, were part of the atavistic "revolt against civilization." While he lambasted experimental modernism as a "cult of the primitive," he viewed primitivism as equivalent to "proletarian culture," just as he considered the biological doctrine asserting racial equality to be "proletarian biology"; for Stoddard, antiracism and revolutionism were one and the same, in both politics and aesthetics. The conservative humanist Stuart Sherman, in a 1923 polemic tellingly entitled *Americans*, argued that the great "tradition of revolt" in American letters had nothing in common with "the militant hostility of alien-minded critics." The radicals' call for "an international society," Sherman concluded, had its corollary in "treasonable and anarchical innovation" in the realm of the arts. The popular novelist Gertrude Atherton, decrying the nation's loss of "class pride" in the current epidemic of "democratic flu," merged older and newer forms of racist nationalism in her plea that contemporaneous writers of "Nordic" stock read their Ripley and their Grant. "There is no forgetting of the cephalic index," she cautioned. Although the nation is "thus far too unenlightened to sterilize . . . and exterminate [the Alpines and the Mediterraneans]," she continued, writers should not "miss the opportunity" to follow the example of Booth Tarkington and represent exclusively Nordic types in their novels. The nation's failure to commit genocide could at least partially be atoned, it would seem, by racially correct mimesis. First targeting democracy in her diatribe, Atherton ended by giving primacy to race: "Let [the younger school of writers] realize before they begin to write to what *race* their characters belong. *Class* is of vastly less importance." Defining the parameters of whiteness was the primary responsibility of American writers, and the "cephalic index" was to be their unerring guide. Although the boyish charm of Tarkington's Penrod is inseparable from his aura of class privilege, Atherton's emphasis is significant, displaying the extent to which her antipathy toward democracy was, like Stoddard's, first and foremost racialized.[18]

Nativist impulses were voiced, albeit less bluntly, by literary commentators in the mainstream as well. The Columbia University English professor John Erskine, attributing the tendency of U.S. writers to "live in a world of ideas" because they "are without a sense of the soil," rejected the melting pot as an alternative cultural ideal. "[N]ot the most optimistic of us can expect any lasting good future for our own country," he lamented, without access to "the peasant point of view, . . . that elemental wisdom of the soil." The *Nation* literary editor and prominent liberal Carl Van Doren, while conceding that "our literature for generations, perhaps centuries, will have to be symbolized by the melting pot," joined Erskine in regretting the absence of indigenous American traditions. "Indian and negro materials," he declared, "are in our poetry still hardly better than aspects of the exotic. No one who matters actually thinks that a national literature can be founded on such alien bases."

Although Van Doren lectured on American literature in Harlem, he apparently viewed both the nation's aboriginal inhabitants and the descendants of its slaves as foreign to its culture; it is small wonder that Eric Walrond, the associate editor of *Negro World*, would pen a devastating satire on Van Doren in 1922.[19]

By contrast, the novelist Mary Austin lauded the contribution of Indian culture and Western regional writers reflecting this culture; it was Jewish writers who aroused her anxiety and ire. Waldo Frank's *Our America*—which in her view trumpeted the virtues of New York–based writers and ignored finer literary artists from points farther west— revealed the "racial bias" of its author. "Can the Jew," she asked, "with his profound complex of election, his need of sensuous satisfaction qualifying his every expression of personal life, and his short pendulum-swing between mystical orthodoxy and a sterile ethical culture—can he become the commentator, the arbiter, of American art and American thinking?" The Jewish American autobiographer Ludwig Lewisohn manifested, to Austin, the "typically Jewish expectation" that "the really desirable things . . . should come to him like manna for the gathering of it." It is this opportunistic cast of mind, she warned, that "isolat[es] the possessor of it from the American outlook" and "produces the psychological and temperamental base of such economic expedients as Socialism and Communism." For Austin, qualities of temperament inherent in the Jewish make-up—opportunism and laziness—explain the Jew's attraction to radicalism, and vice versa. Less obvious than Kenneth Roberts's equation of Jews with parasites, Austin's formulation plays on the same racialization of radicalism in the political unconscious of her audience.[20]

Statements from the various presidents who presided over the postwar United States gave the stamp of state approval to yoking Americanism with racial purity, on the one hand, and antiradicalism, on the other. In one sense such pronouncements from the White House were nothing new: in 1894 Theodore Roosevelt had proclaimed that "[a]bove all, the immigrant must learn to talk and think and be United States." Postwar presidential utterances, however, lacked the tone of benign paternalism characterizing Progressive Era assimilationism. Wilson coupled his fear of militant blacks with an antipathy to leftist European immigrants, declaring in September 1919 that a "hyphen" was "the most un-American thing in the world," a "dagger" that immigrant radicals were "ready to plunge into the vitals of this Republic." Professing himself especially worried about the loyalty of Jews living on the East Side of New York, Wilson held that "Bolshevism is the negation of everything American." Vice President Calvin Coolidge in 1921 proclaimed in *Good Housekeep-*

ing that "[b]iological laws tell us that certain divergent people will not mix or blend. The Nordics propagate themselves successfully. With other races, the outcome shows deterioration on all sides." He cautioned, "The alien who turns toward America with . . . a set desire to teach destruction" must be excluded. Coolidge also made clear his antipathy to any worker whose outlook was "clouded by class consciousness": labor had no "right" to "monopoly" (i.e., the closed shop), shorter work hours, self-management, or, above all, "slamming the door of production" (i.e., striking). The question of the day, Coolidge declared, was "whether America will allow itself to be degraded into a communistic or socialistic state or whether it will remain American." When Coolidge declared, upon signing the 1924 immigration restriction bill, that "America must be kept American," he was associating racial purity with the unity of labor and capital.[21]

More than any other public figure, however, it was President Warren G. Harding who set the tone for the postwar Thermidor. According to the Klan historian Wyn Craig Wade, Harding, an egregious racist on the personal level, was recruited into the Ku Klux Klan while president, using the White House Bible during his induction ceremony in the Green Room. In a November 1921 speech in Birmingham, Alabama, that would be widely denounced in the leftist and progressive press, Harding approvingly quoted Stoddard's *Rising Tide of Color* and noted that "our race problem here in the United States is only a phase of a race issue that the whole world confronts." The nation's president unabashedly spoke the language of Jim Crow. "Men of both races may well stand uncompromisingly against every suggestion of social equality," he announced, adding, "This is . . . a question of recognizing a fundamental, eternal, inescapable difference. Racial amalgamation there cannot be." Warning of the hemorrhaging of Negro labor produced by the Great Migration, however, Harding admonished white southerners to change their ways and recognize that "[r]estricted immigration will reduce the rate of increase, and force us back upon our older population to find people to do the simpler, physically harder manual tasks. . . . If the South wishes to keep its fields producing and its industry still expanding it will have to compete for the services of the colored man." Moreover, Harding stressed, "the one thing we must sedulously avoid is the development of group and class organizations in this country" that would "array class against class and group against group." He concluded that "[i]n the long era of readjustment upon which we are entering," it was critical that "the nation . . . lay aside old prejudices and old antagonisms, and in the broad, clear light of nationalism enter upon a constructive policy in dealing with these intricate issues." As part of this "constructive policy," Harding attended the 1922 "America's Making Festival" in New York City and praised its planners for the diverse range of ethnic and racial groups recognized for their "contributions to America." Although the president's personal predilections were in accord with the violent logic of Jim Crow and he himself belonged to an organization that would "array . . . group against group," he evidently saw no irreconcilable contradiction between preaching the value of segregation, on the one hand, and of diversity, on the other, so long as both qualified as forms of Americanism. This contradiction—and its validation in the "broad, clear light of nationalism"—is relevant to the project of the cultural pluralists considered in chapter 4.[22]

One might argue that the upsurge of anti-immigrant sentiment, fueled by statements from the White House and codified in the immigration restriction bills of the early 1920s, illustrates the autonomous character of racist ideology: even though capitalists stood to profit from the lowering of the price of labor that would accompany continuing immigration, they were so caught up in the tide of xenophobia that they ignored their own class interests. The notorious steel magnate Judge Gary, who, fresh from the smashing of the great steel strike of 1919, knew how valuable foreign-born labor was to capital, strongly opposed the government's efforts to restrict immigration; he was among those industrialists targeted in Davenport's allusion, in a letter to Gould, to "those unworthy citizens who would get rich quickly at the expense of America." But the argument for ideological autonomy reduces class interest to economic immediacy and ignores the more strategic imperatives of class rule. While the statements of Wilson, Coolidge, and Harding reveal the prevalence of racist antiradicalism in ruling-class political discourses of the day, it must not be forgotten that these presidents also spoke as executives for the ruling class. As such, they expressed the widespread but by no means irrational fear that, unless there was a blanket exclusion of immigrant workers—any of whom could be the carrier of the revolutionary incubus—there was the real possibility that revolution or at least large-scale and uncontrollable labor rebellion would occur in the United States. Moreover, the linkage of anti-Negro racism with fears of proletarian insurgency, explicit in Harding's speech, points to the principal ideological task that the rhetoric of racist antiradicalism was intended to perform— namely, the othering of any opposition to 100 percent Americanism and the taming of native-born (that is, white) labor. As Coolidge's statement suggests, the main target of the 1921 and 1924 restriction and exclusion laws was, arguably, not so much radical European immigrants as their native-born counterparts. The "Americanization"—that is, the simultaneous racialization and suppression—of the native-born, white working class was the primary concern of business and government in the wake of 1919, underpinning the conversion of industrial democracy into industrial relations, of Reconstruction into the American Plan. The dual signification of the term *Red Summer*—to the attacks on Socialists and Communists, on the one hand, and the blood, mainly of African Americans, that flowed in the nation's streets, on the other—can be extended to a triple signification, in which blood is seen as the carrier of the virus of discontent. The various presidents' declarations of racial and nationalist essentialism, while no doubt uttered from the heart, served above all to interpellate U.S. (white) workers as members of the (white) body politic—to pay out the "psychological wages of whiteness," however paltry these might be, and convince their recipients that these wages possessed more than symbolic value.[23]

"[We Must] Prevent This International Blight from Finding Root in the Soil of the United States": Nativism, Eugenics, and American "Roots"

Science provided the legitimacy for racist antiradicalism, and government converted it into policy; I now examine the discursive field in and through which ideology was further naturalized. The metaphor of the melting pot—adumbrated by Crèvecoeur in his 1782 statement that in America "individuals of all nations are melted into a new race"; taken up by Frederick Jackson Turner in his 1893 statement that the frontier was a "crucible" where "the immigrants were Americanized, liberated, and fused into a mixed race"; and brought into common parlance in 1908 by Israel Zangwill in his play *The Melting-Pot*—would be met with near-universal rejection by eugenicists and nativists. The publicist George Creel, who during the war had headed up the Committee on Public Information, became a fervent advocate of postwar immigration restriction. "Close the Gates!" he intoned. "The overwhelming majority of immigrants for the last twenty years has proved to be just so much slag in the melting pot." The immigrants, "[o]pposed at every point to the American or Nordic stock, both in traditions and ideals, . . . do not enter into solution, but coagulate in alien masses." In a possible allusion to Walt Whitman's claim, in "Crossing Brooklyn Ferry," to have been "struck from the float forever held in solution," Creel indicated that, in the new era, the nation's chemical solution was overloaded with unassimilable elements; to maintain its pristine character, it must reject the infusion of additional foreign matter. In a comparable vein, Clinton Stoddard Burr, in *America's Race Heritage* (1922), declared that "America is not, nor must ever be, the melting pot. . . . Most of the hordes of immigrants who have been pouring into the United States from countries of South and Eastern Europe, from lands inhabited by races impregnated with radicalism, Bolshevism, and anarchy, belong for the most part to the lower strata of humanity." He challenged, "Do we desire a mongrel population in America such as that which gave birth to Sovietism in Russia?" Although Burr's metaphor became somewhat tangled—the connection between the melting pot and the tidal wave is unclear, and the immigrants are both feminized in their impregnation by radicalism and masculinized as a semenlike "flood"—its diffused paranoia was clearly premised on a revulsion against admixture of any kind. The melting pot had outlived its usefulness.[24]

Given the conservatives' eagerness to don the mantle of science, one might suppose that the melting-pot trope, which bore the stamp of industrialization—or, in Crèvecoeur's usage, at least of a chemical, and hence by association scientific, paradigm—would be replaced by one still more resonant of modernity. A variety of tropes was in fact deployed to describe the cataclysmic demographic shifts at issue: animality (mongrelization); war (weapons, beleaguered fortresses); forces of nature (floods, tides, fires); disease (parasites, germs); and sexuality (impregnation, rape, sterility). Above all, however, nativist ideology in the era of the Bolshevik Revolution was marked by the recrudescence of romantic metaphorical language and in particular of an organic trope that functioned allegorically to link soil with nation, seed with stock, root with belonging, and fruit with citizenry. This trope was nothing new, being a staple of nineteenth-century "folkish" nationalism at least as far back as Johannes Herder. Moreover, the use of the term *naturalization* to describe the process of acquiring citizenship had been incorporated into U.S. law as early as 1790. Gobineau had used a botanical analogy to represent the role of the "Teutonic race" in history. "I have become convinced that everything in the way of human creation, science, art, civilization, all that is great and noble and fruitful on the earth," he declared, "points toward a single source, is sprung from one and the same root, belongs to only one family, the various branches of which have dominated every civilized region of the world." Gobineau's family tree, of course, was hardly that of universal humanity; its branches signify not diversity in unity but the organic necessity for imperial rule by "advanced" races. Just as important as the manifest content of Gobineau's trope, however, was the almost literal status of his metaphor, which indicated, as Tzvetan Todorov has noted, that he saw no real difference between the natural and human worlds: "Civilizations are male and female, they are born, they live, they die, they have seeds and roots and can be grafted."[25]

The Darwinian Ernst Haeckel turned the family tree to different uses, proposing that all life could be mapped by a single evolutionary tree with roots in the distant past: "The thousands of green leaves on the tree that clothe the younger and fresher twigs, and differ in their height and breadth from the trunk, correspond to the living species of animals and plants; these are the more advanced, the further they are removed from the primeval stem. The withered and faded leaves, that we see on the older and dead twigs, represent the many extinct species that dwelt on the earth in earlier geological ages, and come closer to the primeval simple stem-form, the more remote they are from us." Unlike Gobineau's, Haeckel's tree analogy posited the interrelatedness of all life forms. Nonetheless, it presupposed hierarchy, insofar as "inferior races" were closer to the "primeval simple stem-form." The connection between this elaborate botanical conceit and Victor Berger's more candid assertion that African Americans inhabit a lower place than whites on the evolutionary scale is clear.[26]

While nineteenth-century uses of the organic trope rationalized social inequality, they tended to do so by means of explicit analogy: elements in the imagistic constellation—root, branch, leaves, seed, soil—were characteristically referenced for allegorical purposes. What distinguished the use of the organic trope in the discursive field of postwar racist antiradicalism was its subliminal allusive mode. The implied referent was so politically charged that the mere mention of *soil* could conjure up the spectre of illicit planting and rooting. Thus the *Literary Digest*, heaving a relieved sigh at the suppression of the Seattle general strike, quoted approvingly the *Louisville Courier-Journal* to the effect that "'Bolshevism has no root in America. It does not take root and thrive in American soil. Indeed, the Bolshevism of Russia is largely a transplant from America, which may germinate Bolshevism, but does not develop it.'" *Current History*, less sanguine about the nation's safety from revolutionary transplanting, featured a photograph of Ellis Island in a 1920 article about the deportation of radicals with the caption "Ellis Island, New York, where 50 per cent. of all European immigrants first set foot on American Soil, and whence the deported 'Reds' are shipped home." The Lusk Committee, in its investigations into New York radicalism, reported that the seeds of socialism had, unfortunately, "taken root" at the Rand School—which, despite its location on Lower Manhattan's asphalt, was now apparently a seedbed of insurgency. Peter Roberts—after portraying the breezes of doctrine lashing the souls of radicals and passing over the sick and bankrupt European patient—settled down to a less metaphorically hysterical elaboration of the organic trope in relation to the United States. The propaganda of radicals finds "fertile soil" and "takes root," he lamented, in the minds of those who "do not think" and are unacquainted with the "family tree" that embodies "[the nation's] traditions, its purposes, its future." In the fight to stamp out immigrant radicalism, both soil and tree—nation and race—were at stake. Separate elements in the organic trope invoked a discursive field so ideologically saturated in essentialist concepts of race and nation that the trope could work on an unconscious, or at least preconscious, level; allegory was implied but did not need to be extended to reference the entire set of relevant ideas.[27]

That the organic trope could be deployed in contradictory ways and still allude to the discursive field of racist antiradicalism is evidenced in its utility in invoking anti-Semitism. R. M. Whitney, in *Reds in America* (1924), argued for the termination of laws extending civil liberties to Communists because of the need to "preven[t] . . . this international blight . . . from finding root in the soil of the United States." Here the disease threatening the soil of the U.S. is designated as "international"— a term barely coding its anti-Semitic overtones. The Imperial Ku Klux Klan Wizard Hiram Wesley Evans, by contrast, feared the opposite quality in Jews, their presumed rootlessness. It was because "[t]he Jew produces nothing anywhere on the face of the earth" and "does not till the soil," he lamented, "that "ninety-five per cent of bootleggers are jews." For Evans, it was separation from the soil that, apparently, enabled Jews to take advantage of Prohibition, merchandizing without conscience the product of the grape. Mary Austin expressed the fear—in only slightly less polemical language—that the "tap-rooted" American would be subjected to "invasive intimacy" with the Jew, whose embrace of radical political doctrines "ha[s] a root in Jerusalem." For Whitney, Evans, and Austin, as for the compositors of *The Protocols*, the Jew could be stigmatized for both Bolshevism and capitalist parasitism, rootlessness and unwelcome rootedness.[28]

The equation of nation with race could also be conveyed through a macabre gendering of the organic trope. In *The Fruit of the Family Tree* (1924), the eugenics enthusiast Alfred Wiggam urged wives and mothers in "the higher classes" to recognize their duty to serve as vessels of the nation's destiny. "They are the ones who ought most of all to heed this call of the blood which has tingled in every truly womanly woman's veins since the gates of Eden opened upon a world of knowledge, which is always the world of duty," he sermonized. If the genes of the "higher classes" could define the "family tree" that was the nation, he prophesied, then the nation could return to the prelapsarian state: "The Garden of Eden is not in the past, it is in the future." The tree of knowledge, once implicated in the fall, can now nourish humanity (a.k.a. America). In *America: A Family Matter* (1922)—published as a companion volume to Brigham's *Study of American Intelligence*—Charles W. Gould described uncontrolled immigration as a violation of the land. "Already the plunderers, availing themselves of the importation of cheap labor, without thought of replanting, have recklessly swept away great forests," he declared, "wantonly careless of providing for those who are to come after them, and thus leave, as their fitting memorial, vast reaches of barren acres and a diminished water supply." In Gould's formulation, greedy employers might be responsible for the "plunder" of the land, but it was the immigrants, "mongrel people" genetically unable to "replant," who were draining the soil of present nutrients and future harvests. "Naturalization" thus entailed a violation of the nature that is the nation. Gould's elaborate conceit also concealed a sexualized anxiety: the immigrant "plunderers" are "wanton" in their ruination of the land, which they leave "barren," no longer able to bear. André Siegfried, in his *America Comes of Age: A Fresh Analysis* (1927), explored the continuation of this rape fantasy in the American imagination. "It is a question whether the measures against foreign penetration have not been taken too late," he opined, since "these heterogeneous seeds will continue to grow once they have been planted." Where Gould's nightmare describes a nation rendered infertile through the rape of immigration, Siegfried's metaphorical scenario displays the fear that the nation has been "penetrated" and "impregnated" by "foreign invaders," producing illegitimate offspring that will do further mischief. Both Gould's and Siegfried's gendering of the nation as feminine—and vulnerable—contrasts dramatically with Grant's portrayal of the nation as a huge militarized phallus and calls to mind Palmer's warning about immigrant radicals "crawling into the sacred corners of American homes" and "seeking to replace marriage vows with libertine laws." Central to the conjoined discourses of nativism and eugenics was the conception of the nation as at once feminized and genetically pure, a notion further promoted by metaphorically equating woman with land. When the *Crisis* and the *Crusader*—and, later, the *Messenger*—featured portraits of winsome but distinctly maternal women on their covers, they were reacting against such discursive attempts to secure the iconography of chaste motherhood for 100 percent (white) Americanism.[29]

The association of nation with soil, and of both with female essence, is a legacy of romantic nationalism. As Laura Doyle has pointed out, William Wordsworth's proposition that poetic language displaying "'the essential passions of the heart'" finds a "'better soil'" in the "'humble and rustic'" life of peasants than in the urbanized existence of intellectuals is closely linked with a view of the peasant as "'in his person attached, by stronger roots, to the soil of which he is the growth.'" In the discourse of competitive "racial patriarchy," she observes, nations are "vast family trees, with some being simply more 'thrusting,' more manly, than others." But nations are given identity, spatial and temporal, primarily through mothers. Because of the "mother's alignment with the body," argues Doyle, "and her function as reproducer of the group as a social body, [she] comes to signify . . . a bodily and collective past." This received romantic association of organicism with native land was, in the American context, compounded historically by the exceptionalist discourse that represented the nation as uniquely fertile—whether in the Puritan mission of planting a New World garden, the Revolutionary War–era identification of the new nation with a sturdy young pine, Crèvecoeur's view of Americans as plants thriving or failing according to their environment, or the pioneer conceit of penetrating a virgin wilderness. As Annette Kolodny has argued, what is probably the nation's "most cherished fantasy" involves an experience of the land as essentially feminine—that is, not simply the land as mother but the land as woman: the "total female principle of gratification—enclosing the individual in an environment of receptivity, repose, and painless and integral satisfaction." In the postwar era, however, the gendered discourse linking nation and nature took on added metonymic force, for now not all the would-be citizens inhabiting the soil were welcome additions; to protect mother earth was to identify with whatever disciplinary laws and practices the fatherland might devise. Although the *combinatoire* of terms constituting the inherited nativist/ eugenicist use of the organic trope is not identical with that of racial patriarchy, their overlap underwent a process of intense ideological overdetermination in the era of "war and revolution, struggle and change."[30]

Let me here interpose a methodological proviso about the nature and extent of my claims about the signifying capacity of the organic trope in the discourse of racist antiradicalism. I am not arguing that this discourse was dependent on the organic trope in order to be communicated; nativists and eugenicists used language in all sorts of ways—including other tropes, as well as plenty of straightforward assertions—to get their points across. Nor am I proposing that every term in the constellation constituting the discursive field of the organic trope or for that matter the entirety of the constellation can signify in only one way. The invocation of "American soil" in the 1919 *Literary Digest* possessed quite a different valence than the phrase would have evoked, say, by the Union Army during the Civil War. Nor am I suggesting that, even in the context of the intense ideological warfare of 1919 and its aftermath, the trope could invoke only a single discursive field. As will be seen in the next chapter, root and tree, seed, soil, and fruit could be deployed abstractly to reference cause and effect (that is, the notion of "root cause") or even allegorically to reference the process by which proletarian internationalism moves toward revolution (that is, the notion of "spreading seeds"). However complex their meanings, words used metaphorically can resignify to a degree that words used nonmetaphorically cannot. What I am arguing, however, is that, in the particular historical conjuncture of 1919, the discursive field of racist antiradicalism was so ideologically saturated that, when either race or nation was invoked through one or more elements of the organic trope, an entire *combinatoire* of associated ideas and assumptions—often gendered—could also be invoked, without a shred of argument having been made. This rhetorical overdetermination would pose a formidable challenge to cultural pluralists who would attempt to recruit the organic trope into the service of a progressive and inclusive—that is, a "good"—nationalism.

While all this talk about roots and soil functioned primarily as metaphor, it could also be deployed quite literally by policymakers who, concerned about social unrest, proposed holding out the possibility that real people might settle on real land. Striving to update the obsolete Turner frontier thesis, one school of thought held that the expectation of rural land settlement should continue to furnish a "safety-valve" for restive immigrants. Frederic C. Howe, New York's wartime immigration commissioner, wrote in the war's aftermath that "the alien will Americanize himself if he is given the opportunity to do so. . . . The best antidote for Bolshevism is not deportation but a home, a farm, a governmental policy of land settlement." Feri Felix Weiss, a former immigration official as well as a self-proclaimed believer in the "religion of Eugenics," advocated in 1921 that "the Nation finance the small farmer, the worker who is willing to till the soil in the summer and work in the mill in the winter! Let Congress create a real farmer's 'credit' to take the toiler back to the soil, the foundation of all national wealth, health, and happiness." Weiss's portraiture of the modern American tiller of the soil combines a romantic invocation of the land with a shrewd appreciation of the necessity for government subsidization of seasonal rural workers. Giving his book the metaphorically provocative title *The Sieve; or, Revelations of the Man Mill, Being the Truth about Immigration,* Weiss viewed immigration as a straining process that would permit only the most fit to enter the "complex industrial beehive of the nation." Through such a policy, he maintained—summoning up still another metaphor—the "new dawn [of Industrial Democracy]" would negate the "red dawn of Sovietism."[31]

In *A Stake in the Land* (1921), part of a government-sponsored Americanization studies series, Peter A. Speek explicitly linked land ownership, Americanism, and anti-Bolshevism. "There is no other tie that binds a man so closely to a country as his home," wrote Speek. "In direct distinction, the word 'homeless' has implications of aimless drifting, of destitution and misery, and of the indifference of a 'homeless' man to 'his' country. Certain advocates of cosmopolitanism in their agitation against patriotism often take advantage of the importance of home in the relation of a man to his country when they appeal to the 'proletarians': 'Do you own anything? Do you even have a home in this country?'" "From the viewpoint of Americanization," Speek concluded, whether the government could actually deliver on the promise of a homestead to every immigrant family wanting one—a promise that, he admitted, might pose practical problems—was less important than "the certainty in the mind of an immigrant that there is a stake in the land for him." "A stake in the land," in Speek's formulation, functioned ideologically for immigrants by offering an antidote, however illusory, to their "rootlessness." The "cosmopolitanism" of the immigrant proletarian, defined as "homeless-[ness]," was to be combated by the promise of belonging. But whether actual land was to belong to the immigrant was left unresolved; immigrant laborers might not be able to drive a physical stake signaling ownership of their own plot of land, but they would have a psychological stake in the nation all the same. Speek had nothing to say about African Americans in relation to the land that they already tilled; the notion that they might even participate in the dream of moving from tenancy to ownership was beyond his ken.[32]

For Howe, Weiss, and Speek, the relationship between Americanization and land was more than simply metaphorical; "soil" was not just an element in an organic trope. But their hesitancy in attaching to the referent a promise of possession—and, in Speek's case, the admission that the pledge of land settlement was not a metaphor but a lie—puts their association of rooting with belonging on a continuum with other more evidently fanciful uses of the trope. What is "at stake" (as it were) in both the literal and the metaphorical usages is the notion that the immigrant's identification with the land and the germination of seed in the nation's soil is what would produce and sustain a laboring population loyal to the lords of the land. That this population would be white—whatever its place of European origin—went without saying.

"The Biological Unity of the Human Race":
The Boasians, Antiracism, and Cultural Relativism

Culture would prove the crucial wedge concept by which the opponents of 100 percent Americanism would attempt to invade and capture the rhetorical field of racist antiradicalism. Foundational to the discourse of cultural pluralism that would guide these oppositional projects—especially that of the New Negroes—was the concept of cultural relativism, as it was being worked out by Franz Boas and other pioneers in the field of cultural anthropology. Culture would be used to refute the evolutionist paradigm of a hierarchy of civilizations, disarticulate race from nation, and call into question essentialist notions of citizenship. The central importance of Boasian doctrine to the artists and theorists of the Harlem Renaissance has often been noted; what has not yet been adequately examined, however, is the Boasians' relation to contemporaneous leftist thinking, much less to the various contradictions and gaps informing that thinking.

The Boasians mounted a concerted attack on the citadel of racist pseudoscience. Boas's early work with skull measurements refuted the claims of Ripley and other craniometrists who purported to demonstrate the iron laws of biological determinism. Davenport's fetish of "quantitative findings" was returned to him in spades: if skull shape and size could vary widely among members of ethnic and "racial" groups and could change dramatically in one generation as a result of new environmental conditions, Boas reasoned, the famous "cephalic index"—so dear to the hearts of Palmer, Atherton, and other 100 percenters—could pretend to little explanatory power. "Variations in cultural development can as well be explained by a consideration of the general course of historical events," Boas argued, "without recourse to the theory of material differences of mental faculty in different races." Boas's comparisons of the cultural achievements of different groups led him to testify to "the remarkable development of industry, political organization, and philosophic opinion," as well as "the frequent occurrence of men of great willpower and wisdom among the negroes in Africa." As Du Bois was to note, his own desire to explore African history was sparked partly by Boas's 1906 Atlanta University commencement speech on the subject. Besides refuting racist arguments frontally, Boas's pioneering fieldwork among "primitive" peoples produced challenges to contemporary evolutionary theory that in turn created a paradigmatic shift—from the physical to the cultural—throughout the entire field of anthropology. Boas's landmark *Mind of Primitive Man* (1911) demonstrated that "primitive" was differ-

entiated from "civilized" humanity only insofar as the former manifested its creative impulses in different cultural forms. Lampooning as
"Nordic nonsense" the attempt to analogize animal and human species
through such notions as "mongrelism," Boas polemicized against the
evolutionist postulation of "lower" and "higher" races. The cultures of
different groups should be studied synchronously, as instances of different, rather than hierarchical, human activities, Boas urged. *Culture* thus
possessed a dual valence. Cognitively, it supplied a rubric for examining
different civilizations without preconceived notions of value; epistemologically, it supplied the means to undermine essentialist notions of race,
for it was a term that demanded to be used in the plural: *cultures*. Boas
both removed the empiricist figleaf from contemporaneous racist ideology—his reviews of Grant's and Stoddard's work were devastating—and
supplied an alternative paradigm accounting for human variability. As
Thomas Gossett, a historian of racism, observes, "[T]he racists of the
1920s rightly recognized Boas as their chief antagonist."[33]

Some of the younger practitioners of the new cultural anthropology
extended the antiracist and egalitarian implications of Boas's findings.
Edward Sapir, discussing the "mythology of all races," wrote that race
itself was a social rather than a biological concept and that, as a result of
the new anthropology, "[p]rimitive humanity now stands revealed as what
we had always sneakingly felt it was—simply ourselves, caught in the
net of other geographical and historical circumstances. Its psychology is
our psychology, no more archaic and no less variable." Alexander Goldenweiser, challenging the evolutionist view that all civilizations must
pass through the same series of stages, asserted that "[n]o proof has been
forthcoming of the inferiority of the other racial stocks to the white."
Goldenweiser rejected "the prevailing view" that "man is many and civilization one, meaning by this that the races differ significantly in potential ability and that only one, the white race, could have and has achieved
civilization." Instead, he proposed in what was to become a famous
phrase, "*Man is one, civilizations are many.*" Robert M. Lowie argued
that "the unilinear theory which assumes that mankind must everywhere
conform to the same laws of evolution, every step being necessary at a
certain stage of development" had been "long discredited among profes-
sional anthropologists." Moreover, he rejected "all significant connection
between racial and cultural factors"—a radical denial that would spark
Alain Locke's opposition. The work of the Boasians made it increasingly
possible from a scientific standpoint to decouple the primitive from the
atavistic and to refute linkages between the "destruction of civilization"
and racial regression.[34]

The pioneering cultural anthropologists all tended toward the left, a number of them being self-described socialists. Boas himself, the offspring of radicals of 1848, was inspired by egalitarian social values that enabled him to discern the elitist premises underlying the theories of the academic racists. Boas observed that the "race instinct" evoked in many whites by the presence of mulattoes was not a "physiological dislike" but "an expression of social conditions that are so deeply ingrained in us that they assume a strong emotional value." "[U]ltimately," Boas declared, "race instinct" is "a repetition of the old instinct and fear of the connubium of patricians and plebeians, of the European nobility and the common people, or of the castes of India." Boas lampooned the complacency of those intellectuals who "assume that their own mentality is, on the average, appreciably higher than that of the rest of the people." "The masses in our modern city populations," whose "desires . . . are in a wider sense more human than those of the classes," he declared, "are less subject to the influence of traditional teaching." By "traditional teaching," Boas clearly meant something like dominant ideology; the educated "classes," he implied, were more susceptible to rationalizations of the status quo than were the "masses" not benefiting from present power relations. Writing to the *Nation* in October 1918, Boas urged its readers to vote Socialist to "rehabilitat[e]" the civil liberties lost under the Federal Espionage Act and "similar State laws." Lowie viewed intellectual rigor as inseparable from leftist politics. Where Stoddard prophesied that eugenics would liberate humankind from the clutches of atavistic radicals, Lowie proposed that the new anthropology would serve as a "universal prophylactic against loose thinking"; particularly "as applied to matters such as private property, women, and the Negro," the new discipline would "preclude views that are intellectually unsound and socially pernicious but which the untutored mind almost automatically embraces because of their meretricious reasonableness." Sapir declared in 1919 that "the great majority of us . . . are slave-stokers to fires that burn for demons that we would destroy, were it not that they appear in the guise of our highest benefactors." Comparing the "harmonious" culture of "the civilization of a typical American Indian tribe" with the "spurious" culture of the United States, Sapir wrote that the cardinal "illusion" was "that because the tools of life are today more specialized and refined than ever before, it necessarily follows that we are in like degrees attaining to a profounder harmony of life, to a deeper and more satisfying culture." Linking the upsurge of 1919 to a notion of "maladjustment" comparable with the Marxist notion of alienation, Sapir concluded that "the present world-wide labor unrest has as one of its deepest roots some sort of dim perception of the cultural fallacy of the present form of industrialism. For this reason it should be welcomed. A civilization that has attained to such ethical consciousness as we now possess and yet is, for the most part, based on helotry is hardly worth saving."[35]

Although the cultural anthropologists directed their critique of evolutionism primarily toward decoupling race from culture, they also understood the critique's implications for the reformist theory, prevailing in the right wing of the Second International—and, after 1919, in the SPA—that every revolution must go through prescribed "stages," including full-fledged capitalist development, to succeed. Lowie thus observed that the recent working-class revolution in Russia's largely peasant society showed that "to regard a preceding era of industrialism as indispensable is to exalt the discarded theory of an earlier generation into an immutable dogma." Melville J. Herskovits argued that the findings of both Lowie and Goldenweiser led inevitably to the conclusion that the theory of necessary stages was as irrelevant to modern political developments as it was to the history of humankind. "It is nothing short of fantastic to talk of the predetermined failure of the Russian revolution because Russia skipped a step in the fixed economic development of nations," Herskovits wrote in the *Liberator* in 1923. "Our greater understanding of the organisation, industry and ideas of primitive communities, makes it difficult to speak of 'stages' of development, of 'higher' or 'lower' cultures. The biological unity of the human race, the equal potentialities of racial groups, stand out sharply, no less than does the fact that culture, being human, refuses to be neatly pigeon-holed and filed away for future consultation." For Herskovits—who wore an IWW button during his undergraduate days at Columbia—belief in the "equal potentialities of racial groups" had a direct corollary in confidence that the Russian Revolution could succeed. Just as racism and antiradicalism were mutually implicated in the discourse of the nativists, antiracism and political egalitarianism were, for Boas, Lowie, and Herskovits, similarly intertwined. And just as Davenport recognized the implication of his doctrines ("No Bolsheviki need apply"), most of the cultural anthropologists were well aware of the political consequences of their antievolutionary stance: they were refuting the doctrine of "non-historical peoples" and the stagist theory of social change to which it was attached.[36]

"Nordic Nonsense": The Limitations of the Boasian Critique

For all their careful research and eloquent polemics, however, Boas and his followers hardly managed to bring down the temple of racist pseudo-

science during the postwar Thermidor. Their influence was restricted partly because, particularly in the early 1920s, they were simply overwhelmed
by superior force. The scientific racists enjoyed almost unlimited back-
ing in the mass media. While Boas and company were publishing in the
Dial and the *Nation*, as well as scientific journals with even less of a popular audience, the *Saturday Evening Post*, the largest circulation magazine
in the country, brought to its two million readers—for weeks on end—the
wisdom of Kenneth Roberts and Lothrop Stoddard. The cultural anthropologists' limited influence in the early 1920s can also be traced to the
cowardice of the rest of the scientific community, which largely declined
to enter into public debate with the eugenicists, even though by decade's
end the majority had grown increasingly skeptical of the legitimacy of the
racists' claims. External constraints thus operated powerfully to limit the
Boasians' influence in the wake of 1919; as the statements of Wilson, Harding, and Coolidge make clear, racist antiradicalism received unequivocal support from the ruling elite in the early 1920s.

The cultural anthropologists' impact in delegitimating racist pseudoscience was also constrained by various contradictions internal to their
arguments. As various scholars have noted, the Boasians themselves were
not fully exempt from the racism and elitism pervading contemporaneous social and scientific theory. Boas's early writings in particular show
him not only accepting at face value the notion of race but also struggling between acceptance and rejection of current doctrines of Negro
inferiority. In 1909, he conceded the "slightly inferior size, and perhaps
lesser complexity of structure of [the Negro's] brain." Boas undercut the
otherwise antiracist conclusions of *The Mind of Primitive Man* he drew
from his own study of African civilizations when he noted, "We might,
therefore, anticipate a lack of men of high genius [among blacks] but
should not anticipate any lack of faculty among the great mass of Negroes
living among whites and enjoying the leadership of the best men of the
race." This "men of high genius" proviso does not acknowledge any differential in the intelligence levels among the masses of different "races"
but leaves room for the supposition that the white race would produce
slightly more people of great talent than would the colored ones. During
the 1900s and 1910s, Boas characteristically hedged, as when he wrote
in his foreword to Mary White Ovington's *Half a Man* that "no proof can
be given of any material inferiority of the Negro race; . . . without doubt
the bulk of the individuals composing the race are equal in mental apti-
tude of the bulk of our own people. . . . [A]lthough their hereditary apti-
tude may lie in slightly different directions, it is very improbable that the
majority of individuals composing the white race should possess greater

ability than the Negro race." Lowie, too, at times straddled the egalitarian fence. Although he argued that "the ethnologist cannot solve his
cultural problems by means of the race factor," he hypothesized that
"extraordinary deviations from the norm" discoverable in vast populations might produce "significant cultural results." "A *little* greater energy or administrative talent may be just sufficient to found a powerful
state," he wrote. "[A] *slightly* greater amount of logical consistency may
lead to the foundation of geometrical reasoning or of a philosophical system." Lowie, like Boas, was—at least initially—unable fully to break with
the dominant paradigms guiding thinking about genetics and intelligence.
Although the entire burden of the cultural relativist argument was that
race itself was a social construction, this final small step would at first
prove a large one to take.[37]

More crucial, however, the Boasians' influence in the immediate
postwar period was limited by their failure fully to appreciate the political—that is, *ideological*—dimension of the struggle in which they were
engaged. To varying degrees, they were hobbled by the same conceptual
constraints that delimited the ability of the Left as a whole to forge an
antiracist and internationalist theory and practice. To begin with, the
Boasians based their explanations for the hegemony of racist thinking on
the same pragmatist conception of psychology that at once shaped and
confined other early-twentieth-century leftists' efforts to formulate the
social and political origins of consciousness. In Sapir's proposition that
"[primitive humanity's] psychology is our psychology, no more archaic
and no less variable," the term *psychology* means simply "group consciousness," without reference to the power relations that historically
determine its contents. For all his sharpness in spotting a racist argument
when he saw one, Boas's own comments on the material foundations of
racism had inadequate explanatory value. Prejudice, he asserted, "is
founded essentially on the tendency of the human mind to merge the
individual in the class to which he belongs, and to ascribe to him all the
characteristics of his class. . . . We find this spirit at work in anti-Semitism as well as in American nativism, and in the conflict between labor
and capitalism. We have recently seen it at its height in the emotions
called forth by the world war." The "negro problem," in particular, must
be understood as the acting out of an inherent human need—a "psychological" need—to categorize and differentiate:

> It is claimed by many that the negro problem is economic rather than
> racial, that the fear of negro competition causes racial opposition. Obvi-
> ously, this explanation also would not hold good if the tendency did not
> exist to treat the negro as a class, not as an individual. I do not wish to

deny that the economic conflict may be a contributing cause that accentuates the pre-existing feeling of the contrast between whites and negroes. This feeling may be emphasized in many ways—by economic interest, by questions of social privilege, or by any other social process that brings about conflicts of interest between large groups of whites and negroes. It would, however, be an error to seek in these sources the fundamental cause for the antagonism; for the economic conflict, as well as the other conflicts, presupposes the social recognition of classes.

Boas's formulation shares a number of premises with the statements on the relation of race to class voiced by other progressives of his day. As in the assertions of James Weldon Johnson, Stephen Graham, and William Pickens examined in chapter 1, *class* signifies simultaneously "classification" and "social group"; analysis of social location blurs into taxonomy. To his credit, Boas rejected the jobs competition thesis, popular among Socialists, for valid reasons. "Fear of economic competition," he aptly pointed out, does not explain "the pre-existing feeling of the contrast between whites and negroes." Yet neither did he supply an alternative materialist analysis of where this "pre-existing feeling" comes from. His reference to the "social process that brings about conflicts of interest among large groups of whites and negroes" suggests agreement with (or at least accession to) the view—espoused by Kate Richards O'Hare—that such "conflicts of interest" reflect real "interests" rather than ideological constructions of benefit functioning as social control mechanisms facilitating the exploitation of black and white alike. Moreover, rather than press for a deeper understanding of the relationship between "economic conflict" and "the social recognition of classes," Boas resorted, at this crucial juncture, to ahistorical and idealist assertions about the "tendency of the human mind." "Economic conflict," instead of being broadened into class struggle, at once material and ideological, recedes in his formulation to the status of merely one of several "contributing cause[s]"; a potentially totalizing causal paradigm dissipates into a congeries of "factors." The substitution of "economic" for class analysis, coupled with the substitution of "psychology" for ideology, reveals that, like many other leftists and progressives of the day, Boas did not possess an analytical vocabulary permitting him to view race as a concept serving class ends.[38]

The Boasians' formulation of the "propaganda" nature of racist doctrine further displayed their limited understanding of the social function of racist pseudoscience. In a famous riposte to Grant, Boas referred to Grant's "purely imaginary" fear of racial amalgamation as "Nordic nonsense." Grant more than deserved Boas's contempt. But Boas's formulation trivialized the political import of the nativist/eugenicist argument.

He dubbed Stoddard's *Rising Tide of Color* "vicious propaganda" but analyzed its "amateurish" and "dogmatic . . . self-admiration of the white race" as a reflection of the writer's own "emotional prejudice" rather than as a doctrine the 100 percenters used in their campaign for racist antiradicalism. As in his diagnosis that the modern "race instinct" is a "repetition of the old instinct and fear of the connubium of patricians and plebeians," Boas viewed the propaganda aspect of Stoddard's and Grant's books as consisting primarily of the authors' own logic-defying and passion-burdened prejudices. Along with other progressive critics of the day, Boas lacked access to a theory of the role of ideology in class formation that would have enabled him to appreciate more fully the political inflection—and performative potential—of his opponents' racist rhetoric.[39]

Boas's thinking about nationalism was similarly contained within the limits of the Deweyan group psychology that framed current theorizing about social consciousness at many points along the political spectrum. Commenting on the tragic outcome of the various nationalisms both preceding and following World War I, Boas blasted essentialist equations of race with nation, pointing out that "[u]nity of national descent does not bring about national cohesion." He also concluded that "imperialistic nationalism" was highly dangerous and could never serve the "general human interests" of "the mass of the people." "Nationalism in large states cannot flourish unless it is continually rekindled by education, and preached in and out of season," he declared. "[F]or these reasons it finds its home chiefly among the educated classes, while the masses merely follow the impetus that is given to them by 'propaganda' designed to arouse strong patriotic emotions." Although Boas's understanding of the class interests served by "strong patriotic emotions" enabled him to grasp the blatant nationalism of ruling-class propaganda, his inability—once again—to grasp the role of ideology as a social control mechanism led him to the strikingly inaccurate conclusion, revealed in its patent erroneousness by the recent war, that the masses could never fully embrace a nationalism that ran counter to their interests. Moreover, Boas did not repudiate national identification as such: "[D]istinct racial elements may combine and form a nation of great solidarity," and "nationality"—as distinct from "nationalism"—"is one of the most fruitful sources of cultural progress." Replacing religion as the bond uniting people in the modern era, "national feeling finds its natural basis" in "the common interest of the people in the history of their ancestors." Like most other progressives and socialists of the 1910s and 1920s, Boas thus distinguished "bad" nationalism from "good." Accompanying this distinction was—once again—the pragmatist differentiation of propaganda and psychology: "imperialistic nationalism" was served by the former, while "great solidarity" producing "cultural progress" was enabled by the latter. Just as Spargo insisted on the inherence of nationalism in the psychology of the masses—and called on the SPA to support U.S. entry into the war on this basis—Boas, although reaching quite different political conclusions, held that nationalism was in some sense a natural phenomenon of consciousness. Moreover, he embraced a view of the nation as integrated body politic. Even as he declared that "patriotism must be subordinated to humanism" and advocated "the equal rights of all members of mankind," he admitted that he did not "consider absolutely unrestricted immigration as right, because the very respect that I have for the individuality of each nation implies that each has the right to maintain its individuality if it seems threatened by the course of human migration." Assumed here is the notion of nation as unitary entity also premised in the theory of self-determination; that the "equal rights of all members of mankind" might not be articulable within the discourse of a "good" nationalism, one presumably unburdened by class conflict and imperialist superexploitation, was evidently beyond his ken. Indeed, he concluded, "the idea of social justice appears as the foundation of Americanism."[40]

Finally, the Boasians' theorizing of "culture" itself—as opposed to the pluralist notion of "cultures"—contained a critical ambiguity, one that would be carried over into the discourse of the New Negro (and *The New Negro*). While Boas insisted that cultural stages were a function of history rather than of race, his Herderian definition of culture as folk genius implied an essentialist notion of group collectivity that threatened to let in through the ontological back door the linkage of culture with race that had been ushered out the epistemological front door. Sapir, retreating in 1924 from the revolutionary implications of his 1919 condemnation of a class-stratified civilization based on "helotry," wrote that the United States had the pluralist potential to be the site of various "genuine" cultures, even if its national culture was, he still maintained, "spurious." "[A] 'genuine' culture must embrace those general attitudes, views of life, and specific manifestations of civilization that give a particular people its distinctive place in the world," he now argued. Commenting on the current burgeoning of cultural nationalisms, Sapir noted that the "development of culture" took place in "comparatively small, autonomous groups"; in the United States, the ideal to be striven for was the emergence of "linked autonomous cultures" in the "major urban centers." Bringing together pluralism, cultural autonomy, and urbanization, Sapir's 1924 formulation foreshadowed Locke's project of delineating Harlem as the "culture capital" of a nation within a nation in *The New Negro*.

Continually articulating the Boasian critique of biologism, Sapir maintained that, as opposed to the "current assumption that the so-called 'genius' of a people is ultimately reducible to certain inherent hereditary traits of a biological and psychological nature," careful investigation reveals that "what is assumed to be an innate racial characteristic" routinely turns out to be "the resultant of purely historical causes." Nonetheless, in contrasting the "spurious" cultures of modernity, alienated and fragmented, with the disappearing "genuine" cultures of American Indian tribes, Sapir deployed the discourses of both nationalism and naturalization. "A healthy national culture," he opined, "is never a passively accepted heritage from the past, but implies the creative participation of the members of the community"; it should therefore be "looked upon as a sturdy plant growth, each remotest leaf and twig of which is organically fed by the sap at the core." That the organic trope should figure as Sapir's vehicle for conveying his deradicalized 1924 formulation suggests the powerful hold that the discourse of a naturalizing soilness had on the imagination of progressive intellectuals committed to outlining the counterdiscourse of "our America."[41]

The Boasians' principal legacy was an antiracist formulation of cultural relativism that powerfully refuted their opponents' arguments for a hierarchy of civilizations and hence of races. As social scientists, they eventually decimated the evolutionist premises of the eugenicists. But the anti-essentialism guiding their delinking of race and culture did not extend to their theorization of race as such, which they still accepted as a category possessing explanatory value, if only in relation to physical features presumably shared by members of racial groups. This failure fully to theorize race as a social construction was accompanied by a failure to construe it as an *ideological* construction—that is, to grasp the relation between epistemology and ideology. It may be that the Boasians' inability—at least initially—to part company with their own residual racism was inextricably connected with or even grounded in their failure to appreciate fully the ideological function served by racism under capitalism. Moreover, although their cultural relativism disarticulated race from nation, thereby de-essentializing the notion of *patria*, the cultural anthropologists did not sufficiently grasp the ways in which *nation*—even if construed in relation to nationality rather than nationalism—might be reembedded in a presumably progressive counterdiscourse that would be nonetheless built on resuscitating essentialist notions of race. For all its deconstructive power, the Boasians' formulation of cultural relativism would prove assimilable to the loyal oppositionist nationalism—and, as will be seen, the revived racial essentialism—constituting the pluralist response to 100 percent Americanism. It is to a consideration of the discourse and rhetoric of cultural pluralism, which would profoundly shape Locke's project in *The New Negro,* that I now turn.

4 Metonymic Nationalism, Culture Wars, and the Politics of Counterdiscourse

> In many cases the writers had grown up in a still raw
> West or had returned from Paris in search of "roots,"
> that shy and impalpable quiddity the lack of which they
> felt had made them frequently shallow and generally
> restless. No word was more constantly on their lips un-
> less it was the native "soil" or earth and this obsession
> lay deep in the minds of the urban cosmopolitans whom
> one saw toiling now and then with spade and pick.
>
> —Van Wyck Brooks, *Days of the Phoenix: The Nineteen-
> Twenties I Remember* (1957)

Having explored the substance and rhetoric of racist antiradicalism, the dominant ideology informing political discourse and rationalizing state and business repression amidst the social upheavals of
1919 and its Thermidorian aftermath, I now examine various attempts
by progressives and leftists to construct counterdiscourses that would
use the master's tool of pluralist democracy to dismantle the master's
house of 100 percent Americanism. The culture wars of the early 1920s
were waged on various fronts, all of which cannot be treated here. To
understand the forces that would decisively influence the transmutation of the New Negro as leftist warrior into the New Negro as culture
hero, however, I focus on three principal participants in the battles of
the day: liberal cultural pluralists, left-leaning Young Americans, and

the cultural Left associated with the SPA and the fledgling CP, here designated as the *Liberator* radicals.

"Seeded in the Earth Like a Deep Clean Tap Root": Metonymic Nationalism

A concept guiding the discussion from this point forward is what I call "metonymic nationalism," by which I mean a representational practice that treats a social group within a nation as empowered to signify the larger totality that is the nation. Invoking a signifying chain connecting folk with soil with region with nation, the term *metonymic nationalism* points to the ideologically saturated character of American nationalist rhetoric in the historical conjuncture under consideration. The relevance of the trope of metonymy to the historical phenomenon of nationalism has been noted previously. Homi Bhabha, speaking of the construct of the nation, has noted that "[i]t is the mark of the ambivalence of the nation as a narrative strategy—and an apparatus of power— that it produces a continual slippage into analogous, even metonymic categories, like the people, minorities, or 'cultural difference' that continually overlap in the act of writing the nation." But where Bhabha— with a nod toward Benedict Anderson—holds out the possibility that what he calls "counter-narratives" can "disturb ideological manoeuvres through which 'imagined communities' are given essential identities," I argue that "ambivalence" and "counter-narrative" hold forth only the most limited potential for critique. The notion of ambivalence valorizes— or at least codifies as a valorized epistemological stance—the state of ironic oscillation between a dominant discourse and its subversive other; neither negation nor sublation is seen as important, much less necessary, for its oppositional character to be felt. Similarly, the notion of counter-narrative (like its close cousin, counterdiscourse) signifies that prevailing ideological paradigms can give rise to oppositional alternatives that are not themselves connected with a historical process engaged in dialectical negation of those ruling paradigms. Both of these suppositions, I argue, are called into question by the accommodationist workings of the discourse of postwar cultural pluralism, which provided the paradigm shaping the practice of many putatively oppositional critics of the day. What the notions of ambivalence and counternarrative/discourse expose but then mask is a series of incompatible propositions about nation, race, and class that produce not so much irony and complexity as confusion. Metonymic nationalism, I contend, is constituted by a series of aporias generated by the inevitably class-collaborationist character of nationalism and the discourses by which it claims legitimation. Its culturalist premise is thus inseparable from its political functionality as the discourse of loyal oppositionist Americanism.[1]

I use the term *metonymy* rather than *metaphor* to point to a quality distinctive to metonymy, namely, its tendency, as C. Carroll Hollis puts it, to "remind us of what we already know," whereas metaphor more generally invokes "what we do not know or had not thought of until that moment." Wai-chee Dimock, along comparable lines, argues that metonymy "would seem to be a cognitive form especially open to cultural conditioning, since the notions of the 'representative,' the 'generalizable,' invariably carry with them a silent set of normative assumptions." I refer to the distinction between metonymy and metaphor with some hesitation, for I do not want to engage in the formalistic exercise of claiming that metonymy is inherently reactionary and metaphor inherently progressive—not least because the inverse has been claimed. My purpose in specifying the discursive operation I am investigating as "*metonymic nationalism,*" not simply "metaphorical nationalism," is to highlight the particular capacity for redundancy and overdetermination that is invested in metonymy. As David Simpson has argued in a discussion of Walt Whitman as the figure in U.S. literary history quintessentially practicing and embodying metonymy in the service of nationalism, metonymy is "the trope of self-sufficient independence: each person or thing is imaged by a part or attribute of himself." Metonymy is especially useful in communicating connections and relations that have an "always already" quality to them: one *re*-cognizes the embeddedness of one thing in another. Metonymy thus usefully describes the signifying chain through which the cultural pluralists sought to link the part to the whole, the local to the national. To show that the first item in the chain—whether soil, folk, or region—belongs in the last or that the last is always already constituted by the first is to portray by means of an aesthetic of inclusive representation what should be acknowledged—that is, taken for granted —as a politics of inclusive representation. Coupled with nationalism, metonymy is thus especially suited to speak to the liberal conscience of an imagined democratic body politic. It is also positioned to construe those features of a social group that are "re-cognized" as features of, specifically, *identity.* Charles Taylor, one of the key founding theorists of contemporary identity politics, has made explicit the connections among recognition, nationalism, and multiculturalism: "A number of strands in contemporary politics turn on the need, sometimes the demand, for *recognition.* The need, it can be argued, is one of the driving forces behind nationalist movements in politics. And the demand comes to the fore in a number of ways in today's politics, on behalf of minority or 'subaltern' groups, in some forms of feminism, and in what is today called the politics of 'multiculturalism.'" One of my goals in designating the characteristic representational practice of postwar cultural pluralists as "metonymic nationalism" is not only to describe the links they established between nationalism and culturalism in the wake of 1919 but also to suggest their continuing relevance to the project of late-twentieth-century identity politics.[2]

Central to my analysis of metonymic nationalism in 1919, however, is the essentialization of race, the fetishization of place, and the characteristic function of the organic trope in mediating between the two. My argument targets a key irony: it was largely the embrace of nationalism by leftists and progressives, black and white, that ended up facilitating the perpetuation of the very notions of racial difference that these critics hoped to eradicate by asserting the Negro's claim to full citizenship. Where the nativists would declare that the nomad, cosmopolitan doctrines of proletarian radicalism could—or at least should—never take root in American soil, their opponents would contend that the germination and sprouting of multifarious folk cultures were essential elements in a full national harvest. Where the eugenicists would assert that certain racial groups bore bad seeds that could never grow into trees bearing authentic American fruit, the cultural pluralists would insist on the ease of transplantation and the benefit to the nation of diversified cultivation. The healthy—and ineradicable—rootedness of non-Anglo-Saxon culture(s) in the nation's soil, a trope pervasive in cultural pluralist discourse of the 1920s, feeds readily into a second central trope: namely, the portrayal of these cultures' distinctive "gifts" as "contributions" to the nation. Although cultural pluralist doctrine entered into debate with prevailing racist and xenophobic ideologies to point up the contingency— that is, the socially constructed nature—of 100 percent Americanism, it often produced the counterdiscourse of "our America"—the well-chosen title of Waldo Frank's 1919 manifesto—in the terms of a folkish primitivism that fell back on reified conceptions of race. The progressives' call for the inclusion and belonging of a soil-soaked folk in the nation could— and frequently did—usher in the back door the notions of inexpungable racial difference that, as explicit statements of racial hierarchy, had been denied entry through the front. The pluralist notion that different groups bring different "gifts" to the nation's democratic feast could easily blur into the essentialist notion that each group was by nature "gifted" in distinct and unique ways. A social constructionist conception of "America" did not necessitate social constructionist conceptions of its component parts. The part/whole paradigm central to both the politics and the epistemology of metonymic nationalism presupposed the irreducible and contradiction-free nature of the various units constituting the constructed totality. Although culturalism—epitomized in the project of *The New Negro*—was intended to eradicate notions of racial hierarchy, the nationalist linkage of culture with soilness—embedded in the etymological connection between "culture" and "cultivation" of the earth—produced a logic that worked in the opposite direction.

I attempt to get at some of the key aporias in metonymic nationalism through a series of related binaries: nationalism versus internationalism, evolutionism versus revolutionism, immediacy versus mediation, nature versus history, idealism versus materialism, formalism versus realism, roots as belonging versus roots as structural cause. Many of these oppositions derive from a Marxist paradigm for approaching the relationship of discourse to ideology and do not stem directly from the problematic of metonymic nationalism as such. Without imposing homologous equivalences among these binaries, however—and creating my own kind of metonymic reductionism—I demonstrate that, in the debates over cultural pluralism versus 100 percent Americanism in the early 1920s, the discourse of metonymic nationalism habitually called on several of these oppositions, in one or another combination. Although I make no claim for its equivalent explanatory force in other times and places, I propose metonymic nationalism as an informing rubric for understanding ideological contradiction at this singular historical conjuncture. Providing an epistemological bridge between class struggle and political doctrine, on the one hand, and literary representation, on the other, the concept of metonymic nationalism performs a dual explanatory function in my argument. On the level of ideological analysis, it enables me to examine the links among liberalism, nationalism, and racial essentialism. On the level of methodology, it grounds discourses in material causality, thus offering a historically specific—and adequately mediated—instance of the base-superstructure paradigm indispensable to Marxist cultural inquiry.

Let me emphasize how I am viewing "rootedness" as the carrier of an especially heavy load of ideological freight in the various pluralist counterdiscourses constituting metonymic nationalism. I am not asserting that every metaphorical reference to plant growth in all of literature —or even all of the literature produced in the particular historical conjuncture under consideration—has to summon up the full agenda of metonymic nationalism. In T. S. Eliot's "Waste Land," for instance, the symbolic use of roots—"What are the roots that clutch, what branches grow

/ Out of this stony rubbish?"—extends to metaphysical considerations of "belonging" that take in a good deal more than nation. Similarly, in William Carlos Williams's "Spring and All," the deeply rooted plants that "stir / And begin to awaken" signify life forces beyond those in northern New Jersey or, for that matter, the United States. By contrast, Arna Bontemps's deployment of the organic trope in "A Black Man Talks of Reaping" requires a historically specific decoding. After declaring that he has "sown beside all waters in my day" and "planted deep," the poem's speaker bitterly concludes:

> Yet what I sowed and what the orchard yields
> My brother's sons are gathering stalk and root,
> Small wonder then my children glean in fields
> They have not sown, and feed on bitter fruit.

The phrase "my brother's son" signifies not the family of man but the family of man in the Jim Crow South, where mulatto and white "brothers," inheriting the biological legacy of the rape of black women, inherit differential portions of the wealth yielded by the land. Those who sow as sharecroppers do not reap as owners. Bontemps's use of the organic trope does not celebrate a folk close to the land but instead lays bare the racist antagonisms—which are simultaneously class antagonisms—that make his "black man" who "speaks of reaping" unsuited to represent a seamless national polity. Like Carita Owens Collins's "This Must Not Be!" (see chapter 1), Bontemps's poem introduces metaphors of planting and harvest to accent the alienation of black people from the system that denies them the product of their labor. Its metaphorizing procedure thus differs significantly from that ordinarily followed in the discourse of metonymic nationalism and challenges the fetishized rhetoric of "rootedness" which often accompanied that discourse.[3]

The tropes deployed by writers working in the crucible of 1919 were thus not simply "determined" by the dominant discourse—at least, not in the sense of "determination" that implies inevitability. But to say that the dominant discourse was dominant means just that: it possessed the rhetorical advantage. As seen in the previous chapter, nativism and eugenics were widely promoted through the various ideological state apparatuses of the day. I argue here that, in the context of 1919 and its aftermath, the organic trope possessed an ideological charge such that even attenuated usages, invoking relatively few elements in the trope's constellation of constituent terms, would invoke the discourse of metonymic nationalism. The political crisis encountered by capitalism in the aftermath of the war was severe enough to engender a discourse of racist antiradicalism aimed at interpellating the average American as a loyal (white) patriot. This rhetorically overdetermined discourse, often projected through the organic trope, was signaled by a quality that I call the "hyper-materiality of the signifier." By this phrase, I designate an aura of extreme—one might say, excessive—concreteness in the representation of the elements constituting the trope, such that vehicle overwhelms, and at times conflates with, tenor. As an example, I adduce Aloysius Coll's "Washington," which appeared in William Stanley Braithwaite's *Anthology of Magazine Verse for 1920*. In this aptly titled poem, the buildings of the capital city are heralded for their promise of democracy: compared to a "white ship" on a "maiden trip" down a "universal river," the Capitol dome in particular inscribes the nation as a "clean new Rome of an unwritten epic." Lodged amidst these quite conventional images, however, is a startling use of the organic trope: the Capitol is said to be "Seeded in the earth like a clean deep tap root—/ The granite in the oak of her boughs today!" By a quite extraordinary imagistic feat, the round-domed stone seat of Congress takes on organic qualities; it is "rooted" in the land and thus lays claim to a "natural" basis for its claim to be the new Rome.[4]

Striking in itself, Col's use of the organic trope here takes on added importance when one considers the aesthetic-cum-political argument embedded in other poems in Braithwaite's anthology. The volume is prefaced by Carl Van Doren's lament that U.S. culture lacks "tap-rooting" in inherited traditions; rejecting as "exotic" both Native American and Negro cultures, Van Doren bemoans the necessity of settling for rootedness in a shallower soil. Among many other poems debating the meaning of Americanism, the volume also contains Carl Sandburg's harshly unpatriotic "Tangibles," which portrays the Capitol as evanescent and unreal. Can a woman who has lost a beloved man in the recent carnage of the war, asks Sandburg, "find ... here ... something ... men die for," or must she instead "go sad, singing and red out of the float of this dome?" (Sandburg's ellipses). Col's poem answers such doubts by proclaiming that the stone of state power and the root of personal belonging are one and the same; the image's hyper-materiality, verging on the grotesque, cannot be fully grasped apart from this ideological context. The discourse of rootedness, brought to the fore by the rhetoric of racist antiradicalism, has, as it were, gone into the groundwater of the political unconscious; Col's invocation of this discourse to assure doubters and questioners is as saturated in the rhetoric of nationalism as are his poem's more explicit declarations of fealty to *patria*. Such subliminal workings of the organic trope were, as will be seen, prevalent in the discourse of many postwar progressives and leftists, revealing the confluence of nationalism, culturalism, and, not infrequently, essentialist notions of race, even as the first two of these were thought to have superseded the last.[5]

The notion that a "good" self-determinationist nationalism can be deployed to counter the noxious influence of "bad" imperialist and racist nationalism has its genesis in the era of 1919. It continues to crop up to this day—even in texts that passionately seek to dissociate themselves from the tragic consequences wrought in the twentieth century by nationalism, both the reactionary and putatively progressive kinds. In *The Black Atlantic: Modernity and Double Consciousness* (1993), Paul Gilroy laments, "Marked by its European origins, modern black political culture has always been more interested in the relationship of identity to roots and rootedness than in seeing identity as a process of movement and mediation that is more appropriately approached via the homonym routes." Hybridity, he argues, offers an alternative to the racial essentialism attendant upon notions of identity fixated on place. In his more recent *Against Race: Imagining Political Culture beyond the Color Line* (2000), Gilroy presses his argument against the rhetoric of rootedness, proposing that "invocations of organicity . . . forg[e] an uncomfortable connection between the warring domains of nature and culture," making "nation and citizenship appear to be natural rather than social phenomena—spontaneous expressions of a distinctiveness that was palpable in deep inner harmony between people and their dwelling places." The alternative, he now proposes, is the notion of "diaspora," which he finds "a useful means to reassess the idea of essential and absolute identity precisely because it is incompatible with that type of nationalist and raciological thinking." He elaborates in an extended metaphorical and genealogical commentary:

> The word comes closely associated with the idea of sowing seed. This etymological inheritance is a disputed legacy and a mixed blessing. It demands that we attempt to evaluate the significance of the scattering process against the supposed uniformity of that which has been scattered. Disapora posits important tensions between here and there, then and now, between seed in the bag, the packet, or the pocket and seed in the ground, the fruit, or the body. By focusing attention equally on the sameness within differentiation and the differentiation within sameness, diaspora disturbs the suggestion that political and cultural identity might be understood via the analogy of indistinguishable peas lodged in the protective pods of closed kinship and subspecies being. Is it possible to imagine how a more complex, ecologically sophisticated sense of interaction between organisms and environments might become an asset in thinking critically about identity?[6]

Traced to its etymological origin signifying "sowing seed," Gilroy's trope of diaspora offers a paradigm for formulating identity clearly superior to that contained in the "nationalist or raciological thinking" embedded in the trope of roots and rootedness, dependent as this latter trope is on constructions of selfhood formed within the "protective pods of closed kinship and subspecies being." Moreover, Gilroy's conception of diaspora avoids the implication of biological purity that is embedded in the notion of hybridity, which, it has been pointed out, affirms the very essentialism that it would transcend. Nonetheless, it is questionable whether even "diaspora," imagistically and conceptually wedded as it is to the hyper-materiality of its underlying organic metaphor, manages to negate and supersede the fetishization of place—and hence of nation—conveyed by a botanical trope still reliant on the notion of seeds if not seed, soils if not soil. The point at issue here is more than a quibble over metaphor (or metonymy). While Gilroy's glossing upon "diaspora" asserts that the trope directs attention equally to the "here and there" and the "then and now," its emphasis on geographical dissemination not only links identity with place more than with history but also suggests a randomness in the cause for dispersal: the vagaries of historical conjuncture, rather than the structural imperatives of capitalism, have sown the seeds of global migration. Moreover, as with the argument for "routes" over "roots" in *The Black Atlantic*, the argument for "diaspora" as the key to identity in *Against Race* retains the biologistic implication that a distinct people, as carriers of a distinct seed, have come to inhabit a distinct terrain (or, more accurately, terrains). Although potentially alluding to the radically antinationalist—that is, "cosmopolitan"—tendency within proletarian internationalism that specifies imperialism as the source of inequality and urges the workers of the world to unite, Gilroy's use of the term *diaspora* more closely resembles the formulation of "nation" by Otto Bauer in the early-twentieth-century debates over the national question—that is, as a "people" possessing "a common psychology and a common fate," even if they have been scattered to the winds. The notion of diaspora thus fails to exempt itself from, and in fact subtly confirms, the very "nationalist or raciological thinking" that Gilroy evidently aspires to negate and transcend. But the blame hardly rests at Gilroy's door, for, in its echo of Bauer, his notion of diaspora invokes that position within the discourse of internationalism (that is, inter-*nation*-alism) that, originating in the debate over self-determination and the national question among the early-twentieth-century Left, also carried within itself, and failed to sublate, that which it would supersede. That the distinction between good and bad nationalisms should continue, at century's end, to shape even such explicitly antinationalist arguments as those advanced by Gilroy should help place in context the enormous appeal that the rhetoric of self-determination would hold for progressives and leftists in 1919 and its immediate aftermath. Then the contradictions of self-determinationist nationalism were present only *in nuce,* and its historical consequences were unforeseen.[7]

"Multiplicity . . . in Unity": Cultural Pluralism and Liberalism

Although the dominant ideology in the era of 1919 equated nation with race and the dominant practice was one of ruthless repression, not all members of—or ideologists for—the ruling elite saw 100 percent Americanism as the most effective way to banish the spectre of the Seattle Soviet or the gun-brandishing New Negro. The liberal alternative to 100 percent Americanism initially voiced the anxieties of policymakers who feared that excessive repression and antiradicalism instead of squelching workers' revolts would fan the flames of class discontent and rebellion. The industrialist and wartime dollar-a-year man Alexander Bing deplored his fellow capitalists' "invitations to violence" against striking workers and warned that repression would only stoke the fires of the "uncompromisingly revolutionary" IWW. Urging his peers to recognize unions and engage in arbitration—taking a page, it would appear, from the right-wing Socialists—Bing concluded, "An attitude of irreconcilable hostility [to unions] by big business interests runs contrary to the processes of social evolution." The former labor organizer turned journalist Frank Tannenbaum, displaying the new concern with psychology among industrial relations experts, called on industrialists to study the "psychology of the labor movement" and listen to the workers' grievances. If properly handled and directed toward "cooperation" rather than "economic struggle," the labor movement, he asserted, could take on "a highly conservative function . . . transmut[ing] economic interests to spiritual values and mak[ing] progress pragmatic rather than violently revolutionary." The labor historian John R. Commons, although favoring immigration restriction in the case of foreign-born radicals, advocated collective bargaining with the moderate trade union leadership and urged an end to capitalist "despotism." Capitalists should concentrate on "Americanizing" native-born workers, not immigrants, he recommended; the main danger to business stability consisted not in agitators from overseas but in U.S. workers rising up angry. The liberal journalist Ray Stannard Baker—who, having served as Woodrow Wilson's press attaché in Paris, knew something about the discourse of self-determination—commented in 1920 that "there never was before in America such a number of revolutionary groups, or so widespread a propaganda of radicalism." The repressive tactics used by Judge Gary and his henchmen during the great steel strike, he warned, might "make for the very revolution which they think they are preventing." These liberal appeals to a kinder and gentler notion of the national interest were explicitly linked to the fear of intensified class struggle.[8]

Even as plans were being hatched for the Americanization of obstreperous native-born labor, the call was also being issued for a more humane and inclusive approach to the foreign-born. American cultural pluralism, which rewrote anticolonial self-determination as the American exceptionalist celebration of ethnic difference, was an important concomitant to the postwar co-optation of and assault on labor. Thus in 1920 the public education theorist Isaac Berkson decried "melting-pot" theories of Americanization premised on a normative Anglo-Saxon ideal that required immigrants to "forge[t] other languages and other traditions" and "sever [their] loyalty to the past lived on a foreign soil." What was needed, Berkson declared, was a "positive" Americanization based on a recognition that "[t]o conceive of America as belonging exclusively to one race, because priority of habitation has given it a divine right to possession of the land, is a notion contrary to democracy." Not assimilation, Berkson concluded, but "self-determination" is the "quintessence of democracy." Implicitly aligning his project with the struggle of the American revolutionary opponents of monarchy and with current movements for national liberation, Berkson portrayed the U.S. immigrant population as the bearer of modernity. In his formulation, the self-determination of multiple racial and ethnic groups, while signaling the socially constructed nature of "America," in no way contradicted the notion of *e pluribus unum*. Where Lenin had hailed the gathering of workers from all lands in the capitalist metropoles as a demographic shift that would break down national barriers and foster the development of class consciousness—and hence hasten proletarian revolution—Berkson's invocation of self-determination implied quite the opposite conclusion: cultural pluralism would at once maintain separate national identities and enhance loyalty to the newly gained capitalist nation. Berkson's ideal of a multiply-rooted citizenry was the inverse of Mary Austin's nightmare vision of the Jew with roots extended to Jerusalem; both, however, had as their goal strengthened ties between populace and polity.[9]

Berkson's ideals were codified in the government-sponsored publishing project, begun in 1921, entitled "Americanization Studies: Acculturation of Immigrant Groups into American Society." The texts published under the rubric of this project all contained a preface advocating that "Americanization should perpetuate no unchangeable political, domestic, and economic regime delivered once for all to the fathers but a growing and broadening national life, inclusive of the best wherever found." In *Old World Traits Transplanted* (1921), the series's inaugural volume, the sociologists William H. Thomas, Robert E. Park, and Herbert A. Miller proposed that "a wise policy of assimilation, like a wise educational policy, does not seek to destroy the attitudes and memories that are there, but to build upon them." Opposing the conservatives' demand for a "quick and complete Americanization through the suppression and repudiation all the signs that distinguish [the immigrant] from us," the authors suggested that the nation's strength rested with its diversity. In *The Immigrant's Day in Court* (1923), the civil libertarian Kate Holladay Claghorn chastised the government for the postwar repression and pointed out that immigrants whose civil liberties had not been violated would make better citizens and more pliable workers. A comparable set of texts called the "Contributions Series"—including such texts as George Cohen's *Jews in the Making of America* and W. E. B. Du Bois's *Gift of Black Folk*, both published in 1924—sought to expand tolerance for both immigrants and racial minorities by delineating these groups' distinctive donations to America. Du Bois's designation of the distinctive African American offering as the "gift" of laughter reveals the peculiar compatibility of near-essentialist notions of race with the socially constructed notion of gift as a contribution to the pluralist homeland. His own "contribution" to the Americanization series constitutes, arguably, one of the most conservative and least analytically probing texts in Du Bois's remarkably zig-zagging career as writer and theorist.[10]

It is widely acknowledged that the theoretical rationale for the cultural pluralists' ecumenical conception of citizenship was provided in large part by the Columbia University sociologist Horace Kallen, who, in a highly influential pair of 1915 *Nation* articles tellingly entitled "Democracy versus the Melting-Pot," brought into widespread use the term *cultural pluralism* to denote this new and improved version of nonassimilationist Americanism. Alluding to such advocates of immigration restriction as Edward A. Ross, Kallen noted that "what troubles [them] is not really inequality, [but] . . . difference." Yet "multiplicity in . . . unity," he argued, was exactly what makes for the "orchestration of mankind." Kallen then produced the extended metaphor that would become the *locus classicus* of cultural pluralist doctrine:

As in an orchestra every type of instrument has its specific timbre and tonality, founded in its substance and form; as every type has its appropriate theme and melody in the whole symphony, so in society, each ethnic group is the natural instrument, its spirit and culture are its theme and melody, and the harmony and dissonances and discords of them all may make the symphony of civilization. With this difference: a musical symphony is written before it is played; in the symphony of civilization the playing is the writing, so that there is nothing so fixed and inevitable about its progressions as in music, so that within the limits set by nature and luck they may vary at will, and the range and variety of the harmonies may become wider and richer and more beautiful—or the reverse.

Kallen's utopian portrait of human community—which would exercise considerable influence on progressive/liberal thinking about race, ethnicity, and nation for more than a decade—was clearly premised on the celebration rather than the eradication of difference. With his emphasis on performativity ("the playing is the writing") and his view of the symphony of civilization as fluid and uncontrolled by any totalizing score ("there is nothing so fixed and inevitable about its progressions as in music"), Kallen voiced an early formulation of "jouissance" that suggestively links the rhetoric of liberal pluralism with that of postmodernism.[11]

Kallen's cultural program provided grounds for contesting the reactionary agenda of the 100 percenters. He was aware of the value of racist and xenophobic doctrine to ruling elites, ending his 1915 orchestra analogy with the query, "[D]o the dominant classes in America want such a society?" In 1918, contemplating the slaughter during the Great War, he wrote that "the society we live in is basically a system of taboos . . . set by class for mass, by property for humanity." Kallen castigated the Humphreys of *Mankind: Racial Values and the Racial Prospect* for being a member of the "Pan Germanist priesthood" and decried the "total absence of anthropological and archaeological evidence" behind Humphreys's claim that all great civilizations had been "Aryan." In 1924, Kallen observed that the multiplying "literature on race" functioned as "capitalist apologetics." Mobilizing the organic trope beloved by the evolutionists, Kallen turned the metaphor of the tree of humanity against his antagonists. Rejecting Gobineau's claim that the only "family tree" worth mention was the "Nordic" one, Kallen observed, "Speculation has it that the races of men are diversified fruits of a single seed. They have crossed, separated, and recrossed from before history, and they have grown in number and in kind." Kallen's sympathetic presentation of the view that all people are "diversified fruits of a single seed," possessing a "common heritage," called into question the eugenicists' claims of racial hierarchy.

Where Wilson had envisioned the hyphen as a dagger in the entrails of the nation, Kallen argued that the hyphen "connects instead of separates." Enlisting to cultural pluralist ends the nativists' favored tropes and catch-phrases, Kallen formulated a counterdiscourse aimed at destabilizing his antagonists' linguistic hegemony in the project of defining Americanism.[12]

Nonetheless, Kallen's proposal that human unity derives from diversity was neither free of biological reductionism nor premised on egalitarianism. As Werner Sollors and Walter Benn Michaels have pointed out, Kallen's notion that the different instruments in the orchestra of the nation possess fundamentally different timbres and tonalities—qualities intrinsic to the instruments—reinforced essentialist notions of racial difference. Moreover, Kallen's assurance that his version of "democracy" would entail not forced miscegenation but the provision of the "conditions under which each [of the existing ethnic and cultural groups] might attain the cultural perfection that is proper to its kind" hardly amounted to the call for an end to segregation. In his critique of Humphreys, Kallen distinguished sharply between what he called "racial mythology" and "legitimate eugenics." "That the superior are for a variety of reasons infertile, that the multiplication of the inferior is excessive," he wrote, are "matters deserving the deepest attention of the classes concerned with the conservation of the race, in whatever nation." Implying his own identification with these superior but insufficiently fertile "classes," Kallen embraced a eugenic program not altogether different from that set forth in Wiggam's *Fruit of the Family Tree*.[13]

While Kallen's proponents routinely praise his championing of democratic pluralism, his call for a progressive—that is, inclusive—American nationalism was explicitly based on what he viewed as the failure of socialist internationalism. "The history of the 'International' prior to the Great War, the present *debacle* in Europe are indications of how little 'class-consciousness' modifies other types of consciousness, including consciousness of nationality and patriotism," he remarked. "[S]imilarity of class rests upon no inevitable external condition: while similarity of nationality has usually a considerable intrinsic base. Hence the poor of two different peoples tend to be less like-minded than the poor and the rich of the same peoples." Like the right-wing SPA theorist John Spargo, Kallen evidently believed that nationalistic bonding could be traced not to the impress of bourgeois ideology but to an innate human need—notably, a "psychological" need—to ally and identify on the basis of common biological and geographical lineage. The global trend toward cultural nationalism and self-determination, he wrote, is an "inevitable" consequence of the "democratic principle" upon which the United States is fortunate enough to have been founded. While he might dub Nordicist ideology "capitalist apologetics," he apparently viewed capitalism as separable from democratic government. In 1924, he opined that "any citizen of the United States who . . . uses his citizenship to the disadvantage of his own country for the sake of an enemy is properly called traitor and deserves to be treated as such." As an enraged *Liberator* reviewer observed, "This means that those who opposed the entrance of this country into the European war against the wishes of Morgan were traitors and that those who carried on a propaganda to get this country into war were patriots." Carrie Bramen has pointed out that Kallen "universalized the minority position as quintessentially American, so that subcultural uniqueness became a source of national exceptionalism." To this insight I would add that Kallen's advocacy of both cultural pluralism and American exceptionalism was premised on a rejection of proletarian internationalism. Sollors and Michaels correctly point out the racist overtones accompanying Kallen's orchestra analogy; Michaels in particular argues that cultural pluralism, Kallen-style, not only essentialized race but also racialized culture. What these critiques overlook, however, is the role played by nationalism in hitching culture to race. The conception of the nation's culture as fluidly constituted and pluralistic was premised on the conception of its components as marked by fixed capacities; Kallen's social constructionist notion of the nation did not simply permit but actually required essentialist notions of its component races and ethnicities.[14]

The organic trope figured significantly in the discursive field of postwar liberalism and more than any other displaced the metaphor of the melting pot favored by the prewar Progressive assimilationists. The authors of *Old World Traits Transplanted*, as their title indicates, viewed immigrants as bearers not of alien spores or soil-sapping parasites but of mature and hardy (and presumably fruit-bearing) plants that simply required rerooting in the hospitable soil of the United States. The editors of *American Hebrew* opted for the symbol of the nation as a tree to encode immigrants' contributions (see figure 16). Immigration, the drawing asserts, is the trunk bringing nutrients to the nation's various fruits. Where Gobineau's racial tree excludes all "races" but the Nordic, Haeckel's evolutionary tree posits some groups closer to the primeval stem than others, and Wiggam's "family tree" comprises only Anglo-Saxon and upper-class branches, the tree pictured in *American Hebrew* declares that all groups "belong" to the nature that is the nation. Yet in proposing that "old world traits," when "transplanted" to American soil, would preserve their unique characteristics, the Chicago sociologists were suggesting that different cultures possess the distinctness of botanical species;

WOODMAN, SPARE THAT TREE.

"Woodman, spare that tree!   In youth it shelter'd me,
Touch not a single bough!   And I'll protect it now."

Figure 16. "Woodman, Spare That Tree," by Israel, *American Hebrew*, January 1916 "difference" still retained the stamp of biology. The editors of *American Hebrew*, while demonstrating the fallacy of equating the nation with Anglo-Saxon heritage, suggest that the labor of the worker is, as one more piece of fruit, equivalent to the occupation of the lawyer or the businessperson. Ostensibly providing a better, because more inclusive, representation of social relations, the tree analogy actually obscures the structural relation of classes. The politics of "contribution" thus at once perpetuated race-based notions of innate difference and clouded the reality of the exploitation that gave rise to this difference—indeed, to the very idea of race—in the first place. Pluralism, racism, and capitalist exploitation found in the ideologically saturated organic trope mutually accommodating means of representation.[15]

Paralleling in cultural policy what the proponents of labor co-optation were urging in public policy, Kallen and like-minded pluralists clearly diverged, in both substance and rhetoric, from the nativists and the eugenicists; liberals and conservatives were proposing quite different versions of the American Plan. For the nativists and eugenicists, the "other" of 100 percent Americanism was mongrelization and radicalism; for their pluralist opponents, it was, in Kallen's phrase, "Kultur Ku Klux Klan": the culture war was real. Nonetheless, these groups converged in their vision— their advocacy—of a nation untroubled by internal schisms. Americanism entailed an *e pluribus unum* in which diverse groups would not conflict but instead would contribute their respective mites—"gifts"—to the nation's productivity and wealth, cultural and material. A minority discourse in the aftermath of 1919, cultural pluralism would war for hegemony through the decades to come; as multiculturalism, it would attain the status of dominant ideology by century's end. From the outset, however, it was always an opposition loyal to American democratic capitalism, whose "other"—cosmopolitan communism—was unthinkable.[16]

"The First International Nation": Young America

The loyal oppositionist tendency among the postwar critics of American nationalism is epitomized in the avant-garde group calling itself, appropriately, Young America. Not to be confused with the mid-nineteenth-century New York circle surrounding Evert Duyckinck and George Duyckinck, the Young Americans of the late 1910s and early 1920s took as their project the creation of a national culture that would provide—in Van Wyck Brooks's oft-repeated term—a "usable past." Initially clustered around the *Seven Arts*—which proclaimed in 1916 that "we are living in the first days of a renascent period"—and such short-lived "little magazines" as *Others, Soil, Prairie,* and *Nomad,* the Young Americans took shape as a self-consciously counterdiscursive movement that would encourage and nurture "an expression of our American arts which shall be fundamentally an expression of our American life." The best-known representatives of this group advocating a recapture of the "our" in "our American life" were Van Wyck Brooks, Waldo Frank, Hart Crane, Lewis Mumford, Alfred Stieglitz, and the prematurely deceased Randolph Bourne; others included Harold Stearns, Paul Rosenfeld, James Oppenheim, Gorham Munson, and, briefly, Jean Toomer. Young America based much of its understanding of the malady besetting the nation on Brooks's Freudian-inflected 1915 diagnosis that U.S. cultural history had been shaped by the unfortunate dual legacy of "puritans" and "pioneers." The former, Brooks argued, had promoted a repressed ethic of self-denial and authoritarianism, while the latter had sublimated the citizenry's energies into the pursuit of material welfare. Young America, by contrast, saw itself as, in Frank's words, the first generation of Americans consciously engaged in "spiritual pioneering"—a formulation linking their project with not the rejection but the revision of manifest destiny. Linking the recent discourse of cultural pluralism with inherited traditions of literary regionalism, the Young Americans laid out the logic of metonymic nationalism and signaled the centrality of the organic trope to the counterdiscourse through which they aspired to represent "our America" and contest the hegemony of "Kultur Ku Klux Klan." Through Locke and Toomer, their impact on the New Negro movement would be considerable: the "Young" in Young America would bear suggestive parallels with the "New" in New Negro.[17]

Self-styled inheritors of the mantle of American romanticism, several of the Young Americans voiced a pastoral yearning barely distinguishable from a Thoreauvian revulsion against commercialism and the machine. Although Munson, in the early 1920s infatuated with dadaism, viewed the machine as the embodiment of progressive modernity, Mumford's ideal of the city was shaped in contradistinction to the "new form of human barbarism" embodied in the industrial city of the "Machine Age." Brooks opined that U.S. civilization had been "bled and flattened out by the Machine Process." If the Young Americans differed in their estimates of industrialism, however, all of them considered themselves well left of center—at least in the immediate postwar years—and stipulated one or another form of socialism as integral to their program for revivifying the national culture. In *America's Coming-of-Age* (1915), Brooks conjoined his vision of individual development with a recognition of collective need. If "self-fulfillment as an ideal" is to be "substituted for self-assertion as an ideal," he wrote, "[o]n an economic plane this implies socialism. On every other plane it implies something which the majority of Americans in our day certainly do not possess—an object in living." Socialism, he concluded—invoking a somewhat odd trilogy—is "based on those three things in the world which have the most dignity—hunger, science, and good will." In a 1921 *Freeman* article, Brooks expressed support for the Russian Revolution and proposed that writers should be valued for the extent that they "have . . . presented to the workers of America . . . images of a greater, a freer, a more beautiful life than they are capable themselves of associating with reality." Mumford praised the "Marxian analysis of society" for "presenting a great dream—the dream of a titanic struggle between the possessors and the dispossessed in which every worker had a definite part to play." Moreover, he chided socialists for their reformism: "By a revolution [the socialists] do not mean a transvaluation of values. They mean a dilution and spreading out of established practices and institutions." That even such mild social critics as Brooks and Mumford should consider themselves opponents of capitalism testifies to the leftward trend of the period. Looking back on the early 1920s, Brooks later commented, "Every writer I came to know called himself a radical, committed to some program for changing and improving the world."[18]

Bourne, more explicitly anticapitalist than either Brooks or Mumford, wrote about exploitation in broadly Marxian terms: "[T]he very food we eat, the clothes we wear, the simplest necessities of life . . . have their roots somewhere, somehow, in exploitation and injustice. It is a cardinal necessity of the social system under which we live that this should be so, where the bulk of the work of the world is done, not for human use and happiness, but primarily and directly for the profits of masters and owners." There were even Leninist undertones to Bourne's 1918 essay "The State," famous for its repeated declaration, "War is the health of the State." Distinguishing between the country and the state, Bourne argued that the state is an instrument of coercion and that especially in times of war, when the "revolutionary proletariat" is baited as "heretics," the "sanctity of the State becomes identified with the sanctity of the ruling class and the latter are permitted to remain in power under the impression that in obeying and serving them, we are obeying and serving society, the nation, the great collectivity of all of us." The flag, Bourne asserted, is "not a symbol of the country as a cultural group, following certain ideals of life, but solely a symbol of the political State, inseparable from its prestige and expansion. . . . The flag is primarily a banner of war." Bourne unabashedly analyzed society in class terms and repudiated the pseudo-collectivity promulgated in patriotic propaganda. At the same time, Bourne's distinction between the country and the state, accompanied by his view of the country as a "cultural group, following certain ideals of life," indicates his espousal of Deweyan categories of social analysis. Bourne's formulation of culture was essentially "cultura*list*": culture consisted in "democratic cooperation in determining the ideas and purposes and industrial and social constitutions of a country." For Bourne, then, culture served at once to expose the ideological stratagems of the ruling class and to propose a national unity beyond class altogether.[19]

Frank's *Our America* (1919), more than any other text the manifesto of Young America, uttered a clarion call for democratization at once cultural and social. Its critique of capitalism was based partly on a romantic rejection of modern technology. "The average New Yorker is caught in a Machine," Frank declared; "if he resists the Machine will mangle him." Yet Frank's campaign for revolutionary culture was premised on fundamental political and economic transformation. "Whatever consciousness we have had so far has been the result of vast and deliberate exclusions," he wrote. This consciousness "would fit the citizen for pioneering, prepare him to exploit, or to remain the victim of exploitation." Moreover, Frank adopted a radical political criterion when he praised the "buried culture" of Native Americans for its collectivity. "The uncorrupted Indian knows no individual poverty or wealth," asserted Frank. "All his tribe is either rich or poor." Speaking of the present, Frank praised such midwestern writers as Sandburg and Edgar Lee Masters for realizing that "the 'land of the brave' was in fact a land of greedy and unscrupulous exploiters, and that the 'home of the free' was in fact becoming a people of economic serfs." The rags-to-riches myth only reinforced the worker's continuing entrapment. "[N]ot each American can become a capitalist," warned Frank. "Labor in this country is cheated of its own resurgence by the common myth that any worker may reach the employer's class." For Frank, modernity was retrograde, even neo-feudal, so long as workers remained in thrall—materially and psychologically— to the regime of capital. But, he asserted, "[i]ndustrialism holds the seeds of its own destruction because it can satisfy but a tithe of the humans whose suffrage it requires." The closing words of *Our America*—"In a dying world, creation is revolution"—called for a better world that would be among other things socialist; it is no accident that the section on Chicago writers was reprinted in the SPA's *Call* in March 1920. According to Frank's close associate Munson, *Our America* was written "from a consciously socialist point of view," and its title was intended to differentiate the America of the Young Americans from "Their America," the America of the 100 percenters. An occasional lecturer at the Rand School, Frank openly identified himself with the organized Left—and would do so for many years, serving as the head of the Communist-organized League of American Writers in the mid-1930s.[20]

Answering Kallen's call for cultural pluralism, the Young Americans repudiated the patrician association of nation with race in the doctrines of the Anglo-Saxonists and treated as exemplary the texts of hitherto marginalized social groups—both ethnic minorities and inhabitants of regions removed from the cultural hegemony of New England. Brooks, stressing the promise held in the nation's heady mixture of peoples, analogized the United States with a "vast Sargasso Sea." Frank stressed the centrality of the "buried cultures" of Indians and hispanics to the definition of the oppositional America he was claiming as "ours." Bourne, whose 1918 formulation of a "trans-national America" was directly influenced by Kallen, borrowed Kallen's orchestra metaphor to represent his vision of ideal cultural production and argued that the "Jewish ideal of Zionism" was "the purest pattern and the most inspiring conceptio[n] of trans-nationalism." The United States, site of the gathering of many diasporic peoples, was "the first international nation, already the world-federation in miniature." Moreover, Bourne's definition of culture as entailing "democratic cooperation in determining the ideas and purposes and industrial and social constitutions for a country" meant that his prescription for change was premised on culture as praxis. Stearns, introducing the 1922 anthology *Civilization in the United States,* also envisioned cultural pluralism as the route to freedom. "[W]hatever else American civilization is," he wrote, "it is not Anglo-Saxon. . . . [W]e shall never achieve any genuine nationalistic self-consciousness as long as we allow certain financial and social minorities to persuade us that we are still an English Colony. Until we begin seriously to appraise and warmly to cherish the heterogeneous elements which make up our life, and to see the common element running through all of them, we shall make not even a step toward true unity." Including pieces on—if not by—African Americans and immigrants, Stearns produced the first anthology in the history of American letters that could make a claim to multiculturalism. That he viewed the cultural pluralists' project of wresting "American civilization" from the grasp of "financial and social minorities" to be a continuation of the American colonies' rebellion against the English testifies to his status as loyal opposition. To battle Anglo-Saxonism was to manifest "genuine nationalistic self-consciousness." For Stearns and his colleagues, the most effective way to undermine 100 percent Americanism was to demonstrate the superiority of a pluralistically reconceived "our America."[21]

"The Soil Stands Ready To Be Turned": Troping the Nation

Although the Young Americans used various images and metaphors to convey their mission, their deployment of the organic trope most fully displays the assumptions—and the aporias—accompanying their contribution to the cultural pluralist project. On rare occasions, an imagistic matrix involving roots and soil, plants and fruit appeared in the writings of the Young Americans to delineate relations of a structural and historical nature. Bourne's statement that everyday commodities "have their roots in economic injustice," for example, implies a metaphorical reading of roots as causal foundation; tenor and vehicle can be related only if we abstract from both the common quality of derivation and view this as having primarily a structural character. The materiality of roots here consists in their referencing a historical causality that is operative in time rather than a process of nourishment anchored in a given place. Frank's assertion that "[i]ndustrialism holds the seeds of its own destruction" uses the trope of seeds to suggest, again, systemic causal analysis. Implying that industrialism contains the forces that will lead to its demise, Frank's metaphor recalls Marx's famous metaphor in the *Communist Manifesto*—premised on a troping of earth as something other than site of cultivation and cyclical renewal—that capitalism creates its own gravediggers. Perhaps not coincidentally, these abstracted usages of the organic trope by the Young Americans occur when their assertions are most explicitly historical materialist.

More often, however, the Young Americans used the organic trope to signify the notion of belonging to and in a physically defined place: soil, region, nation. As Brooks later recalled with a touch of self-satire, even in their personal lives the writers with whom he associated in the postwar years—mainly in ex-urban Connecticut—were, like himself, preoccupied with the notion of having (or acquiring) roots: "[I]n many cases the writers had grown up in a still raw West or had returned from Paris in search of 'roots,' that shy and impalpable quiddity the lack of which they felt had made them frequently shallow and generally restless. No word was more constantly on their lips unless it was the native 'soil' or earth and this obsession lay deep in the minds of the urban cosmopolitans whom one saw toiling now and then with spade and pick." The hyper-materiality that "roots" would acquire in the discourse of postwar cultural pluralism evidently had a lived counterpart. Writers metonymically preoccupied with "soilness" also wanted direct contact with the thing itself; presumably many of them could afford the "stake in the land" that Speek and Howe would have the government dangle before potentially restive immigrants.[22]

The Young Americans' obsession with soilness derived partly from their alienation from the mainstream culture that was, in their view, incapable of nourishing the art of modernity. Brooks introduced the organic trope as early as 1908 in *The Wine of the Puritans*, where he reiterated the still earlier complaints of Nathaniel Hawthorne and Henry James regarding the sterility of American culture. "[W]e Americans have no bonds with a remote antiquity, no traditions of the soil old enough as yet to have become instincts," Brooks lamented. In his contribution to Stearns's 1922 anthology, his complaint became more emphatic:

> The creative will in this country is a very weak and sickly plant. . . . Of the innumerable talents that are always emerging about us there are few that come to any sort of fruition: the rest wither early; they are transformed into those neuroses that flourish on our soil as orchids flourish in the green jungle. . . . If our creative spirits are unable to grow and mature, it is a sign that there is something wanting in the soil from which they spring and in the conditions that surround them. Is it not, for that matter, a sign of some more general failure in our life?

Stearns voiced the same complaint in the same anthology using almost the same language:

> [The genteel tradition], which has stolen from the intellectual life its own proper possessions, gaiety and laughter, has left it sour and *deraciné*. It has lost its earthy roots, its sensuous fullness. Thought is nourished by the soil it feeds on, and in America today that soil is choked with the feckless weeds of correctness. Our sanitary perfection, our material organization of goods, our muffling of emotion, our deprecation of curiosity, our fear of idle adventure, our horror of disease and death, our denial of suffering—what kind of soil of life is that?

The "extraordinary feminization of American social life," Stearns added, was the heart of the problem. Since the "pioneer" tradition consigned men exclusively to the business of earning money, "[t]o an extent almost incomprehensible to people of other older cultures, the things of the mind and the spirit have been given out, in America, to the almost exclusive custody of women." The only hope for a national literature, Stearns averred, consisted in the "germinal energy that may yet push its way through the weeds." While Brooks does not share Stearns's misogyny—fructifying seed and barren soil do not constitute a gendered binary for the older writer—it is significant that both men theorize the relation of writer to nation as one in which place supplies or at least ought to supply both energy and identity.[23]

As Young America gained momentum as a self-conscious movement, its participants' use of the organic trope to describe their cultural pluralist mission conveyed an increasingly messianic message. In *Port of New York* (1924), the music critic Paul Rosenfeld observed that the "seed" of European modernism initially "did not take root" in the United States, because it "had its roots in a past which was not ours, and which we might never adopt." Through the efforts of "a dozen or more of artists to find the values again here on the soil, to restate ideas of work and growth and love," however, artists of his generation "have taken root." The poet Alfred Kreymborg—author of the radical call for blood-brotherhood between blacks and whites that was published in the *Crisis* in 1918—also stressed the fertility of New York, where he first came into contact with the "dream of the new soil" being brought into reality by Brooks and Rosenfeld. "No longer did [the aspiring writer] have to dig up a good part of his best energies toward providing manure for the soil," he wrote happily in 1925; Young America itself was fertilizing the land. This process apparently turned the writer—urban citizen though he might be—into an authentic tiller of the nation's soil: Kreymborg dubbed the last chapter of his autobiography "A Folk Tale."[24]

Brooks, Stearns, Rosenfeld, and Kreymborg pressed the organic trope into the service of their nationalist projects by nearly literalizing it: writers formed a "usable past"—one that they could belong to and that could belong to them—by becoming one with the terrain. Culture was the product of cultivation in a sense that went beyond trope: without closeness to, and definition through, the land, it seemed, there could be no meaningful culture at all. Yet the notion that the writers themselves might supply the rich soil to be used for the planting of other writers' seed implied a certain circularity, headed toward aporia: rootedness in place was being conflated with rootedness in culture—which was, however, rooted in its cultivators, who then furnished the needed creative place for one another. The claim that they themselves constituted a "folk," whimsically implied in Kreymborg's autobiography, could not be taken very far.

"To Lift America into Self-Knowledge": Frank and Culturalist Manifest Destiny

It was in the work of Frank that the contradiction between place-based and text-based notions of cultivation would emerge with particular clarity, partly because he was the Young American most fully reliant on the organic trope to announce that revolution above all else was a cultural—indeed culturalist—praxis. Frank praised the "kinetic energy of revolt" he felt in the work of midwestern writers like Sandburg. "Here is water," declared Frank. "[H]ere is the elemental seed. . . . Something is indeed pushing high from the black loam of the prairie[,] [h]igh through the smudge and steel." This conjunction of the urban and the agrarian was central to Frank's vision of a national art and literature, for it was writers gathered from all parts of the United States in New York who, "desir[ing] to create a world of their own to live in," had renewed the cultural life of the nation as a whole. "The vast horizontal Stream that fertilized a continent strains now to become vertical," wrote Frank, "in order to fertilize a heaven." The task facing Frank's generation of "spiritual pioneers" was thus not simply to plant their own seeds and keep them watered but to cultivate and plow and "make loam for the growing prairie. . . . The materialism of the middle-generation falls back to the despair that gave it birth. . . . It burned down the stubble of ancient harvests: it cleared the fields for the new planting. The soil stands ready to be turned."[25]

That Frank envisioned his culturalist program to be profoundly radical is evident from his ringing assertion that "in a dying world, creation is revolution." Yet, for all its pretension to democratic inclusiveness, *Our America* omits any reference to—let alone treatment of—Negro culture; this lack would irk Jean Toomer and inspire him to create, in *Cane*, this crucially missing component in the text of his friend and mentor. The racism manifested in the exclusion of African Americans from his manifesto also surfaced in Frank's discussion of the "buried cultures" of the Southwest; his praise of the egalitarianism of the "uncorrupted Indian" is alloyed by a paternalistic primitivism leading him to conclude that the Indian "has no politics." The excessive concreteness of Frank's use of the organic trope helps occlude the history of oppression that Frank proposes to transcend: "The lowly Mexican is articulate, the lordly American is not. For the Mexican has really dwelt with his soil, cultivated his spirit in it, not alone his maize. He has stooped to conquer. And when you enter the homes of the occasional intelligent Americans of the South-West, you realize how truly the whipped race has won. The walls that cool or warm you, the rug you step on, the food you eat proclaim the Mexican master." That middle-class intellectuals in Taos eat tacos in adobe-walled houses measures the victory of the "lowly Mexican," whose poverty is apparently invisible because he has "cultivated his spirit . . . in his soil." Moreover, Frank's insistent characterization of the emerging generation of writers as "spiritual pioneers" hinged on the occlusion of the past role played by actual pioneers in preparing the way for the industrial urbanization that Frank so distrusted—as well as in entombing the "buried cultures" that Frank wished to revive as carriers of the nation's discursive legacy. The unpleasant parts of national history had to be forgotten— or, more precisely, remapped onto adobe villas—if the nation were to be reappropriated and represented through Young America's cultural pluralist program. Moreover, while Frank's description of seeds germinating in the newly turned soil, pushing high up from the black loam of the prairie, appears to unite space and time, geography and history, the time that it invokes is cyclical rather than historical: "Here is the *eternal* seed" (emphasis added). Finally, Frank's notion that ancient Aztec and Native American civilizations had been "buried" not only ignored their continuity into the present but also identified culture with the land: presumably these ancient civilizations were providing some of the "loam" enabling modern writers to draw sustenance from the terrain as they looked under their bootsoles for a usable past. In this context, Frank's extraordinary vision of the Mississippi River upended, now reaching to the skies, obscured the role of historical actors in modernity's cultural revolution. Were they acting purposively as agents, or were they naturalized emanations from the nation's terrain?[26]

Because of the very relentlessness with which it asserts a utopian conception of belonging, Frank's text perhaps most fully displays the aporias accompanying the counterdiscourse that he and his colleagues were aspiring to formulate. His proposition that marginalized people—"whipped races"—possess privileged status as spiritual pioneers clearly challenges the worldview of the Gertrude Athertons and Stuart Shermans. His exuberant valorization of "buried cultures" contests the pessimistic—and uninterrogated—Eurocentrism of John Erskine and Carl Van Doren. But Frank's formulation entails a reassertion of manifest destiny: the notion that folk cultures are at the core of modernity can become operative in Frank's schema only if the historical fates of those cultures are occluded. The conviction that socialism is necessary to any genuine cultural revolution is problematized, moreover, by the inconsistent approach to class contradiction in Frank's text. Although he opined that the "land of the free" was inhabited by "economic serfs," he envisioned for these serfs no agency in abolishing their servitude. Instead, he mused:

> America is a turmoiled giant who cannot speak. The giant's eyes wander about the clouds: his feet are sunk in the quicksands of racial and material passion. . . . His need is great, and what moves across his eyes is universal. But his tongue is tied.

We know the meaning of this. We know that utterance is a step in consciousness. We know that if America is dumb, the reason is that consciousness within America has not yet reached that pitch where the voice bursts forth. . . . [T]he problem is . . . to lift America into self-knowledge that shall be luminous so that she may shine, vibrant so that she may be articulate.

Frank here invokes a staple simile of early-twentieth-century socialist discourse—comparing labor to a chained giant, unable to liberate itself because it is unaware of its own strength. As Upton Sinclair's stand-in for Eugene Debs puts it in *The Jungle,* Labor is

despised and outraged; a mighty giant, lying prostrate—mountainous, colossal, but blinded, bound, and ignorant of his strength . . . haunted by . . . a dream of resistance, hope battling with fear; until suddenly he stirs, and a fetter snaps—and a thrill shoots through him, to the farthest ends of his huge body, and in a flash the dream becomes an act! He starts, he lifts himself; and the bands are shattered, the burdens roll off him; he rises—towering, gigantic; he springs to his feet, he shouts in his new-born exultation—

The "turmoiled giant" in *Our America* is described as having feet "sunk in the quicksands of racial and material passion"; Frank recognizes, as Sinclair's Debsian speaker apparently does not, that racist and consumerist false consciousness contributes crucially to the giant's powerlessness. But Sinclair's giant liberates himself—and comes to speech—by making a "dream of resistance" into a reality; his praxis may be aided by the evolution of the forces of production, but class-conscious activity is a crucial element in his breaking the fetters of capitalism. Frank's giant, by contrast—who, it is stipulated, represents not the working class but the nation—achieves speech by being "lifted into self-knowledge"; class struggle plays no part in an awakening to potentiality that appears to be guided by artists and cultural critics alone. Moreover, by a deft rhetorical sex-change the male giant, with his conventional proletarian muscularity, is transformed, upon attaining "self-knowledge," into a female, "luminous, . . . shin[ing], . . . articulate," a voluble Statue of Liberty. Frank's representation of the nation as woman, passively awaiting the gift of speech from the enlightened male artist, suggests the reliance of his utopian nationalist project on a gendered binary opposition less noxious, but no less potent, than the one suggested by Stearns.[27]

Although in various places *Our America* couples some of the least progressive aspects of SPA nationalism with Frank's distinctive style of mystical ranting, the text presents itself as the harbinger of socialist modernity. Frank appropriates the rhetoric of revolutionary self-determination for immediately culturalist ends, even renarrating the Bolshevik Revolution as culture war. "In Russia," he writes, "the oppressive system permitted no careers in the open world to [meet] men's need of service and of creation. There was vast spiritual force in Russia. It was not allowed to grapple with reality." But the "mystical experience of Russia nursed the people through centuries of oppression; bore the will at last to throw them up into the light. Heaven was transferred from death to life. Revolution followed with logical precision." By contrast, in the United States "American energy . . . fled equally from the soil of the land and from the soul of man," leaving the people "more backward than the Magyar or the Slav, because we lack that spiritual substance which creates Faith and which moves mountains." Russian peasants have emerged as history-making people, in other words, not simply in spite of but because of their proximity to the soil, itself conceived as the mystical mother rather than the site of exploitation. Americans, however—and here Frank explicitly invokes a parallel with Magyars and Slavs, the "non-historical peoples" conventionally cited by such nation-as-people theorists of the Second International as Otto Bauer—are "backward" to the extent that they lack an organic link to the land. Rootlessness—the very characteristic that, in Karl Kautsky's formulation, made the proletariat countryless and therefore revolutionary—figures, for Frank, as something the proletariat must overcome if it is to be a revolutionary agent. Lenin considered the occurrence of the first proletarian revolution in Russia to be at least a problematic that Marxism must confront; such leftist sympathizers as Robert Lowie and Melville Herskovits saw the triumph of antievolutionism over stagism in Russia as having happened in spite of, rather than because of, the country's largely peasant population. For Frank, by contrast, closeness to the land was—at least culturally, and that was what mattered most—an important, indeed, the most important, vanguard characteristic.[28]

Despite its many internal contradictions, the cultural pluralist program associated with Young America appealed to many progressive and left-leaning intellectuals and artists of the day and significantly influenced the Harlem Renaissance. Young America's espousal of socialism, however vague, indicated that only a classless society could fully implement Young America's cultural program. Its proposal that groups traditionally marginalized in U.S. society should occupy its center, moral and aesthetic, entailed a strategy of representation at once antiracist and democratic, deconstructive and inclusive; the debate over who constituted a "true American" carried both political and epistemological impli-

cations. Young America's enthusiastic appropriation of a discourse drawn
from nature to criticize the capitalist present demonstrated its unwillingness to surrender "nature" to the discourse of eugenics. Its insistence
that the loam of the prairie lay beneath the city meant that the modern
artist was not forced to choose between the metropolitan and the pastoral, the cosmopolitan and the folk; the appreciation of the folk *as* the folk
was precisely what enabled the modern to know itself as new. Young
America's hope that "our America" could prevail over "their America"
inspired the emergence of new culture heroes, free to choose ancestors
from whom to claim lineage and terrain in which to set down roots. The
Young Americans held out the possibility that a national culture at once
revived and redefined would supply the needed remedy to capitalist alienation and facilitate the eventually socialist—and "inter-national"—transformation of society.

Yet Young America's program reproduced many of the features of the
hegemony that it sought to undermine. Its attempt to appropriate the
naturalizing discourse of the nativists and eugenicists issued in a biolo-
gized primitivism that inadvertently resuscitated certain features of the
very racism that it presumed to critique. Its commitment to a "good"
nationalism involved a rearticulation, rather than an interrogation or
repudiation, of manifest destiny. Its embrace of a protomulticulturalist
politics of identity precluded a grasp of exploitation as the keystone of
capitalist rule. Its celebration of inclusion and belonging through an organic trope linking soil with nation, seed with artist, and tree with humanity implied a fetishization of place as the source of consciousness that
discouraged structural and historical analysis. At the same time, Young
America's notion that culture supplied the basis of cultivation implied a
logical circularity: were artists to be rooted in the land, or in other artists, or even, perhaps, in themselves? Although Young America offered
a pluralistic alternative to 100 percent Americanism and was critical of
various aspects of capitalist rule, it was dependent on the dominant discourses, political and aesthetic, that it proposed to contest. It could not
move beyond a politics of antinomy or an aesthetics of irony.

"A Mighty National Art Cannot Rise Save out of the Soil of the Masses": Nationalism, Internationalism, and the Liberator Radicals

The writers and critics clustered around the *Liberator*—strongly identified with opposition to the war, enthusiasm for the Bolshevik Revolution, advocacy of social equality for African Americans, and the left wing

of the SPA—were considerably more cautious in proclaiming the merits of nationalism than were the Young Americans. Indeed, the *Liberator* was the principal cultural organ in the wartime and immediate postwar period through which to glimpse the haunting spectre of the international proletariat, transplanted not by controlled cultivation but by the seeds of capitalist contradiction sown to the winds of the world. Many cartoons, drawings, commentaries, and poems in the *Liberator* satirize not just 100 percent Americanism but "Americanism" as such. A May 1920 drawing by Art Young depicting the jailing of antiwar dissidents carries the ironic caption "Lessons in Americanism." An August 1921 Robert Minor drawing entitled "America Today" depicts cossacks persecuting serfs, thereby equating U.S. police forces with the czar's army and striking U.S. workers with revolutionary Soviet peasants and workers. A February 1924 drawing by Fred Ellis entitled "Selective Immigration" stresses the anti-radicalism underlying the drive to cut off immigration. John Reed's coverage of the 1918 trial of the IWW—complete with Art Young's satiric illustrations—ruthlessly lampoons the prejudicial behavior of the judges and prosecutors and cites the IWW preamble: "The working class and the owning class have nothing in common." Max Eastman's February 1920 column, "Examples of 'Americanism,'" links the government's persecution of radicals with lynching, calling attention to the dual signification of the term *Red Summer*. Martha Foley's March 1922 poem "Americanizing Haiti" castigates U.S. imperialism in the Caribbean. Hazel B. Poole's March 1922 sonnet "The Alien," prompted by the observation of a "thronging multitude" in whose veins "[f]lows crimson . . . the racial tide," repudiates the "patriot thrill of pride" at the word "'American!'":

> The alien—I? I know not whence I came,
>   Nor of what races blent. All who could know
>   Have crumbled into dust. Yet from this band
> A face, a vibrant accent, or a name
>   Has power to kindle in my heart a glow
>   Warm, strange, compelling, for an unknown land.

Where Stoddard would see a rising tide of color threatening the nation with inferior genetic material, Poole's speaker reacts to the "crimson . . . racial tide" with warmth and curiosity. Dubbing herself—ignorant of her own "racial" origins—more "alien" than the newcomers, the speaker experiences a paradoxical sense of homecoming upon seeing this denizen of an unknown land. The poem thus valorizes the rootless, the un-American, the cosmopolitan—the nomad proletarian whose identity is defined not by belonging on a given patch of earth, an "unknown nation," but by being inserted as a producer into capitalist relations of production.[29]

Liberator commentators frequently criticized the liberalism of the cultural pluralists and the Young Americans. In a mordant review of Frank's *Our America* in January 1920, Floyd Dell regretted that he could not hail the book "as the work of a comrade." While Frank's text "is a gallant effort to give young and lonely idealists a background," Dell remarked, it missed the central point that "the literature of America is above all a literature of protest and rebellion." He concluded, "It is hard for me to realize [the] common identity of our cause; it is easy to see the differences which separate us." Mike Gold in April 1920 scored Stearns's *Liberalism in America* for its portrayal of intellectuals as the source of change, declaring that "the working class, which suffers most under capitalism, alone can develop the desire and strength to destroy this system." Also indicating a divide between the *Liberator* radicals and the Young Americans, Max Eastman in August 1921 took Brooks to task for what he considered Brooks's elitist confidence in the ability of poets to lead revolutionary movements. T. J. O'Flaherty's September 1924 review of Kallen's *Culture and Democracy in the United States* bluntly accused the founder of cultural pluralism of "putting the hood on the class war."[30]

Yet the *Liberator* also propounded its own version of American nationalism—alternative and oppositional but nationalism nonetheless. The March 1920 issue carried a picture of a Pueblo Indian by Maurice Stern bearing the caption "100% American"; ridiculing Anglo-Saxonist claims to stand for the nation, the drawing redefined rather than jettisoned patriotism. Well before the Popular Front, Abraham Lincoln was appropriated in the service of a leftist nationalism. While the January 1918 cover featured a picture of Lenin, the next month's cover carried a portrait of Lincoln, accompanied by a quotation from the Great Emancipator: "The strongest bond of human sympathy, outside of the family relation, should be one uniting all working people of all nations and tongues and kindred.'" Hardly a proletarian internationalist, Lincoln meant here simply that the "working people" of all nations should recognize their commonality—a humanist sentiment most apposite to the increasingly global aspirations of U.S. industrialists during the years of his presidency. Dell, in his riposte to Frank, explicitly valorized Lincoln, noting in his critique of *Our America* that his own America was that of Debs and Lincoln. "We only slowly come to learn that what we sometimes contemptuously call 'American' is not American at all; that it is, astonishingly enough, we who are American."[31]

The contradiction between nationalism and internationalism embodied in the *Liberator*'s graphic and editorial statements was inscribed in the images and symbols appearing in the magazine's cartoons and poems.

Some drawings and poems invoked the organic trope to express antiracism and international proletarian solidarity. A December 1918 cartoon
captioned "'Will Raymond Robins Please Come Out?'" portrays the head
of the Red Cross mission in Russia clutching his anti-Bolshevik writings
and ensconced within the ruined trunk of a "reactionary tree" about to
be ignited by the torch held by the "U.S. Socialist and Labor Interests."
The aged tree trunk, sprouting two scrawny, leafless branches, represents
a past in need of obliteration; it embodies no venerable traditions, and
no nourishment for the working class can be culled from it. Jeannette
Pearl's November 1923 poem, "Negro Bodies," presents an irreconcilable
antagonism between a tree's natural beauty and its horrific social use:

> I love the tree.
> I love the soothing of its green and the fragrance of its
>   sweetness. . . .
> I love the hidden power of its roots and the grandeur of its
>   imposing height.
> And now, I turn from the tree in fear,
> Lest the body of my love swing from that height
> The same as other Negro bodies of his kin
> The wild sport of frenzied mobs, nurtured in secret strength.

The "hidden power" of the tree's roots may sustain its "imposing height,"
but it cannot prevent the horror of lynching carried out by a mob possessing its own "secret strength." The tree cannot stand for a moral order beyond itself, for history—as in the song "Strange Fruit" that Billie
Holiday would make famous some twenty-five years later—operates in
a register wholly removed from that of nature.[32]

Some of the metaphors involving roots and soil, seeds and plants in
Liberator texts represented the possibilities for revolutionary transformation of the social order. For example, Harry Kemp's "Rune of the Sower"
in February 1920 transforms its biblical epigraph—"And One Went Forth
to Sow"—into an explicitly revolutionary parable of cosmopolitan proletarian internationalism:

> I am the Sower
> Of the Seed
> Unto harvests
> Of Thought and Deed. . . .
>
> I have no roof
> To cover my head;
> They drive me forth
> To beg my bread . . .

The knaves, their own
Posterity
Will house and feed
Themselves through Me. . . .

Blindly I cast
The seeds about:
Never the God
Within I doubt,

For 'tis not mine
To see or know
What fruit shall be
What harvest grow. . . .

Mine only 'tis
To sow and sow. . . .
MINE ONLY 'TIS
TO SOW AND SOW!

The sower's homelessness is not metaphysical but a function of his class status: after laboring for the "knaves and their posterity," he is cast out to wander and starve. "The Rune of the Sower" is written in the spirit of the hammer and sickle, stressing not the peasant's closeness to the land but his alienation from its product, not his identification with place but his definition through labor. To the extent that his identity is diasporic, it seeks articulation primarily through the relation of "now" to some future "then" rather than through the relation of "here" to "there."[33]

Elsa Gidlow's August 1921 "Declaration" invites interpretation as an allegory of the insurgent and uncontrollable energies that have germinated—and await full growth and reaping—as a consequence of the Bolshevik Revolution:

I am a seed in the dust,
    A live root bedded in night,
And I am filled with a lust
    For something the worms call light.

From what seed-pod I was blown
    Matters little to me:
Why and by whom I was sown,
    Or what the reaping will be. . . .

If published in a less radical journal than the *Liberator*, "Declaration" might be read as invoking a broad discursive field in which allusions to planting and harvesting signify processes of growth including, but not limited to, social change. Read in the context offered by such texts as

"The Rune of the Sower," however, the poem affirms the proletariat's irrepressible yearning for revolution. What "matters" to the proletarian's seed is its "lust [f]or . . . light," not its belonging in place; not its predi-asporic ethnic derivation ("what[ever] seed-pod"), but its need for a realization beyond the ken of those imprisoned, like worms, in the darkness of class relations.[34]

In *Liberator* poems focused on African Americans' experiences of Jim Crow and migration, the organic trope sometimes highlights racial oppression but at other times obscures its causes. James Weldon Johnson, in his April 1918 riposte to Dell's review of his *Fifty Years and Other Poems*, quoted one of his own poems to make the point that there is no such thing as "a Negro way of looking at a sunset." The basis of African Americans' claim to belonging in the United States, Johnson asserted, was not their exotic epistemological stance but their investment of labor in a land that had never belonged to them:

> This land is ours by right of birth,
> This land is ours by right of toil.
> We helped to turn its virgin earth
> Our sweat is in its fruitful soil.

As in Ethel Trew Dunlap's *Negro World* poem "The Toiler," rhyming "toil" with "soil" stresses the role of black agrarian labor in generating wealth; one is reminded that Johnson's understanding of the political economy of racism was at this time shaped partly by Marxism. At the same time, the speaker's claim to the land—besides anticipating Woody Guthrie's Popular Front anthem "This land is your land, / This land is my land"—in its allusion to "virgin earth" subliminally calls up the patriarchal discourse of manifest destiny. Moreover, this claim rests on a politics of contribution and belonging, as well as an invocation of the doctrine of bourgeois "right": the "we" in Johnson's poem demands not the abolition of private property and wages but inclusion within the inherited system of property ownership.[35]

In Clement Wood's "Alien," published in November 1918, the Negro's definition through his relation to land is at once socially constructed and essentialist:

> I saw a negro in the snow—
> His vast face dark and pondering,
> Shoulders whitened, and head hunched low.
>
> What vagabonding lust could bring
> You from the cotton-field's soft glow,
> The white magnolia drifts of Spring?

The thin sun here will whiten your face,
The lean, long winters ruthlessly
Wither your slouching jungle grace.

Our nights grow longer; better flee
This callous and transforming place
Or would you grow no more than we?

Wood utters nativism's counterdiscourse: it is the environment of modernity—"this callous and transforming place"—rather than the alienated migrant that is "alien." Moreover, "whitening"—that is, the formation of racial identity—is a cultural process rather than a biological fact:
not only the Negro's clothes but also his "vast, dark face" will be "whit-
ened" by the northward move. Yet the notion that the Negro would have
migrated from the Jim Crow South out of "vagabonding lust" rather than
economic necessity or lynch terror oddly recalls Davenport's postulation
of a gene for nomadism. Moreover, the seductive representation of the
South as a place of softly glowing cotton fields and white magnolia drifts
summons up the conventions of plantation romance, while the attribution of a "slouching jungle grace" suggests a biological component to his
"belonging" somewhere other than the city—not just the South but Africa. In Wood's formulation, modernity is not so much a historical conjuncture as a place; its temporal antithesis would appear to be not an
earlier moment of history—let alone a future moment free of class contradiction—but a mythic site, the jungle, beyond history altogether.[36]

The contradictions in the *Liberator*'s stance on nationalism and internationalism, nature and history, are epitomized in Mike Gold's February 1921 "Toward Proletarian Art"—an essay that would come to be
seen as a key early manifesto of the literary proletarianism that attained
maturity in the next decade. Proclaiming that "[w]e are prepared for the
economic revolution of the world, but what shakes us with terror and
doubt is the cultural upheaval that must come," Gold counterposes the
literature produced by the petty bourgeoisie with that generated by the
working class. "Art is the tenement pouring out its soul through us, its
most sensitive sons and daughters," he declares. The "intellectuals," by
contrast, "have no roots in the people. The art ideals of the capitalistic
world isolated each artist as in a solitary cell, there to brood and suffer
silently and go mad." By contrast, "[t]he masses are still primitive and
clean, and artists must turn to them for strength." The pallid offerings
contained in the *Little Review* and the *Seven Arts*, Gold judged, were
being surpassed in Russia, where Prolet-Kult had "grow[n] from the soil
of life" as an "organized attempt" to cultivate the art that had "always
flourished secretly in the hearts of the masses."[37]

Gold's use of the organic trope captures the blend of national and class identifications informing his ideal conception of the artist "rooted" in the proletariat. "A mighty national art cannot rise save out of the soil of the masses," he writes. "It is not in [the] hot-house air [of the studios] that the lusty great tree will grow. Its roots must be in the fields, factories, and workshops of America—in the American life." Gold unequivocally valorizes the life of the proletarian masses, rural and urban, and the art representing that life. The "roots" of the "lusty tree" of proletarian art draw sustenance from the "soil" of the masses; by contrast, the art of the petty bourgeoisie has germinated and grown in the "hot-house" of privilege. Yet the soil that is the masses is also "the American life," and the art rooted in that soil is simultaneously proletarian art and a "great national art." The place-based character of Gold's nationalism asserts itself in the hyper-materiality of his guiding metaphor. Even as Gold nods to internationalism in comparing U.S. proletarian art with Soviet Prolet-Kult, this invocation of cultural activity in the USSR only underlines his point that nationalism—albeit the progressive nationalism of popular self-determination—constitutes the site where *internationalism* is concretely embodied and therefore made possible. In Gold's 1921 formulation, proletarian literature is closely aligned with primitivism, on the one hand, and a kind of leftist patriotism, on the other. Although Locke's 1925 formulation of the New Negro as quintessentially rooted in the nation's soil would drop class out of the equation altogether, to be reconfigured as "folk," the links between his project and that of Gold, both genealogical and political, should not be overlooked.[38]

The "Most Specific Correspondence of National Character to National Geography": "Old Walt" and Metonymic Nationalism

The beatification of John Brown codified the leftward and centripetal energies of revolt emerging from the crisis of 1919; postwar representations of the martyr of Harper's Ferry raised the spectre of another civil war fought to free the oppressed from slavery—this time, from the slavery of the wage relation. By contrast, the canonization of Walt Whitman revealed the containing and centrifugal force of a reformist nationalism that, in the aftermath of 1919, would shore up the center and ensure that it held. With the centenary of his birth falling in May 1919—hardly a month of quietude in the class struggle, national or global—the debate over the legacy of the good gray poet serves as a touchstone for the different political tendencies vying for hegemony in contemporaneous cultural debates.

Voices from all points along the political spectrum sought to enlist Whitman on their side. Conservatives cited him as they expounded their nativist versions of Americanism. As an epigraph to *America's Race Heritage,* Clinton Stoddard Burr included passages from Rudyard Kipling, John Greenleaf Whittier, and, at greatest length, Whitman:

> We primeval forests felling,
> We the rivers stemming, vexing we and piercing
>   deep the mines within,
> We the surface broad surveying, we the virgin
>   soil upheaving,
> Pioneers! O pioneers!

Landscape functions here not metaphorically but literally: for Burr, Whitmanian pioneering unproblematically connotes appropriation of the riches of the earth. Presumably the destruction of nature—compared, predictably, with the penetration of virgin soil—is the "race heritage" of U.S. Caucasians. The conservative critic Stuart Sherman, in a more subtle maneuver, argued that liberals and radicals had misread Whitman to suit their own needs. "The 'ruling class,' the statesmen, in all nations, will find their mission and their honor progressively dependent upon their capacity for bringing the entire body of humanity into one harmonious and satisfactory life," he wrote. Sherman concluded that if Whitman had been alive "in these years of the Proletarian Millennium," he "would have been hanged as a reactionary member of the bourgeoisie" instead of being a Bolshevist.[39]

Well before the era of the Popular Front—when Whitman would acquire near-canonical status on the left—he was enthusiastically claimed by radicals of various stripes. The *Liberator* featured Whitman on its cover in May 1920; in a special issue of the *Call*'s Sunday literary supplement devoted to Whitman, Clement Wood declared him a "red poet." Lola Ridge, the editor of *Broom,* invoked "Out of the Cradle Endlessly Rocking" in her call to industrial workers:

> Out of the mouths of turbines,
> Out of the turgid throats of engines,
> Over the whistling steam,
> You shall hear me shrilly piping.
> Your mills I shall enter like the wind,
> And blow upon your hearts,
> Kindling the slow fire.

For Max Eastman, who expatiated on Whitman in *Colors of Life* (1918), Whitman had set the course for "the poetry of the future." Gold, in "To-

ward Proletarian Art," declared that Whitman was the model for the proletarian artist, because the bard of Brooklyn "dwelt among the masses,
and from here . . . drew his strength." Although, in Gold's view, Whitman
made "one mistake"—namely, "dream[ing] the grand dream of political
democracy, and [thinking] it could express in completion all the aspirations of proletarian man"—Whitman "knew the masses too well to believe that any individual could rise in intrinsic value above them." The
SPA leader William English Walling, also conceding that Whitman's "fatal
fallacy" was to think that "the America of small property owners that
he knew was already leading the world into a new civilization," nonetheless dubbed Whitman "the world's foremost poet of democracy."
Among radicals, Floyd Dell was relatively isolated in his view that Whitman, like other idealists from Emerson to Tolstoy, had a philosophy that
was "Utopian, unsocial, and except in its final implications antisocial."[40]

If radicals occasionally qualified their approval of Whitman, cultural pluralists and Young Americans did not. Berkson prefaced *Theories of
Americanization* with an epigraph from *Democratic Vistas:* "'I refer to
a Democracy that is yet unborn.'" For Brooks, it was Whitman who "laid
the cornerstone of a national ideal" capable of the project of "releasing
personality and of retrieving for our civilization . . . the only sort of 'place
in the sun' really worth having." For Frank, who also included an epigraph from Whitman in *Our America*, Whitman was less an influence
or even a progenitor than an embodiment of the nation itself. Frank took
Whitman's claim, "I embrace multitudes," as an occasion for meditat-
ing on those contemporary writers who were fulfilling Whitman's democratic promise. In his February 1920 *Dial* essay "Poetry—The First
National Art," the poet and critic James Oppenheim asserted that Whitman embodied the America of Debs and Lincoln, as opposed to that of
Roosevelt and Wilson; the following year he dedicated *The Mystic Warrior* to Whitman: "Your book walks in the light: let mine be the shadow
beside it." The educator Winifred Kirkland, addressing herself to the
"teacher of Americanization" in the *Dial*, wrote that "[t]he mere name
of Whitman brings an instant exhilaration like the sudden sight of the
stars and stripes billowing in the breeze," imparting the "[p]ride of place
[that is] a foundation element in patriotism." For Kirkland, the "only
'place in the sun' worth having" was defined in unambiguously nationalistic terms: Whitman's lesson was that "genuine patriotism is always
expressive of place in no vague, but in most specific correspondence of
national character to national geography."[41]

That Whitman should have attracted such a wide spectrum of partisans reveals not only his own chameleon quality but also the overlapping

nationalist proclivities of right, left, and center at the time of the Whitman centenary. For Sherman and Burr, Whitman legitimated the manifest destiny that facilitated the expansion of capital. For leftists, Whitman provided assurance that socialism and communism were not alien
imports brought from overseas by rootless cosmopolitans but structures
of feeling intrinsic to American culture. To liberals, Whitman represented
the spirit of inclusion essential to U.S. democracy, pure and simple. That
Whitman's own favored symbol should be leaves of grass—constituting
simultaneously his oeuvre and the nation described in that oeuvre—both
reinforced and was reinforced by the American exceptionalist nationalism pervading political discourse from right to left during this period.
Beyond the content of his work, however, was the notion that Whitman
himself pluralistically embodied the United States—that he functioned
metonymically to signal the congeries of social groups and historical
forces in the nation. John Brown, whose star had risen briefly in the revolutionary upsurge of 1919, signified polarization that would tear the
nation asunder; Whitman, by contrast, signified cohesion and synthesis.
Where Brown stood for the heightening of contradiction, Whitman stood
for its effacement. The contest between the two figures in the postwar
political imagination of leftists and progressives was thus epistemological as well as doctrinal. But the enthusiastic invocation of Whitman by
nearly all the participants in the culture war that followed the Great War
signifies the limits to the metonymic nationalist counterdiscourse articulated by much of the Left of the day and heralds the emergence of the
nationalist culturalism that would link representation in the sphere of
politics with representation in the sphere of aesthetics.

5 From the New Negro to The New Negro

> The young Negro writers dig deep into the
> racy peasant undersoil of the race life.
> —Alain Locke, "Negro Youth Speaks" (1925)

Returning to the question raised at the outset of this inquiry, how did the arms-bearing, anticapitalist New Negro of 1919 get transmuted into the culture hero of *The New Negro* (1925)? While the causal threads are many, Alain Locke's guiding role is clearly of central importance. In this chapter, I investigate the bodies of theory Locke brought to the making of his anthology; examine his pragmatist theory of "secondary race consciousness" and the aporias attendant upon it; demonstrate the expunging of radicalism and the consolidation of nationalism— simultaneously Negro and American—in his creation of *The New Negro* out of its *Survey Graphic* predecessor; and examine the ideological function of the organic trope in articulating the connections among soil, folk, race, and nation in *The New Negro*'s metonymic nationalist program. Even though Locke was several degrees removed from Marxism—both temporally and doctrinally—by the time he published *The New Negro*, the process from which his text emerged cannot be understood apart from the larger contradictions shaping the theory and practice of leftist politics in 1919 and its aftermath.

The concept of the folk, I argue, figures as the central conceptual mechanism helping Locke to shift the New Negro movement from politics to culture, self-determinationist militancy to quietistic pluralist patriotism. Drawing on folk origins to lay claim to the Negro's Americanism was in one sense nothing new to discourses addressing the problematics of African American identity, going back at least as far as Du Bois's 1903 declaration, in *The Souls of Black Folk*, that the African American folksong was "the singular spiritual heritage of the nation and the greatest gift of the Negro people." But the notion that the folk constitute the core identity of any nation—and that black folk might play this role in and for the United States—took on particular resonance in the wake of 1919, when the various discourses of nationalism—self-determinationist, liberal pluralist, and 100 percent Americanist—competed for popular legitimacy and elite support. Locke's reconceptualization of the newly migrated proletariat as a folk figured centrally in his turn from class consciousness to class collaborationism.[1]

"The Black Arts of Interpretation": Vernacular Theory and Its Critique

Before examining the ideological crucible from which *The New Negro* emerged, it bears noting that some of the issues in the debate over the nature and extent of the Negro's belonging in the United States and in Locke's seizing on the category of the folk to argue his case during the New Negro movement of the mid-1920s remain today. Locke's treatment of the folk as a privileged entry point into the definition of African American culture has been carried forward into the vernacular theories of African American literature that—espoused by such influential critics as Bernard Bell, Houston Baker, and Henry Louis Gates—have done much over the past twenty years to shape not only the canon of African American literature but also the paradigms through which this literature is routinely studied. Bell, who notes that the wartime and postwar migration and urbanization led "[r]ace conscious intellectuals to tap the roots of their ethnic heritage with varying degrees of ambivalence," argues that Herderian notions of folkishness have definitively influenced African American literature from its inception as a self-conscious tradition. "Herder's belief that the highest cultural values are to be found in the lowest orders of society," contends Bell, informed the most significant developments in African American literature from the early twentieth century through the black arts movement. Baker, echoing Du Bois, writes that "a FOLK is always, out of the very necessities of definition, possessed of a guiding or tutelary spirit—an immanent quality of aspiration that is fittingly sounded in its treasured rituals." Seeing an act of "radical marronage"—that is, maroon rebellion—in Locke's declaration that American Negroes constituted "not a 'problem' but a NATION," Baker treats *The New Negro* as an exemplary instance of "guerrilla warfare." For Baker, the vernacular approach to African American literature is explicitly linked with self-determinationist nationalism; the "national impulse valorized by Locke, Du Bois, and Washington is best described . . . as Afro-American spirit work."[2]

Gates has argued that critics of African American literature should focus on "the black vernacular tradition" so that they can "isolate the signifying black difference through which to theorize about the so-called discourse of the Other." Only then, he contends, can the African American critic "know and test the dark secrets of a black and hermetic discursive universe that awaits its disclosure through the black arts of interpretation." Gates's emphasis on "signification" as a rhetorical strategy distinctive to the African American literary tradition is thus premised on the centrality of the folk in his interpretation of the genesis of that tradition: the vernacular, which "informs and becomes the foundation for formal black literature," contains principles of "repetition" and "revision" that enable it to be a "meta-discourse, a discourse about itself." For Gates, the intrinsically deconstructive features of African American literature—at least as laid bare by the "black arts of interpretation"—are associated, somewhat paradoxically, with a distinctly nondeconstructive view of the "black discursive universe" as "hermetic." As laid out by these and other critics, the vernacular theory of African American literature currently dominates pedagogical and critical practice, having produced the *Norton Anthology of African-American Literature*, on the one hand and, on the other, critical approaches stressing tricksterism and linguistic subversion as near-inherent qualities of black American literature.[3]

The vernacular paradigm and the valorization of the folk on which it is usually based have been subjected to various critiques over the years. Nathan Huggins has argued that, with the exception of Jean Toomer and a few other artists who successfully engaged in what he calls a "forthright search for the roots of the Negro self," the Harlem Renaissance was above all marked by an "ethnic provincialism," routinely expressed as a naive primitivism that ended up "limit[ing] the possibility of achieving good art." For the great majority of African American intellectuals as well as their Euro-American counterparts, Huggins argues, "culture . . . had nothing to do with folk roots." Wilson Moses, locating the "golden age" of black nationalism in the pre-Renaissance years usually derided as the era of the Old Negro, has objected to the proposition that the most significant African American literature has its origins in "plantation folklore, the blues style and proletarian iconoclasm." Hazel Carby, insisting on distinguishing the last two of these from the first, has argued that the designation of literature based on folk traditions as "a natural expression of the Afro-American experience" has involved an act of selection that is "neither . . . inevitable nor . . . natural." By invoking "one mythical rural existence" as definitive of this experience, she argues, critics have not only "conflate[d] . . . two very distinct modes of production, slavery and sharecropping," but also effaced the crucial effects of urbanization and proletarianization on African American life and culture alike.[4]

More recently, the vernacular doctrine espoused by Bell, Baker, and Gates has been criticized for its essentialist homogenization of difference and effacement of intragroup conflict. Kenneth Warren worries that "vernacular critique" leads to "the depoliticization of black cultural discussion and the tendency to suppress and discredit internal dissent." J. Martin Favor, highly skeptical of black nationalism, notes a troublesome similarity between "the dynamics of positing authenticity" practiced alike by "a group bent upon racial nationalism for destructive, even genocidal, purposes" and by "a group using notions of authenticity to combat racism itself." He also complains that "privileg[ing] the African American folk and its cultural forms in the discourse of black identity" has resulted in a kind of "anti-elitist elitism," whereby "racial authenticity" is said to inhere only in persons and texts "privileging the folk." The consequence of this "positing too-concrete bonds between authenticity, culture, color and class," Favor argues, has been to "ris[k] reliance on a vision of identity so dependent on marginality as its legitimizing feature that it can never effectively deconstruct the center, which, in turn, may hold the margins to be inauthentic." David Nicholls similarly faults vernacular approaches for treating the folk as "unmediated," an "assumed category of person rather than as a contested vision of collectivity." Instead, he proposes, there are "many folks," corresponding to "many modernities," including even a "rural modernity" that need not "look to a vanished past in order to assert its claim to continuing importance." The lesson to be learned from the "many modernities" that emerge from a rehistoricized examination of the "plural" representations of the folk in African American literature, Nicholls argues, is the necessity of recognizing the folk as "a historically contingent constituency" and dispensing with "master narratives" of the emergence of the folk into modernity that are derived from the European model of national development. Unlike Baker's invocation of "traceable ancestry" and Gates's "dark secrets of a black and hermetic discursive universe," these formulations insist on the incapacity of *any* master narrative—Eurocentric or Afrocentric—to do justice to the diversity and plurality of African American experience.[5]

202 Spectres of 1919

These statements contain useful admonitions regarding the perils of essentialism, romanticization, and historical distortion to which vernacular theory, as well as the fetishization of the folk on which it is commonly based, can fall prey. In some important respects, however, the debate between the advocates and the opponents of the folk/vernacular approach to African American literature has not managed to break free from the constraints by which it has been hobbled from the time of Locke to the present—and for reasons not unrelated to its genesis in the political struggles of the 1920s. In particular, the problematic of nationalism— can there be a "good" nationalism that evades the pitfalls of "bad" nationalism?—continues implicitly to structure the debate, even when the category of nationalism is no longer directly invoked and at times may even be explicitly repudiated. The older critics of the folk/vernacular thesis were forthrightly nationalist, in either the African American or the American mode. Huggins asserted that the Harlem Renaissance largely failed because its participants did not "appreciate . . . the positive implications of American nativity" and "clai[m] their *patria.*" Moses held up as an alternative to proletarianitis an unabashedly conservative black nationalism explicitly premised on a politics of "civilizationism," acculturation, and identification with the "genteel tradition in English letters." By contrast, the nationalism shaping the vernacular theories of African American literature tends more toward self-determinationism, now recast as the necessity of embracing a strategic essentialist politics of identity. Thus both Baker and Gates—the former explicitly, the latter implicitly—take self-determination as a premise in their calls for a criticism based on *"marronage"* and the "black arts of interpretation."[6]

Yet even the critics of Baker and Gates embrace aspects of the nationalist homogenization that they claim to disavow. Warren displays a conception of "black folks" as a unified entity that contradicts his complaint that Baker and Gates suture class and ideological differences among African Americans. Although Favor notes parallels between the ways in which both genocidal and antiracist nationalisms commonly "seek to create unity in the face of an 'other,'" he hastily qualifies his assertion: "This is not to say that all forms of nationalism are equally beneficial or detrimental. Without nationalism and its corresponding senses of cultural and communal identity, anticolonialist movements might never win the people's right to self-determination and nondomination." Favor faults Bell, Baker, and Gates for embracing essentialist—as well as reverse elitist—notions of black authenticity as residing in the folk and its speech. His own valorizing rhetoric, however—"cultural and communal identity," "the people"—proclaims the need for African Americans to see themselves as a holistic body, presumably capable of unitary consciousness and agency. That the success or failure of twentieth-century "anticolonialist movements" based on "a people's right to self-determination" bears no scrutiny further indicates nationalist premises. For all the radical panache accompanying Favor's repudiation of "'grand unified theor[ies]' of black identity," his brief on behalf of the black middle class, past and present, recapitulates a good deal of the elitism—as opposed to "anti-elitist elitism"—informing the more straightforward formulations of Huggins and Moses.[7]

Nicholls goes further than Warren and Favor in repudiating essentialism—not just that imposed by the master narrative of European historical development but also that embedded in any alternative master narrative that would locate what is distinctive in African American experience in its construction of a "unitary tradition" out of "folk materials." "[I]f we are to believe the stories of European cultural development," he asks, "what people did not?" Instead, Nicholls argues, what is distinctive about the trajectory of African American history is that it "profoundly disrupts and reshapes the transition narrative provided by the European Enlightenment," thereby "retrofitting Eurocentric notions of cultural development with the particularity of African-American experiences and location." Nicholls thus invests the African American historical experience with a tricksterish power to undermine the dominant discourse; the critic's own narrative of African American emergence into modernity takes on the deconstructive subversiveness that Gates associates with the verbal "signification" derived from the black folk tradition itself. The "plurality" and "contingency" that Nicholls discovers in his own dispersed and "non-totalizing" narrative thus projects onto the screen of historical process the disruptive quality of the vernacular that he has denied to the folk tradition as such. Although Nicholls's move here is not expressly a nationalist one—indeed, it sharply criticizes the "totalizing" tendencies of both U.S. and African American nationalisms—his formulation functions epistemologically as an extension of the nationalist thesis in that it is premised on the doctrine of group exceptionalism: what characteristically marks African American representations of the folk is their uncanny ability to subvert the monologism of the dominant "great modes of production narrative." Divested of residually progressive content, the self-determinationist paradigm here turns not only against Marxism but also, ironically, against itself. Whereas leftist proponents of self-determination in the crucible of 1919 had in view a revolutionary process in which nationalism, a passing stage, would be negated and superseded by proletarian internationalism, contemporary spokespersons for the self-determinationist argument—here recast as totality-defying dissemination and dispersal—take as their implicit opposition *any* attempt to frame a "master discourse" that would presume to articulate the particular within a generalizing unified field. That nationalism, along with Marxism, ends up being targeted as reductive and authoritarian is, I would suggest, a paradoxical consequence of the Left's own accession to the "good" nationalism of self-determinationism many decades ago; the chickens of exceptionalism have come home to roost.[8]

The repudiation of racial essentialism and master narratives in recent poststructuralist-influenced forays into the realm of African American literary study fails to deliver on its promise of shattering old paradigms and providing new ones. For all the energy with which they deconstruct their forebears, Favor's and Nicholls's formulations of what is distinctive in the African American tradition lack a good deal of the verve motivating the predecessor theories and narratives—whether of Huggins and Moses, on the one hand, or Bell, Baker, and Gates, on the other—which, whatever their elitist or essentialist shortcomings when viewed in retrospect, expressly contested the racism of the dominant culture in their postulation and valorization of alternative paradigms for approaching African American literature. Nor have these most recent totality-defying formulations proven to be exempt from the strategic essentialism—and hence the difference-suturing nationalism—from which they purport to be free. Although the millennial analyses are several steps removed from early-twentieth-century debates over the national question, they remain haunted by the spectre of nationalism, albeit a spectre that has gone through multiple incarnations, reemerging most recently as a generalized antipathy to totality of any and all kinds. The aporias and contradictions inscribed in contemporary attempts to liberate the study of African American literature from the toils of essentialism and identity politics remain, like the precursors of these attempts some eighty years ago, historically determinate. In the examination of the transmutation of the New Negro into *The New Negro*, it will thus be useful to practice a certain historical humility, recognizing that the culture wars of the 1980s and 1990s have been fought over much of the same terrain as those of the 1920s largely because most progressives and radicals have not yet managed to move beyond the antinomies of discourse and counterdiscourse generated by the continuing oscillation of would-be emancipatory movements within the poles of "good" and "bad" nationalism. That U.S. racism—perhaps less virulent than that in the Jim Crow era but potent nonetheless—continues to supply much of the driving force behind the felt need for "good" nationalism should also leaven any sense of superiority one might feel toward those who emerged from the crucible of 1919.

"Apologia for Prevailing Practice" or "Operative Factor in Culture"? Locke, Cosmopolitanism, and Socialism

Alain Locke's intellectual training and experiences positioned him expertly to negotiate among the paradigms that he would bring into alignment in the 1925 anthology. It was at Harvard—where Locke met his classmate Van Wyck Brooks and began his friendship with Horace Kallen, then a graduate instructor in philosophy—that he came into contact with the pragmatist philosophy and empiricist psychology of John Dewey and William James, influences that would shape the cultural pluralism of several key figures of his generation. (The term *cultural pluralism*, usually attributed to Kallen because of his famous elaboration on it in his *Nation* articles of 1915, was actually coined by Locke.) First encountering Boas's critique of racial essentialism in England, where he traveled on a Rhodes fellowship in 1907, Locke spent several years studying in Oxford and Berlin. Upon his return to the United States, Locke completed his Harvard dissertation on the epistemological and valuational procedures involved in classification, read the Boasians more extensively, plunged into his teaching at Howard, kept abreast of the emerging body of cultural commentary by the Young Americans, and established the ties with the Harlem bibliophile Arthur Schomburg that would deepen his interest in recovering African American history and promoting African American culture. The Locke who would be contacted by *Opportunity*'s editor Charles S. Johnson to host the historic 1924 Writers Guild dinner bringing together many to-be-famous figures of the Harlem Renaissance, as well as by *Survey Graphic*'s editor Paul U. Kellogg to edit the special issue in March 1925 resulting in *The New Negro* some nine months later, had synthesized an impressive body of contemporaneous thinking on race and culture.[9]

Less frequently remarked on is the cosmopolitan radicalism with which Locke came into contact during his years overseas. While at Oxford, Locke not only heard William James's Hibbert lectures on pluralism but also established ties with anticolonial radicals who shaped his understanding of imperialism as an economic system requiring racism as its ideological rationale. His relationships with the H. E. Alaily, president of the Egyptian Society of English; Pa Ka Isaka Seme, a black South African law student; and the Indian revolutionaries Har Dayal, Shyamaji Krishnavarma, and Damodar Savarkar acquainted him with not just socialist internationalism but also debates within the Left over the relation of the class contradiction to the national question. That Locke's name appeared in 1908 on the editorial masthead of the *Oxford Cosmopolitan*, a short-lived journal published by students of non-European background, suggests the readiness with which he flung himself into these debates. On the political agenda of Locke's anticolonial associates would have been the question of whether the peasantry—the folk—could be thought of as agents in history or merely "non-historical peoples," as well as the debate between Lenin and Luxemburg over the potential risks and benefits of colonial movements for self-determination and Bauer's notion of nation-hood as potentially constituted by the "common fate and common char-acter" of "a group of human beings." In Berlin, Locke was exposed to de-bates surrounding the Marxist doctrine of class conflict through the teachings of Gustav Schmoller, and the heightening ethnic tensions on the European continent brought to his attention the divide-and-conquer dynamics of racial discrimination at work among populations in which all the affected groups could be designated as "white." The Left-inflected intellectual and experiential framework gained in Locke's sojourn over-seas would profoundly shape his first efforts at mapping the nature of—and possible solution to—the "race problem" in the United States.[10]

Also insufficiently examined are Locke's earliest writings, in which he analyzed the questions of race and class, culture and nation, in terms quite different from those that would shape his discussion in *The New Negro*. In "The American Temperament," published in the *North Amer-ican Review* in 1911, Locke sounded the note of democratic optimism that would resound in the 1925 text. Paying tribute to Whitman as the only "literary genius" who had "found it possible to accept. . . . the startling divergencies and instinctive antipathies" flowing from the "insatiable curiosity and . . . surplus of individual energy" constituting the "Ameri-can temperament," he argued that culture supplied the route to national health and progress. Although the "ideal loyalty to a national character and belief in a national will and destiny" could be whipped up by jour-nalism as "jingoistic patriotism," this loyalty could also, in the hands of able practitioners of the "reflective and representative arts," create "sound [national] traditions." At the same time, Locke warned that "[s]ociety is quite at the mercy of the class that paints its portrait" and that a "leisure class" identified with "the Anglo-Saxon type of civilization" had depict-ed the "national character" as being "at leisure," thereby imposing its own self-conception on "the whole life of the people who supported the lei-sure class." Locke here lambasted Anglo-Saxonism as rationalizing not just racial exclusion but also class hegemony. Mixed in with his Whitmanesque call for a poetic discourse embracing multitudes was a quasi-Marxist critique of nationalist ideology as both race- and class-bound, dependent on the exploitation of those who make possible the "leisure" of those who have the power to dictate who will be represented and how.[11]

Locke viewed World War I as imperialist. Speaking before the Yonkers Negro Society for Historical Research in September 1914, Locke angrily decried the racialization of nationality. Remarking that the war was "not a conflict over differing aims or systems," let alone about "civilization"—as the principal antagonists, Germany and Great Britain, were both "hysterical[ly] assert[ing]"—he argued that "it is not as nations but as empires" that the two "rival each other." He also commented on the dual racial paradoxes laid bare by the outbreak of world war. On the one hand, the barbarism of the conflict negated the "pretensions of European civilization to world-dominance and eternal superiority." No longer could the "divine right of certain nations to govern others" be invoked; the "imperial pretensions of a whole race perished therefore with the quarrel." On the other hand, the war was a "war to the death rivalry between two arms of the same civilization[,] the same race." Even though "in each country the common folk . . . posses[s] often a common culture and tradition," they "feel their existence is in jeopardy" and are "forced to regard themselves as bitterly estranged. The epithet of barbarian and enemy of civilization is hurled at blood brothers[;] the idea of Empire, the nemesis of alien races, has turned upon its authors." Articulated here was not just an analysis of the Great War as imperialist in its origins—prior to Lenin's *Imperialism*—but also a recognition that race is a category of consciousness that rulers can conflate with nation at their warmongering will, even when the nations in question are populated by people of the same racial classification. That Locke declared this "bitter estrange[ment]" ran counter to the interests of the "common folk" of Germany and Great Britain alike and consisted of something very like dominant ideology shows him substantially to the left of the European parties of the Second International.[12]

The Marxist inflection in Locke's 1911 and 1914 commentaries on race, class, and nation was substantially accented in both the text and the notes of his 1916 Howard University lecture series, "Race Contacts and Interracial Relations." Invoking the Boasians, Locke asserted that "any true history of race must be a sociological theory of race," because race "amounts practically to social inheritance," even though it "parades itself as biological or anthropological inheritance." "As applied to social and ethnic groups," he observed, the notion of race "has no meaning at all beyond that sense of kind, that sense of kith and kin which undoubtedly is somewhat of an advantage to any ethnic group that can maintain [it]. . . . And yet, useful as it is, it is not to deny its usefulness that we call it an ethnic fiction." Moreover, he noted, conceptions of racial superiority and inferiority are the result of "imperialistic dominance." "[T]he color-line . . . is essentially the line drawn by the practice of what I call commercial imperialism," which "the United States practices as much as Germany or England or France or Russia." Although "race antipathy" was, he believed, "instinctive," it was not "spontaneous"; on the contrary, "it is cultivated, very often deliberately cultivated, and much is not only cultivated but controlled and modified. . . . [When] left to itself, it subsides." He continued, "Race groups, like class groups, compete for the same social good." Even though "these race struggles and race issues generate a perfect vortex of more fundamental antagonisms that are very often regarded as so ultimate and beyond solution that they seem distinct from class questions, . . . they are common differing only in degree. They are very violent, . . . but the very fact that they sometimes break into class issues proves that they are only a very virulent kind of class question, after all." The racism experienced among workers "compet[ing] for the same social good," in other words, is traceable to the class exploitation of all workers. "Color prejudice," Locke further observed, "is a strange sort of aberration which seems peculiar to the modern mind," a product of the past two centuries. Noting its "enigmatical nature as a peculiar phenomenon in democratic societies," he argued that "its relation to social solidarity" was "not to be minimized"—an assertion suggesting that the "social solidarity" accompanying Jim Crow racism was integral to the paradoxical existence of democracy as a form of political rule. But precisely because racial antipathy was a historical product, Locke concluded, it was "of necessity to be regarded as eradicable and to be eradicated."[13]

That the Locke of the 1916 lectures was significantly influenced by Second International theorizing over the origins of racism is patent. Locke was significantly ahead of almost all his socialist contemporaries in his materialist understanding that not just "racial antipathy" but also the "ethnic fiction" of race itself served to reinforce ruling-class hegemony, as well as in his observation that the concept of race could be deployed to stir up antagonism even among members of the "same" racial or ethnic group. Nonetheless, in the last of the 1916 lectures, Locke retreated dramatically from the materialist and potentially revolutionary implications of his theorization of the relation of race to class. Anticipating the strategy of transvaluation and redefinition that would guide the culturalism of *The New Negro*, Locke argued, unlike those who "feel that race is so odious a term that it must be eradicated from our thinking and from our vocabulary," that "a word and an idea covering so indispensable[,] useful[,] and necessary a grouping in human society will never vanish, never be eradicated, and that the only possible way in which a change will come about will be through a substitution of better meanings for the meanings which are now so current under the term." Curiously, he now declared chimerical what he had previously specified as the desired end of recognizing the historicity of race—namely, "eradicat[ion]," a term itself premised on the metaphorizing of roots as structural cause. *Race,* he now argued, has both positive and negative meanings. "What men mean by 'race' when they are proud of race, is not blood race, but that kind of national unity and national type which belongs properly not to the race but to the nation." Although "some reactionary nationalism" invokes race to "legitimate empire," he wrote, this practice is to be distinguished from the "historical concept of race," which can "justify the historical group sense and . . . stimulate men into that sense or corporate destiny which is . . . an essential part of any healthy national unity." Introducing the term *social race* to describe the "only kind of race that is left to believe in"—that is, the "civilization type or civilization kind"—Locke now proposed that the older, negative notion of race was the residuum of a "caste system" grounded in preindustrial society. "We must pin a great deal of faith in the modern industrial and economic order," he declared, because "a competitive industrial order means that one generation rarely occupies the same social position as the generation immediately before or after." Locke reversed his earlier contention that consciousness of race was a distinctly modern phenomenon, genealogically linked to the emergence of democracy; now it was the modern capitalist system, based on competition and democracy, that would expunge the racial antipathies so harmful to the "health" of the nation.[14]

Secondary race consciousness was the term Locke chose to designate this "revised" sense of *social race*—the "counter-theory" or "counter-doctrine"—for which he was issuing his call. "This race pride or secondary race consciousness seems to be the social equivalent to self-respect in the individual moral life" and is "a doctrine peculiarly [appropriate] to this generation of the Afro-American," he wrote, for in collective political life "such race consciousness has been a feature of national revivals in European politics and European art . . . and in political propaganda for recognition of the right to self-determination." Citing the example of Poland under Russian domination, he noted that the Poles were fighting for the right to determine just what kind of recognition they receive. They wanted to be "free to maintain and to operate what is best and noblest in their cultural tradition and . . . have found it necessary to recreate the national type." "The prologue of political recognition of submerged nationalities," he observed, "has been their separate struggle for artistic expression. . . . [Such movements] by which the submerged classes are coming to their expression in art . . . are . . . the gateways through which culture-citizenship can finally be reached." Applying this model specifically to the situation of the Negro in the United States, Locke rejected the notion of the melting pot and called instead for "the development of social solidarity out of heterogenous elements." At the same time, he denied that what he was advocating was either "race isolation" or "race integrity." Rather, he was proposing a notion of "culture-citizenship" that would involve the merging of different "race-types" into a "civilization-type" in a process of "race adjustment" that would blend "two heterogeneous elements into a homogeneity of which either one in itself would have been incapable without the collaboration and help of the other." Secondary race consciousness was thus not an end in itself but a way station on the path to "race progress"; heterogeneity would lead to a new and higher national homogeneity. He concluded with a consummately pragmatic pronouncement: "Whatever theory [or] practice [moves] toward [race progress] is sound; whatever opposes and retards it is false."[15]

Several elements of the culturalist program that would be fully synthesized in *The New Negro* are present here: the strategic essentialism guiding Locke's theorization of "social race"; his view of the centrality of culture to "race progress"; and his conception of American democratic pluralism as the means to effect "race adjustment" through "culture-citizenship." This early formulation is also significant for what it reveals about the process of censorship and revision by which Locke would arrive at the more mature formulation of 1925. The contradictions noted above suggest that Locke had to wrestle down his original conviction that race was an "ethnic fiction," to be "eradicated" rather than sustained, as well as his earlier view that racist doctrine was essentially modern, a product of capitalism and imperialism—clearly a notion that he would have to dispense with if he were to envision contemporaneous American capitalism as a privileged site for Negro self-expression and hence full social and political acceptance. Locke's fragmentary notes for the course syllabus especially demonstrate that he was well aware of the extent to which his proposed path to "race adjustment" aligned him with conservatives, both white and Negro, hardly bent on desegregation. "[T]he biracial organization of . . . societies [is] a typical modern solution," he pondered, "essentially a transitional form—its immediate advantages often cause its adoption even by the group discriminated against—Booker

Washington's acceptance of it notable—as a means to an ultimate end it has appealed to many statesmen having to deal with race problems acutely affecting large groups." In addition, the notion of class—specifically, a concern for the "submerged classes"—is omnipresent throughout the 1916 text. Locke was at times somewhat blurry in his formulation of the relation of race to class to nation: it is not clear how "race issues can be broken up into class issues," and his slippage between "submerged classes" and oppressed nations is unrigorous. Nonetheless, it is apparent that—at least in all lectures except the last—he saw consciousness of race as a tool used by rulers to control the ruled, and—again, in all lectures except the last—*nation* as the expression of great power chauvinism and the agent of imperialist oppression. Such ideas would be expunged from his program by the time he produced *The New Negro*. The absence of a concept key to the 1925 text—*the folk*—should also be noted, particularly since the appearance and full elaboration of this term in Locke's thought —in effect, its substitution for the term *submerged classes*—would constitute the conceptual breakthrough enabling him to complete the deradicalization of his project.[16]

The insight into the making of *The New Negro* afforded by Locke's 1916 syllabus and lecture notes suggests that his 1925 text was a creative synthesis of significant proportions; those who castigate Locke for foreclosing debate over the identity of the New Negro should not deny that he was an original and powerful thinker. But it detracts nothing from Locke's project—indeed, it only enhances the project's historical and ideological importance—to note the extent to which its limitations were to a significant degree the limitations of the current leftist thinking that substantially influenced his work. To begin with, Locke was constrained by the lack of a comprehensive notion of ideology around which to organize his various insights into the functioning of "race antipathy." His notion that a feeling of solidarity based on race was "instinctive"—a proposition embraced by early-twentieth-century socialists from Spargo to Boas—flew in the face of his argument that it was "cultivated," "controlled," and "modified." Moreover, Locke's tendency to conflate class with race, rather than to explore their mutual articulation, suggestively relates his argument to those of other Socialist—or Socialist-influenced—theorists, from Debs to Pickens to Randolph, who similarly underestimated the broad social control function of racism within capitalism. The revealing formulation that competition for the same social good establishes the link between class issues and race issues suggests that he, like many of his contemporaries, was bound by the limits of the labor competition thesis as he sought to formulate a materialist analysis of the causes for "race antipathy."

Furthermore, Locke's various reversals of earlier arguments in the last lecture of the series, instead of expressing a confusion or inconsistency that was merely individual, reflect historically and politically determinate contradictions that not only were shared by other leftists and progressives of his day but also have had far-reaching consequences for leftist politics in the United States. Thus his proposal that race consciousness needed to be not "eradicated" but "revised" by means of a "counter-theory" or "counter-doctrine" not only links his stance with that of contemporaneous proponents of an "our America" seeking to contest and subvert the hegemony of "their" America but also casts a long shadow to the end of the century, when the counterdiscourses of various forms of identity politics would still be invoked as the alternative to mainstream racist ideology. In addition, Locke's somewhat peculiar belief that the United States, even if guilty of "commercial imperialism," nonetheless possessed a "competitive industrial" economic system that would do away with "race antipathy" reveals an affinity with the stagist doctrine that trusted the full development of capitalism would prepare the way for social equality—a doctrine endorsed not only by right-wing Socialists who embraced American exceptionalism in the era of 1919 but also by many present-day proponents of U.S. multiculturalism, at least of the mixed salad or patchwork quilt variety. It is perhaps no accident that the single appearance of the term *Afro-American* in the lecture series coincides with Locke's proposition, in the last lecture, that secondary race consciousness is a necessary stage in the "generation of the Afro-American": the reacceptance of "race" as a meaningful category for social analysis—and policy—is inextricably linked with Locke's recharacterization of U.S. capitalism as the favored site of "progress" and "opportunity." At the same time, Locke's closing paean to self-determination not only links political progress with cultural "group-expression" but also recalls the pragmatism with which Lenin and the Bolsheviks approached the colonial question. That Locke's pragmatism came with a Harvard pedigree and was intended to strengthen U.S. capitalist democracy, while Lenin's derived from the exigencies of anti-imperialist class struggle and was meant to hasten the abolition of capitalism worldwide, does not dispel the fact that *self-determination* was invoked by both. The implicit distinction between "good" nationalism and "bad" nationalism that underwrites Locke's program—and paves the way for the transmutation of politics into aesthetics—thus links it with the traditions of both the right wing and the left wing of contemporaneous socialism.

"Race Operates as Tradition, as Preferred Traits and Values":
The Roots of Culturalism

Several of Locke's writings from the early 1920s show him groping toward the culturalism of *The New Negro* and increasingly distancing himself from the radicalism that sporadically cropped up in the 1916 lecture series. In "Steps toward the Negro Theatre," published in the *Crisis* in December 1922, Locke deployed an extended organic metaphor to describe the conditions needed to nurture a Negro drama in which Negro actors would be able to exercise their talent:

> Culturally we are abloom in a new field, but it is yet decidedly a question as to what we shall reap—a few flowers or a harvest. . . .
> The Negro actor without the Negro drama is a sporadic phenomenon, a chance wayside flower, at mercy of wind and weed. He is precariously planted and still more precariously propagated. . . . Not that we would confine the dramatic talent of the race to the fence-fields and plant-rooms of race drama, but the vehicle of all sound art must be native to the group—our actors need their own soil, at least for sprouting. . . . Our art . . . must be safe somewhere from the exploitation and ruthlessness of the commercial theatre and in the protected housing of the art-theatre flower to the utmost perfection of the species.

While Locke was clearly enamored here with images of seed, soil, and fruit, planting and harvesting, it bears noting that the motif functioned allegorically, not naturalistically. That is, neither the Negro actor nor Negro drama was associated with soilness; there was no suggestion that rootedness in a folkish earthiness was to supply the source of Negro dramatic talent. Although Locke claimed to abjure an art cultivated in "fence-fields and plant-rooms," his conclusion that Negro drama might require the "protected housing of the art-theatre flower" suggested quite the opposite. In "The Ethics of Culture" (1923), an address delivered to freshmen at Howard, Locke espoused a comparably elitist notion of the origin and function of art and literature. Drawing on Matthew Arnold's definition— "'Culture is the best that has been thought and known in the world'"— he reminded his young listeners that "the highest intellectual duty is the duty to be cultured." Defending culture from the charge of being "*artificial, superficial, useless, selfish, over-refined,* and *exclusive,*" he urged his students, as "Americans," to "raise the low average of cultural tastes." This task had a specifically racial dimension, since "[a]s a race group we are at the critical stage where we are releasing creative artistic talent in excess of our group ability to understand and support it"; evidently Locke saw the necessity of developing an audience for what he would soon be calling a "renaissance" in Negro art and literature. In a text sprinkled with allusions to Holbein, Bacon, and Goethe, however, Locke was principally preparing his listeners to join "the educated classes" by acquainting themselves with the "ideals" of a "humanism" here defined in unabashedly Eurocentric terms. The notion that "soilness" signals the essence of the "race group" and that the culture his students needed to absorb was based in the folk was as yet absent from his formulation.[17]

In a 1924 essay entitled "The Concept of Race as Applied to Social Culture," published in the *Howard Review*, Locke manifested an intimate acquaintance with the Boasians—and the subtle distinctions among them—when he articulated a definition of the relation of race to culture that anticipated *The New Negro* in significant ways. At the end of the essay, he concluded with the formulation that the three principles making up "the methodological foundation and platform of the newer science of social culture" are the "*principle of organic interpretation*," the "*principle of cultural relativity*," and the "*dynamic and social interpretation of race*." The tortuous logical process by which he reached this conclusion, however, warrants scrutiny. Locke initially subscribed enthusiastically to various Boasian doctrines: cultural differences among peoples must be linked to social and historical, as opposed to physical, causes; and the "evolutionary formula" leading to a "grading of cultures" must be rejected. Nonetheless, Locke objected to Robert Lowie's "extreme cultural relativism," which, he warned, "denies all significant connection between racial and cultural factors." Referencing instead Edward Sapir's notion of "the genius of a people," Locke attempted to stake out a terrain on which the concept of "race"—shorn of any association with biology—would retain explanatory value in accounting for cultural difference. After emphasizing that physical anthropology's attempts to link culture with biology were "pseudo-scientific," he speculated:

> Nevertheless though there is lacking for the present any demonstrable explanation, there are certain ethnic traits the peculiarly stable and stock character of which must be interpreted as ethnically characteristic. They are in no sense absolutely permanent, the best psychological evidence as yet gives us no reason for construing them as inherent, yet they are factors not without an integral relationship one to the other not satisfactorily explained as mere historical combinations. Indeed it seems difficult and in some cases impossible to discover common historical factors to account for their relative constancy.

Locke's use of suasive verbs ("must," "seems") to substitute for argument, as well as his heavy deployment of negatives ("in no sense," "no reason," "not without," "not satisfactorily explained"), signaled his hesitancy: he was not about to proclaim race as causal of culture. Rather than reject the notion of race altogether, however, he proposed, following Alexander Goldenweiser, that "instead of regarding culture as expressive of race," race should be "regarded as itself a culture product." This "redefinition" of race as "a fact in the social or ethnic sense" made it susceptible, he argued, to "the independent investigation of its differences and their causes apart from the investigation of the factors and differentiae of physical race." But this formulation was ambiguous: if the phrase "its differences" means "the differences of race" and the phrase "their causes" means "the causes of the differences of race," but if race is itself an expression of culture, it is not clear how race, even if redefined as "a fact in the social or ethnic sense," can be seen as causal of culture, since culture is what causes it to begin with. Locke's rhetorical contortions suggest that he was on some level aware of the logical fallacies in his argument for a strategically essentialist notion of "social race."[18]

The circularity in Locke's reasoning in the 1924 essay became all the more patent when he declared:

> Confident that this is the correct scientific conception of culture and its most warrantable scientific basis of approach and study, we return to the consideration of whether or not by such interpretation the concept of race is not entirely relegated from serious consideration in connection with it. So considerable is the shift of emphasis and meaning that at times it does seem that the best procedure would be to substitute for the term race the term *culture-group*. But what has become absolutely disqualified for the explanation of culture groups taken as totalities becomes in a much more scientific and verifiable way a main factor or explanation of its various cultural components. Race accounts for a great many of the specific elements of the cultural heredity, and the sense of race may itself be regarded as one of the operative factors in culture since it determines the stressed values which become the conscious symbols and tradition of the culture. Such stressed values are themselves factors in the process of culture making, and account primarily for the persistence and resistance of culture traits. . . .
>
> Race operates as tradition, as preferred traits and values, and when these things change culturally speaking ethnic remoulding is taking place. Race, then, so far as the ethnologist is concerned, seems to lie in that peculiar selective preference of certain culture-traits and resistance to certain others which is characteristic of all types and levels of social organization.

Although Locke repeatedly claimed the "scientific" validity of his redefinition of race, assertion supplanted demonstration. Even if race operates through the "soft" determination of setting boundaries rather than the "hard" determination of bringing realities into being, it is evident that he was now insisting, on the one hand, that race *causes* the "peculiar selective preference" manifested in culture and, on the other, that "race is . . . itself a culture product." In his assertion that "race accounts for a great many of the specific elements of cultural heredity," even the essentialist language of biologism had crept in through the back door. Whereas in the 1916 lectures Locke posited the notion of secondary race consciousness as a temporary palliative—needed to supply African Americans with the psychological means to embrace a strategy of self-determination that would be superseded by inclusion within the "civilization-type" of the "homogeneous" nation—here he proposed a far more permanent notion of race, one valorized as immutable difference. Although stagism in politics, taking the form of a secondary race consciousness enabling self-determination, had been intended to supersede and negate the racist doctrine that African Americans constituted a "non-historical people," lower on the scale of both cultural and biological evolution, it ended up compounding the racial essentialism it had set out to delegitimate. *The New Negro* would be born out of this paradox.[19]

While a number of conceptual threads in Locke's writings from the early 1920s would be gathered in *The New Negro*, it bears noting that an explicit repudiation of communism would number among them. A July 1923 review of *Public Opinion in War and Peace* by Abbot Lawrence Lowell—then president of Harvard—reveals that there was an integral relationship between culturalism and anticommunism in Locke's coalescing world outlook. Locke attacked Lowell's patrician qualities—his "distrust of large-area democracy, his abhorrence of moral and doctrinaire issues in politics, his disapprobation of the idea of class struggle, his downright phobia of mass control and the unreason of the crowd." Lowell's "managerial conception of social institutions" prevented him from "entertaining . . . any view that would make the forms of society themselves grow out of the cleavages of opinion and the clash of group purposes," wrote Locke. Lowell's universe was guided by the "naive aristocratic view that God and the upper classes in consultation or pre-established harmony ordained and planned society." Lowell's study, "platitudinous and almost specious in basic theory and ground conclusions," could do little more than "predict the past," Locke scathingly concluded. Although Locke made no mention of Lowell's stewardship at Harvard, lurking in the background of his polemic was the recent scandal over Lowell's aggressive role in preventing several Negro freshmen from living in campus housing—as well as, no doubt, Locke's own bitter experiences with Harvard's racism during his student days in the first decade of the century.[20]

But even as Locke castigated Lowell's aristocratic worldview, which presumably blinded him to the drift of history, Locke's own formulation of the relationship of leaders to the "mass movements [that] gather momentum with each decade" was hardly free of elitism:

> It is more and more true that the leader is the man who knows which way the crowd is going or is likely to go; to manage means largely to be in a position to profit by, rather than actually to make or direct or control social forces. In other words, just as we have had to revise our conception of mind as only a small part intelligence and rationality and in larger part impulse and groping, so must we give [up] the pet fictions of minority direction and moulding of society, and view the classes as the creatures of the masses, even when they are their masters, and see society as the expression of the common mind.

Locke's notion of the relation of "classes" to "masses" is at first glance puzzling: how can the former be "creatures" of the latter and at the same time be their "masters"? What concept of "management" informs that proposition that the leader of the masses is one who can "profit by . . . social forces," without making, directing, or controlling them? Moving toward formulation here but not yet explicit is a view of culture as the site at which the "common mind" gains articulation, at once making the masses the key to the "direction and moulding of society" while still allowing the classes to occupy the position of masters. In this context, particular significance attaches to a comment that Locke makes in passing about an issue on which he and Lowell agree—namely, his belief that Lowell's "warning against the ultra-collective interpretation of society is somewhat sound," for this "ultra-collective interpretation of society"— presumably communism—would not sustain but instead would abolish the reciprocity between classes and masses that Locke saw as vital to the growth and development of the cultural movement that was taking shape in his mind and that he, as a "leader" cognizant of the motion of the masses, might be "in a position to profit by." Locke might abhor Lowell's "pet fictio[n] of minority direction and molding of society," but he seemingly saw eye to eye with his antagonist on the danger of "ultra-collectiv[ity]" to the social order consisting of classes and masses, creatures and masters.[21]

The "Maturing Speech of Full Racial Utterance": Locke's Discovery of the Folk

Although Locke's writings from the early 1920s show him poised to make the culturalist breakthrough, his approach to the relation of race to culture—especially in "The Concept of Race as Applied to Social Culture"—still appealed to scientific canons of legitimacy. The argument for culturalism was not itself "culturalist"; there was no invocation of "roots" or "soilness" as central to the metonymic nationalist project that would make Negro self-determination equivalent to other self-determinationist programs, both cultural and political, of the day. The crucial concept enabling Locke to complete the transition from politics to aesthetics would be the folk. This notion had figured centrally in Du Bois's discussion of the folk as group "genius" and hence as an antidote to "double consciousness" in *The Souls of Black Folk*. Whereas for Du Bois the folk bore multiple traces of its Herderian origins, for Locke the concept retained a trace of these origins—both Boas and Sapir wrote of the "genius" of different peoples—but functioned in a distinctly modern way. Locke's deployment of the folk cannot be understood apart from contemporaneous postwar debates over the relation of race to nation, colonial self-determination to great power nationalism.[22]

In "Harlem: Mecca of the New Negro"—the full title of the March 1925 *Survey Graphic* version of *The New Negro*—Locke's introductory essay, "Harlem," announced the centrality of the folk to the paradigm guiding his anthologizing project:

> If we were to offer a symbol of what Harlem has come to mean in the short span of twenty years it would be another statue of liberty on the landward side of New York. It stands for the folk movement which in human significance can be compared only with the pushing of the western frontier in the first half of the last century, or the waves of immigration which have swept in from overseas in the last half. . . . Harlem represents the Negro's latest thrust towards Democracy. . . . [It is] a deliberate flight not only from countryside to city, but from medieval America to modern.
>   Harlem is. . . . a race capital. . . . The tide of Negro migration, northward and city-ward, is not to be fully explained as a blind flood started by the demands of war industry coupled with the shutting off of foreign migration, or by the pressure of poor crops coupled with increased social terrorism in certain sections of the South and the Southwest. . . . The wash and rush of this human tide on the beach line of the northern city centers is to be explained primarily in terms of a new vision of opportunity. . . .
>   In Harlem, Negro life is seizing upon its first chances for group expression and self-determination. . . . Without pretense to their political significance, Harlem has the same role to play for the New Negro as Dublin has had for the New Ireland or Prague for the New Czechoslovakia. . . .
>   These moving, half-awakened newcomers provide an exceptional seedbed for the germinating contacts of the enlightened minority.[23]

In his assertion that the nation's most recent "folk movement" is from the Middle Ages into modernity, Locke's essay gestured toward a Marxist modes of production narrative, one that would theorize the migrants' diasporic movement as historical as well as geographical, structural as well as spatial. This was merely a nod, however, for throughout his discussion the migrants signify not as "workers" but only as a "folk"; Locke's 1916 designation of the African American masses as "submerged classes" had, it seems, been left behind. History was seen in a general way to create the conditions effecting the Great Migration, but such flagrantly material causal factors as the draw of wartime jobs in northern industry, the devastation wrought by the boll weevil, or the "terrorism" of lynching were mentioned only to be repudiated. Moreover, the migrants' newfound belonging in the metropolis of New York affirmed their status as citizens in both the self-determining black nation and the larger nation. African Americans might have made their first migration across the Atlantic under conditions of compulsion, but the beacon of their modern migration was, like that calling to their European counterparts, the Statue of Liberty. Locke's troping of the migration as a "human tide" co-opted Stoddard, but Locke reassured his readers that *this* "rising tide of color" was not one they should fear, for it was motivated by the same "vision of opportunity" that is held before—and presumably available to—all Americans. These migrants were associated with the pioneers involved in the "pushing of the western frontier" in the previous century; like Waldo Frank, Locke conveniently elided the history of native genocide in his celebration of a new kind of pioneering in a newly conceived kind of America. Above all, Locke's migrants were bearers of a culture; Harlem was a "race capital" because it was a "nascent cente[r] of folk-expression and self-determination." Even if the bearers of folk culture were only "half-awakened," they provided "an exceptional seed-bed for the germinating contacts of the enlightened minority"; one is reminded of Frank's description in *Our America* of the nation as "a turmoiled giant who cannot speak," awaiting the voice of the enlightened nationalist writer who will "lift America into self-knowledge." The description of Harlem as the capital of a nation within a nation rendered its role in promoting Negro self-determination in terms that are both geographical and aesthetic. But the folk were saved from the fate of being a "non-historical people" not by engaging in vanguard action as their Russian counterparts did—that is, aiding the proletariat in smashing the bourgeois state—but by bringing their soilness to the doorsteps of the "enlightened minority" that would then plant the seeds of the culture of modernity. The folk, in

Locke's formulation, do not engage in class struggle; they engage in song. The conceptual currency through which Locke negotiated the Negro's entry into modernity—the price of inclusion—guaranteed good behavior; not equality but the chance at "opportunity" was the migrants' felt need. Although the black citizenry of Washington might have driven through the streets brandishing guns during the "Red Summer," the proud citizens of Harlem would not destroy the city on the hill that represented their triumphal self-determination. Harlem had definitively replaced Bogalusa as the metonymy for a better world.

Locke clearly had in place the guiding role played by the folk by the time he brought out the *Survey Graphic* version of his anthology. More than extension and amplification were involved, however, in the production nine months later of *The New Negro*, which represents a concerted effort to efface—to "e-radicate"—almost all traces of a class politics from its culturalist reassessment—"re-vision"—of its title subject. Since space considerations prevent a full examination of the differences between the two versions, I highlight only those points that most suggestively reveal the politics guiding Locke's revisionary project.

Locke's alterations in and additions to his own contributions to the volume reveal that he subjected not just the work of his contributors to critical scrutiny. In the *Survey Graphic* version, Locke's pieces consisted of "Harlem," "Enter the New Negro," "Youth Speaks," and a two-paragraph essay on "The Arts of the Ancestors." In *The New Negro*, most of the paragraphs constituting the first two of these were merged to form the famous signature essay, "The New Negro"; the comments on African art were expanded into a feature-length essay, "The Legacy of the Ancestral Arts"; "Youth Speaks" was revised as "Negro Youth Speaks" in minor but significant ways; and "The Negro Spirituals" was added. Locke also added a foreword stressing the key features of his anthology:

> This volume aims to document the New Negro culturally and socially,— to register the transformations of the inner and outer life of the Negro in America that have so significantly taken place in the last few years. There is ample evidence of a New Negro in the latest phases of social change and progress, but still more in the internal world of the Negro mind and spirit. Here in the very heart of the folk-spirit are the essential forces, and folk interpretation is truly vital and representative only in terms of these.

Where the *Survey Graphic* version began with a discussion of Harlem as a site of world-historical demographic change, the book version stipulated that the "internal world of the Negro mind and spirit" is the locus of interest. Moreover, the later text brought in the folk not as the collective agent of a "folk-movement" but as the repository of a "folk-spirit" that needed to be subjected to "folk interpretation" if the "essential forces" of change—now described as residing "in the internal world of the Negro mind and spirit"—were to be fully appreciated. The aestheticist and quietist implications of this reformulation are apparent.[24]

The foreword then expanded on the American nationalist implications of the emergence of the culture-bearing New Negro:

> Yet the New Negro must be seen in the perspective of a New World, and especially of a New America. Europe seething in a dozen centers with emergent nationalities, Palestine full of a renascent Judaism—these are no more alive with the progressive forces of our era than the quickened centers of the lives of black folk. America seeking a new spiritual expansion and artistic maturity, trying to found an American literature, a national art, and national music implies a Negro-American culture seeking the same satisfactions and objectives. Separate as it may be in color and substance, the culture of the Negro is of a pattern integral with the times and with its cultural setting.

Where the *Survey Graphic* version had dubbed Harlem the "Mecca of the New Negro"—a formulation with cosmopolitan, indeed Orientalist, overtones—here it was a site for producing the pure products of America. Moreover, even though the notion of Harlem as the site of discovery of a "new soul" suggested a Baueresque notion of African Americans as a nation in diaspora, Locke insisted that the New Negro's project of self-determination was entirely "integral" with the larger goal of creating a "national art." At a stroke, Locke asserted the Negro's unproblematic loyalty to the nation yet raised no anxieties that Negro self-determination—"separate . . . in color and substance"—would intrude on—"integrate"—the rest of the nation's space, either cultural or geographical. The foreword ended with a bold rhetorical flourish: "Negro life is not only establishing new contacts and founding new centers, it is finding a new soul. There is a fresh spiritual and cultural focusing. We have, as the heralding sign, an unusual outburst of creative expression. There is a renewed race-spirit that consciously and proudly sets itself apart. Justifiably, then, we speak of the offerings of this book embodying these ripening forces as culled from the first fruits of the Negro Renaissance." Not only did Locke define *creative expression* as the supremely meaningful mode of praxis; he also posited that the instances of it included in his volume constituted a "renaissance," a term he had not used in the *Survey Graphic* version of his anthology. He also deployed the organic trope to emphasize the relation of culture to geography: the "first fruits" constituting the "offerings" of the "race-spirit" had been produced on a soil—a nation within a nation—that "proudly sets itself apart."[25]

Locke's increased reliance on folk and soil as mediating categories in the signifying chain of metonymic nationalism was underlined by various changes that he made in *The New Negro*'s version of "Negro Youth Speaks," his manifesto heralding the arrival of the young New Negro writer as culture hero. Where in the *Survey Graphic* version Locke had written that "when youth speaks, the future listens," in *The New Negro* he significantly expanded his claim: "The Younger Generation comes, bringing its gifts. They are the first fruits of the Negro Renaissance. Youth speaks, and the voice of the New Negro is heard. What stirs inarticulately in the masses is already vocal upon the lips of the talented few, and the future listens, however the present may shut its ears. Here we have Negro youth . . . foretelling in new notes and accents the maturing speech of full racial utterance." Building on the notion of "offerings" in the foreword, this formulation played on the dual notion of "gift" that pervades the anthology: those who possess particular "gifts"—a term bearing strong implications of innateness—happily contribute them to the nation's common store. Accompanying the conflation of race with culture was an implied economic model that portrayed the nation's different peoples not as wage earners engaged in the production of commodities for profit but as happy participants in a kind of ongoing potlatch, in which their distinctive "racial utterance" was their contribution to the national party.[26]

Jean Toomer figured prominently in Locke's revision of "Negro Youth Speaks." While the earlier text simply commented that Toomer "gives a folk-lilt and ecstasy to the American modernists," in *The New Negro* version the commentary on Toomer was significantly expanded, turning Locke's former protégé into a crucial spokesperson for the emerging generation of diggers into the "exceptional seed-bed" that is the folk: "[T]he young Negro writers dig deep into the racy peasant undersoil of the race life. Jean Toomer writes: 'Georgia opened me. And it may well be said that I received my initial impulse to an individual art from my experience here. For no other section of the country has so stirred me. There one finds soil, soil in the sense the Russians know it,—the soil every art and literature that is to live must be imbedded in.'" Locke ended his tribute to the coming generation by stressing its ability to conjoin "the sophistications of modern style" with "a fresh distinctive note that the majority of them admit as the instinctive gift of the folk-spirit." Locke's tautological play on the word *racy*, compounded by Toomer's own tautological play on *soil,* suffused with hyper-materiality the relation of race to place. Locke's formulation thus laid bare the process by which he was constructing the metonymic chain whereby region and soil supply the critical links between race and nation. If rural blacks are peasants, and peasants are folk, and folk are connected to the soil through their culture, and if soil constitutes region, and if the nation is made up of its regions, then the United States could be defined—typified—through the culture of its most oppressed and impoverished racial minority. Any potentially revolutionary association signaled by Toomer's reference to Russia was canceled out, for Locke's argument was that, instead of signaling exotic otherness, the vernacular of southern black folk—and the project of the writers representing this vernacular—was quintessentially American. That the black peasantry's role in this process was "instinctive" only enhanced the value of the "gift" blacks were contributing to the nation's cultural feast.[27]

In "The Negro Spirituals," Locke declared that the songs Du Bois dubbed the "sorrow songs" "are really the most characteristic product of the race genius as yet in America. But the very elements which make them uniquely expressive of the Negro make them at the same time deeply representative of the soil that produced them. Thus, as unique spiritual products of American life, they become nationally as well as racially characteristic. It may not be readily conceded now that the song of the Negro is America's folk-song; but if the spirituals are what we think them to be, a classic folk expression, then this is their ultimate destiny." A cagey Hegelian, Locke valorized the art of the African American rural masses by claiming that, if not at present then in the days to come, the spirituals would be "America's folk-song." Once their regional quality—their being "deeply representative of the soil that produced them"—was fully granted, they would assume their metonymic status and role; the "always already" character of the metonymic chain was thus projected into the future. But even as he specified the historically conditioned character of this signifying process—that is, the socially constructed nature of the nation—Locke stipulated that the spirituals reflected "qualities put there by instinct." The spirituals were "racially characteristic" and "produced" by "the soil." The category of soilness thus permitted Locke to move back and forth at will between essentialist and social constructionist notions of racial identity. This category also permitted Locke to pass over the blues—the principal musical expression of the newly proletarianized migrants whom he insistently celebrated as a folk—as a competitor for the mantle of typicality. The manifestation through soil of "spirit" not only guaranteed the spirituals' authenticity but also validated their claim to folk, and hence nationally significant, status. For all his claim to be getting down in the dirt with (or of) the masses, Locke guaranteed that the folk would be represented not by a rowdy earthiness but by a soulful soilness.[28]

Even as Locke stressed what was "racially characteristic" in American Negro literature and art, however, he balked at the primitivistic attribution of artistry to innateness when it came to the analysis of African art. "The lesson of a classic background, the lesson of discipline, of style, of technical control pushed to the limits of technical mastery," Locke declared, constituted the legacy of African art. The spirit embodied in "Aframerican" art, by contrast, was "exactly the opposite. What we have thought primitive in the American Negro—his naivete, his sentimentalism, his exuberance and his improvizing spontaneity are then neither characteristically African nor to be explained as an ancestral heritage. They are the result of his peculiar experience in America and the emotional upheaval of its trials and ordeals. . . . [T]hey represent essentially the working of environmental forces rather than the outcropping of a race psychology." African art, Locke acknowledged, was being appreciated primarily by artists of European origin, who had inherited it "by tradition only, and through the channels of an exotic curiosity and interest." Although he wanted to sunder any biological knot imagined to exist between African and "Aframerican" art, Locke argued that, "once known and appreciated," African art "can scarcely have less influence upon the blood descendants, bound to it by a sense of direct cultural kinship." The challenge facing the Negro artist was to discover the "slumbering gift of the folk temperament that most needs reachievement and reexpression." Once recovered, this "gift" would reveal that it had always been present, simply biding its time, like Sleeping Beauty, until its modern prince came.[29]

"The New Frontage on American Life": From The Survey Graphic to The New Negro

The culturalist contradictions informing Locke's own contributions to *The New Negro* informed his selections for the rest of the anthology, especially as it was revised from its original *Survey Graphic* version. It bears noting, however, that the *Survey Graphic* version of the anthology itself represented a reshaping—and in some key respects a taming—of Locke's original intent. Correspondence between Locke and the *Survey Graphic*'s editor, Paul Kellogg, reveals that, in its initial conception, the Harlem issue was supposed to consist of the "Introductory Article by

Locke"; "The New Negro"; a handful of poems arranged under the rubric "Poems of Attitude"; and then three main sections, designated as "The New Stage, The New Problem, The New Solution." The first of these sections was to consist of three prose pieces that survived into the special Harlem issue—by James Weldon Johnson, Rudolph Fisher, and W. A. Domingo—as well as two that did not—a piece by Eric Walrond called "The Mirrors of Harlem" and one by the British writer Rebecca West entitled "Harlem as a Foreigner Sees It." The second section—alternately designated "The Negro Expresses Himself"—would have consisted of the articles by Eunice Hunton, J. A. Rogers, Arthur Schomburg, Albert C. Barnes, W. E. B. Du Bois ("The Negro Brings His Gifts"), and Locke ("Youth Speaks") that did appear in the *Survey Graphic.* The final section—originally entitled "Black and White: Studies in Race Contact and Reactions"—would have comprised the pieces by Melville Herskovits, Walter White, Kelly Miller, Charles S. Johnson, and Elise McDougald that also appeared in the *Survey Graphic.* The original plan also included a piece by the Harlem Socialist leader Hubert Harrison, entitled "The White Man's War," that did not make it into the *Survey Graphic* issue. The editors' description of this never-published article is worth quoting in full: "The effect of the war upon the Negro, and the analysis of the disillusionment of the treatment inconsistent with the principles of democracy and self-determination, reaction among the generation that took part in it toward the church, the state, and capitalism. The points of radical indictment and the forces of agitation and protest,—the attitude of radical organizations toward the Negro, and of the Negro to radical social programs." Kellogg, responding to Locke's proposed outline, expressed enthusiasm for the first two sections but remarked that the last section had aroused concerns at a *Survey Graphic* staff meeting because it was "disproportionately long." It is surely no coincidence, however, that it was Harrison's piece that fell under the axe, even though it had been accorded one of the shortest word limits (2,200) of all the pieces under consideration. Perhaps Harrison's "radical indictment" of "capitalism"—a word that would not make it into the *Survey Graphic,* much less *The New Negro*—was too much for Kellogg and his colleagues. There is no evidence that Locke contested this decision.[30]

Apparently not content with eliminating an explicitly leftist voice from the anthology, Locke undertook revisions of the *Survey Graphic* version that redirected in an aestheticist direction the more sociological mode of the earlier version, which had contained several decidedly noncelebratory pieces. Kelly Miller's "Harvest of Race Prejudice" and Eunice Hunton's "Breaking Through" stressed the negative aspects of the social forces that were making the new Harlem. Miller opined that Harlem, "the most gigantic instance of racial segregation in the United States," was "a fair specimen of the harvest of race prejudice"; his invocation of the organic trope suggested a less than enthusiastic estimate of the fruit being gathered from the soil of this "city within a city." Hunton proclaimed at the outset of her essay—which was originally to be called "Breaking through the Ghetto Bonds"—that "Harlem is a modern ghetto." Utilizing the trope of enclosure to describe the deleterious effects of race prejudice, Hunton observed that Harlem might be "a small city, self-sufficient, complete it itself—a riot of color and personality, a medley of song and tears, a canvas of browns and golds and flaming reds," but that its inhabitants were nonetheless "bound," unable to leave "its narrow confines." For Miller and Hunton, Harlem neither could nor should stand for the nation as a whole. Similarly, Winthrop D. Lane's anecdotal commentary, "Ambushed in the City: The Grim Side of Harlem," depicted this "Mecca" as a den of hustlers and thieves bent on stripping the migrants of their paltry savings. Rudolph Fisher's "The South Lingers On" depicts Jake Crenshaw, a refugee from Jim Crow, whose status as migrant evokes only contempt in the clerk who stands between him and a job. There is no place for Jake, representative of a deracinated folk, in the asphalt jungle: "He looked up at the buildings. They were menacingly big and tall and close. There were no trees. No ground for trees to grow from." The Harlem set forth in these pieces cast doubt on the notion that migrants could readily reroot themselves in the asphalt of cosmopolitan modernity, much less retain the aura of soilness that would enable the "enlightened minority" of artists and writers to drop seeds among them. Apparently there was a negative aspect to the "laboratory of race-welding" that was Harlem; pieces that dwelled too insistently on this aspect would have to be eliminated from Locke's text.[31]

Besides scrapping various pieces that suggested the difficulties of folk transplantation, Locke, when converting the special Harlem issue into *The New Negro*, added several essays that built on the theme of the Negro's distinctive contribution to the national culture. It is perhaps significant that, next to "soil" and "fruit," the trope most commonly appearing in *The New Negro* was "gift." *The New Negro* featured a new piece entitled "The Gift of Laugher" by Jessie Redmon Fauset, the literary editor of the *Crisis*. Comparing the Negro with "the Irish, the Russian and the Magyar" in "the conviction that . . . he has some peculiar offering which shall contain the very essence of the drama," Fauset argued that "the black man bringing gifts, and particularly the gift of laughter, to the American stage is easily the most anomalous, the most inscrutable figure of the century." Aware that stereotyping had "befogged and misted" this "great gift," Fauset nonetheless maintained its reality. In an essay on Negro drama, the Howard Players theatrical director Montgomery Gregory argued that "the same racial characteristics that are responsible for [the Negro's folk-music] are destined to express themselves with similar excellence in the kindred art of drama." Harvard's president emeritus Charles William Eliot, he continued, "recently expressed the inspiring thought that America should not be a 'melting-pot' for the diverse races gathered on her soil but that each race should maintain its essential integrity and contribute its own special and peculiar gift to our composite civilization: not a 'melting-pot' but a symphony where each instrument contributes its particular quality of music to an ensemble of harmonious sounds." Although he mistakenly attributed to Eliot the orchestra metaphor originated by Kallen and elaborated by Randolph Bourne, Gregory demonstrated its ideological compatibility with the notion of "gift" as innate proclivity, as well as its connection to the discourse of cultural pluralism. That this discourse was given the stamp of approval by the past president of Harvard, site of the recent scandal over discrimination in campus housing, appears not to have roused Gregory's suspicions about why cultural pluralism might so readily accommodate the notions of "gift" and "essential integrity."[32]

In addition to foregrounding *The New Negro* as a contribution to the nation's common cultural till, Locke undertook strategic revisions—from retitlings to larger alterations—in several articles reprinted in the later version of his anthology. Walter White's piece on passing—called "The Psychology of the Color Line" in the planning outline and "Color Lines" in the *Survey Graphic*—was retitled "The Paradox of Color." James Weldon Johnson's essay "The Making of Harlem" became "Harlem: The Culture Capital"; with the elimination of Miller's and Hunton's pieces critical of ghettoization, there was little remaining opposition to Johnson's closing claim that "New York guarantees its Negro citizens the fundamental rights of American citizenship and protects them in the exercise of those rights. In return the Negro loves New York and is proud of it, and contributes in his way to its greatness." Charles S. Johnson's "Black Workers in the City"—accompanied in the *Survey Graphic* by a drawing by Mahonri Young of a strapping male Negro proletarian entitled "The Laborer" that was eliminated in the 1925 book—became "The New Frontage on American Life." Omitted from the revised version of Johnson's essay was a paragraph detailing the "grim shadows" of inadequate health care in the lives of Harlemites, as well as an explicit reference to the Socialist *Messenger* as the essay's source of information about the racist deficiencies of labor unions. The finale to the revised text of Johnson's piece subtly shifted the ground of its argument. The *Survey Graphic* version ended with the restrained pronouncement that "a common purpose is integrating these energies and once leashed to a purposeful objective, it is not improbable that in industry and in the life of the city the black workers will compensate in utility and progressiveness for what they lack in numbers and traditions." The *New Negro* version noted that "just as these currents move down and across and intersect, so may one find an utter maze of those rationalizations of attitudes of differently placed Negro groups toward life in general, and their status in particular. But a common purpose is integrating these energies born of new conflicts, and it is not at all improbable that the culture which has both nourished and abused these strivings will, in the end, be enriched by them." During the nine-month gap between the two texts, "black workers" had been replaced by "differently placed Negro groups." Moreover, the goal of changing the position of these workers "in industry and in the life of the city" had turned into the goal of enriching "the culture which has both nourished and abused these strivings." Culturalism was now the principal—it would seem, the only—socially transformative praxis.[33]

Neither version of Locke's anthology paid much attention to the New Negro who was not male. As it appeared in the *Survey Graphic*, however, Elise Johnson McDougald's "Double Task: The Struggle of Negro Women for Sex and Race Emancipation" observed that single mothers faced particular "stress and struggle," insofar as they lived in neighborhoods where "rents are large, standards of dress and recreation high and costly, and social danger on the increase." In the *New Negro* version, retitled "The Task of Negro Womanhood," this sobering assessment was toned down by an additional comment:

> One cannot resist the temptation to pause for a moment and pay tribute to these Negro mothers. And to call attention to the service she is rendering to the nation, in her struggle against great odds to educate and care for one group of the country's children. If the mothers of the race should ever be honored by state or federal legislation, the artist's imagination will find a more inspiring subject in the modern Negro mother—self-directed but as loyal and tender as the much extolled, yet pitiable black mammy of slavery days.

Coupled with the 1925 anthology's new frontispiece of a Winold Reiss portrait of mother and child called "The Brown Madonna," McDougald's revised text indicated that a crucial component of *The New Negro*'s mission was to recruit the image of the Negro woman as mother, suitably dignified and domesticated, to the cause of the "good" nationalism

Locke's text espoused. Where the stereotype of the mammy "loyal and tender" to the slavemaster had been "pitiable" and was justly relegated to the dustbin of history, the "modern Negro mother" was also "loyal and tender," viewing her maternal task as a contribution to both family and nation.[34]

In their differing portrayals of the African diaspora, the two versions of W. A. Domingo's discussion of Caribbean immigrants tellingly revealed the editorial hand of the cultural pluralist as patriot. The *Survey Graphic* version, entitled "The Tropics in New York," read:

> Within Harlem's seventy or eighty blocks, for the first time in their lives, colored people of Spanish, French, Dutch, Arabian, Danish, Portuguese, British and native African ancestry meet and move together.
>
> A dusky tribe of destiny seekers, these brown and black and yellow folk, eyes filled with visions of their heritage—palm fringed sea shores, murmuring streams, luxuriant hills and vales—have made their epical march from the far corners of the earth to Harlem. They bring with them vestiges of their folk life—their lean sunburnt faces, their quiet, halting speech, fortified by a graceful insouciance, their light, loose-fitting clothes of ancient cut telling the story of a dogged, romantic pilgrimage to the El Dorado of their dreams.

In the revised text—entitled, notably, "Gift of the Tropics"—Domingo wrote:

> Almost unobserved, America plays her usual rôle in the meeting, mixing and welding of the colored peoples of the earth. A dusky tribe of destiny seekers, these brown and black and yellow folk, eyes filled with visions of an alien heritage—palm-fringed seashores, murmuring streams, luxuriant hills and vales—have made an epical march from the far corners of the earth to the Port of New York and America. They bring the gift of the black tropics to America and to their kinsmen. With them come the vestiges of a quaint folk life, other social traditions, and as for the first time in their lives, colored people of Spanish, French, Dutch, Arabian, Danish, Portuguese, British and native African ancestry meet and move together, there comes into Negro life the stir and leavening that is uniquely American.

In the later version, Domingo's re-presented Caribbean migrants were exoticized; their heritage was "alien," their traditions "quaint." Yet these qualities were presented as no bar to the migrants' being welcomed in the nation; four times in as many sentences there were reminders that the migrants were now in America. The United States here emerged as the crucible of Pan-Africanism. What need was there for Garveyism—or for that matter colonial self-determination, much less proletarian internationalism—if the United States performed for even its darkest new inhabitants its time-honored role of welcoming the world's huddled masses? Domingo made no mention here of the racially exclusionary immigration acts of 1921 and 1924, even though less than six months earlier he had published in *Opportunity* a searing critique of the 1924 act, which, he charged, "places Negro blood in despite" by its discriminatory assignment of differential immigration quotas to Caucasians and Negroes. The Harlem of *The New Negro* was the capital of a nation within a larger nation with which it appeared to be on excellent diplomatic terms.[35]

The contributions to Locke's project by several white critics and commentators epitomized the contradictory ideological proclivities guiding Locke's editorial project. "Difference" was valorized as the key to citizenship in Konrad Bercovici's "Rhythm of Harlem." Opining that what he had seen and felt in Harlem was "a different culture, a different music, a different art, of which the Negroes are capable and which should be like a gift to the races they live with," Bercovici concluded that Negroes "are not inferiors. They do not have to strive for equality. They are different. Emphasizing that difference in their lives, in their culture, is what will give them and what should give them their value." Alfred C. Barnes's "Negro Art and America"—positioned in *The New Negro* right after Locke's opening essay—offered a more frankly essentialist account of the origins of Negro art in "a primitive nature upon which a white man's education has never been harnessed." The Negro, Barnes asserted, was "a poet by birth," whose art "is so deeply rooted in his nature that it has thrived on a foreign soil where the traditions and practices tend to stamp out and starve out both the plant and its flowers." By contrast, "[m]any centuries of civilization" had "attenuated [the white man's] original gifts," and he had "wandered too far from the elementary human needs and their easy means of natural satisfaction." Because the Negro was "simple, ingenuous, forgiving, good-natured, wise and obliging," however, he would "consent to form a working alliance with us for the development of a richer American civilization to which he will contribute his full share." In Barnes's view of Negro primitivism as the needed antidote to white overcivilization, allusions to "nature" and "gift" were integral to a politics of culturalist "contribution"; the organic trope expressed allegiances to both racialism and nationalism. For Bercovici and Barnes alike, recognizing "difference" involved not a call for equality but a notion of complementarity that implied the need to continue those patterns of segregation that could help sustain what was unique—and so beneficial to the nation at large—in the Negro's particularity. Bercovici was quite explicit on the subject. "To pile up wealth as the white man

has done will not further [the Negroes]," he wrote. "To pile up industrial organizations, institutions, universities, charities and armies will not
do it." What will do it, he opined, was "[a] different culture, a different
music, a different art, of which the Negroes are capable and which should
be like a gift to the other races they live with."[36]

The New Negro's correlative culturalist arguments for the Negro's
"belonging" in the mainstream of American democracy were hardly more
emancipatory, for they simply overlooked the "difference" produced by
racism, if not race. In "The Negro's Americanism," the Boasian disciple
Melville J. Herskovits described a recent trip to Harlem, during which
"it occurred to me that what I was seeing was a community just like any
other American community. The same pattern, only a different shade!"
He pondered, "Where, then, is the 'peculiar' community of which I had
heard so much? To what extent, if any, has the Negro genius developed
a culture peculiar to it in America? I did not find it in the great teeming
center of Negro life in Harlem, where, if anywhere, it should be found.
May it not then be true that the Negro has become acculturated to the
prevailing white culture and has developed the patterns of culture typical of American life?" As various scholars have pointed out, Herskovits—
partially at Locke's prompting—would later effect a 180-degree turnabout,
arguing forcefully for the centrality of African survivals in American black
culture. What is noteworthy in Herskovits's 1925 statement, however,
is not simply his blindness to what he would later see as obvious but also
his insistence that "social pattern" consisted in culture as such—an assumption making him apparently impervious to the economic hardship
and demographic trauma that had drawn the attention of Fisher, Hunton, Miller, and Lane. The radical cultural anthropologist who as a youth
had sported an IWW button and, in 1919, had celebrated the Bolshevik
Revolution as proof against stagism was now turning the Boasian doctrine that race does not produce culture into the conclusion that capitalism does not produce racism.[37]

That culturalism could result in not just obliviousness to racist inequality but also an alibi for not contesting such inequality at all was
manifested in the contribution to the volume attributed to the *Survey
Graphic* editor Paul Kellogg, "Negro Pioneers." Kellogg, a liberal advocate of national self-determination who envisioned the special Harlem
issue as an extension of other issues of the magazine focusing on Ireland,
Mexico, and even Russia, was from the outset well aware of the political
implications of his and Locke's shared project in the March 1925 issue.
As he wrote to Locke, they were advocating "a new approach, different
from the economic-educational approach of Hampton and Tuskegee on

the one hand; and on the other hand, different from the political approach of Negro rights, lynching, discrimination, and so forth. We are interpreting a racial and cultural revival in the new environment of the northern city: interpreting the affirmative genius of writers, thinkers, poets, artists, singers and musicians, which make for a new rapprochement between the races at the same time that they contribute to the common pot of civilization." While the "racial and cultural revival" based on "the affirmation of genius" would distance itself from the tradition of Booker T. Washington, it would not bear any relation to programs advocating "Negro rights" and opposing "lynching" and "discrimination." If the Negro were to "contribute to the common pot of civilization," Kellogg opined, "genius" would not manifest itself in "political" form, and strategic debates over Negro liberation would be carefully sutured over in the celebration of nationalist cultural contribution.[38]

"Negro Pioneers" spelled out the metonymic nationalist logic underpinning the supersession of antiracist struggle by culturalism. Conceptualizing the New Negro within the paradigm developed by Van Wyck Brooks and Waldo Frank, the essay described the migrants as "pioneers," whose movement northward was "more than a migration, it is a rebirth." The Negroes' mass migration was in the American grain: "By way of the typical American experience, they become for the first time a part of its living tradition." The New Negro Renaissance, the essay concluded, was part and parcel of a revivified American nationalism that recast the Great Migration as manifest destiny: "[T]hough this latest experience of the American Negro is properly a promisefully racial revival, more fundamentally even it is an induction into the heritage of the national tradition, a baptism of the American spirit that slavery cheated him out of, a maturing experience that Reconstruction delayed." Not only was the New Negro Renaissance construed as a near-religious ritual, distinct only in its having a history in slavery, but also Reconstruction, the most radical moment in the struggle for economic and political enfranchisement in African American history, was seen as having "delayed" the real "maturity" signaled by the emergence of culturalism. Even as the theorists of postwar "industrial relations" were claiming the rhetoric of Reconstruction to co-opt and eliminate subversive elements in the labor movement, "Negro Pioneers" theorized the actual Reconstruction as injurious to black folks, preventing their emergence as responsible adult—that is, discursive—actors on the historical stage. The essay's culturalist definition of the New Negro did not simply depoliticize the term *Reconstruction* and efface its recent leftist resonance in the discourse of insurgent labor activists; it repudiated that moment in the previous century when African Americans had most effectively and forcefully confronted the U.S. ruling elite.[39]

Although it would be tempting to attribute this peculiarly conservative take on Reconstruction to Kellogg's limitations as a white person schooled in the dominant ideology about the American past, it was probably Locke himself, not Kellogg, who penned the final paragraph of "Negro Pioneers" in which this statement appears. Writing to Kellogg in October 1925 as he was putting last-minute touches on the book, Locke thanked his colleague "heartily" for the article, saying that he "like[d] it very much," admitting that he had "taken up [Kellogg's] permission to tinker editorially by a final sketch paragraph which you may in turn do what you want with." Kellogg's original draft had apparently ended with the statement—in what is now the penultimate paragraph—that Reiss's portraits depicted for the book's readers not only "plain people . . . such as they knew on the street" but also "poets, philosophers, teachers and leaders, who are the spearheads of a racial revival." The reason for his revision, Locke stated, was his "fear that the average reader might miss the main point in your closing—concentrating as it does on Reiss and the leaders rather than the mass movement." He remarked that he had gotten the "nucleus" for his revision from the "generous and fine paragraph contributed to A. L.'s introduction 'Harlem'—so I am 'borrowing' back from Paul." Locke's statement reveals that if it was Kellogg who authored the often-quoted opening to "Harlem" cited earlier, their collaboration must have been close. More important, however, the statement attests to Locke's determination to cast the migration in nationalist terms rather than in the class-based terms, which was more readily suggested by the grand modes of production narrative implicit in the assertion that the Negro had moved from the Middle Ages into modernity. While he did not want to leave the reader with Kellogg's more elitist formulation, Locke's reframing of Reconstruction as an era of *backward* movement by extension reframed the Left-inflected militancy of 1919 as a phenomenon to be similarly superseded. There were apparently mass movements and, then again, mass movements.[40]

That Locke was anxious to bury other debates in *The New Negro* was evidenced in his approach to including pieces by both Du Bois and R. R. Moton, Washington's successor at Tuskegee and the quintessential Old Negro in the discourse of the African American Left. Congratulating Kellogg for having "gotten in touch with Mr. Moton and [having] tactfully arranged to have him have his say," Locke told him that he thought Moton's piece should "be quite separate—for our sakes as well as his." He suggested that Kellogg "run a special follow up on Negro Education, using Moton and the Moton cut, DuBois defense of his position and the DuBois cut, and if you want, I will even referee the match, trying to point out that the two programs only 'seem to conflict.' But let's leave them out of this issue—there is no use bringing in through the back-door what we have so ceremoniously bowed out of the front." Referring the current embroilment of both figures in educational issues—Moton being "in the heat of the Tuskegee-Hampton campaign, with more hat-in-hand arguments than ever," and Du Bois being "center-stage with the Fiske issue"—Locke asserted that "we ought to keep these controversial issues out." Although Du Bois's contribution to the *Survey Graphic* version of the anthology had been "The Negro Brings His Gifts," a satiric assertion of the New Negro's bid for full recognition as an educated and cultured being, Locke's decision to mute any debate between Du Bois and Moton may have influenced his decision to change Du Bois's contribution to *The New Negro* to the resolutely internationalist "The Negro Mind Reaches Out"—which, while politically further left than "The Negro Brings His Gifts," invited no comparison whatsoever with Moton's contribution, "Hampton-Tuskegee: Missioners of the Masses." Having "ceremoniously bowed out of the front" of his book any debate between the Left and the Right, he was reluctant now to allow debate even between the Right and the center. Any diversity of standpoint exhibited in *The New Negro* would reflect individual differences rather than doctrinal polemics.[41]

That Locke was well aware of the debate embedded in still other contributions to the *Survey Graphic* version of the anthology is indicated by his including an italicized sidebar that explicitly counterposed Herskovits's rejection of the view that cultural differences can be attributed to "the racial factor" with the conclusions reached by Bercovici:

> *Looked at in its externals, Negro life, as reflected in Harlem registers a ready—almost a feverishly rapid—assimilation of American patterns, what Mr. Herskovits called "complete acculturation." It speaks well both for the Negro and for American standards of living that this is so. Internally, perhaps it is another matter. . . . In the article which follows this Mr. Bercovici tells of finding, by intuition rather than research, something "unique" in Harlem—back of the external conformity, a race-soul striving for social utterance.*

However, Locke eliminated "The Rhythm of Harlem" from *The New Negro*, along with his own mediating comments. Although the anthology continually shifted ground between its assertions of Afrocentric distinctness and its claims to full American citizenship, debate between the juxtaposed standpoints of Herskovits and Bercovici was seemingly too explicit for comfort.[42]

The aporial logic of *The New Negro*, which limns in microcosm the contradiction between abolishing race and reifying it that underwrites the entire project of New Negro culturalism, cannot be separated from the dual valence of the folk in the discourse of metonymic nationalism, which itself cannot be understood apart from the conjunction of different notions of "good" nationalism—self-determinationist and democratic-inclusive—in the discourse of leftists and progressives in the wake of 1919. Locke's formulation of African Americans as a folk enabled them at once to stand for the body politic—as when Locke called the spiritual "America's classic folk song"—and to signify their own unique contribution to the multifaceted totality that was the nation. The self-determination of African Americans as a Negro nation consisting of a folk marked by racial distinctness—and signified in their distinct regional capital, Harlem—thus coexisted with their belonging in the soil—the earth, land, states, regions—of the nation as a whole. The aestheticism accompanying the trope of soilness—through which, as a folk, African Americans would be defined—thus stemmed not so much from a racial essentialism accompanying uninterrogated primitivism as from the place-based formulation of group identity accompanying contemporaneous doctrines of self-determination. That the politics of self-determination, designed to supersede racist doctrines of evolutionism, would prove compatible with a primitivism saturated (soil-soaked) in racialist assumptions was apparently an eventuality that Locke, as strategic essentialist advocate of "secondary race consciousness," was prepared to accept.

Various critics have noted throughout Locke's anthology the contradictory claims, on the one hand, that Negroes possessed a distinct "race-soul" and, on the other, that racial categorizations possessed little explanatory validity because Negroes were as American—and as forward-looking and history-making—as any other social group. Sieglinde Lemke has complained that *The New Negro* splits into two incompatible parts, the first section "stressing cultural difference (contrasting Nordic sterility with Negro rhythm) to show that Negro Americans have something unique to contribute to American civilization" and the second emphasizing "cultural sameness" in an attempt to "prove that blacks are just as 'modern' as European immigrants." These simultaneous claims are, Lemke concludes, in a play on Du Bois, "the two unreconciled—and paradoxical—strivings at the heart of *The New Negro*." Astrid Franke, while sympathetic with Locke's attempt to "combin[e] 'group-expression' and 'self-determination' and thus the artistic and the political," wonders why "someone who is obviously aware of the dangers and abuses of stereotypes still proclaim[s] a new essentializing image." She also notes that "Locke's frequent recourse to 'folk' when describing the specific black contribution to modernism can be regarded as a way to avoid talking about the urban masses he started out with . . . [and] seems to have more to do with a rural, perhaps mythical, past than with the contemporary urban black working class in Harlem." Christopher Mott observes that the contradiction in Locke's anthology pervades the discourse of 1920s Harlem intellectuals, whose "attempt simultaneously to undo race and to promote racial pride" produced a "cognitive dissonance" that "created a great deal of tension in the movement" and eventually proved its undoing.[43]

But even critics who have defended Locke's move as a legitimate pragmatist gesture concede it is problematic. Leonard Harris, who praises Locke's project as "a tool of resistance to racism," which needs to be read as a "polemic" in a "battle [against] racist stereotypes of black people as having static, unchangeable cultural characteristics," admits that *The New Negro* does portray the Negro as having "an ontological identity" that "appears rooted in an essence engendered by a culture." Harris's brief on Locke's behalf, which rests on an opposition between an essentialist "strong atavism" and what he calls Locke's pragmatist "weak atavism," is thus somewhat uneasy; with its biologistic overtones, "atavism" remains atavism, whatever the size of the dosage. Nancy Fraser, who views Locke's project as "redemptive" and forthrightly celebrates Locke as, "in Gayatri Spivak's terms, a 'strategic essentialist' *avant la lettre*," argues that "Locke's mature cultural nationalism . . . appears as a strategy aimed at overcoming a form of racial domination that he understood as ultimately economic and political." She admits the failure of Locke's culturalist program—"[t]he extraordinary flowering of Black cultural production he envisioned and promoted did not serve to win civil and political rights"— as well as the inconsistency in Locke's simultaneously endorsing "both the melting-pot vision and the view of a modern civilization type as comprehending a plurality of social cultures." But she defends Locke's embrace of "race-pride" as a "pragmatic transitional strategy for realizing the long-term goal of assimilation." Both the 1916 lectures and *The New Negro*, Fraser concludes, "expos[e] the false symmetry of approaches that assume that all groups and individuals stand in essentially the same relation to the problem of recognition of difference. Locke reminds us, rather, that systematically dominated social groups have pragmatic political needs for solidarity that differ from the needs of others." However, Fraser's praise of Locke as a cagey Deweyan pragmatist rests on the somewhat patronizing assumption that different epistemological standards must be applied to different social groups: "they" cannot afford to see the fallacy of positing an essentialist unity, while "we" must allow them their error. Explicitly linking pragmatism with racial essentialism, Fraser thus suggestively connects pragmatism and racial essentialism, on the one hand, with self-determination and nationalism, on the other. The notion that the "solidarity" of "systematically dominated social groups" produces a coherent and unitary subject position replicates in the realm of epistemology the political proposition that oppressed nations and peoples can and should act as unfissured entities when issuing the call for self-determination. Fraser's comment reveals that the occlusion of class conflict entailed in Locke's 1916 formulation of secondary race consciousness, which would culminate nine years later in *The New Negro*, continues to influence arguments for a strategic essentialist identity politics nearly a century later.[44]

"So Would I Live in Rich Imperial Growth": The New Negro Rooted in Verse

Not surprising, the poems Locke selected for *The New Negro* strenuously avoid the militant anticapitalist themes of poems that had been published in the *Messenger*, the *Crusader*, and the *Liberator* and instead insist on the Negro's membership in the democratic polity. In portraying the Negro as already a quintessential American, Locke appears to have gone out of his way to choose for his anthology poems that foreground the organic trope as a carrier of the thematics of rootedness as belonging. The poems by Jean Toomer that Locke settled on, "The Song of the Son" and "Georgia Dusk," are the two pieces of verse in *Cane* that— especially when taken out of context and paired with each other—can be most readily viewed as depoliticized celebrations of the South as a site where hardy Negro peasants are barely distinguishable from the "racy peasant undersoil" that they till. Even in poems not explicitly addressing the thematics of folkishness, however, the hyper-materiality of the organic trope functions metonymically to naturalize identity as a function of place, thereby largely occluding both historical and structural understandings of the "roots" of racism.[45]

In "The Fruit of the Flower," Countée Cullen develops a botanical analogy that traces the speaker's own hedonistic proclivities—"To do a naked tribal dance / Each time he hears the rain"; to write "[o]f love and lovers, broken heart / And wild sweet agony"—to the repressed sexual impulses of his parents. If his father is "haunt[ed]" by the "languid ghost

/ Of some still sacred sin" and if his mother's flesh is "[s]et all aquiver" by "a bit of checkered sod" (presumably the grave of a former lover), then his own tumultuous physical passions should be no surprise:

> Who plants a seed begets a bud,
> Extract of that same root;
> Why marvel at the hectic blood
> That flushes this wild fruit?

On one level, "The Fruit of the Flower" appears to use the organic trope as part of a naturalizing discourse: the son's wild behavior can be accounted for by his genetic inheritance; a given root, seed, and bud will inevitably produce a given fruit. On another level, however, where Cullen is describing not just sexual adventurism but also homosexual experience, the imagistic nexus takes on a different meaning. Now the inevitability implied in the botanical analogy undermines biological determinist narratives of sexuality. All desires, straight and gay, manifest themselves through comparable behaviors; the issue at stake is thus not the form of the behaviors but whether they remain repressed or are freely acted out. Cullen's evident satisfaction at the "hectic blood / That flushes this wild fruit" of his own conduct leaves little doubt about the poet's own position. In "The Fruit of the Flower," the organic trope contests homophobic notions of sexual essence and suggests a universal human need to permit the development of whatever contradictions inform a given person or process.[46]

But "Fruit of the Flower" also reflects on representation as the discovery of sameness, of what is always already part of one's heritage. The speaker's difference from his origins is a matter of appearance, not essence: his derivation from the "seed" of his forebears guarantees his oneness with them. The poem thus asks to be read as a reminder of his and his parents' common "belonging" to an unrepressed African past where all engage in "a naked tribal dance." The speaker's insistence on self-expression is an act of personal self-determination that will emancipate his parents from the cultural domination of puritanism/colonialism. At the same time, his remaining on the terrain where they have raised him suggests that sexual self-determination—here manifested culturally as engagement in dance—can be enacted as readily in the United States as in Africa. The poem's sexual radicalism is thus framed and made safe within a racial essentialism that is framed within the discourse of nationalist cultural pluralism. Similarly, in "To a Brown Boy," the assertion of homosexual identity is linked with belonging on a given soil. Celebrating the addressee's "clean, brown limbs" and lips that "know better how to kiss / Than how to raise white hymns," the speaker proposes his friend's oneness with the common soil:

> And when your body's death gives birth
> To soil for spring to crown,
> Men will not ask if that rare earth
> Was white flesh once, or brown.

Invoking Whitman's "look for me under your boot-soles," the poem links soil and nation with the freedom from sexual repression proclaimed by the good gray poet who also heard America singing. As in "Fruit of the Flower," "good" nationalism—albeit projected into the future—will supply the ground for untrammeled sexuality.[47]

Cullen's "In Memory of Colonel Charles Young" deploys the organic trope more directly to address the politics of historical memory. Brooding by the grave of the Negro hero of the famous Fighting 369th Infantry of the Great War, the speaker bemoans the racist expunging of the historical record that deepened Young's despair and hastened his death: "The great dark heart is like a well / Drained bitter by the sky." He predicts, however, that the truth will come out:

> No lie is strong enough to kill
> The roots that work below;
> From your rich dust and slaughtered will
> A tree with tongues will grow.

The conduit through which Young's "rich dust" will be communicated to posterity is the many-tongued tree of the poet's own verse; as with Toomer's "singing tree" in "The Song of the Son," art will be the means by which Jim Crow will be avenged. Unproblematized, however, is the patriotism for which Young had been renowned and which had led Randolph and Owen—in their radical phase—to condemn Young's postwar boosting of the American Legion as "servile, sycophant, slavish, silly, stupid and senseless." In Cullen's tribute, the nation's soil is enriched by its pluralistic history; by insisting on recognition of the Negro's contribution to this history—and withholding criticism of the imperialist slaughter to which Young's "slaughtered will" contributed and which his continuing political allegiance defended—the New Negro poet makes a bid for respect and inclusion. There is, to say the least, no space for critique of U.S. foreign policy.[48]

In Anne Spencer's "Lady, Lady," the potential for class-based critique embedded in the trope of "roots" is dissipated when the poet simply abandons the earth for the sky. The speaker apostrophizes an elderly laundress whose lifetime of labor has warped her hands:

> Lady, Lady, I saw your face,
> Dark as night, withholding a star . . .
> The chisel fell, or it might have been
> You had borne so long the yoke of men.
>
> Lady, Lady I saw your hands,
> Twisted, awry, like crumpled roots,
> Bleached poor white in a sudsy tub,
> Wrinkled and drawn from your rub-a-dub.
>
> Lady, Lady, I saw your heart,
> And altared there in its darksome place
> Were the tongues of flame the ancients knew,
> Where the good God sits to spangle through.

"Hands" here signal exploitation; they are "crumpled" by their rootedness not in nature but in history—where, provocatively, it is suggested that the old African American laundress shares the fate of a "poor white." But the closing reference to the saving grace of "the good God" (presumably of Western Christianity) and to the woman's closeness to the "ancients" (presumably of Africa) assigns her emancipation "from the yoke of men" to a realm beyond history and structural class analysis altogether.[49]

Langston Hughes's "An Earth Song" also invokes various elements in the organic trope's discursive field to suggest links between botanical and biological processes and the inexorability of social change:

> And I've been waiting long for a spring song.
> Strong as the shoots of a new plant
> Strong as the bursting of new buds
> Strong as the coming of the first child from its
>   mother's womb.

As in Harry Kemp's "Rune of the Sower," the historical is analogized with the natural. Hughes may have in mind here Marx's use of the metaphor of childbirth in *The Communist Manifesto* and other writings describing the old order as pregnant with the new. The long-awaited change will come not through human agency, however, but through the cyclical passage of the seasons and the natural process of childbirth. People need neither sow nor harvest; nor does there appear to be any necessity for a midwife—even though Marx had stipulated that the mother of capitalism could not deliver the child of communism without the assistance of revolution.[50]

Locke evidently was intent on excluding the voice of the radical
Hughes from *The New Negro*. Opening with a direct allusion to Whitman's "I Hear America Singing," the speaker in "I, Too," the "darker
brother" who has been excluded from the nation's table, proclaims:

> Tomorrow
> I'll sit at the table
> When company comes
> Nobody'll dare
> Say to me,
> "Eat in the kitchen"
> Then.
>
> Besides, they'll see how beautiful I am
> And be ashamed,—
>
> I, too, am America.

A culturalist manifesto both assuming and asserting metonymic nationalism, the poem attributes the Negro's induction into full membership
in the family that is the nation to an aesthetic moment: the rest of the
family's recognition of "how beautiful I am." The causal role played by
the speaker's "beauty" here is ambiguous, since apparently it is only *after* the "darker brother" has found his seat "at the table" that the rest of
the family, seeing "how beautiful" he is, will "be ashamed." As in Locke's
own contributions to *The New Negro*, the exact role to be played by art
in transforming social reality—that is, making it possible for the "darker brother" to gain that seat—is not specified; metonymic nationalism
invests his possession of the seat with an aura of the always already. But,
with its deliberate Whitmanian echo, clearly the poem advocates aesthetic representation as the key to political representation. Where Bontemps's
"Black Man Talks of Reaping" places primacy on the reappropriation of
the harvest illegitimately seized by his "brother's sons," Hughes's speaker
trusts in a change of heart. Notably absent among Hughes's contributions
to the anthology are such class-conscious poems as "Johannesburg
Mines," "Steel Mills," "Rising Waters," and "God to Hungry Child," in
which revolutionary proletarian internationalism is prominent and both
culturalism and American nationalism significantly absent.[51]

Since Claude McKay was by 1925 the best-established of the poets
associated with the New Negro movement, Locke had in his oeuvre a still
more substantial body of work from which to make his selections for *The
New Negro* than was the case with Hughes. But McKay was widely
known as a revolutionary poet. Passing over such popular—and frequently
reprinted—poems as "If We Must Die" and "The Lynching," as well as

the many militantly pro-Soviet and anticolonialist poems that McKay had published in the *Messenger* and the *Liberator*, Locke settled on a relatively introspective and lyrical grouping of texts. Even the angriest of these, "White Houses"—which describes the speaker's encounter with "Your door . . . shut against my tightened face," and his need to "keep my heart inviolate / Against the potent poison of your hate"—lost considerable political force through Locke's decision to change its title from "The White House." Locke's retitling qualitatively changed the import of the poem, which with its original title had unambiguously targeted the federal government, seat of ruling-class power, and not simply racist mass consciousness, as the quintessential site of Jim Crow. "Like a Strong Tree" typifies those features of McKay's work that Locke wanted to impress on the readers of *The New Negro:*

> Like a strong tree that in the virgin earth
> Sends far its roots through rock and loam and clay,
> And proudly thrives in rain or time of dearth,
> When the dry waves scare rainy sprites away;
> Like a strong tree that reaches down, deep, deep,
> For sunken water, fluid underground,
> Where the great-ringed unsightly blind worms creep,
> And queer things of the nether world abound:
>
> So would I live in rich imperial growth,
> Touching the surface and the depth of things,
> Instinctively responsive unto both,
> Tasting the sweets of being and the stings,
> Sensing the subtle spell of changing forms,
> Like a strong tree against a thousand storms.[52]

"Like a Strong Tree" does not immediately invite a racially specific reading; indeed, were it published in a venue not specified as Negro, the sonnet could be interpreted as a commentary on a human condition beyond race altogether. In the context of Locke's volume, however—especially in view of the editor's own stated admiration for Negro art growing from a "racy peasant undersoil"—the poem invites being read as an exploration of the role of racial heritage in arming the African American, perhaps especially the African American artist, against oppressive circumstance. If the speaker is the New Negro, then his roots, reaching "in the virgin earth . . . deep, deep," signify his reliance on the past to endure the present. Unlike the alienated speaker in "The Waste Land," who envisions roots clutching the dry earth but unable to find water, McKay's speaker has access to "sunken water," enabling him to intuit "the depth of things." He is like one of Frank's "spiritual pioneers," for whom plumbing deep into the unconscious of the individual is coterminous with digging deep into the common memory of the folk. Where the oxymoronic "dry waves" of drought scare away the "rainy sprites" capable of inhabiting only a well-watered terrain—the speaker refers to people, probably affluent whites, less accustomed than he to grappling with hardship—he prevails by virtue of his deep rooting in the racial past.

But the notion of time in "Like a Strong Tree" has little to do with historical specificity; the "subtle spell of changing forms" suggests not the negative dialectic of historical process but seasonal oscillation within the overall stasis embodied in the tree's fixity. The aspect of the tree's rootedness that dominates the poem is not so much its strength as its integral relation to place; all that it needs for nourishment exists where it stands, if only it will go deep enough. If the tree is a figure for the New Negro, then, its dogged insistence on remaining where it is and thriving in spite of myriad attacks by the harsh weather testifies to the capacity of the soil to provide all that it needs. Read as an assertion of the Negro's deeply rooted belonging in American soil and placed in the context of the American nationalism pervading Locke's text, McKay's poem can even be interpreted as an updated version of Booker T. Washington's famous parable about the need for the Negro to cast down his bucket where he is. Whatever elements of antiracist critique McKay voiced in "Like a Strong Tree"—embedded, for example, in the references to "rain" and "time of dearth"—can thus be subordinated to the poem's testimony to the Negro's powers of endurance, as well as to the availability of fructifying nutrients in the nation's soil, if only one is willing to penetrate deeply enough. Although the poem hardly invokes the pastoral image of "[t]he workman . . . [h]appy and grateful in his peaceful toil" that McKay had lambasted in "Labor's Day," "Like a Strong Tree" engages in a "singing of the fertile soil." While "soil" need not connote Fatherland more than Mother Earth, the poem's subtly gendered rhetoric leagues the speaker with those who take possession of the "virgin earth" to complete an "imperial" design.

Context is clearly key to how one reads the organic trope in McKay's sonnet: if the poem had appeared in such a venue as the *Liberator* or the *Messenger*, juxtaposed poems and articles might have supplied a more cosmopolitan and proletarian reading of the metaphor of survival and triumph. Framed by the other materials in Locke's anthology, however, the poem obliquely asserts an identification with the project of an inclusive and pluralist manifest destiny, even as it proclaims the speaker's identification with the deeply rooted—and presumably nationless— wretched of the earth. Locke's decision to include this poem—rather than, for example, "Birds of Prey," "Labor's Day," or "Exhortation"—reflects not just his priorities in shaping the McKay canon but also his distinct preference for the soil-soaked discourse of metonymic nationalism over the class warfare rhetoric of 1919. As Kellogg had urged, the priorities of the anthology stressed "affirmative genius," not protest against the capitalists who tear out the organs of the multiracial working class or summonses to look to the Soviet East for the future direction of humanity. In "Like a Strong Tree," the hyper-materiality of the signifier wards off a historical materialist critique of social relations.

Coda: Du Bois and "That Vision Splendid of 1918"

Arnold Rampersad has pointed out that the one piece in *The New Negro* that does not quite fit into Locke's culturalist mold is W. E. B. Du Bois's closing essay, "The Negro Mind Reaches Out." In both argument and rhetoric, this essay departed from the rest of the volume in significant ways. Pursuing the line of inquiry taken up a decade earlier in his wartime *Atlantic Monthly* series, "The African Roots of War," Du Bois's contribution to Locke's anthology offered a marked contrast to the celebratory American nationalism otherwise informing the volume. Contemplating whether the white working class of the United States would go the way of South Africa or Russia, Du Bois remarked on the "terrible, ceaseless propaganda" barraging the U.S. white worker in the form of the "myth of mass inferiority of most men." The white worker, "[b]orn into such a spiritual world," was "absolutely at the mercy of its beliefs and prejudices." "Color hate," Du Bois observed, "easily assumes the form of a religion and the laborer becomes the blind executive of the decrees of the masters of the white world," thereby "giving white capital the power to rule all labor, white and black." Du Bois noted that immigration restriction, which enabled Negro laborers to supply "cheap labor for the industries of the white land," had made African Americans "silently elated," even if they found "extraordinary bed fellows" in "white capitalists" and "'Nordic' fanatics.'" Nonetheless, he concluded, it was "colored labor" that understood the nature of exploitation most clearly and that, as it "becomes more organized and more intelligent it is going to spread this grievance through the white world."[53]

Discussing the origins of the Great War, Du Bois played on a meaning of "roots" that comprises historical and structural causality, on the one hand, and the "routes" of imperial conquest, on the other:

> Fruit of the bitter rivalries of economic imperialism, the roots of that catastrophe were in Africa, deeply entwined at bottom with the problems of the color line. And of the legacy left, the problems the world inherits

hold the same fatal seed; world dissension and catastrophe still lurk in
the unsolved problems of race relations. . . .

    Modern imperialism and modern industrialism are one and the same
system; root and branch of the same tree.

Du Bois's metaphor was allegorical and abstract, describing cause-and-
effect relationships that evaded naturalization; emphatically, the organic trope cannot be read here as alluding to the discursive field of metonymic nationalism. Nor was Du Bois's tree that of racial heritage;
instead, it signified the global capitalist economic order, understood as a
structured totality. This order's root was colonialism and imperialism,
especially the exploitation of Africa; its branch was the industrial capitalism enabled by the primitive accumulation of capital; and its seed was
the drive to profit. Geographical location supplied the terrain where this
process of capital accumulation was transpiring, but—whether as region
or nation—place possessed in itself no determining power. The only "rich
imperial growth" possible here was that which added to the coffers of the
oppressor; the organic trope served Du Bois not to invest with hyper-
materiality a politics of belonging to a soil, a region, or a nation but to
delineate the need for a politics of anticapitalist internationalism.[54]

    Du Bois then gave a backward glance toward the war years:

To some persons—to more human beings than ever before at one time
in the world's history, there came during the Great War, during those
terrible years of 1917 and 1918, a vision of the Glory of Sacrifice, a dream
of a world greater, sweeter, more beautiful and more honest than ever
before; a world without war, without poverty and without hate.

    I am glad it came. Even though it was a mirage it was eternally true.
To-day some faint shadow of it comes to me again.

He closed by noting his location on a ship bound for Africa:

My ship seeks Africa. . . . And now we stand before Liberia; Liberia that
is a little thing set upon a Hill;—thirty or forty thousand square miles
and two million folk; but it represents to me the world. Here political
power has tried to resist the power of modern capital. It has not yet succeeded, but its partial failure is not because the republic is black, but
because the world has failed in this same battle; because organized industry owns and rules England, France, Germany, America and Heaven.
And can Liberia escape the power that rules the world? I do not know;
but I do know unless the world escapes the world as well as Liberia will
die; and if Liberia lives it will be because the World is reborn as in that
vision splendid of 1918.

    And thus again in 1924 as in 1899 I seem to see the problem of the 20th
century as the Problem of the Color Line.

Du Bois's allusion to "a world greater, sweeter, more beautiful and more honest than ever before" was ambiguous. He might have been referring to the Wilsonian program of a world made safe for democracy through a League of Nations committed to self-determination; it had been in the hope of supporting this program, after all, that he had urged African American participation in the war. Given the militant tenor of his postwar *Crisis* editorial proclaiming, "We Return Fighting," however, as well as his repeated expressions during the early 1920s of enthusiasm for the fledgling workers' state in the USSR, it is at least equally probable that the "mirage," the "faint shadow" toward which he was gesturing—that "vision splendid of 1918"—was the hope emerging from the Bolshevik Revolution, which not only had freed Russian workers and peasants from the regime of capital but had promised to emancipate colonized peoples of color from imperialist domination as well.[55]

It is crucial, however, that the place on earth currently embodying for Du Bois the potential of being the "city on a hill" to which the African diaspora might look for spiritual citizenship was Liberia. Liberia was hardly the offspring of anticolonial rebellion; it was the creature of a U.S. foreign policy based on a global vision of manifest destiny. In 1918, Yekutiel Gershoni observes, Liberia's north had witnessed an "all-out revolt" against Americo-Liberian rule; by 1925, the year Du Bois published his paean, the hinterland had been opened to labor recruiters who were imposing a regime of forcible labor exportation that differed little from the capture and sale of slaves in past centuries. Du Bois's suppression of any reference to such practices, along with the occlusion of class categories in his closing invocation of "Liberia" and "the World" and his echo of the pilgrim father John Winthrop in his allusion to the "city on a hill," ran directly counter to the spirit of anti-imperialism and proletarian internationalism elsewhere informing the essay. Du Bois's final proclamation of allegiance to the Pilgrims brought his essay into alignment, however, with the other contributions to *The New Negro.* Even as he wondered whether Liberia could "escape the power that rules the world," the structural inequalities produced by capitalism were largely elided as they were displaced onto a geographically based strategy for emancipation. That Liberia figured above all else as homeland suggested that routes must be followed to regain roots; the "Color Line," earlier invoked to describe the racism at the foundation of imperialism, ended up delineating a zone of reentry and return.[56]

In *The New Negro,* cultural pluralism was pressed to deliver on its promise of inclusiveness. The egregious racial gaps occurring even in Young America's most eloquent calls for diversity—Bourne's "Trans-National America," Frank's *Our America*—were to be filled by texts proclaiming the Negro's right to full representation in the nation's polity—and profile. Rather than play to racist exoticism, primitivism was to link the soilness of black folk to their rootedness in southern terrain and to demonstrate they were always already citizens, even if denied basic rights and discursive visibility. The organic trope was to stress not the oneness of black folks with a "nature" arrested at a lower place on the evolutionary scale or their status as "non-historical people" but, rather, their belonging to and in a region that in turn belonged to and in the nation. The trope invoked a signifying chain that asserted the ability of black folks to stand for the nation as much and as well as any other group. African American folk culture was to challenge any notion that the nation lacked the rich loam from which a modern national culture might be cultivated. This folk culture was to be the basis for the New Negro's simultaneous claims to self-determination as a "people" and full citizenship as Americans. Both the New Negro and *The New Negro,* the products of such cultural cultivation, were to frame a counterdiscourse that would appropriate the rhetoric of the racists to antiracist ends. In the atmosphere of reaction dominated by the discourses of nativism and eugenics as well as the politics of the American Plan, immigrant exclusion, and a burgeoning Ku Klux Klan, this project of re-presentation was no small task and no mean achievement.

Yet, I have argued, the pluralist counterdiscourse of African American soilness could not negate the hegemonic discourse of 100 percent Americanism and in fact would end up validating key features of the dominant ideology, largely because this counterdiscourse had carried within itself too many of its opponent's foundational premises. The neoromantic image of a peasantry rooted in the land was consonant with the class politics—if not the racial proclivities—of the 100 percenters. The strategic essentialism accompanying the notion of soilness left intact the notion of racial types, even as it sought to invert racial stereotypes. Pragmatism, instead of specifying race as an ideological category, reintroduced reified notions of race; that cultural pluralism entailed a socially constructed notion of the nation as the site of continual flux and reordering did not mean the different races and ethnicities constituting the nation would be freed from essentialist construction. For pluralists from Kallen and Bourne to Locke and Kellogg, social constructionism on the national scale implied quite the opposite on the local scale. Metonymic nationalism thus played a powerful ideological role in redirecting the potentially revolutionary energies invested in antiracist self-determinationism into an American exceptionalism that posed no threat to—indeed, buttressed —existing relations of power. The relative ease with which Locke could carry out his program of censoring and reshaping the New Negro as *The New Negro* indicates that he was co-opting rather than confronting whatever opposition he might have encountered from the Left.

But this opposition was, by 1925, minimal. W. A. Domingo—who had been cited at length by the Lusk Committee for advocating working-class revolution in 1919 and warning Socialists about the urgent necessity of including African Americans in the revolutionary fold—now appeared content to celebrate the "gift" that Caribbean migrants were contributing to the nation. A. Philip Randolph and Chandler Owen—whose earlier calls for black-white unity had focused on the need for workers to fight exploitation at the point of production—now praised Locke's project for "the spirit which gave it birth," namely, its having been "planned by black and white intellectuals, . . . as it should be." Culturalism, it would seem, was supplying an egress from the contradictions of capitalism not just for Locke, whose relationship with the Left had always been tenuous, but also for some of the leading African American revolutionaries of 1919. One could of course posit, with Theodor Adorno, that falling away from revolutionary purpose and turning toward culture as the zone of opposition were inevitable reactions to the diminishing of left-wing possibility in the aftermath of 1919. Recalling my earlier citation of Marx, I grant that revolutionary ideas require the existence of a revolutionary class; a left-wing culture cannot continue to produce and be produced, to any significant degree, if there is no mass political movement to sustain that culture. But *Spectres of 1919* has made the case that contradictions internal to the Left itself—combined with the impact of the postwar Thermidor—contributed crucially to the ease with which the New Negro as cultural pluralist could supersede the New Negro as class-conscious warrior. That culturalism would supplant class struggle was not a foregone conclusion but a particular product—if a highly mediated one—of the particular politics guiding class struggle in the era and aftermath of 1919.

Yet Du Bois's "vision splendid of 1918" would continue to animate revolutionary movements in the decades ahead. The resurgence of militant class warfare and antiracist struggle some half-dozen years after the publication of Locke's anthology indicates that culturalism would have limited power to contain the fundamental social contradictions endemic to capitalism. The rest of the twentieth century would witness both tremendous advances and tremendous defeats for those Locke had once called "the submerged classes" of the earth. And while the movement for "a better world" remains to this day hamstrung—not only by ruling-class repression but also by limitations inherited from the twentieth-century Left—Du Bois's glimpsed future, a "mirage eternally true" that emerged in a moment of sudden and brilliant clarity in the crucible of the Great War and the Bolshevik Revolution, remains a necessity for the "submerged classes." The spectres of 1919, threatening always to become flesh, continue to haunt those whose hold on political power and pursuit of capital accumulation are founded on racist division and exploitation—in the United States and around the world. It is to be hoped that a fuller understanding of both the failures and the achievements of those pursuing the "vision splendid" in the past will aid us as we continue along the winding path of our collective journey toward that better world.

NOTES

Preface

1. John Dos Passos, *The Big Money* in *U.S.A.* (New York: Random House, 1937), 103.

Chapter 1: The New Negro and the Left

1. Alain Locke, "The New Negro," in *The New Negro: An Interpretation*, ed. Alain Locke (1925; reprint, New York: Simon and Schuster, 1992), 11–12, 15.

2. Ibid., 11; Anthony Dawahare, *Nationalism, Marxism, and African American Literature between the Wars: A New Pandora's Box* (Jackson: University Press of Mississippi, 2003), 41; John Hope Franklin, *From Slavery to Freedom: A History of Negro Americans*, 4th ed. (New York: Alfred A. Knopf, 1974), 375; Ann Douglas, *Terrible Honesty: Mongrel Manhattan in the 1920s* (New York: Farrar, Straus, and Giroux, 1995); Steven Watson, *The Harlem Renaissance: Hub of African-American Culture, 1920–1930* (New York: Pantheon Books, 1995); Mark Helbling, *The Harlem Renaissance: The One and the Many* (Westport, Conn.: Greenwood, 1999); Michael North, *The Dialect of Modernism: Race, Language, and Twentieth-Century Literature* (New York: Oxford University Press, 1994); J. Martin Favor, *Authentic Blackness: The Folk in the New Negro Renaissance* (Durham, N.C.: Duke University Press, 1999); Chidi Ikonné, *From Du Bois to Van Vechten: The Early New Negro Literature, 1903–1926* (Westport, Conn.: Greenwood, 1981); Robert Bone, *Down Home: Origins of the Afro-American Short Story* (New York: Columbia University Press, 1988), 109–38; Cheryl A. Wall, *Women of the Harlem Renaissance* (Bloomington: Indiana University Press, 1995); Gloria Hull, *Color, Sex, and Poetry: Three Women Writers of the Harlem Renaissance* (Bloomington: Indiana University Press, 1987); Claudia Tate, *The Selected Works of Georgia Douglas Johnson* (New York: G. K. Hall, 1997); Cary Wintz, *The Harlem Renaissance, 1920–1940*, 7 vols. (New York: Garland, 1996–98); Houston Baker Jr., *Modernism and the Harlem Renaissance* (Chicago: University of Chicago Press, 1987); Walter Kalaidjian, *American Culture between the Wars: Revisionary Modernism and Postmodern Critique* (New York: Columbia University Press, 1993); Robert Stepto, "Afro-American Literature," in *Columbia Literary History of the United States*, ed. Emory Elliot (New York: Columbia University Press, 1988), 785–99; Carla Cappetti, *Writing Chicago: Modernism, Ethnography, and the Novel* (New York: Columbia University Press, 1993); Eric J. Sundquist, "Red, White, Black and Blue: The Color of American Modernism," *Transition* 70

(Summer 1996): 94–116; George Hutchinson, *The Harlem Renaissance in Black and White* (Cambridge, Mass.: Belknap Press of Harvard University Press, 1995); Jean Toomer, *Cane* (New York: Horace Liveright, 1923). See also Eloise E. Johnson, *The Rediscovery of the Harlem Renaissance: The Politics of Exclusion* (New York: Garland, 1997); and Maria Balshaw, *Looking for Harlem: Urban Aesthetics in African American Literature* (London: Pluto, 2000). The *locus classicus* of the hostile take on Harlem Renaissance interracialism remains Harold Cruse, *The Crisis of the Negro Intellectual* (New York: William Morrow, 1967).

3. Nathan Irvin Huggins, *Harlem Renaissance* (London: Oxford University Press, 1971), 54, 303; Theodore Kornweibel, *No Crystal Stair: Black Life and the Messenger, 1917–1928* (Westport, Conn.: Greenwood, 1975), 107; Theodore Vincent, *Voices of a Black Nation: Political Journalism in the Harlem Renaissance* (San Francisco: Ramparts, 1973), 62; David Levering Lewis, introduction to *The Portable Harlem Renaissance Reader*, ed. David Levering Lewis (New York: Viking, 1994), xv. For more on the historical parameters of the Harlem Renaissance, see Sundquist, "Red, White, Black and Blue"; and Robert Stepto, "Sterling Brown: Outsider in the Harlem Renaissance?" in *The Harlem Renaissance: Revaluations*, ed. Amritjit Singh, William S. Shiver, and Stanley Brodwin (New York: Garland, 1989), 73–74.

4. Henry Louis Gates Jr., "The Trope of a New Negro and the Reconstruction of the Image of the Black," *Representations* 24 (Fall 1988): 136, 147; Arnold Rampersad, introduction to *The New Negro*, ed. Locke, xxi. For more on the many choices that went into the making of *The New Negro*, see chapter 5.

5. Faith Berry, *Langston Hughes before and after Harlem* (New York: Citadel, 1992); Clyde Taylor quoted in James A. Miller, "African-American Writing of the 1930s: A Prologue," in *Radical Revisions: Rereading 1930s Culture*, ed. Bill Mullen and Sherry Linkon (Urbana: University of Illinois Press, 1996), 79; William J. Maxwell, *New Negro, Old Left: African-American Writing and Communism between the Wars* (New York: Columbia University Press, 1999), 49. James Smethurst holds out for the necessity of retaining a sharp distinction between the decades in *The New Red Negro: The Literary Left and African American Poetry, 1930–1999* (New York: Oxford University Press, 1999).

6. The logic of the mid- to late-1930s Communist Party's view of communism as "twentieth-century Americanism" is laid out in Earl Browder, *The People's Front* (New York: International, 1938). For differing interpretations of the Popular Front, see Michael Denning, *The Cultural Front: The Laboring of American Culture in the Twentieth Century* (London: Verso, 1996); and Barbara Foley, *Radical Representations: Politics and Form in U.S. Proletarian Fiction, 1929–1941* (Durham, N.C.: Duke University Press, 1993).

7. "Manifesto of the Communist International to the Workers of the World" (6 March 1919), in *Theses, Resolutions and Manifestoes of the First Four Congresses of the Third International*, ed. Alan Adler (London: Ink Links, 1980), 27–36 (quote on 27); "Nation-Wide Dynamite Conspiracy," *New York American*, 1 May 1919, 1; "Reds Blamed in Bomb Plot," *New York American*, 1 May 1919, 2; "Deportation for All Bomb Suspects," *New York American*, 3 May 1919, 1; Lothrop Stoddard, *The Rising Tide of Color against White-World Supremacy* (New York: Charles Scribner's Sons, 1920), xxx. For more on the impact of Japan's rise on African American radicals, see Marc Gallicchio, *The African American En-*

counter with Japan and China: Black Internationalism in Asia, 1895–1945 (Chapel Hill: University of North Carolina Press, 2000).

8. David Montgomery, *The Fall of the House of Labor: The Workplace, the State, and American Labor Activism, 1865–1925* (Cambridge: Cambridge University Press, 1987), 388; broadside quoted in Jeremy Brecher, *Strike!* (San Francisco: Straight Arrow Books, 1972), 111; Boris Brasol, *Socialism versus Civilization* (New York: Charles Scribner's Sons, 1920), 202; "Bolsheviki in the United States," *Literary Digest* 60 (22 February 1919): 11; William MacDonald, "The Seattle Strike and Afterwards," *Nation* 108 (29 March 1919): 470.

9. John Graham Brooks, *Labor's Challenge to the Social Order: Democracy Its Own Critic and Educator* (1920; reprint, New York: Macmillan, 1923), 5; Wilson quoted in Gary Gerstle, *American Crucible: Race and Nation in the Twentieth Century* (Princeton, N.J.: Princeton University Press, 2001), 98; Frank Tannenbaum, *The Labor Movement: Its Conservative Functions and Social Consequences* (1921; reprint, New York: Arno, 1969), 111, 114. Theresa S. McMahon, writing more soberly, remarked that the Seattle general strike "had none of the earmarks of a revolution. It possessed all the distinguishing features of a craft strike" ("The Strike in Seattle," *Survey* 41 [March 1919]: 822). For more on the Seattle general strike, see Harvey O'Connor, *Revolution in Seattle: A Memoir* (New York: Monthly Review, 1964); and Robert L. Friedheim, *The Seattle General Strike* (Seattle: University of Washington Press, 1964). For more on the great steel strike, see William Z. Foster, *The Great Steel Strike and Its Lessons* (1920; reprint, Arno, 1969); and Brecher, *Strike!* 118–28. Another typically fearful response to the labor militancy of 1919 is contained in Alexander M. Bing, *War-Time Strikes and Their Adjustment* (New York: E. P. Dutton, 1921).

10. Robert Minor, "Soviets on Earth," cited in Joint Legislative Committee Investigating Seditious Activities, *Revolutionary Radicalism: Its History, Purposes, and Tactics,* 4 vols. (Albany, N.Y.: J. B. Lyon, 1920), 2:1378–84. For more on industrial democracy, see David Montgomery, "'Industrial Democracy or Democracy in Industry?' The Theory and Practice of the Labor Movement, 1870–1925," in *Industrial Democracy in America: The Ambiguous Promise,* ed. Nelson Lichtenstein and Howell John Harris (Cambridge: Cambridge University Press, 1993), 20–42; Joseph A. McCartin, *Labor's Great War: The Struggle for Industrial Democracy and the Origins of Modern American Labor Relations* (Chicago: University of Chicago Press, 1997); James Weinstein, *The Decline of Socialism in America, 1912–1925* (New Brunswick, N.J.: Rutgers University Press, 1984); Theodore Draper, *The Roots of American Communism* (New York: Viking, 1957); Lillian Symes and Travers Clement, *Rebel America: The Story of Social Revolt in the United States* (New York: Harper Brothers, 1934); Melvin Dubofsky, *We Shall Be All: A History of the Industrial Workers of the World,* 2d ed. (Urbana: University of Illinois Press, 1988); and Philip S. Foner, *The Bolshevik Revolution: Its Impact on American Radicals, Liberals, and Labor* (New York: International, 1967). For more on the view of Lenin as pragmatist, see Brian Lloyd, *Left Out: Pragmatism, Exceptionalism, and the Poverty of American Marxism, 1890–1922* (Baltimore: Johns Hopkins University Press, 1997), 376–408.

11. Joint Legislative Committee Investigating Seditious Activities, *Revolutionary Radicalism,* 2:1441; Gerstle, *American Crucible,* 92–97 (quote on 97). For more on the wartime and postwar political repression, see Julian F. Jaffe, *Crusade against*

Radicalism: New York during the Red Scare, 1919–1924 (Port Washington, N.Y.: Kennikat, 1972); Robert Justin Goldstein, *Political Repression in Modern America: From 1870 to 1975* (1978; reprint, Urbana: University of Illinois Press, 2001); and Howard Abramowitz, "Historians and the Red Scare of 1919–1920 in Detroit," in *Anti-Communism: The Politics of Manipulation,* ed. Judith Joël and Gerald M. Erickson (Minneapolis: MEP, 1987), 87–118; David H. Bennett, *The Party of Fear: From Nativist Movements to the New Right in American History* (Chapel Hill: University of North Carolina Press, 1988), 193–217; and John Higham, *Strangers in the Land: Patterns of American Nativism, 1860–1925* (New York: Atheneum, 1969), 220–82. See also the contemporaneous accounts in Jerome Davis, *The Russian Immigrant* (New York: Macmillan, 1922), 161–72; and Joseph Mereto, *The Red Conspiracy* (New York: National Historical Society, 1920).

12. For more on the Elaine cases, see James Weldon Johnson, "The Real Causes of Two Race Riots," *Crisis* 19 (November 1919): 56–62; Walter White, *A Man Called White: The Autobiography of Walter White* (New York: Viking, 1948), 46–50; and Herbert Seligmann, *The Negro Faces America* (New York: Clarence S. Nathan, 1920), 218–52. Philip S. Foner places the number of dead in Elaine at one hundred and notes that, besides those killed outright in the struggle, twelve more sharecroppers were sentenced to death and seventy-seven to lengthy prison terms (*Organized Labor and the Black Worker, 1919–1981,* 2d ed. [New York: International, 1982], 146–47). The role of lynch violence in precipitating the migration northward is discussed in contemporaneous accounts: Emmett Scott, *Negro Migration during the War* (New York: Oxford University Press, 1920), 79–80; and Carl Sandburg, *The Chicago Race Riots: July 1919* (New York: Harcourt, Brace and Howe, 1919), 26. The thesis that lynching played a preponderant role in the Great Migration was challenged in 1923 by Charles S. Johnson, "How Much Is Migration a Flight from Persecution?" *Opportunity* 1 (September 1923): 265–70, and has been more recently revisited by Stewart E. Tolnay, E. M. Beck, and James L. Massey, "Black Lynchings: The Power Threat Hypothesis Revisited," *Social Forces* 67 (March 1989): 605–23. The role of black scabs in breaking the great steel strike is discussed in Foster, *The Great Steel Strike and Its Lessons,* 205–12; and Michael Reich, *Racial Inequality: A Political-Economic Analysis* (Princeton, N.J.: Princeton University Press, 1981), 253–56. For more on crowding as a precipitant of race riots, see W. E. B. Du Bois, *Darkwater: Voices from within the Veil* (New York: Harcourt, Brace and Howe, 1920), 81–104.

13. Richard Wright, "The Ethics of Living Jim Crow," in *Uncle Tom's Children,* by Richard Wright (1940; reprint, New York: Perennial Books, 1993), 1; Wilson quoted in David S. Foglesong, *America's Secret War against Bolshevism* (Chapel Hill: University of North Carolina Press, 1995), 42; Joint Legislative Committee Investigating Seditious Activities, *Revolutionary Radicalism,* 2:1489–1510 (quote on 1504); Palmer quoted in Theodore Kornweibel, *"Seeing Red": Federal Campaigns against Black Militancy, 1914–1925* (Bloomington: Indiana University Press, 1998), xiv; "For Action on Race Peril: Radical Propaganda among Negroes Growing, and Increased Mob Violence Set Out in Senate Brief for Federal Inquiry," *New York Times,* 5 October 1919, 10; "Planned Negro Uprising," *New York Times,* 28 June 1919, 1. For more on the Houston case, see David Levering Lewis, *W. E. B. Du Bois: Biography of a Race, 1868–1919* (New York: Henry Holt, 1993), 540–42.

14. NAACP quoted in Foner, *Organized Labor and the Black Worker*, 138; detective firm quoted in Breecher, *Strike!* 125; A. Philip Randolph and Chandler Owen, "The Cause of and Remedy for Race Riots," *Messenger* 2 (September 1919): 14–22. For more on the emerging black-white unity in the stockyards, see William Z. Foster, *American Trade Unionism: Principles and Organization, Strategy and Tactics* (New York: International, 1947). For more on Bogalusa, see Seligmann, *The Negro Faces America*, 196–203; and Philip S. Foner and Ronald C. Lewis, eds., *The Black Worker from 1900 to 1919* (Philadelphia: Temple University Press, 1980), 483–89. *Reconstruction* is discussed in McCartin, *Labor's Great War*, 173–98. For an example of the use of the term *reconstruction* in the discourse of black radicals, see Editorial, "The Negro and the New Social Order: Reconstruction Program of the American Negro," *Messenger* 2 (April 1919): 3–11.

15. Charles Conant Josey, *Race and National Solidarity* (1923; reprinted as *The Philosophy of Nationalism* [Washington, D.C.: Cliveden, 1983]), 95–96; Tannenbaum, *The Labor Movement*, 80; J. Brooks, *Labor's Challenge to the Social Order*, 278. McCartin discusses the American Plan in *Labor's Great War*, 199–200. See also Dos Passos's acerbic portrayal of Taylorism as "The American Plan" in *The Big Money*, 19–25.

16. Muret quoted in Wilson Moses, *The Golden Age of Black Nationalism, 1950–1925* (Oxford: Oxford University Press, 1978), 254; Winston James, *Holding Aloft the Banner of Ethiopia: Caribbean Radicalism in Early Twentieth-Century America* (London: Verso, 1998), 122; William T. Ferris, "Negro Renaissance," *Negro World*, 11 February 1922, 2, quoted in Tony Martin, *Literary Garveyism: Garvey, Black Arts, and the Harlem Renaissance* (Dover, Mass.: Majority, 1983), 6; J. Miller, "African-American Writing of the 1930s," 81. For more on Pan-Africanism in relation to African American political debates, see Eric J. Sundquist, *To Wake the Nations: Race in the Making of American Literature* (Cambridge, Mass.: Belknap Press of Harvard University Press, 1993), 540–62; Tony Martin, *Race First: The Ideological and Organizational Struggles of Marcus Garvey and the Universal Negro Improvement Association* (Westport, Conn.: Greenwood, 1976); and Manning Marable, *W. E. B. Du Bois: Black Radical Democrat* (Boston: Twayne, 1986), 89–120.

17. Dos Passos quoted in Weinstein, *The Decline of Socialism in America*, 199–200; Brooks, *Labor's Challenge to the Social Order*, 5.

18. Booker T. Washington, *A New Negro for a New Century* (1900; reprint, New York: Arno, 1969); August Meier, *Negro Thought in America: Racial Ideologies in the Age of Booker T. Washington* (Ann Arbor: University of Michigan Press, 1969), 258; Gates, "The Trope of a New Negro and the Reconstruction of the Image of the Black," 135; David Krasner, *Resistance, Parody, and Double Consciousness in African American Theatre, 1895–1910* (New York: St. Martin's, 1997), 20–21. See also Wilson J. Moses, "The Lost World of the Negro, 1895–1919: Black Literary and Intellectual Life before the 'Renaissance,'" *Black American Literature Forum* 21 (Spring–Summer 1987): 61–84. Joel Williamson argues that the term *New Negro* was used as early as 1889 by racial "Radicals" (that is, extreme biological racists) to describe the emerging generation of young adults who, "unsupported by the enforced moral behavior of slavery, . . . was reverting to a native savagery" (*The Crucible of Race: Black-White Relations in the American South since Emancipation* [New York: Oxford University Press, 1984], 111).

19. *Amsterdam News* quoted in Milton C. Sennett, *Bound for the Promised Land: African American Religion and the Great Migration* (Durham, N.C.: Duke University Press, 1997), 52–53; "Negroes of the World United in Demanding a Free Africa," *Crusader* 1 (December 1918): 13; Kelly Miller, "Radicalism and the Negro," circa 1920, 1, 5, microfilm #41251, Miscellaneous Monographs and Pamphlets, Library of Congress, Washington, D.C.; Kelly Miller, "The Negro in the New Reconstruction," circa 1919, 2, 6, microfilm #41250, Miscellaneous Monographs and Pamphlets, Library of Congress; Miller quoted in Moses, *The Golden Age of Black Nationalism*, 247. Moton reported in his autobiography that his exact words were "You will go back as you have carried yourselves over here—in a straightforward, manly and modest way. If I were you, I would find a job as soon as possible and get to work. To those who have not already done so, I suggest that you get hold of a piece of land and a home as soon as possible, marry and settle down. . . . I hope no one will do anything in peace to spoil the magnificent record you have made in war" (quoted in Moses, *The Golden Age of Black Nationalism*, 244). Besides authoring *Negro Migration during the War*, Scott coauthored, with Lyman Beecher Stowe, *Booker T. Washington: Builder of a Civilization* (New York: Doubleday, 1917). As part of the Wilson administration, Scott had the job of defending a president highly unpopular with African Americans. See, for example, "The Negro under Wilson," in *Republican Campaign Textbook, 1916* (Washington, D.C.: Republican National Committee 1916), 3–14, a sharp critique composed by Henry Lincoln Johnson, recorder of deeds (and husband of the poet Georgia Douglas Johnson). For more on the Negro Sanhedrin, see Mark Solomon, *The Cry Was Unity: Communists and African Americans, 1917–1936* (Jackson: University Press of Mississippi, 1998), 29–33. For more on Howard University as a center of black intellectual life and activism, see Rayford W. Logan, *Howard University: The First Hundred Years, 1867–1967* (New York: New York University Press, 1969).

20. "Plan Memorial for Negro Soldiers," *Washington Bee*, 20 December 1919, 1; "An Appeal to Republicans," *Washington Bee*, 20 December 1919, 8. For more on the *Bee*, see Hal Chase, "William C. Chace and the Washington *Bee*," *Negro History Bulletin* 36 (December 1973): 172–74. Frederick Detweiler recorded that by 1921 there were 492 Negro periodicals in the United States and estimated that they reached some million readers (*The Negro Press in the United States* [1922; reprint, College Park, Md.: McGrath, 1962]). For another contemporaneous commentary on the consciousness-raising role of the black press in 1919, see Robert T. Kerlin, *The Voice of the Negro: 1919* (New York: E. P. Dutton, 1920).

21. Editorial, "Negro-Phobia," *Washington Bee*, 27 February 1915, 8; William Pickens, *The New Negro: His Political, Civil, and Mental Status and Related Essays* (1916; reprint, New York: Negro Universities Press, 1969), 235 ("colored soldier" quote); William Pickens, "Jim-Crowed," *Socialist Review* 9 (July 1920): 75–76 ("[the Negro] was human" quote); William Pickens, "The American Congo" (New York: American Civil Liberties Union, 1921), excerpted in the *Bee*, 21 July 1921, 2 (remaining quotes). The article was also published as "The American Congo—The Burning of Henry Lowry," *Nation* 109 (23 March 1921): 426–28. Pickens also tried his hand at fiction in *The Vengeance of the Gods and Three Other Stories of the Real American Color Line* (1922; reprint, New York: AMS, 1975). Philip Foner designates Pickens a "socialist" (*Organized Labor and the Black Worker*, 148). Pickens offered a quasi-Marxist analysis of how racist oppression of blacks

negatively affects the material welfare of whites in "The Negro and the Community," *Opportunity* 2 (August 1924): 229–31. For more on the Congo, particularly the role of African American journalists and missionaries in publicizing the Congo genocide, see Adam Hochschild, *King Leopold's Ghost: A Story of Greed, Terror, and Heroism in Colonial Africa* (Boston: Houghton Mifflin, 1998).

22. James Weldon Johnson, "What the Negro Is Doing for Himself," *Liberator* 1 (June 1918): 30; James Weldon Johnson, "The Obvious Thing to Do," *New York Age*, 29 November 1919, 4. On Johnson and the *Crusader* radicals, see Kornweibel, *"Seeing Red,"* 32. Joyce Moore Turner reports that the ABB also contributed funds for McKay's trip to the USSR (Joyce Moore Turner, "Richard B. Moore and His Works," in *Richard B. Moore, Caribbean Militant in Harlem: Collected Writings, 1920–1972*, ed. W. Burghardt Turner and Joyce Moore Turner [Bloomington: Indiana University Press, 1988], 47). On the party for McKay, see James Weldon Johnson, *Along This Way: The Autobiography of James Weldon Johnson* (1933; reprint, New York: Viking, 1961), 376.

23. Quoted in Editorial, "Lynchings in the United States," *Crisis* 4 (February 1922): 167; Walter White, *Rope and Faggot* (1929; reprint, New York: Arno, 1969), 82; Walter White, *The Fire in the Flint* (New York: Alfred A. Knopf, 1924), 126. White described his investigation into the Elaine killings in "'Massacring Whites' in Arkansas," *Nation* 109 (6 December 1919): 426. The findings from White's many investigations are contained in the NAACP's *Thirty Years of Lynching in the United States, 1889–1918* (1919; reprint, New York: Arno, 1969). See also Robert L. Zangrando, *The NAACP Crusade against Lynching, 1909–1950* (Philadelphia: Temple University Press, 1980).

24. Clifford quoted in Foner and Lewis, *The Black Worker from 1900 to 1919*, 455–56; Carrie Williams Clifford, *The Widening Light* (Boston: Walter Reid, 1922), 20 (tribute to Mary Turner quotes), 15 ("Race-Hate" quote), 16 ("Silent Protest Parade" quotes). The Negro clubwoman Leila Amos Pendleton referred to Clifford in 1912 as "a well-known elocutionist and club woman who has written a book of poems" (*A Narrative of the Negro* [1912; reprint, Freeport, N.Y.: Books for Libraries, 1971], 204). For a classic statement of the uplift mission of Negro clubwomen, see Fannie Barrier Williams, "The Club Movement among Negro Women," *Voice of the Negro* 1 (March 1904): 99–107.

25. Quoted in Dickson D. Bruce Jr., *Archibald Grimké: Portrait of a Black Independent* (Baton Rouge: Louisiana State University Press, 1993), 240. "Her Thirteen Black Soldiers" was singled out by the Justice Department as evidence of the *Messenger's* "dangerous radicalism" (ibid., 238). For more on the *Crisis's* refusal to print the poem, see Editorial, "Mr. Grimké and 'The Crisis,'" *Messenger* 2 (October 1919): 8. Grimké signed the call for the SPA-organized Friends of Negro Freedom in May 1920 (Philip Foner, *American Socialism and Black Americans: From the Age of Jackson to World War II* [Westport, Conn.: Greenwood, 1977], 314). See also Kornweibel, *"Seeing Red,"* 95–96.

26. Mary White Ovington, *Half a Man: The Status of the Negro in New York* (1911; reprint, New York: Hill and Wang, 1969); Mary White Ovington, *The Shadow* (New York: Harcourt, Brace and Howe, 1919); Mary White Ovington, "Bogalusa," *Liberator* 2 (January 1920): 33; letter to *Messenger* 2 (July 1918): 14. See also Ovington's retrospective on the NAACP, *The Walls Came Tumbling Down* (New York: Harcourt, Brace, 1947).

27. Seligmann, *The Negro Faces America*, 152, 201; Hoover quoted in Kornweibel, *"Seeing Red,"* 23.

28. James Weldon Johnson, "The Riots: An NAACP Investigation," *Crisis* 18
(September 1919): 241–43; Editorial, "Slavery," *Crisis* 22 (May 1921): 6 ("Negroes
are held" quote); W. E. B. Du Bois, "The Rising Truth," *Crisis* 22 (June 1921): 54
("shrill cry" quote); drawing of migrant, *Crisis* 19 (March 1920): 264. Governor
Hugh Dorsey's pamphlet *The Negro in Georgia* was published on April 22, 1921,
clearly in response to the "death farm" scandal. For more on the representation
of women on the cover of the *Crisis*, see Anne Stavney, "'Mothers of Tomorrow':
The New Negro Renaissance and the Politics of Maternal Representation," *African American Review* 32 (Winter 1998): 533–61.

29. Editorial, "The Amazing Major," *Crisis* 19 (November 1919): 345; Editorial, "The Real Causes of Two Race Riots," *Crisis* 19 (December 1919): 56; Alfred
Kreymborg, "Red Chant," *Crisis* 18 (November 1918): 31; Anonymous, "As Europe Sees Us," *Crisis* 21 (January 1921): 125 (Reed report); Claude McKay, "Exhortation," *Crisis* 21 (March 1921): 266; Joint Legislative Committee Investigating Seditious Activities, *Revolutionary Radicalism*, 2:1318.

30. Carter G. Woodson, *The Negro in Our History* (Washington, D.C.: Associated Publishers, 1922), 329–31; Benjamin Brawley, *A Social History of the American Negro* (New York: Macmillan, 1921), 349.

31. Stephen Graham, *The Soul of John Brown* (New York: Macmillan, 1920),
266–67; Oswald Garrison Villard, *John Brown, 1800–1859: A Biography Fifty Years
After* (Boston: Houghton Mifflin, 1911), 589. Graham's "Marching through Georgia" appeared in *Harper's* 140 (December 1919): 612–20, and 140 (May 1920): 813–
23.

32. Geroid Robinson, "The New Negro," *Freeman* 1 (2 June 1920): 278–80
(Palmer quoted on 279); Editorial, "Lynching: An American Kultur?" *New Repub-
lic* 18 (13 April 1918): 311–12; Anonymous, "The Week," *New Republic* 19 (30
July 1919): 405; Anonymous, "The Week," *New Republic* 21 (3 December 1919):
2. The *New Republic* also published an excerpt from Du Bois's *Darkwater*, "On
Being Black" 21 (18 February 1921): 339.

33. Editorial, *Nation* 112 (6 April 1921): 496; John Spargo, *Bolshevism: The
Enemy of Political and Industrial Democracy* (New York: Harper and Brothers,
1919), n.p.; Joint Legislative Committee Investigating Seditious Activities, *Revolutionary Radicalism*, 1:113. The Lusk Committee also included the *Dial*—
which regularly published articles by Thorstein Veblen, Helen Marot, Albert Rhys
Williams, and other left-leaning intellectuals associated with the Rand School—
among its group of "dangerous" magazines. Seligmann published his powerful
commentary on the "death farm," "Slavery in Georgia, A.D. 1921," in the *Nation* 112 (20 April 1921): 591.

34. W. E. B. Du Bois, "The Problem of Problems," *Intercollegiate Socialist* 6
(December 1917–January 1918): 7; W. E. B. Du Bois, "The African Roots of War,"
Atlantic Monthly 115 (May 1915): 707–14, quoted in Lewis, *W. E. B. Du Bois*, 504;
W. E. B. Du Bois, "Socialism and the Negro," *Crisis* 22 (October 1921): 247. See
also W. E. B. Du Bois, "The Negro and Radical Thought," *Crisis* 22 (July 1921):
103. Du Bois was roundly criticized by the wartime New Negroes for his "closing ranks" stance; according to Jeffrey Perry, it was Hubert Harrison who initiated the attack (introduction to *A Hubert Harrison Reader*, ed. Perry, 6–7). Perry

considers Harrison the "foremost Black organizer, agitator and theoretican" of New Negro radicalism in the 1910s and early 1920s (2). For more on Harrison, see James, *Holding Aloft the Banner of Ethiopia*, 122–84.

35. W. E. B. Du Bois, *John Brown*, rev. ed. (New York: International, 1962), 395 ("abolition of hard and fast lines" and "the inspiration which America owes" quotes; after aligning himself with communism, Du Bois dramatically revised his 1909 edition of *John Brown*, adding new material in italics; the quotations here are in regular type, indicating they were in the 1909 edition); W. E. B. Du Bois, "The Song of the Smoke" (1907), in *The Oxford W. E. B. Du Bois Reader*, ed. Eric J. Sundquist (New York: Oxford University Press, 1992), 55; Du Bois, *Darkwater*, 159; W. E. B. Du Bois, *The Gift of Black Folk: The Negroes in the Making of America* (Boston: Stratford, 1924), 78.

36. W. E. B. Du Bois, "Returning Soldiers" (May 1919), in *The Oxford W. E. B. Du Bois Reader*, ed. Sundquist, 380–81; Du Bois, "The Negro and Radical Thought," 103; W. E. B. Du Bois, *The Negro* (1915; reprint, Millwood, N.Y.: Draus-Thompson, 1975), 241; Du Bois, *Darkwater*, 70; W. E. B. Du Bois, "Georgia: Invisible Empire State," *Nation* 120 (21 January 1925), reprinted in *Struggling to Shake Off Old Shackles: Twentieth-Century Georgia*, ed. William F. Holmes (Savannah, Ga.: Beehive, 1995), 92–93; Lewis, *W. E. B. Du Bois*, 420–21, 540; Military Intelligence Division quoted in Kornweibel, *"Seeing Red,"* 71. For an interpretation of Du Bois's career stressing its continuing leftist strain, see Marable, *W. E. B. Du Bois*. For more on the contradictions informing Du Bois's politics, as well as errors of various historians in locating and naming these politics, see Adolph L. Reed Jr., *W. E. B. Du Bois and American Political Thought: Fabianism and the Color Line* (New York: Oxford University Press, 1997), especially 71–89.

37. Alain Locke, "The Great Disillusionment," appendix to *Race Contacts and Interracial Relations: Lectures on the Theory and Practice of Race*, ed. Jeffrey C. Stewart (Washington, D.C.: Howard University Press, 1992), 110 ("foolish[ness]" quote), 108 ("for the utopia of empire" quote); Alain Locke, "Race Contacts and Interracial Relations" (lecture text), in ibid., 54 ("[Race antipathy]" and "and much is" quotes), 68 ("divergent sects" quote), 70 ("[r]ace issues" quote); Alain Locke, "Race Contacts and Inter-Racial Relations: A Study in the Theory and Practice of Racism" (syllabus notes), in *The Critical Temper of Alain Locke: A Selection of His Essays on Art and Culture*, ed. Jeffrey C. Stewart (New York: Garland, 1983), 408 ("false race theory," "apologia," "practice of race," and "competitive and industrial basis" quotes), 411 ("eradicable" and "in the ethnological" quotes), 412 ("sociological" quote), 407 ("false conceptions" and "an obstacle" quotes). For more on Locke and pragmatism, see G. Hutchinson, *The Harlem Renaissance in Black and White*, 33–61; Everett H. Akam, "Community and Crisis: The 'Transfiguring Imagination' of Alain Locke," *American Literary History* 3 (Summer 1991): 255–76; Helbling, *The Harlem Renaissance*, 43–67; and Johnny Washington, *Alain Locke and Philosophy* (Westport, N.Y.: Greenwood, 1986). It bears noting that sociology was viewed as a seedbed of socialism by the Lusk Committee, which targeted the sociology departments at City College of New York, Columbia, and New York University in its investigations into "academic and scholastic socialist activities" (Joint Legislative Committee Investigating Seditious Activities, *Revolutionary Radicalism*, 1:112–22).

38. Alain Locke, "Racial Progress and Race Adjustment," in *Race Contacts and*

Interracial Relations, ed. Stewart, 84–99; Jeffery Stewart, introduction to *Race Contacts and Interracial Relations,* xix–lix (quote on xlii). The Howard University Library was threatened with being closed largely because it contained a copy of Albert Rhys Williams's *Russian Soviets: Seventy-Six Questions and Answers on the Workingman's Government of Russia.* For more on the banning of books and political intimidation at Howard, see Logan, *Howard University,* 189–90. Locke leaned back toward the left significantly in the late 1930s. In "The Politics of Alain Locke," Gilbert Belle mentions no political activities on Locke's part prior to the 1924 Negro Sanhedrin (in *Alain Locke: Reflections on a Modern Renaissance Man,* ed. Russell J. Linneman [Baton Rouge: Louisiana State University Press, 1982], 50–62).

39. *Call,* quoted in Foner, *American Socialism and Black Americans,* 285; "Sixty-two Lynchings in U.S. in Year, Says Report," *Call,* 1 January 1919, 1 (on covering lynchings); reprint of lynching advertisement, *Call,* 14 July 1919, 1; Editorial, "Man Hunting in Washington," *Call,* 24 July 1919, 8 ("American capitalism" and "patriotic fakirs" quotes). See also Felix Holt, "Race Riots Are Blamed in Attempt to Split White and Black Workers," *Call,* 25 July 1919, 3.

40. The Dreamer, untitled fable, *Call,* 6 April 1918, 8; John Nicholas Beffel, "Spattering Mud on John Brown's Halo," *Call,* 9 November 1919, 10; David Karsner, "Debs on John Brown, Martyr," *Call,* 22 June 1919, sect. 2:1; Nicholas Feffel, "Your Negro Neighbor," and Alvin Winston, "Poetry of Negroes" (review of J. Johnson, *Fifty Years and Other Poems), Call Magazine,* 2 February 1919, 11.

41. Anise, "The Negro Worker," *Call,* 28 May 1919, 8; Foner, *American Socialism and Black Americans,* 243–47; Editorial, "The New York Call's Fifteenth Anniversary," *Messenger* 5 (June 1923): 737. For more on "ragged-verse" poetry, see Cary Nelson, *Repression and Recovery: Modern American Poetry and the Politics of Cultural Memory, 1910–1945* (Madison: University of Wisconsin Press, 1989), 46–47.

42. Editorial, *Liberator* 1 (March 1918): 3; Esau Jones, "Georgia Saves Her Reputation," *Liberator* 4 (May 1921): 30.

43. Lucy Maverick, "Out of Texas," *Liberator* 5 (June 1922): 28–30; E. Merrill Root, "Southern Holiday," *Liberator* 5 (March 1922): 11; Jeannette Pearl, "Negro Bodies," *Liberator* 6 (November 1923): 28; Daytie Randle, "Lament," *Liberator* 4 (January 1922): 6; Ralph Chaplin, "Wesley Everest," *Liberator* 5 (March 1922): 11; Mary Burrill, "Aftermath," *Liberator* 2 (April 1919): 10–14; Robert Minor, "Exodus from Dixie," *Liberator* 6 (June 1923): 18–19. Lucy Maverick, it turned out, was the pen name of a group of people writing about a state-sponsored lynching in San Antonio, Texas. See Maxwell, *New Negro, Old Left,* 99–100, 212n5.

44. Hugo Gellert, "Negro Boy," *Liberator* 5 (June 1922): 29; Boardman Robinson, "In a Street Car," *Liberator* 5 (April 1922): 7; Stuart Davis, "The Return of the Soldier," *Liberator* 2 (March 1919): 35; Georgia Douglas Johnson, "The Octaroon [*sic*]," *Liberator* 2 (August 1919): 10; J. Johnson, "What the Negro Is Doing for Himself"; Walter White, "What Is Social Equality?" *Liberator* 4 (January 1922): 4–5; Walter White, "The Negro as Poet," *Liberator* 5 (April 1922): 20; Lydia Gibson, review of *The Negro in Our History,* by Carter G. Woodson, *Liberator* 7 (September 1924): 33; Lydia Gibson, "A Voice in the Wilderness," *Liberator* 7 (October 1924): 31; Angelina Grimké to the *Liberator,* n.d., box 38-3, folder 44, Angelina Grimké Papers, Moorland-Spingarn Research Institute, Howard University; advertisement, *Liberator* 5 (May 1922): 31. The description of McKay was peculiar:

"Claude McKay is the foremost revolutionary poet of America, and the fact that he is a pure-blooded Negro adds the piquant flavor of curiosity to his work."

45. Claude McKay, "If We Must Die," *Liberator* 2 (July 1919): 21; Maxwell, *New Negro, Old Left*, 102; Claude McKay, "Home Thoughts," *Liberator* 2 (February 1920): 19; Claude McKay, "To Ethiopia," *Liberator* 2 (February 1920): 7. Winston James points out that the rhetoric of "If We Must Die" is anticipated in McKay's 1912 poem about Jamaican tramcar rioters, "Passive Resistance." He considers McKay's early poems, especially those in *Songs of Jamaica* (1911) and *Constab Ballads* (1912), the "unrivaled foundation for . . . understanding . . . the politics of the young McKay" (*A Fierce Hatred of Injustice: Claude McKay's Jamaica and His Poetry of Rebellion* [London: Verso, 2000], 87–88, xix).

46. Claude McKay, "Birthright," *Liberator* 5 (July 1922): 16 ("the problem," "may be eventually," and "more broadly socialistic" quotes); Cruse, *The Crisis of the Negro Intellectual*, 50–53; Wayne Cooper, *Claude McKay: Rebel Sojourner in the Harlem Renaissance* (Baton Rouge: Louisiana State University Press, 1987), 139; J. Miller, "African-American Writing of the 1930s," 87; Solomon, *The Cry Was Unity*, 9; Maxwell, *New Negro, Old Left*, 103; Claude McKay, *A Long Way from Home* (1937; reprint, New York: Arno, 1969), 149. Maxwell's chapter on McKay (95–124) is indispensable. See also Tyrone Tillery, *Claude McKay: A Black Poet's Struggle for Identity* (Amherst: University of Massachusetts Press, 1992), 55–57. According to the *Izvyestia* of 18 November 1922, while McKay was in Moscow, he affirmed a class analysis of U.S. racism, fulminating against the use of Negroes as "strikebreakers . . . under the protection of the American police who protect them from the wrath of their striking white comrades . . . but prefer not to interfere or else interfere on the side of the white in case the Negroes are treated to 'lynch law.'" On this occasion, McKay also attacked the *Urban League Bulletin*, the precursor to *Opportunity*, for being in collusion with such white millionaires as the "great capitalist, Rosenwald" to spread strikebreaking propaganda among "the masses of unclass-conscious colored people" (Anonymous, "Claude MacKay [sic] before the Internationale," *Opportunity* 1 [September 1923]: 258–59).

47. Robert Minor, "Death or a Program!" *Workers Monthly* 5 (April 1926): 270–73, 287 (quote on 273); William F. Dunne, "The Negroes as an Oppressed People," *Workers Monthly* 4 (July 1925): 395–98 (quote on 397). See also William F. Dunne, "Negroes in American Industry," *Workers Monthly* 4 (March 1925): 206–8, and 4 (April 1925): 257–60. Minor began his attack on Garvey in the last issue of the *Liberator*, in "The Handkerchief on Garvey's Head," *Liberator* 7 (October 1924): 17. For the argument that Garvey "combined the energies of the new urban mass consciousness with those of traditional Pan-Africanism," see Moses, *The Golden Age of Black Nationalism*, 262. For more on communism and black nationalism in the mid-1920s, see Solomon, *The Cry Was Unity*, 3–67; Robin D. G. Kelley, *Race Rebels: Culture, Politics, and the Black Working Class* (New York: Free Press, 1994): 103–21; and Oscar Berland, "The Emergence of the Communist Perspective on the 'Negro Question' in America, 1919–1931: Part One," *Science and Society* 63 (Winter 1999–2000): 411–32. Earl Ofari Hutchinson, working in the Harold Cruse vein, offers a negative assessment in *Blacks and Reds: Race and Class in Conflict, 1919–1990* (East Lansing: Michigan State University Press, 1995), 7–86.

48. Jay Lovestone, "The Great Negro Migration," *Workers Monthly* 5 (February 1926): 179–84; Langston Hughes, "God to Hungry Child," *Workers Monthly* 4 (March 1925): 234; Langston Hughes, "Goodbye Christ," *Negro Worker* (November–December 1932): 32; Langston Hughes, "Rising Waters," *Workers Monthly* 4 (April 1925): 267.

49. Hubert Harrison, "On a Certain Condescension in White Publishers," reprinted in *African Fundamentalism: A Literary and Cultural Anthology of Garvey's Harlem Renaissance*, ed. Tony Martin (Dover, Mass.: Majority, 1983), 23 ("friendly and faithful" quote); "Honorable Marcus Garvey Replies to Article in New York World by Herbert Seligmann," *Negro World*, 10 December 1921, 1 ("a friend of the Negro people" quote); "'Reds Seek Negro Recruits to Help Start Revolution," *Negro World*, 9 July 1921, 1 (on ABB); "New York World Makes Exposé of Ku Klux Klan," *Negro World*, 12 September 1921, 12 (on KKK-UNIA relationship).

50. Perry, introduction to *A Hubert Harrison Reader*, ed. Perry, 2 ("principal radical influence" quote); Marable, *W. E. B. Du Bois*, 117 (quote from *Negro World* on red in UNIA flag); Kornweibel, *"Seeing Red,"* 116 (Garvey on Lenin and Trotsky), 28 (BI investigator); Hubert Harrison, "Wanted—A Colored International," *Negro World*, 28 May 1921, reprinted in *A Hubert Harrison Reader*, ed. Perry, 225; Hubert Harrison, review of *The Folly of Nations*, reprinted in *African Fundamentalism*, ed. Martin, 115; Vincent, *Voices of a Black Nation*, 29 (on *Negro World* circulation); Communist May Day advertisement in *Negro World*, 1 May 1926, 2; Lusk Committee quoted in Kornweibel, *"Seeing Red,"* 106. For more on the relationship between Irish and African American nationalisms, see Tracy Mishkin, *The Harlem and Irish Renaissances: Language, Identity, and Representation* (Gainesville: University Press of Florida, 1998). For more on the leftist aspects of Garveyism through 1921, see Marable, *W. E. B. Du Bois*, 115–18; and James, *Holding Aloft the Banner of Ethiopia*, 122–84.

51. Tony Martin, "General Principles," in *African Fundamentalism*, ed. Martin, 21; Walrond, "Batouala, Art and Propaganda," reprinted in ibid., 32; Fred J. Edwards, "The African Chief," *Negro World*, 19 February 1921, 6.

52. Ethel Trew Dunlap, "In Respect of Marcus Garvey," reprinted in *African Fundamentalism*, ed. Martin, 179–80; Marion S. Lakey, "On Miss Dunlap's Poems," ibid., 66–68 (quote on 68).

53. Andrea Razafkeriefo, "The Rising Tide," ibid., 173–74; Carita Owens Collins, "This Must Not Be!" ibid., 168; Tony Martin, "The Negro Spirit," ibid., 167; Leonard Brathwaite, "Georgia," *Negro World*, 7 May 1921, 6. The *Negro World* featured several other poems on the "death farm": Ethel Trew Dunlap, "The Peonage Horror," *Negro World*, 23 April 1921, 6; Leonard Brathwaite, "Covington, Georgia," *Negro World*, 23 April 1921, 6; and Leonard Brathwaite "To Ethel Trew Dunlap," *Negro World*, 4 June 1921, 6. Covington is the seat of Newton County, where the case was tried. For more on Razafkeriefo, who later became the popular songwriter Andy Razaf, see Maxwell, *New Negro, Old Left*, 13–62.

54. Ethel Trew Dunlap, "The Toiler," *Negro World*, 10 September 1921, 6. For more on the expansion of the UNIA into Washington, D.C., see "Washington U.N.I.A.," *Negro World*, 12 March 1921, 9; and "Washington Landsliding to Garveyism," *Negro World*, 26 November 1921, 1. A number of writers who would become prominent in the Harlem Renaissance published early in their careers in the pages of the *Negro World*: Razaf, Walrond, McKay, and Zora Neale Hurston.

55. Advertisement, *Messenger* 1 (November 1917): 21 ("Only Magazine" quote); Editorial, "Bolshevism and World Democracy," *Messenger* 1 (July 1918): 9 ("the Banquo's ghost" quote); Editorial, "The Negro—A Menace to Radicalism," *Messenger* 2 (May–June 1919): 20 ("[o]rganized labor" quote); Editorial, "The New Negro—What Is He?" *Messenger* 3 (August 1920): 73 ("political equality," "as a worker," and social aim quotes); Editorial, "Labor and Lynching," *Messenger* 2 (February 1920): 2 ("All hail" quote); W. A. Domingo, "Socialism: The Negroes' Hope," *Messenger* 2 (July 1919): 22 ("[American Negroes]" quote). See also W. A. Domingo, "Capitalism: The Basis of Colonialism," *Messenger* 2 (August 1919): 26–27; and W. A. Domingo, "Private Property as a Pillar of Race Prejudice," *Messenger* 3 (April–May 1920): 9–10, and *Messenger* 3 (August 1920): 69–71. As of March 1920, the magazine changed its subtitle to *A Journal of Scientific Radicalism*, Owen and Randolph explained, in part because they had some 10,000 white readers and in part because of the appearance of other black radical journals, especially the *Crusader* (Editorial, "Trend of the Times," *Messenger* 2 [March 1920]: 1). Although Harrison had initiated Randolph and Owen into left-wing politics, he was deeply critical of their affiliation with the SPA, charging in March 1920 that the SPA had "secretly subsidized" the *Messenger* to "cut into the splendid solidarity which Negroes are achieving in response to the call of racial necessity" ("Race First versus Class First," reprinted in *A Hubert Harrison Reader*, ed. Perry, 108).

56. Scott Nearing, "War Shouters and War Contracts," *Messenger* 2 (January 1918): 2; Editorial, "The Hun in America," *Messenger* 2 (July 1919): 5; William Colson, "An Analysis of Negro Patriotism," *Messenger* 2 (August 1919): 24 ("When black officers taught" and "The sentiment" quotes), 25 ("[The] next war" quote); Editorial, "Lynching: Capitalism Its Cause; Socialism Its Cure," *Messenger* 2 (March 1919: 9 ("is used to foster" quote); Editorial, "Peonage, Riots, and Lynching," *Messenger* 3 (August 1921): 232 ("howl of disgust" quote). See also Editorial, "The Causes of and Remedy for Race Riots," *Messenger* 2 (September 1919): 14–21. It should be noted that the numbering of the issues of the *Messenger* is confusing, since volume 2 extended from January 1918 through December 1920, whereas volume 1 took in only October–December 1917, while volume 3—which began in January 1921—and all subsequent volumes took in one year apiece.

57. *Messenger* 2 (September 1919): 17; "Following the Advice of the 'Old Crowd' Negro," *Messenger* 2 (June 1919): 16; "The 'New Crowd Negro' Making America Safe for Himself," *Messenger* 2 (July 1919): 17; untitled cartoon, *Messenger* 2 (December 1919): 15; "Workers of the World Unite!!" *Messenger* 2 (August 1919): 4; "Congressman Byrnes of South Carolina Alarmed at Banquo's Ghost of the New Crowd Negro," *Messenger* 2 (August 1919): 12; W. B. Williams, "The Mob Victim," *Messenger* 2 (July 1919): 4; Joint Legislative Committee Investigating Seditious Activities, *Revolutionary Radicalism*, 2:frontispiece.

58. Claude McKay, "Labor's Day," *Messenger* 2 (September 1919): 31; Claude McKay, "Birds of Prey," *Messenger* 2 (December 1919): 23; Claude McKay, "Birds of Prey," in his *Harlem Shadows* (New York: Harcourt, Brace, 1922), 76.

59. Langston Hughes, "Danse Africaine," *Crisis* 24 (August 1922): 167; Langston Hughes, "Johannesburg Mines," *Messenger* 7 (February 1925): 93; Langston Hughes, "To Certain Intellectuals," *Messenger* 7 (February 1925): 103; Langston Hughes, "Steel Mills," *Messenger* 7 (February 1925): 103; Langston Hughes, *The*

Big Sea: An Autobiography (1940; reprint, New York: Hill and Wang, 1963), 29. Other radical poems by Hughes published in the *Messenger* in the mid-1920s include "Grant Park," *Messenger* 6 (March 1924): 75; "Gods," *Messenger* 6 (March 1924): 94; and "Prayer for a Winter Night," *Messenger* 6 (May 1924): 153.

60. Chandler Owen, "The Cabaret—A Useful Social Institution," *Messenger* 4 (August 1922): 461. For the argument that the *Messenger* placed little emphasis on culture as a means of conveying political ideas, see John Brown Childs, "Concepts of Culture in Afro-American Political Thought, 1890–1920," *Social Text* 4 (Fall 1981): 28–43. A recent anthology of writings from the *Messenger*—*The Messenger Reader: Stories, Poetry and Essays from The Messenger Magazine*, ed. Sondra Kathryn Wilson (New York: Modern Library, 2000)—overstresses the magazine's literary contents and deemphasizes its early radicalism.

61. Editorial, "R. R. Moton," *Messenger* 2 (July 1918): 28; Editorial, "Who's Who," *Messenger* 3 (March 1919): 23 ("is to destroy all and build up new ones" quote); Editorial, "Du Bois Fails as a Theorist," *Messenger* 2 (December 1919): 7 ("fails as a theorist" and "is the only alleged leader" quotes); Editorial, "Garveyism," *Messenger* 2 (September 1920): 252 ("it broadens" quote); A. Philip Randolph and Chandler Owen, Editorial, "Marcus Garvey! The Black Imperial Wizard Becomes Messenger Boy of the White Ku Klux Kleagle," *Messenger* 4 (July 1922): 437 ("[I]n all its sinister" and "proclaimed to all" quotes); A. Philip Randolph, "The Human Hand Threat," *Messenger* 4 (October 1922): 499 (threats quotes). The incident was widely reported in the black press; see, for example, "Editor Receives a Human Hand," *Echo* (Red Bank, N.J.), 9 September 1922, 1. The *Messenger* also criticized Pickens for the superficiality of his analysis of capitalism: "He exercises great skill in dressing the 'surface' of our racial wounds, then speaks of his work so admirably you think he has eradicated the evil by purifying the blood" (Floyd J. Calvin, "The Mirrors of Harlem: Studies in 'Colored' Psycho-Analysis," *Messenger* 4 [December 1922]: 545). For more on Randolph and Owen's politics, see J. M. Pawa, "Black Radicals and White Spies," *Negro History Bulletin* 35 (October 1972): 129–33; Foner, *American Socialism and Black Americans*, 265–87; and Jervis Anderson, *A. Philip Randolph: A Biographical Portrait* (New York: Harcourt Brace Jovanovich, 1974).

62. Angelina Grimké to the *Messenger* 2 (December 1919): 29; Seligmann, *The Negro Faces America*, 291–94; letters from Charles Chesnutt and F. Scott Fitzgerald, *Messenger* 5 (June 1923): 753, 749; Kornweibel, *"Seeing Red"* (Palmer quoted on 91, Hoover quoted on 85); W. F. Elkins, "'Unrest among the Negroes': A British Document of 1919," *Science and Society* 32 (Winter 1968): 76; J. Johnson, *Along This Way*, 125; Foner, *American Socialism and Black Americans*, 277. For more on Hoover's antipathy to black radicals, especially the *Messenger* editors, see Mark Ellis, "J. Edgar Hoover and the 'Red Summer of 1919,'" *Journal of American Studies* 28 (April 1994): 39–59. Ted Vincent discusses the popularity of the *Messenger* among young and well-educated African Americans in *Keep Cool: The Black Activists Who Built the Jazz Age* (London: Pluto, 1995), 161. Hull notes that Randolph attended several of Georgia Douglas Johnson's famous "Saturday Nights" at her Washington, D.C., home (*Color, Sex, and Poetry*, 165). The date and address of the Fitzgerald letter are significant because it was at this time that he was conceiving *The Great Gatsby* (1925), which takes place in Great Neck. It is possible that Fitzgerald was influenced in his satirization of Tom Buchanan's fear of the

rising tide of color (which Buchanan attributes to one "Goddard," not Lothrop Stoddard) by the May 1923 issue of the *Messenger*, which contained two blistering commentaries on Stoddard's work: Kelly Miller's review of *The Revolt against Civilization* (703) and Alain Locke's review of *The New World of Islam* (711, 720).

63. Detweiler, *The Negro Press in the United States*, 71. The ABB is discussed in Joyce Turner, "Richard B. Moore and His Works," 1–108; Solomon, *The Cry Was Unity*, 1–31; Maxwell, *New Negro, Old Left*, 35–37; Kornweibel, "*Seeing Red*," 133–52; Robert A. Hill, "Racial and Radical: Cyril V. Briggs, the *Crusader* Magazine, and the African Blood Brotherhood, 1918–1922," in *The "Crusader": A Facsimile of the Periodical*, 3 vols. (Newark and London: Garland, 1987), 1:v–lxvi; and James, *Holding Aloft the Banner of Ethiopia*, 155–84. Solomon, Hill, and James offer different dates for the *Crusader* editors' joining the Communist Party.

64. James, *Holding Aloft the Banner of Ethiopia*, 160; George Wells Parker, "The Children of the Sun," *Crusader* 1 (November 1918): 11; Editorial, "Our Far-Flung Challenge," *Crusader* 1 (September 1919): 8 ("Whether the caucasian" quote); Editorial, "The Salvation of the Negro," *Crusader* 4 (April 1921): 8 ("race genius" quote), 9 ("oppressive capitalist system" quote); Editorial, "Rising Tide of Color Sets White World A-Trembling," *Crusader* 2 (July 1920): 14–15. Parker's thesis regarding "blood" was not consistent: he also opined that "[t]he mixed race has always been the great race" and that "the pure race" had been "always the stagnant one" ("The Children of the Sun," part 5, *Crusader* 1 [August 1919]: 5 ["[t]he mixed race" quote], 28 ["always the stagnant" quote]). That the view of African American women as mothers of the race could take an egregiously sexist turn was manifested in the *Crusader* editors' denigrating comments about the "flat-chested girl" (Editorial, "The Sin of Being Unattractive," *Crusader* 1 [August 1919]: 19). The *Crusader* routinely advertised the works of the Afrocentric historian J. A. Rogers, as well as such works about Christianity as W. L. Hunter's *Jesus Christ Was Part Negro* (*Crusader* 1 [December 1918]: 22).

65. Cyril Briggs, "Dr. Du Bois Misrepresents Negrodom," *Crusader* 1 (May 1919): 1; Editorial, "Stand by Soviet Russia!" *Crusader* 5 (December 1921): 8; Boulin quoted in Kornweibel, "*Seeing Red*," 31.

66. Cyril V. Briggs, "The Negro's Place Is with Labor," *Crusader* 2 (December 1919): 6; Richard B. Moore, "Bogalusa," reprinted in *Richard B. Moore*, ed. Turner and Turner, 140–42 (quote on 140); Foner, *Organized Labor and the Black Worker*, 149

67. Andrea Razafkeriefo, "Don't Tread on Me," *Crusader* 1 (May 1919): 7.

68. Anise, "To Stir up Race Hatred," *Crusader* 6 (January–February 1922): 27

69. Editorial, "The Crusader," *Messenger* 2 (November 1919): 6; Editorial, "The Great Illusion," *Crusader* 1 (November 1918): 5–6; "From the Radical Press," *Crusader* 4 (May 1921): 13; "The Liberator Admitted to Second-Class Mails," *Negro World*, 4 June 1921, 1; Anonymous, "Radicals," *Crisis* 19 (November 1919): 46; Joint Legislative Committee Investigating Seditious Activities, *Revolutionary Radicalism*, 2:1505, 1518–19. On Domingo's resignation from the UNIA, see his notice in the *Messenger* 2 (September 1919): 32.

70. The *Crisis* coverage of the Valdosta lynchings was reprinted in the *Crusader* 1 (October 1918): 31–32; "Capitalism and Race Prejudice" was reprinted from the *Messenger* in the *Call*, 19 March 1919: 8; "Out for Negro Tools!" was reprinted from the *Crusader* in the *Call*, 30 April 1919, 8; the *Call*'s coverage of the Coates-

ville deportations was reprinted in the *Crusader* Digest of News, "Deportation," *Crusader* 1 (April 1919): 23; "The White Press—the Greatest Menace of the Negro Race" was reprinted from the *Negro World* in the *Call*, 26 July 1919, 8; Garvey's critique of the League of Nations having been reprinted there in March 1919; Franz Boas's *Nation* review of Lothrop Stoddard's *Rising Tide of Color* was reprinted in the *Crusader* 3 (January 1921): 6, and, under the headline "Supposed Inferiority of Darker Races Proved Baseless," in the *Negro World*, 16 April 1921, 1, 5; Esau Jones's sardonic commentary on the "death farm" was reprinted from the *Liberator* in the "From the Radical Press" column in the *Crusader* 4 (July 1921): 4–5. McKay's "If We Must Die" was reprinted twice from the *Liberator* in the *Messenger* (September 1919 and July 1921) and three times in the *Crusader* (September 1919, May 1920, and January 1921).

Chapter 2: Nation, Class, and the Limits of the Left

1. Theodor Adorno, *Prisms*, trans. Samuel Weber and Sherry Weber (Cambridge, Mass.: MIT Press, 1983), 32; Karl Marx and Frederick Engels, *The German Ideology*, ed. C. J. Arthur (New York: International, 1970), 65.

2. Werner Sombart, *Why Is There No Socialism in the United States?* (1906; reprint, White Plains, N.Y.: M. E. Sharpe, 1976); Louis Hartz, *The Liberal Tradition in America: An Interpretation of American Political Thought since the Revolution* (New York: Harcourt, Brace and World, 1955); Frederick Jackson Turner, *The Significance of the Frontier in American History* (New York: Continuum, 1991); Seymour Martin Lipset, *Continental Divide: The Values and Institutions of the United States and Canada* (New York: Routledge, 1990).

3. Warren Susman, *Culture as History: The Transformation of American Society in the Twentieth Century* (New York: Pantheon, 1984); Lizabeth Cohen, *From Town Center to Shopping Center: The Reconfiguration of Community Marketplaces in Postwar America* (Washington, D.C.: American Historical Association, 1996); T. J. Jackson Lears, *Fables of Abundance: A Cultural History of Advertising in America* (New York: Basic Books, 1994), 9. See also Lawrence Glickman, *A Living Wage: American Workers and the Making of a Consumer Society* (Ithaca, N.Y.: Cornell University Press, 1997).

4. Patricia Cayo Sexton, *The War on Labor and the Left: Understanding America's Unique Conservatism* (Boulder: Westview, 1991), 38; Mike Hill, *Prisoners of the American Dream: Politics and Economy in the History of the U.S. Working Class* (London: Verso, 1986), 3–51; David Roediger, *The Wages of Whiteness: Race and the Making of the American Working Class* (London: Verso, 1991); David Roediger, *Towards the Abolition of Whiteness: Essays on Race, Politics, and Working Class History* (London: Verso, 1994); Reich, *Racial Inequality*; Alexander Saxton, *The Rise and Fall of the White Republic: Class Politics and Mass Culture in Nineteenth-Century America* (London: Verso, 1990); Theodore Allen, *The Invention of the White Race*, 2 vols. (London: Verso, 1994, 1998); Montgomery, *The Fall of the House of Labor*; Brecher, *Strike!* Michael Goldfield, *The Color of Politics: Race and the Mainsprings of American Politics* (New York: New, 1997).

5. Goldstein, *Political Repression in Modern America*, 153; Bennett, *The Party of Fear*; Abramowitz, "Historians and the Red Scare of 1919–1920 in Detroit," 87–118; Sexton, *The War on Labor and the Left*.

6. Marianne DeKoven, *Rich and Strange: Gender, History, Modernism* (Princeton, N.J.: Princeton University Press, 1991), 24; Huggins, *Harlem Renaissance*; Lewis, introduction to *The Portable Harlem Renaissance Reader*, ed. Lewis, xxiv. Fredric Jameson designates an "arrested dialectic" with respect to what he calls the "antinomies of postmodernism" (*The Seeds of Time* [New York: Columbia University Press, 1994], 1–71). But if one views the contradictions informing postmodernism as an extension of, rather than qualitative departure from, those informing modernism—a position that elsewhere Jameson rejects—the formulation of the "arrested dialectic" has abiding usefulness (*Postmodernism: The Cultural Logic of Late Capitalism* [Durham, N.C.: Duke University Press, 1991], chapter 2).

7. Kalaidjian, *American Culture between the Wars*, 77; Douglas, *Terrible Honesty*, 324.

8. Nelson, *Repression and Recovery*; Douglas Wixson, *Worker-Writer in America: Jack Conroy and the Tradition of Midwestern Literary Radicalism, 1898–1990* (Urbana: University of Illinois Press, 1994); Chip Rhodes, *Structures of the Jazz Age: Mass Culture, Progressive Education, and Racial Disclosures in American Modernism* (New York: Verso, 1998); Berry, *Langston Hughes before and after Harlem*; J. Miller, "African-American Writing of the 1930s," 78–90; Maxwell, *New Negro, Old Left*; Dawahare, *Nationalism, Marxism, and African American Literature*.

9. Hughes, *The Big Sea*, 228. For more on dialectics, see Bertell Ollman, *Dialectical Investigations* (London: Routledge, 1993); and Ira Gollobin, *Dialectical Materialism: Its Laws, Categories, and Practice* (New York: Petras, 1986).

10. For analysis of Hughes's self-censorship in composing *Not without Laughter*, see John P. Shields, "'Never Cross the Divide': Reconstructing Langston Hughes's *Not without Laughter*," *African American Review* 28 (Winter 1994): 601–13; and H. Nigel Thomas, "Patronage and the Writing of Langston Hughes's *Not without Laughter*: A Paradoxical Case," *CLA Journal* 42 (September 1998): 48–70. For more on the categories of the residual and the emergent, see Raymond Williams, *Marxism and Literature* (Oxford: Oxford University Press, 1977), 121–27.

11. For criticisms of the SPA's line and practice regarding race, see Foner, *American Socialism and Black Americans*; Weinstein, *The Decline of American Socialism in America*, 63–74; Roediger, *The Wages of Whiteness*; and Solomon, *The Cry Was Unity*, 3–51. Instances of the critique of Marxism as class reductionist include Kalaidjian, *American Culture between the Wars*; David Theo Goldberg, *Racist Culture: Philosophy and the Politics of Meaning* (Oxford: Blackwell, 1993); and Michael Omi and Howard Winant, *Racial Formation in the United States: From the 1960s to the 1980s* (New York: Routledge and Kegan Paul, 1986).

12. The CPUSA formed out of the left wing of the SPA after the 1919 split. It was constituted by the conjunction of the Communist Party and the Communist Labor Party, which joined within a year after the split within the SPA. The Communists were underground until 1923; their aboveground organization was the Workers Party. For more on the early CPUSA, see Draper, *The Roots of American Communism*. For more on the relationship between the CPUSA and African American leftists, see Solomon, *The Cry Was Unity*; R. Hill, "Racial and Radical," 1:v–lxvi; Joyce Turner, "Richard B. Moore and His Works," 1–108; Kelley, *Race Rebels*, 103–21; and Berland, "The Emergence of the Communist Perspective on the 'Negro Question' in America." Solomon and Hill particularly refute Draper's notion that no African American Communists were part of the CPUSA

from its outset. See also James, *Holding Aloft the Banner of Ethiopia,* 155–73. For more on "bad" versus "good" nationalism, see Étienne Balibar and Immanuel Wallerstein, *Race, Nation, Class: Ambiguous Identities,* trans. Chris Turner (London: Verso, 1991), especially 47–54.

13. On *determination,* see Raymond Williams, *Keywords: A Vocabulary of Culture and Society* (New York: Oxford University Press, 1976), 87–91. For an instance of scholarship largely occluding the role of the Left in working-class cultural history, see Denning, *The Cultural Front.* Brian Lloyd, by contrast, argues that the reformist and nationalist weaknesses of the early-twentieth-century Socialists definitively set the limits within which the class struggle would take shape (*Left Out*).

14. *Appeal to Reason* and Victor Berger quoted in Mark Pittenger, *American Socialists and Evolutionary Thought, 1870–1920* (Madison: University of Wisconsin Press, 1993), 180, 191; Kate Richards O'Hare, "'Nigger' Equality," in *Kate Richards O'Hare: Selected Writings and Speeches,* ed. Philip S. Foner and Sally M. Miller (Baton Rouge: Louisiana State University Press, 1982), 46 ("We Socialists" quote), 47 ("rich and fertile" quote), 48 ("Let us give" quote). Sally M. Miller argues that the left-wing Socialists were more likely to be antiracist than the right-wing Socialists, but the example of O'Hare (a left-winger) would seem to qualify this proposition at least through 1912 ("The Socialist Party and the Negro," *Journal of Negro History* 66 [July 1971]: 220–29). Apparently oblivious to O'Hare's early racism, Randolph and Owen praised her when she was sent to prison in 1918, declaring that she was being punished for "showing the farmers how to stop the blood sucking speculators from robbing them of the fruits of their labor" (Editorial, "Kate Richards O'Hare," *Messenger* 2 [July 1918]: 30). Writing in 1919, Domingo noted key differences on racism between the SPA's left and right wings but considered the entire SPA benighted about the importance of winning black workers to its ranks. See the text of his critique of the SPA, reproduced in its entirety by the tireless Lusk Committee in Joint Legislative Committee Investigating Seditious Activities, *Revolutionary Radicalism,* 2:1489–1511.

15. James Oneal, *The Next Emancipation* (1922; reprint, New York: United Colored Socialists of America, 1929), 19; *Call* quoted in Foner, *American Socialism and Black Americans,* 246–47; Goldman quoted in Foner, *American Socialism and Black Americans,* 247; Domingo quoted in Joint Legislative Committee Investigating Seditious Activities, *Revolutionary Radicalism,* 2:1510, 1504. *The Next Emancipation* was reproduced in the *Messenger* in five installments between June and November 1922. Randolph and Owen considered it "a tract which every Negro and white American should read, . . . one of the most original and valuable pieces of literature on the subject" (Editorial, "James Oneal," *Messenger* 5 [October 1923]: 831). For more on the SPA's improved record on race after 1913, see Foner, *American Socialism and Black Americans,* 254–64; and Weinstein, *The Decline of Socialism in America,* 63–74.

16. John E. Glassburg, "Eugenics and the Layman," *Call,* 16 September 1923, 9; S. J. Holmes, *Studies in Evolution and Eugenics* (New York: Harcourt, Brace, 1923), 250, 248; Zelda Stewart Charters, "Is the Rapist in the Mulatto the Black Man or the White Man?" *Call,* 30 May 1920, 4; William J. Fielding, "Stoddard and His 'Under Man,'" *Call,* 28 January 1923, 10, 25 (quote on 25). For more on Stoddard, see chapter 3 herein. Foner compares the New York–based *Call* with other SPA publications (*American Socialism and Black Americans,* 261–63).

17. Floyd Dell, review of *Fifty Years and Other Poems,* by James Weldon Johnson, *Liberator* 1 (March 1918): 32–33; Amanda Hall, "Coon Town," *Liberator* 3 (May 1920): 25; Fenton Johnson, "The Sunset," *Liberator* 1 (August 1918): 25; Keene Wallis, "A Harvest Stiff Comes Back to Town," *Workers Monthly* 4 (November 1924): 17–18.

18. Herbert Seligmann, "The Negro in Industry," *Socialist Review* 8 (February 1920): 169–72 (quote on 172); Max Eastman, introduction to *Harlem Shadows,* by McKay, xiv.

19. Scott Nearing, *The Super Race: An American Problem* (New York: B. W. Huebsch, 1912), 45 ("Modern society" quote), 48–49 ("the seed has been neither" and "seed bed" quotes), 77–78 ("admirable blending" quote), 44 ("guaranteeing a good heredity" quote). For more on the appeal of eugenics to progressives and leftists before World War II, see Mark H. Haller, *Eugenics: Hereditarian Attitudes in American Thought* (New Brunswick, N.J.: Rutgers University Press, 1963).

20. Claude McKay, *The Negroes in America,* trans. Robert J. Winter, ed. Alan L. McLeod (1923; reprint, Port Washington, N.Y.: Kennikat, 1979), 10–11; Walling quoted in Pittenger, *American Socialists and Evolutionary Thought,* 179; Mary White Ovington, *Black and White Sat Down Together: The Reminiscences of an NAACP Founder* (New York: Feminist Press, 1995), 46. Seligmann had abandoned his hesitancy in proclaiming black equality by 1925, as is manifested in a sharp critique of biological racism entitled "Race Prejudice" (*Opportunity* 3 [February 1925]: 37–40). Brian Lloyd points out that Walling, who quit the SPA over its antiwar stance, moved further and further to the right and ended up an outright racist and proponent of U.S. nationalism (*Left Out,* 380–81).

21. Eugene V. Debs, "The Negro in the Class Struggle," *International Socialist Review* 4 (November 1903): 260; Eugene V. Debs, "The Negro: His Present Status and Outlook," *Intercollegiate Socialist* 6 (April–May 1918): 11–14 (quotes on 12, 13); Editorial, "The Great 'Gene," *Messenger* 2 (August 1919): 8. Randolph and Owen also praised Debs in "Gene Debs and the Negro," *Messenger* 2 (February 1920): 3; and in "The *Messenger* and Its Mission," *Messenger* 5 (May 1923): 716. Debs was featured on the cover of the *Messenger* in November 1920. For more on Debs's antiracism, see Foner, *American Socialism and Black Americans,* 258–60.

22. Foner, *American Socialism and Black Americans,* 238–64; Jack Conroy, *The Disinherited: A Novel of the 1930s* (1933; reprint, Columbia: University of Missouri Press, 1991); Ovington, *Black and White Sat Down Together,* 115.

23. A. Philip Randolph and Chandler Owen, *Terms of Peace and the Darker Races* (New York: Poole, 1917), 15. For more on the SPA's view of African Americans as a "non-historical people," see Joyce Turner, "Richard B. Moore and His Works," 41–42. Du Bois also believed there were more and less "advanced" societies (albeit unconnected to biological notions of race). As late as 1945, he said that "vast numbers of backward peoples have made notable cultural advances under the colonial regime" (quoted in A. Reed, *W. E. B. Du Bois and American Political Thought,* 78).

24. Karl Kautsky, *The Class Struggle (Erfart Program),* trans. William E. Bohn (1892; reprint, New York: W. W. Norton, 1971), 117; Laurence Gronlund, *The Cooperative Commonwealth* (1884; reprint, Belknap Press of Harvard University Press, 1965), 151; Crystal Eastman, "The Socialist Party Convention," *Liberator* 3 (July 1920): 24–29 (quote on 24).

25. John Spargo and George Louis Arner, *Elements of Socialism: A Text-Book* (1912; reprint, New York: Macmillan, 1916), 135; Foner, *American Socialism and Black Americans*, 284, 285 (*Call* quote).

26. Montgomery, *The Fall of the House of Labor*, 388–93.

27. A. Philip Randolph, "Lynching: Capitalism Its Cause, Socialism Its Cure," *Messenger* 2 (March 1919): 9–12 (quotes on 9).

28. Oneal, *The Next Emancipation*, 25–26 ("Human labor" quote), 28 ("The other way" quote), 29 ("The future" quote).

29. Karl Marx, "Critique of the Gotha Programme," in *Selected Works*, by Karl Marx and Frederick Engels, vol. 1 (New York: International, 1968), 315–35 (quotes on 319). For more on the definitions of labor and labor power, see Tom Bottomore, ed., *A Dictionary of Marxist Thought* (Cambridge, Mass.: Harvard University Press, 1983), 265–67.

30. Scott Nearing, *Labor and the League of Nations* (New York: Rand School, 1919), 13, 16; Irwin Granich, review of *Liberalism in America*, by Harold Stearns, *Liberator* 3 (April 1920): 47.

31. W. J. Ghent, *Mass and Class: A Survey of Social Divisions* (London: Macmillan, 1904), 57; M. Hill, *Prisoners of the American Dream*, 14; Thorstein Veblen, *The Instinct of Workmanship and the State of the Industrial Arts* (1914; reprint, New York: A. M. Kelley, 1964); Karl Marx, "The Communist Manifesto," in *Selected Works*, by Marx and Engels, 36. See also Veblen's many writings about production relations appearing in the *Dial* immediately after World War I.

32. Étienne Balibar, *Masses, Classes, Ideas: Studies on Politics and Philosophy before and after Marx*, trans. James Stevenson (New York: Routledge, 1994), 94, 144.

33. Spargo and Arner, *Elements of Socialism*; Oneal, *The Next Emancipation*, 11, 15, 16. For the argument that white workers are hurt by racism, see Goldfield, *The Color of Politics*; Allen, *The Invention of the White Race*; Reich, *Racial Inequality*; and Victor Perlo, *Economics of Racism II: The Roots of Inequality, USA* (New York: International, 1996).

34. Pittenger, *American Socialists and Evolutionary Thought*, 169; Randolph and Owen quoted in Foner, *American Socialism and Black Americans*, 286–87; Randolph and Owen, *Terms of Peace and the Darker Races*, 15; Du Bois, "The Problem of Problems"; Debs, "The Negro: His Present Status and Outlook"; Domingo, "Private Property as a Pillar of Race Prejudice." That the *Messenger* editors felt no embarrassment in equating class analysis with "economic determinism" is evidenced by their concluding an orthodox Socialist account of the need to build "a solid phalanx of black and white labor on the economic and political field" by George Schuyler with the comment, "Here is a basic analysis of economic determinism in the realm of politics" (George S. Schuyler, "Politics and the Negro," *Messenger* 5 [April 1923]: 658–59). Although Schuyler would soon become a virulent anticommunist, he adhered strictly to Socialist doctrine during his first years on the *Messenger*'s staff.

35. A. Philip Randolph and Chandler Owen, "Propaganda," *Messenger* 2 (February 1920): 5; Saxton, *The Rise and Fall of the White Republic*, 7–8. For the thesis that white workers benefit from split labor markets, see Edna Bonacich, "A Theory of Ethnic Antagonism: The Split Labor Market," *American Sociological Review* 37 (October 1972): 547–59. For a trenchant Marxist critique of the labor

competition hypothesis, see Gregory Meyerson, "Marxism, Psychoanalysis, and Labor Competition," *Cultural Logic* 1, no.1 (2000) <http://eserver.org/clogic/back.html>.

36. A. Philip Randolph and Chandler Owen, "Reasons Why White and Black Workers Should Combine in Labor Unions," *Messenger* 2 (July 1918): 14.

37. Randolph, "Lynching," 10, 11.

38. Randolph and Owen, "Propaganda," 5; Ghent, *Mass and Class*, 57; Thorstein Veblen, *The Instinct of Workmanship, and the State of the Industrial Arts* (New York: Macmillan, 1914); Ordway Tead, *Instincts in Industry: A Study of Working-Class Psychology* (Boston: Houghton Mifflin, 1918); B. Harrow, "Instincts versus Industry," *Liberator* 2 (June 1919): 56. For a discussion of how, in the post-war conversion of "industrial democracy" into "industrial relations," Tead's theory of "instincts" would be transmuted into the call for group therapy for insurgent forces diagnosed as "pathological," see William Graebner, *The Engineering of Consent: Democracy and Authority in Twentieth-Century America* (Madison: University of Wisconsin Press, 1987), 70–71.

39. Ordway Tead, "The New Psychology," *Dial* 70 (June 1921): 705–9 (quotes on 708); Randolph, "Lynching," 11; Barbara Fields, "Ideology and Race in American History," in *Region, Race, and Reconstruction: Essays in Honor of C. Vann Woodward*, ed. J. Morgan Kousser and James M. McPherson (New York: Oxford University Press, 1982), 78. See also Charles S. Johnson's discussion of William McDougall's racist and xenophobic *Group Mind*, in which Johnson ably targets "the immaturity of the science of collective psychology" but fails to follow through on the political implications of his closing observation: "Finally, if we are to take his word for it, collective mental life does not mean collective mental life at all, or even group life. National ideals and sentiments . . . 'are formed by the leading spirits (of the nation), the *elite*, and are perpetuated and developed by them, and by them impressed in some degree upon the mass of the people'" (review of *The Group Mind*, by William McDougall, *Messenger* 5 [May 1923]: 698 ["the immaturity" quote], 691 ["Finally, . . . mass of the people'" quote]).

40. Karl Marx, "The London Times on the Orleans Princes in America," *New York Daily Tribune*, 7 November 1861, reprinted in *The Collected Works of Marx and Engels*, trans. Richard Dixon (London: Lawrence and Wishart, 1975–83), 19:30. For an appreciation of Marx as a social constructionist, see David Harvey, *Justice, Nature, and the Geography of Difference* (Oxford: Blackwell's, 1996), 1–116.

41. "Workers of the World Unite!!" (cartoon); Pittenger, *American Socialists and Evolutionary Thought*, 183. As Mark Haller points out, the term *racism* did not even come into the language until the 1930s (*Eugenics*, 76). Randolph and Owen did not devote significant attention to racist pseudoscience in the *Messenger* until May 1923, when Miller's review of Stoddard's *Revolt against Civilization* and Locke's review of Stoddard's *New World of Islam* appeared and commentators writing in the journal's pages began to make more frequent reference to Grant, Stoddard, and their ilk. Although the *Messenger* usually responded to books and events in a timely manner, Miller's review of *The Revolt against Civilization* appeared a year after the book's publication. It was not the journals of the Left but the National Urban League's *Opportunity* that mounted by far the most consistent and thoroughgoing critique of racist pseudoscience. See, for example, Charles S. Johnson, "Mental Measurements of Negro Groups," *Opportunity* 1

(January 1923): 21–25; Howard H. Long, "Race and Mental Tests," *Opportunity* 1 (March 1923): 22–28; Herbert Adolphus Miller, "The Myth of Superiority," *Opportunity* 1 (August 1923): 228–29; Alexander A. Goldenweiser, "Racial Theory and the Negro," *Opportunity* 1 (August 1923): 229–31; Melville J. Herskovits, "The Racial Hysteria," *Opportunity* 1 (June 1924): 166–68; Horace M. Bond, "What the Army 'Intelligence' Tests Measured," *Opportunity* 2 (July 1924): 197–202; and Seligmann, "Race Prejudice."

42. Du Bois, *The Negro*, 242 ("so long as" quote); Du Bois, *Darkwater*, 29–30 ("souls of white folks" and "The discovery of personal" quotes); Hubert Harrison, *The Negro and the Nation* (New York: Cosmo-Advocate, 1917), 33, 34; Wright, "The Ethics of Living Jim Crow," *Uncle Tom's Children*, 1; McKay, *The Negroes in America*, 82, 76–77. McKay made use of Harrison's book, along with Seligmann's, when writing *The Negroes in America* in the USSR (10–11). The anthropologist Mary Kingsley defended the use of the term *fetish* to describe West African religions, maintaining that it signified far more than primitivist animism. "One of the fundamental doctrines of Fetish," she wrote, "is that the connection of a certain spirit with a certain mass of matter, a material object, is not permanent." Relevant to Toomer's romantic treatment of "joujou" in *Cane* is her preference for *fetish* over *joujou* or *juju*: "For all the fine wild sound of it, [*juju*] is only a modification of the French word for toy or doll, *joujou*" (*West African Studies* [1899; reprint, London: Cass, 1964], 96–131 [quotes on 110, 96]).

43. W. E. B. Du Bois, *Black Reconstruction in America: An Essay toward a History of the Part Which Black Folk Played in the Attempt to Reconstruct Democracy in America, 1860–1880* (Newark: Russell and Russell, 1935), 700; James, *Holding Aloft the Banner of Ethiopia*, 127–28 (Harrison quoted on 128).

44. The NAACP pointed out that only 19 percent of lynchings involved allegations of rape and that only 9.4 percent involved "other attacks on women" (*Thirty Years of Lynching in the United States*, 10). McKay did not stress such allegations as the cause of lynching in his Soviet-published set of short stories, *Trial by Lynching*, trans. from the Russian by Robert Winter (Mysore: CCLR, 1977). McKay's suggestion of the centrality of sexuality to racial violence was an early foray in the direction of supplementing Marxism—construed as economic determinism—by psychoanalysis. For further developments in this direction, see Roediger, *The Wages of Whiteness*, chapter 7; and Joel Kovel, *White Racism: A Psychohistory* (New York: Columbia University Press, 1984). For a critique of the argument that Marxism requires this supplementation, see Meyerson, "Marxism, Psychoanalysis, and Labor Competition."

45. Kautsky, *The Class Struggle*, 204; SPA's St. Louis Resolution quoted in Brasol, *Socialism versus Civilization*, 30–31; Joint Legislative Committee Investigating Seditious Activities, *Revolutionary Radicalism*, 1:510; "Workers Resolve to Uphold Rights; Soldiers Beat Boston Socialists," *Call*, 2 July 1917, 1; Eugene Debs, *Eugene V. Debs Speaks*, ed. Jean Y. Tussey (New York: Pathfinder, 1970), 251. For more on elite fears of proletarian internationalism, see Josey, *Race and National Solidarity*; William B. Pillsbury, *The Psychology of Nationalism and Internationalism* (New York: D. Appleton, 1919); and John Oakesmith, *Race and Nationality: An Inquiry into the Origin and Growth of Patriotism* (London: William Heinemann, 1919).

46. A. Philip Randolph, "Japan and the Far East," *Messenger* 2 (July 1918): 22–

23; Chandler Owen, "International Scabbing," *Messenger* 4 (December 1922): 539–40; BI agent Boulin quoted in Kornweibel, *"Seeing Red,"* 31; William Bridges, in *Challenge,* quoted in Joint Legislative Committee Investigating Seditious Activities, *Revolutionary Radicalism,* 2:1488–89; Colson, "An Analysis of Negro Patriotism," 25; cover, *Messenger* 2 (September 1920).

47. John Spargo, *Americanism and Social Democracy* (New York: Harper and Brothers, 1918), v–vi, 200–201; Foster, *The Great Steel Strike and Its Lessons,* 204; Fred Peete, "Nationalism," *Call,* 27 March 1919, 8. For more on the IWW and U.S. nationalism, see Dubofsky, *We Shall Be All,* 147–49.

48. Debs, *Eugene V. Debs Speaks,* 251 ("Wall Street Junkers" quote), 252 ("the real traitors" quote); Nearing, *Labor and the League of Nations,* 28; Bridges quoted in Joint Legislative Committee Investigating Seditious Activities, *Revolutionary Radicalism,* 2:1486. For more on Spargo's opposition to the Bolshevik Revolution, see his *Bolshevism.* Spargo's subtitle, *The Enemy of Political and Industrial Democracy,* indicates an a priori identification of "political" with "industrial" democracy.

49. Editorial, "Manifesto," *Messenger* 2 (March 1919): 26; Editorial, "We Want More Bolshevik Patriotism!" *Messenger* 2 (May–June 1919): 29; Randolph and Owen, "Marcus Garvey! The Black Imperial Wizard Becomes the Messenger Boy of the White Ku Klux Kleagle," 437; Chandler Owen, "Should Marcus Garvey Be Deported?" *Messenger* 4 (September 1922): 479–80 (quotes on 480).

50. Editorial, "The Menace of Negro Communists," *Messenger* 5 (June 1923): 784; Robert Russa Moton, "The Future of Negro Business," *Messenger* 5 (November 1923): 878. The September 1923 issue, designated the "Labor Day Issue," contained "A Message to Negro Workers from None Other Than Samuel Gompers, Head of the AFL" (*Messenger* 5 [September 1923]: 809). The depiction of women in the *Messenger* also sheds light on the magazine's changing class politics. Its first few covers featured clusters of anonymous women, often dark-skinned. During the magazine's period of maximum leftness, the covers featured prominent figures (e.g., Debs); harsh graphics, such as several portraying lynchings; or figures of women—white women—signifying Liberty. Starting in early 1924, the magazine adopted the practice of featuring portraits of individual women—usually well-dressed and light-skinned—belonging to the Negro bourgeoisie. Accompanying the new goal of "Exalting Negro Womanhood" was an announcement of the magazine's intention to showcase women who were "unique, accomplished, beautiful, intelligent, industrious, talented, successful" (Editorial, "Exalting Negro Womanhood," *Messenger* 6 [January 1924]: 7).

51. Cover, *Messenger* 5 (May 1923).

52. Editorial, *"The Survey Graphic," Messenger* 7 (April 1925): 156. The review of *The New Negro* that appeared in the *Messenger* a year later was more sharply critical and more expressly political, describing Locke as "an adherent of the philosophy of 'art for art's sake'" and adjudging the book lacking in "[t]hat virile, insurgent, revolutionary spirit peculiar to the [New] Negro." The reviewer, one U. S. Poston—possibly a pseudonym—asked, "Does not McKay's IF WE SHOULD DIE look as beautiful against an American background of oppression as does James Weldon Johnson's THE CREATOR? Is not the spirit of Garveyism, the N.A.A.C.P. and the Labor Movement agitations by A. Philip Randolph, Frank Crosswaith, and Chandler Owen, Hubert Harrison and other radicals more expressive of the spir-

it of the new Negro than the Sorrow Song and the spirit of Hampton and Tuskegee?" (review of *The New Negro*, edited by Alain Locke, *Messenger* 8 [April 1926]:
118–19 [quotes on 119]). Although this review is clearly to the left of Randolph
and Owen's commentary on the special Harlem issue the year before, its mentioning Garveyism and the NAACP as notable exclusions from the anthology,
along with not mentioning the names of any African American Communists,
indicates a political stance evidently acceptable to the *Messenger* editors in 1926.

53. Chandler Owen, "The Black and Tan Cabaret: America's Most Democratic Institution," *Messenger* 7 (February 1925): 97.

54. Lenin, "A Caricature of Marxism," quoted in Alfred A. Low, *Lenin and the
Question of Nationality* (New York: Bookman Associates, 1957), 36; Lenin quot-
ed in Walker Connor, *The National Question in Marxist-Leninist Theory and
Strategy* (Princeton, N.J.: Princeton University Press, 1984), 35.

55. Connor, *The National Question in Marxist-Leninist Theory and Strategy*,
34. Among Lenin's principal writings on the national question are "Theses on the
National Question" (1913), in *Collected Works*, ed. George Hanna, trans. Yuri
Sdobnikov, 45 vols. (Moscow: Progress, 1960–70), 19:243–51; "Critical Remarks
on the National Question" (1913), ibid., 20:17–51; "The Right of Nations to Self-
Determination" (1914), ibid., 20:393–454; "The Socialist Revolution and the Right
of Nations to Self-Determination" (1916), ibid., 22:143–56; and "The Discussion
on Self-Determination Summed Up" (1916), ibid., 22:320–60. For more on the view
of "backward" peoples as "non-historical nations," see Michael Lowy, *Fatherland
or Mother Earth? Essays on the National Question* (London: Pluto, 1998), 22–27.
For critical discussions of Lenin's approach to the national question, see Low,
Lenin and the Question of Nationality; Ronaldo Munck, *The Difficult Dialogue:
Marxism and Nationalism* (Atlantic Highlands, N.J.: Zed Books, 1986); and Lowy,
Fatherland or Mother Earth? especially 40–42. See also Horace B. Davis, *Toward
a Marxist Theory of Nationalism* (New York: Monthly Review, 1978). Lenin
specifically discussed the parallel between Russian peasants and U.S. blacks in
"Of Capitalism and Agriculture," in *Collected Works*, ed. Hanna, 22:13–102.

56. Kelley, *Race Rebels*, 107. For more on the early appearance of the theory of
African American self-determination among Harlem's radicals, see Solomon, *The
Cry Was Unity*, 3–37; and Joyce Turner, "Richard B. Moore and His Works," 45–
68. Solomon notes that as early as 1917 the soon-to-be Communist Richard B.
Moore promulgated a version of the Negro self-determination thesis in the *New
York Amsterdam News*. For the view that the early Communists were in-
sufficiently appreciative of the necessity for African American nationalism, see
E. Hutchinson, *Blacks and Reds*, 7–78; and Keith P. Griffler, *What Price Alliance?
Black Radicals Confront White Labor, 1918–1938* (New York: Garland, 1995).

57. Otto Bauer, *The Question of Nationalities and Social Democracy* (1907),
quoted in Lowy, *Fatherland or Mother Earth?* 45–50; Joseph Stalin, "Marxism and
the National Question" (1913), in *Works*, vol. 2 (Moscow: Foreign Languages
Publishing House, 1953), 300–381.

58. Rosa Luxemburg, "The National Question and Autonomy" (1908–9), in *The
National Question*, ed. Horace B. Davis (New York: Monthly Review, 1976), 110–
11, 122–23, 135, 141, 140, 290.

59. Amilcar Cabral, leader of the national liberation movement in Guinea Bis-
sau, would ask in 1960 with regard to the notion of self-determination, "Is the ju-

dicial institution which serves as a reference for the right of all peoples who are trying to liberate themselves a product of the peoples who are trying to liberate themselves? Was it created by the socialist countries who are our historical associates? It is signed by the imperialist countries, it is the imperialist countries who have recognized the right of all peoples to national independence, so I ask myself whether we may not be considering as an initiative of our people what is in fact an initiative of the enemy? . . . [T]he objective of the imperialist countries was to prevent the enlargement of the socialist camp, to liberate the reactionary forces in our countries which were being stifled by colonialism and to enable these forces to ally themselves with the international bourgeoisie. The fundamental objective was to create a bourgeoisie where one did not exist, in order specifically to strengthen the imperialist and the capitalist camp" (*Revolution in Guinea: Selected Texts*, trans. and ed. Richard Handyside [New York: Monthly Review, 1970], 58).

60. Domingo, "Socialism: The Negroes' Hope," 22; Eric Hobsbawm, *Nations and Nationalism since 1780: Programme, Myth, Reality* (Cambridge: Cambridge University Press, 1992), 131 ("what looked like" and "play[ed] the Wilsonian card" quotes), 138 ("territory-oriented" quote); Carr quoted in Connor, *The National Question in Marxist-Leninist Theory and Strategy*, 33.

61. C. Eastman, "The Socialist Party Convention," 24–29 (quotes on 25); CP versus CLP quotes in Draper, *The Roots of American Communism*, 189; Joint Legislative Committee Investigating Seditious Activities, *Revolutionary Radicalism*, 2:1378.

62. Locke, "The New Negro," 6–7. The designation of Harlem as the "Mecca" of the New Negro was only in the earlier (March 1925) version of Locke's anthology appearing in the *Survey Graphic*. See chapter 5 herein.

63. Hobsbawm, *Nations and Nationalism since 1780*, 91. See also Craig Calhoun, *Nationalism* (Minneapolis: University of Minnesota Press, 1997); and Ernest Gellner, *Nations and Nationalism* (Ithaca, N.Y.: Cornell University Press, 1983).

Chapter 3: The Rhetoric of Racist Antiradicalism

1. Arthur de Gobineau, *The Inequality of Human Races*, trans. Adrian Collins (New York: Howard Fertig, 1967), 205; Francis Galton, *Hereditary Genius: An Inquiry into Its Laws and Consequences* (New York: St. Martin's, 1978), 338 (on Negro race), 4 (on French). See also George Fredrickson, *The Black Image in the White Mind: The Debate on Afro-American Character and Destiny, 1817–1914* (1971; reprint, Middletown, Conn.: Wesleyan University Press, 1987); Stephen J. Gould, *The Mismeasure of Man* (New York: W. W. Norton, 1981); Thomas F. Gossett, *Race: The History of an Idea in America*, 2d ed. (New York: Oxford University Press, 1997); and Higham, *Strangers in the Land*.

2. Frederick L. Hoffman, *Race Traits and Tendencies of the American Negro* (Philadelphia: American Economic Association, 1896), 312, 188; William Z. Ripley, *The Races of Europe: A Sociological Study* (New York: D. Appleton, 1899), 566 ("predisposition to consumption" quote), 103 ("there was no single European" quote); Edward Alsworth Ross, *The Old World in the New: The Significance of Past and Present Immigration to the American People* (New York: Century, 1914), 285–86, 299; Aldrich quoted in Gossett, *Race*, 306. That Ross's concerns about "race suicide" were linked with concerns about class control is manifest in his

Social Control: A Survey of the Foundations of Order (1901; reprint, London: Macmillan, 1922), a primer for those who would "maintain . . . social order by sweet seduction rather than by rude force" (337).

3. Madison Grant, *The Passing of the Great Race; or, The Racial Basis of European History* (New York: Charles Scribner's Sons, 1918), 18, xx, 8; Haller, *Eugenics*, 218.

4. Stoddard, *The Rising Tide of Color against White World-Supremacy*, 235, 236.

5. Ibid., 218 ("the menace" and "a war" quotes), 219 ("Lenine" quote), 221 ("arch-enemy" and ""renegade" quotes), xxx ("phantoms" quote).

6. Lothrop Stoddard, *The Revolt against Civilization* (New York: Charles Scribner's Sons, 1922), 237, 205, 256, xxx; F. Scott Fitzgerald, *The Great Gatsby* (1925; reprint, New York: Charles Scribner's Sons, 1953), 13; Josey, *Race and National Solidarity*, xi, 51. For more on xenophobia in *The Great Gatsby*, see Walter Benn Michaels, *Our America: Nativism, Modernism, and Pluralism* (Durham, N.C.: Duke University Press), 23–28. That it was the Bolshevik Revolution that galvinized racist hysteria is indicated by the dramatically contrasting measured tone of Stoddard's compendious 1918 *Stakes of the War*, which he described as "an attempt to chart the facts involved in those problems of race and territory which the war has shoved into the foreground of our political and business thinking, which will demand solution at the peace-table." He and his coauthor Glenn Frank had, he assured the reader, "studiously avoided the expression of personal opinions" (*Stakes of the War: Summary of the Various Problems, Claims, and Interests of the Nations at the Peace Table* [New York: Century, 1918], vii–viii).

7. Davenport quoted in Pat Shipman, *The Evolution of Racism: Human Differences and the Abuse of Science* (New York: Simon and Schuster, 1994), 125 ("People" and "[t]he idea" quotes); Charles Davenport, *The Feebly Inhibited: Nomadism, or the Wandering Impulse, with Special Reference to Heredity* (1915; reprint, New York: Garland, 1984), 23 ("simple sex-linked gene" quote), 24 ("tastes and impulses" quote), 10 ("Bushmen . . . livelihood" quotes), 25 ("members of the *nomadic race*" quote).

8. Paul Popenoe and Roswell Hill Johnson, *Applied Eugenics* (New York: Macmillan, 1918), 363; Stoddard, *The Revolt against Civilization*, 30, 56–58, 24; Degler, *In Search of Human Nature*, 44; William McDougall, *Is America Safe for Democracy?* (New York: Charles Scribner's Sons, 1921), 31 ("race-slumpers" quote), 12 ("*[T]he great condition*" quote); Carl C. Brigham, *A Study of American Intelligence* (Princeton, N.J.: Princeton University Press, 1923), 190.

9. Alleyne Ireland, *Democracy and the Human Equation* (New York: E. P. Dutton, 1921), 135; Davenport quoted in Gossett, *Race*, 253; The *Modernist* cited in Joint Legislative Committee Investigating Seditious Activities, *Revolutionary Radicalism*, 2:1303–4.

10. Peter Roberts, *The Problem of Americanization* (New York: Macmillan, 1920), v; Palmer quoted in Kornweibel, *"Seeing Red,"* 119.

11. Anonymous, *The Jewish Peril: Protocols of the Learned Elders of Zion* (London: Eyre and Spottiswoode, 1920); Anonymous, *The Cause of World Unrest* (New York: G. P. Putnam's Sons, 1920), viii–ix; Editorial, "Reaction and the New," *Nation* 111 (3 November 1920): 493; Raker quoted in Gerstle, *American Crucible*, 390; the Grand Dragon quoted in Nancy Maclean, *Behind the Mask of Chivalry: The Making of the Second Ku Klux Klan* (New York: Oxford University Press,

1994), 138; Stoddard, *The Revolt against Civilization*, 151; John R. Commons, *Races and Immigrants in America*, 2d ed. (New York: Macmillan, 1920), xvi, xxii; Palmer quoted in Foglesong, *America's Secret War against Bolshevism*, 41. See also Robert Singerman, "The American Career of the *Protocols*," *American Jewish History* 81 (September 1981): 48–78; and Zosa Szajkowski, *The Impact of the 1919–20 Red Scare on American Jewish Life* (New York: Ktav, 1974), especially 148–65.

12. Kenneth Roberts's *Saturday Evening Post* series was reprinted as *Why Europe Leaves Home* (New York: Bobbs-Merrill, 1922), 15 ("the Jews of Poland" quote), 121 ("continue to exist" and "waifs" quotes). Alain Locke, expressing to Paul Kellogg his astonishment that *The New Negro* had received a somewhat favorable notice in the *Saturday Evening Post*, referred to the magazine as "the American Walhalla," guided by an "almost Ku Klux mindedness" on the part of its editors (Locke to Paul Kellogg, n.d., reel 39, part 1, Survey Associates [microfilm], University of Florida Library [hereafter cited as Survey Associates]).

13. Emery S. Bogardus, *Essentials of Americanization* (1919; 3d rev. ed., Los Angeles: Jesse Ray Miller, 1923), 145; Samuel J. Holmes, *The Trend of the Race: A Study of Present Tendencies in the Biological Development of Civilized Mankind* (New York: Harcourt, Brace, 1921), 263.

14. President Woodrow Wilson quoted in Foglesong, *America's Secret War against Bolshevism*, 42; Seth K. Humphrey, *Mankind: Racial Values and the Racial Prospect* (New York: Charles Scribner's Sons, 1917), 163, 155; Joel Williamson, *New People: Miscegenation and Mulattoes in the United States* (New York: Free Press, 1980), 114.

15. Robert Park, "Education in Its Relation to the Conflict and Fusion of Culture: With Special Reference to the Problems of the Immigrant, the Negro, and Missions" (1918), reprinted in Robert Park, *Race and Culture* (Glencoe, Ill.: Free Press, 1950), 261–83 (quote on 280); Edward Byron Reuter, *The Mulatto in the United States: Including a Study of the Role of Mixed-Blood Races throughout the World* (Boston: Richard G. Badger, 1918), 18 ("backward" quote), 14 ("[f]or the purpose" quote), 102–3 ("unstable" quote), 19 ("the stigma" quote), 394 ("disgruntled agitators" quote), 386 ("[t]he exclusion policy" quote), 385 ("an overwhelming majority" quote), 371 ("plea" quote), 372 ("defeat[ing]," "the effect," and "solidify" quotes).

16. Reuter, *The Mulatto in the United States*, 373 ("stricter," "an advantage," and "[T]he black Negroes . . . leadership" quotes), 384 ("present tendency" quote), 388 ("Agitation gives" and "no longer lives" quotes). Moton stated in 1915 that the Wilsonian segregation of federal office buildings was "bringing Negoes together in a way nothing else could have done and we ought to make the most in some way of any strong sentiment for cooperation among colored people" (quoted in Williamson, *The Crucible of Race*, 377).

17. Reuter, *The Mulatto in the United States*, 389–90. See also F. James Davis, *Who Is Black? One Nation's Definition* (University Park: Pennsylvania State University Press, 1991). It bears noting that the view that mulattoes were an inferior breed could be embraced by Negroes as well; the African American historian Carter G. Woodson held that mulattoes were the offspring of "the weaker types of both races" (quoted in Williamson, *New People*, 117). Reuter apparently reversed his positions about Negro and mulatto inferiority in the years to come,

ending his career at Fisk University. See Stow Persons, *Ethnic Studies at Chicago, 1905–45* (Urbana: University of Illinois Press, 1987), 111–30.

18. Stoddard, *The Revolt against Civilization,* 137–38; Stuart Sherman, *Americans* (New York: Charles Scribner's Sons, 1923), 25, 160; Gertrude Atherton, "The Alpine School of Fiction," *Bookman* 55 (March 1922): 26–33 (quotes on 28, 30, 33).

19. John Erskine, *Democracy and Ideals: A Definition* (New York: G. H. Doran, 1920), 55, 112; Carl Van Doren, "Tap-Root or Melting-Pot?" in *Anthology of Magazine Verse for 1920,* ed. William Stanley Braithwaite (Boston: Small, Maynard, 1920), ix–xii (quote on xi); Eric Walrond, "Junk," in *African Fundamentalism,* ed. Martin, 312–14.

20. Mary Austin, "Up Stream," review of *Up Stream,* by Ludwig Lewisohn, *Dial* 72 (June 1922): 634–39 (quotes on 636). See also Mary Austin, "New York: Dictator of American Criticism," *Nation* 111 (31 July 1920): 129–30; and Jean Toomer, "Americans and Mary Austin," *Call,* 10 October 1920, 2.

21. Roosevelt quoted in Gerstle, *American Crucible,* 53; Wilson quoted in Foglesong, *America's Secret War against Bolshevism,* 41–42, 45; Calvin Coolidge, "Whose Country Is This?" *Good Housekeeping* 72 (February 1921): 13–14, 108–9 (quotes on 14, 109); Coolidge quoted in Laura Doyle, *Bordering the Body: The Racial Matrix of Modern Fiction and Culture* (New York: Oxford University Press, 1994), 15; Coolidge quoted in Gossett, *Race,* 407.

22. Wyn Craig Wade, *The Fiery Cross: The Ku Klux Klan in America* (New York: Simon and Schuster, 1987), 165; Warren G. Harding quoted in *New York Times,* 27 October 1921, 1, 11; John Bodnar, *Remaking America: Public Memory, Commemoration, and Patriotism in the Twentieth Century* (Princeton, N.J.: Princeton University Press, 1992), 71–72. For a discussion of the KKK's deployment of the discourse of diversity by decade's end, see Michaels, *Our America,* 19–23. For more on the creation of a "white" working class, see Allen, *The Invention of the White Race;* Roediger, *The Wages of Whiteness;* and Matthew Frye Jacobson, *Whiteness of a Different Color: European Immigrants and the Alchemy of Race* (Cambridge, Mass.: Harvard University Press, 1998).

23. Davenport to Gould quoted in Elazar Barkan, *The Retreat of Scientific Racism: Changing Concepts of Race in Britain and the United States between the World Wars* (Cambridge: Cambridge University Press, 1992), 71. Gary Gerstle argues that, during the war, U.S. corporations had "used a portion of their wartime government subsidies and profits for capital improvements that yielded advances in mechanization and production efficiency." Their increased productive capacity, coupled with their use of newly migrated black labor and their continued use of Mexican peasant labor (which remained unrestricted), meant that these businesses "no longer required eastern and southern European immigrant labor, and . . . ceased to voice objections to those intent on restricting immigration" (*American Crucible,* 113).

24. Crèvecoeur, Turner, and Zangwill quoted in Philip Gleason, *Speaking of Diversity: Language and Ethnicity in Twentieth-Century America* (Baltimore: Johns Hopkins University Press, 1992), 5, 6, 9; George Creel, "Close the Gates!" *Collier's* 59 (6 May 1920): 9–10 (quote on 9); Clinton Stoddard Burr, *America's Race Heritage* (New York: National Heritage Society, 1922), 3, 6. See also Lawrence Levine, *The Opening of the American Mind: Canons, Culture, and History* (Boston: Beacon, 1996), especially "From the Melting-Pot to the Pluralist Vision."

During the war, Creel—always the pragmatist—defended the foreign-born against the attacks of superpatriots. See George Creel, *How We Advertised America* (1920; reprint, New York: Arno, 1972), 184–99.

25. Tzvetan Todorov, *On Human Diversity: Nationalism, Racism, and Exoticism in French Thought*, trans. Catherine Porter (Cambridge, Mass.: Harvard University Press, 1993), 129–40 (Gobineau quotes on 124). Herder's extensive use of the organic trope to describe the folk's relation to the land was not entirely metaphorical, insofar as he, like many Enlightenment figures, considered "climate"—physical environment—a crucial determinant of a people's intrinsic qualities (see *Reflections on the Philosophy of the History of Mankind*, trans. Frank E. Manuel [Chicago: University of Chicago Press, 1968], 3–78).

26. Haeckel quoted in Shipman, *The Evolution of Racism*, 83. For more on Haeckel's racism, see Pittenger, *American Socialists and Evolutionary Thought*, 258.

27. "Bolsheviki in the United States," 13; Anonymous, "Dealing with 'Red' Agitators: Why the Deportation of Alien Revolutionists Ceased for a Time—A More Stringent Law Enacted," *Current History* 12 (July 1920): 698; Joint Legislative Committee Investigating Seditious Activities, *Revolutionary Radicalism*, 2:1283–84; P. Roberts, *The Problem of Americanization*, 226.

28. R. M. Whitney, *Reds in America* (New York: Beckwith, 1924), 212; Evans quoted in Bennett, *The Party of Fear*, 216 ("[t]he Jew . . . soil" quote), 217 ("ninety-five per cent" quote); Austin, "Up Stream," 636–37.

29. Albert Edward Wiggam, *The Fruit of the Family Tree* (Garden City, N.Y.: Garden City Publishing, 1924), 310, 351; Charles W. Gould, *America: A Family Matter* (New York: Charles Scribner's Sons, 1922), 1, 165; André Siegfried, *America Comes of Age: A French Analysis*, trans. H. H. Hemming and Doris Hemming (New York: Harcourt, Brace, 1927), 129.

30. Doyle, *Bordering the Body*, 43, 6; Annette Kolodny, *The Lay of the Land: Metaphor as Experience and History in American Life and Letters* (Chapel Hill: University of North Carolina Press, 1975), 4.

31. Frederic C. Howe, "The Alien," in *Civilization in the United States: An Inquiry by Thirty Americans*, ed. Harold Stearns (New York: Harcourt, Brace, 1922), 347; Feri Felix Weiss, *The Sieve; or, Revelations of the Man Mill, Being the Truth about Immigration* (Boston: Page, 1921), 191, 209, 302.

32. Peter A. Speek, *A Stake in the Land* (1921; reprint, Montclair, N.J.: Paterson Smith, 1971), 4.

33. Franz Boas, *The Mind of Primitive Man* (1911; reprint, New York: Macmillan, 1920), 29 ("Variations in cultural development" quote); Franz Boas, "Race Problems in America," *Science* 29 (28 May 1909): 848 ("the remarkable development" and "the frequent occurrence" quotes); Franz Boas, "This Nordic Nonsense," *Forum* 74 (October 1925): 507 ("mongrelism" discussion); Du Bois, *The Negro*, 114–15; Franz Boas, "Inventing a Great Race," review of *Passing of the Great Race*, by Madison Grant, *New Republic* 13 (13 January 1917): 305–7; Franz Boas, "The Rising Tide of Color," review of *The Rising Tide of Color*, by Lothrop Stoddard, *Nation* 111 (8 December 1920): 656; Gossett, *Race*, 418.

34. Edward Sapir, "The Mythology of All Races," *Dial* 71 (July 1921): 109; Alexander Goldenweiser, *Early Civilization: An Introduction to Anthropology* (1922; reprint, New York: F. S. Crofts, 1935), 6 ("[n]o proof" quote), 14 ("man is many"

and *"Man is one"* quotes); Robert M. Lowie, "Anthropology Put to Work," *Dial* 65 (15 August 1918): 99.

35. Marshall Hyatt, *Franz Boas, Social Activist: The Dynamics of Ethnicity* (New York: Greenwood, 1990), 3–16; Franz Boas, "The Mental Attitudes of the Educated Classes," *Dial* 65 (2 September 1918): 147; Franz Boas, Editorial, "A Sturdy Protest," *Nation* 107 (19 October 1918): 487; Lowie, "Anthropology Put to Work," 99; Edward Sapir, "Civilization and Culture," *Dial* 67 (30 September 1919): 233–36 (quotes on 234–35). We must remember that Marx's *Economic and Philosophic Manuscripts of 1844*—in which a historical materialist approach to the concept of alienation is first developed—would not be translated into English for many years.

36. Lowie, "Anthropology Put to Work," 99; Melville Herskovits, "Anthropology since Morgan," *Liberator* 5 (February 1923): 28, 30 (quotes on 28).

37. Boas, "Race Problems in America," 848 ("slightly inferior" quote); Boas, *The Mind of Primitive Man*, 51, excerpted in Franz Boas, *A Franz Boas Reader*, ed. George W. Stocking (Chicago: University of Chicago Press, 1976), 316 ("men of high genius" quote); Boas, foreword to *Half a Man*, by Ovington, vii–viii; Robert Lowie, *Culture and Ethnology* (New York: Peter Smith, 1929), 44 (this statement appeared in a lecture from 1917 entitled "Culture and Race"). For a critique of Boas's residual racism, see Gossett, *Race*, xiv–xv; and Vernon J. Williams Jr., "Franz Boas's Paradox and the African American Intelligentsia," in *African Americans and Jews in the Twentieth Century: Studies in Convergence and Conflict*, ed. V. P. Franklin, Nancy L. Grant, Harold M. Kletnick, and Genna Rae McNeil (Columbia: University of Missouri Press, 1998), 54–86. Williams points out, however, that even Du Bois and the prominent African American sociologist Monroe C. Work were proponents of physical anthropology in the early twentieth century. For more on the waning credibility of biological approaches to race in the late 1920s, see Gossett, *Race*, 409–30.

38. Sapir, "The Mythology of All Races," 109; Franz Boas, "The Problem of the American Negro," *Yale Review* 10 (January 1921): 384–95 (quotes on 392–93).

39. Boas, "Nordic Nonsense," 502–11; Boas, "The Rising Tide of Color," 656.

40. Franz Boas, "Nationalism," *Dial* 65 (March 1919): 232 ("[u]nity of national descent" and "[D]istinct racial elements" quotes), 236 ("imperialistic nationalism," "general human interests," "the mass," "national feeling finds," and "is one of the most fruitful" quotes), 235 ("Nationalism in large states" and "[F]or these reasons" quotes), 237 ("the common interest" quote); Franz Boas, "Patriotism" (1917), reprinted in Franz Boas, *Race and Democratic Society* (New York: Biblo and Tannen, 1969), 156 ("patriotism must be subordinated" quote), 157 ("the equal rights" quote), 159 ("consider absolutely" quote); Franz Boas, "Social Justice: Nations" (1916), reprinted in *Race and Democratic Society*, 165 ("the idea of social justice" quote). Boas was also equivocal about the colonial question. He remarked that "[m]andatories have an ugly habit of forgetting their mandate and of considering their temporary charges as permanent property," noted that "[t]he essential motive for interference in foreign countries is the need in our life for the products of these countries," and repudiated the notion that the producers of these products were members of "backward races." Nonetheless, Boas favored a policy of "international protection of the colonies of all countries against exploitation, and their government in the interest of the natives and of humanity."

Clearly Boas was not won to the Bolshevik position of immediate colonial self-determination. Franz Boas, "Colonies and the Peace Conference," *Nation* 108 (15 February 1919): 247 ("[m]andatories"), 248 ("[t]he essential" and "backward races" quotes), 249 ("international protection" quote).

41. Edward Sapir, "Culture, Genuine and Spurious," *American Journal of Sociology* (1924), reprinted in *Selected Writings on Language, Culture, and Personality*, ed. David G. Mandelbaum (Berkeley: University of California Press, 1985), 309–19 (quotes on 310, 318). For a critique of the ways in which Sapir's argument reforges the connection between culture and biology that it aspires to sunder, see Michaels, *Our America*, 35–36, 119–22. Micaela di Leonardo has recently offered a critique of the ways in which American anthropology has "gone wrong" since the 1960s by increasingly acceding to the conflation of race and culture, thereby producing "distorting, victim-blaming visions of class, mobility, power and poverty in America and elsewhere" (*Exotics at Home: Anthropologies, Others, American Modernity* [Chicago: University of Chicago Press, 1998], 9). Even after the victory of the Boasians, the struggle against racist ideology continues, albeit in an altered form that bears, ironically, the legacy of the Boasians themselves.

Chapter 4: Metonymic Nationalism, Culture Wars, and the Politics of Counterdiscourse

1. Homi K. Bhabha, "Dissemination: Time, Narrative, and the Margins of the Modern Nation," in *Nation and Narration*, ed. Homi K. Bhabha (London: Routledge, 1990), 292, 300.

2. Hollis quoted in David Simpson, "Destiny Made Manifest: The Styles of Whitman's Poetry," in *Nation and Narration*, ed. Bhabha, 191; Wai-chee Dimock, "Class, Gender and a History of Metonymy," in *Rethinking Class: Literary Studies and Social Formations*, ed. Wai-chee Dimock and Michael T. Gilmore (New York: Columbia University Press, 1994), 59; Simpson, "Destiny Made Manifest," 191; Charles Taylor, "The Politics of Recognition," in *Multiculturalism: A Critical Reader*, ed. David Theo Goldberg (Oxford: Blackwell, 1994), 75–106 (quote on 75). See also Kenneth Burke's discussion of metonymy in *A Grammar of Motives* (New York: Prentice-Hall, 1945), 503–17. Burke argues that metonymy, as opposed to synecdoche, is reductive, substituting quantity for quality and allowing signification to go in only one direction. I argue that the ideological power of the metonymic chain is that it goes both ways, from nation to folk and from folk to nation.

3. T. S. Eliot, "The Waste Land," in *The Complete Poems and Plays, 1909–1950* (New York: Harcourt, Brace and World, 1962), 38; William Carlos Williams, "Spring and All," in *Selected Poems* (New York: New Directions, 1969), 25; Arna Bontemps, "A Black Man Talks of Reaping," in *The Norton Anthology of African American Literature*, ed. Henry Louis Gates and Nellie McKay (New York: W. W. Norton), 1242. For more on the variety of meanings attached to the motif of roots, especially in early-twentieth-century African American literature, see David Nicholls, *Conjuring the Folk: Forms of Modernity in African America* (Ann Arbor: University of Michigan Press, 2000), 11–17.

4. Aloysius Col, "Washington," in *Anthology of Magazine Verse for 1920*, ed. Braithwaite, 61–62.

5. Van Doren, "Tap-Root or Melting-Pot?" ix–xii; Carl Sandburg, "Tangibles," in *Anthology of Magazine Verse for 1920*, ed. Braithwaite, 62. Containing poems sharply criticizing government repression in 1919—as well as some as patriotic as Col's—the anthology provides a fascinating cross section of contemporaneous political debates. Sandburg considered Braithwaite a "literary log-roller," however, and spoke of the "popery and Kaiserism of [the anthology], the snobbery, flunkey-ism and intrigue"; Claude McKay referred to Braithwaite as the "Booker T. Washington of American literature" (quoted in G. Hutchinson, *The Harlem Renaissance in Black and White*, 352–53). My term *hyper-materiality of the signifier* draws on Walter Benn Michaels's characterization of the modernist concern with the "materiality of the signifier" as "a certain fantasy about the sign—that it might function . . . onomatopoetically, without reliance upon a system of syntactic and semantic conventions" (*Our America*, 2). Whereas Michaels relates this "fantasy about the sign" primarily to the theme of incest that he see as central to what he calls "nativist modernism," I view the notion of materiality to consist more in ideas about the land and the nation. For more on Carl Sandburg's political radicalism in the era of 1919, see Philip R. Yannella, *The Other Carl Sandburg* (Jackson: University Press of Mississippi, 1996).

6. Paul Gilroy, *The Black Atlantic: Modernity and Double Consciousness* (Cambridge, Mass.: Harvard University Press, 1993), 19; Paul Gilroy, *Against Race: Imagining Political Culture beyond the Color Line* (Cambridge, Mass.: Belknap Press of Harvard University Press, 2000), 125.

7. For the critique of hybridity as reessentializing the categories it would deconstruct, see, for example, Samira Kawash, *Dislocating the Color Line: Identity, Hybridity, and Singularity in African-American Narrative* (Stanford, Calif.: Stanford University Press, 1997).

8. Bing, *War-Time Strikes and Their Adjustment*, 281; Tannenbaum, *The Labor Movement*, 175; Commons, *Races and Immigrants in America*, xxviii; Ray Stannard Baker, *The New Industrial Unrest: Reasons and Remedies* (Garden City, N.Y.: Doubleday, Page, 1920), 6, 72.

9. Isaac B. Berkson, *Theories of Americanization: A Critical Study* (1920; reprint, New York: Arno, 1969), 73, 67, 62, 27.

10. William H. Thomas, Robert E. Park, and Herbert A. Miller, *Old World Traits Transplanted* (1921; reprint, Montclair, N.J.: Patterson Smith, 1971), v ("Americanization should perpetuate" quote), 280 ("a wise policy" and "quick and complete" quotes); Kate Holladay Claghorn, *The Immigrant's Day in Court* (New York: Harper and Brothers, 1923); George Cohen, *The Jews in the Making of America* (Boston: Stratford, 1924); Du Bois, *The Gift of Black Folk*. Benjamin Brawley, however, considered *The Gift of Black Folk* one of Du Bois's finest works to date (review of *The Gift of Black Folk*, by W. E. B. Du Bois, *Opportunity* 2 [December 1924]: 377–78), and an editorial in the *Messenger* called the book's display of black cultural achievement "a mortal blow to the Nordic myth of race superiority" ("The Ku Klux Klan Wants Negroes to Join," *Messenger* 7 [May 1925]: 157). Du Bois used the term *gift* as early as 1903 in *The Souls of Black Folk*; it is central to his formulation of the multiple contributions of African Americans featured in his 1913 "Star of Ethiopia" pageant (*The Oxford W. E. B. Du Bois Reader*, ed. Sundquist, 305–10).

11. Horace Kallen, "Democracy versus the Melting-Pot?" (1915), reprinted in

Horace Kallen, *Culture and Democracy in the United States* (1924; reprint, New York: Arno, 1970), 67–125 (quotes on 124–25).

12. Kallen, *Culture and Democracy*, 125 ("[D]o the dominant classes" quote), 28 ("capitalist apologetics" quote), 179 ("Speculation has it" quote), 132 ("connects instead of separates" quote); Horace Kallen, *The Structure of Lasting Peace: An Inquiry into the Motives of War and Peace* (Boston: Marshall Jones, 1918), 183 ("the society we live in" quote); Horace Kallen, "Eugenics—Made in Germany," *Dial* 65 (11 January 1919): 29 ("Pan Germanist priesthood" and "total absence" quotes). Although Kallen has been given credit for having stood by Locke when Locke was excluded by racist southerners from a Thanksgiving celebration while Kallen and Locke were both at Oxford in 1907–8, it bears noting that Kallen did not relinquish his own personal racism. In the aftermath of the incident, he wrote to his Harvard friend Barrett Wendell, "I have neither respect nor liking for [Locke's] race—but individually they have to be taken, each on his own merits and value, and if ever a negro was worthy, this boy is" (quoted in Carrie Bramen, *The Uses of Variety: Modern Americanism and the Quest for National Distinctiveness* [Cambridge, Mass.: Harvard University Press, 2000], 98). Bramen insists that Kallen did not merely "overlook" the exclusion of African Americans from U.S. culture but "used it as the starting point from which to theorize pluralism," which in his discussion consisted entirely of the contributions by different European ethnic groups (314).

13. Werner Sollors, *Beyond Ethnicity: Consent and Descent in American Culture* (New York: Oxford University Press, 1986), 183–86; Michaels, *Our America*, 137–38, 64–65; Kallen, "Eugenics—Made in Germany," 28.

14. Kallen, *Culture and Democracy*, 93–94; T. J. O'Flaherty, "Putting the Hood on the Class War," *Liberator* 7 (September 1924): 31; Bramen, *The Uses of Variety*, 71. Because Kallen is routinely viewed as an important precursor to multiculturalism and identity politics, the pros and cons of his program have been vigorously debated in recent years. See, for example, David A. Hollinger, *Postethnic America: Beyond Multiculturalism* (New York: Basic Books, 1995), 92–99; Michael Lind, *The Next American Nation: The New Nationalism and the Fourth American Revolution* (New York: Free Press, 1995), 237–40; Ross Posnock, *Color and Culture: Black Writers and the Making of the Modern Intellectual* (Cambridge, Mass.: Harvard University Press, 1998), 23–24, 191–97.

15. Cartoon from *American Hebrew*, reprinted in Szajkowski, *The Impact of the 1919–1920 Red Scare on American Jewish Life*, 166.

16. Kallen, *Culture and Democracy*, 43.

17. Van Wyck Brooks, *America's Coming-of-Age* (New York: B. W. Huebsch, 1915); *Seven Arts* manifesto quoted in Arthur Frank Wertheim, *The New York Little Renaissance: Iconoclasm, Modernism, and Nationalism in American Culture, 1908–1917* (New York: New York University Press, 1976), 178; Waldo Frank, *Our America* (New York: Boni and Liveright, 1919), 9. For more on the Young Americans, see Edward Abrahams, *The Lyrical Left: Randolph Bourne, Alfred Stieglitz, and the Origins of Cultural Radicalism in America* (Charlottesville: University of Virginia Press, 1986); and Cary Nelson Blake, *Beloved Community: The Cultural Criticism of Randolph Bourne, Van Wyck Brooks, Waldo Frank, and Lewis Mumford* (Chapel Hill: University of North Carolina Press, 1990). For a discussion of the relationship between Locke and Brooks, see G.

Hutchinson, *The Harlem Renaissance in Black and White*, 94–124; C. Barry Chabot, *Writers for the Nation: American Literary Modernism* (Tuscaloosa: University of Alabama Press, 1997), 139–41; Posnock, *Color and Culture*, 191–92, 197; and Bramen, *The Uses of Variety*, 97–99.

18. Lewis Mumford, "The City," in *Civilization in the United States*, ed. Stearns, 3–20 (quotes on 10–11); V. Brooks, *America's Coming-of-Age*, 121, 34, 180–81; Van Wyck Brooks, "A Reviewer's Notebook," *Freeman* 2 (29 June 1921): 383; Van Wyck Brooks, *An Autobiography* (New York: E. P. Dutton, 1965), 101. Brooks's *Freeman* article prompted a debate with Max Eastman, who argued against overestimating the role artists and writers could play in bringing about revolution. For more on Munson's theory of the Machine, see Gorham Munson, *The Awakening Twenties: A Memoir-History of a Period* (Baton Rouge: Louisiana State University Press, 1985), 201–2. Munson was listed as a contributor to the *Socialist Review* in November 1920.

19. Randolph Bourne, *Youth and Life* (1913; reprint, Freeport, N.Y.: Books for Libraries, 1967), 303 ("[T]he very food" quote); Randolph Bourne, "The State," in *War and the Intellectuals: Essays by Randolph Bourne, 1915–1919*, ed. Carl Resek (New York: Harper and Row, 1964), 71 ("War is" quote), 77 ("revolutionary proletariat" and "heretics" quotes), 91 ("sanctity" quote), 87 ("not a symbol" quote); Randolph Bourne, "Trans-National America," in *War and the Intellectuals*, ed. Resek, 112 ("democratic cooperation" quote). Bourne's biographer Bruce Clayton argues that he became increasingly radical, citing Bourne's words to his friend Esther Cornell toward the end of his short life: "I feel very much secluded from the world, very much out of touch with my time, except perhaps with the Bolsheviki" (quoted in Bruce Clayton, *Forgotten Prophet: The Life of Randolph Bourne* [Baton Rouge: Louisiana State University Press, 1984], 230). Brian Lloyd, by contrast, treats Bourne as, to the end, a "petty-bourgeois idealist" (*Left Out*, 262–76 [quote on 263]).

20. Frank, *Our America*, 114, 125, 179, 232; Munson, *The Awakening Twenties*, 67. "Chicago" appeared in the *Call*, 7 March 1920, 6–8.

21. V. Brooks, *America's Coming-of-Age*, 164; Frank, *Our America*, 93–116; Randolph Bourne, "The Jew and Trans-National America," in *War and the Intellectuals*, ed. Resek, 128 (Zionism quote); Bourne, "Trans-National America," 117 ("the first international" quote), 112 ("democratic cooperation" quote); Harold Stearns, preface to *Civilization in the United States*, ed. Stearns, vii.

22. V. Brooks, *Autobiography*, 57. For more on the Young Americans' favored tropes, see Charles Scruggs and Lee VanDemarr, *Jean Toomer and the Terrors of American History* (Philadelphia: University of Pennsylvania Press, 1998), 73.

23. Van Wyck Brooks, *The Wine of the Puritans: A Study of Present-Day America* (London: Sisley's, 1908), 31; V. Brooks, "The Literary Life," in *Civilization in the United States*, ed. Stearns, 181; Harold Stearns, "The Intellectual Life," in *Civilization in the United States*, ed. Stearns, 148.

24. Paul Rosenfeld, *Port of New York* (1924; reprint, Urbana: University of Illinois Press, 1961), 285 ("seed did not take root" quote), 288 ("had its roots" quote), 294 ("a dozen" quote), 292 ("have taken root" quote); Alfred Kreymborg, *Troubadour: An Autobiography* (New York: Liveright, 1925), 406, 412.

25. Frank, *Our America*, 137, 177, 229.

26. Ibid., 232, 96.

27. Ibid., 4; Upton Sinclair, *The Jungle* (1906; reprint, New York: Signet Classics, 1990), 302–3.

28. Frank, *Our America*, 227, 231. Chabot argues that much of the "soilness" of the Young Americans' project in the 1920s can be traced to the regionalism that increasingly replaced the more optimistic nationalism of the previous decade. This regionalism, he argues, is "either a diminished form of cultural nationalism or an alternative to it" and is "typically shadowed by the memory of some defeat experienced on the larger stage and by worry that a comparable fate is awaiting the little society in which one has temporarily found refuge" (*Writers for the Nation*, 39).

29. Art Young, "Lessons in Americanism," *Liberator* 3 (May 1920): 8–9; Robert Minor, "America Today," *Liberator* 4 (July 1921): 3; Fred Ellis, "Selective Immigration," *Liberator* 6 (February 1924): 18–19; Art Young and John Reed, "The Social Revolution in Court," *Liberator* 1 (September 1918): 20–28 (IWW preamble quoted on 21); Max Eastman, "Examples of Americanism," *Liberator* 2 (February 1920): 13–14; Martha Foley, "Americanizing Haiti," *Liberator* 5 (March 1922): 11–12; Hazel Poole, "The Alien," *Liberator* 2 (January 1920): 36.

30. Floyd Dell, review of *Our America*, by Waldo Frank, *Liberator* 2 (January 1920): 44; Granich [Mike Gold], review of *Liberalism in America*, by Harold Stearns, 47; Max Eastman, "Inspiration or Leadership?" *Liberator* 4 (August 1921): 7–9 (Eastman's polemic responds to the Brooks *Freeman* article mentioned in note 18); O'Flaherty, "Putting the Hood on the Class War."

31. Maurice Stern, "100% American," 3 *Liberator* (March 1920): 4; cover portrait of Lenin, *Liberator* 1 (January 1918); cover portrait of Lincoln, *Liberator* 1 (February 1918); Dell, review of *Our America*, by Waldo Frank, 44.

32. "Will Raymond Robins Please Come Out?" *Liberator* 1 (December 1918): 17; Pearl, "Negro Bodies," 28.

33. Harry Kemp, "The Rune of the Sower," *Liberator* 2 (February 1920): 50.

34. Elsa Gidlow, "Declaration," *Liberator* 4 (July 1921): 27. Other poems by Gidlow use the organic trope to suggest the "natural" growth of lesbian sexuality in an unnatural world. See her *On a Grey Thread* (Chicago: Will Ransom, 1923).

35. James Weldon Johnson, "Negro Poetry—A Reply," *Liberator* 1 (April 1918): 41. These same four lines of poetry were also reproduced in J. Johnson, "This Land Is Ours by Right of Birth," *Messenger* 5 (March 1923): 637.

36. Clement Wood, "Alien," *Liberator* 1 (November 1918): 31. Writing to the *Survey Graphic* editor Paul Kellogg in 1926, Locke referred to Wood's "well-intentioned but blundering atavisms" and noted, "He thinks he has to be primitive out of courtesy to us, I daresay" (Locke to Kellogg, 19 May 1926, reel 39, part 1, Survey Associates).

37. Irwin Granich [Mike Gold], "Towards Proletarian Art," *Liberator* 3 (February 1921): 20 ("[w]e are prepared" quote), 21 ("Art is the tenement" and "intellectuals" quotes), 22 ("[t]he masses" quote), 23 (Prolet-Kult quote).

38. Ibid., 24 ("A mighty . . . American life" quote). The most recent argument for this notion of the Popular Front is Denning, *The Cultural Front*.

39. Burr, *America's Race Heritage*, vi; Sherman, *Americans*, 158.

40. Clement Wood, "Walt Whitman, the Good Red Poet," *Call*, 30 May 1920, 3; Ridge quoted in Alan Golding, *From Outlaw to Classic: Canons in American Poetry* (Madison: University of Wisconsin Press, 1995), 96; Max Eastman, *Colors*

of Life: Poems and Songs and Sonnets (New York: Alfred A. Knopf, 1918), 13; Granich, "Towards Proletarian Art," 23; William English Walling, *Whitman and Traubel* (New York: Albert and Charles Boni, 1916), 36; Floyd Dell, "The Road to Freedom," *Liberator* 2 (May 1912): 42. For more on Whitman's popularity with the interwar Left, see Daniel Aaron, *Writers on the Left: Episodes in American Literary Communism* (1964; reprint, New York: Columbia University Press, 1992); Golding, *From Outlaw to Classic*, 86–102; and Bryan K. Garman, *A Race of Singers: Whitman's Working-Class Hero from Guthrie to Springsteen* (Chapel Hill: University of North Carolina Press, 2000), 43–78. Garman emphasizes the racism and sexism underlying Whitman's notion of "artisan republicanism," which he viewed as a distinctly white and male working-class phenomenon. Echoing Whitman's own comment, Garman argues that Whitman created a hero who was "radical, but not too damned radical" (9).

41. Berkson, *Theories of Americanization*, 8; V. Brooks, *America's Coming-of-Age*, 121; Frank, *Our America*, 202–21; James Oppenheim, "Poetry—The First National Art," *Dial* 68 (February 1920): 238–42; James Oppenheim, *The Mystic Warrior* (New York: Alfred A. Knopf, 1921), n.p.; Winifred Kirkland, "Americanization and Walt Whitman," *Dial* 66 (17 May 1919): 537 ("teacher of Americanization" and "[t]he mere name" quotes), 538 ("only" and "genuine patriotism" quotes). Whitman sometimes took on a religious aura during this period; Will Hayes outrightly equated Whitman with Christ (*Walt Whitman: The Prophet of a New Era* [London: C. W. Daniel, 1921]). For more on Whitman's politics, see Charles Molesworth, "Whitman's Political Vision," *Raritan Review* 1 (Summer 1992): 98–112.

Chapter 5: *From the New Negro to* The New Negro

1. Du Bois, *The Souls of Black Folk*, in *The Oxford W. E. B. Du Bois Reader*, ed. Sundquist, 231. I omit the quotations marks around *folk*, but in my view it is, like *race*, a term possessing problematic powers of reference.

2. Bernard W. Bell, *The Afro-American Novel and Its Tradition* (Amherst: University of Massachusetts Press, 1987), 94 ("[r]ace conscious intellectuals" quote); Bernard Bell, *The Folk Roots of Contemporary Afro-American Poetry* (Detroit: Broadside, 1974), 27 ("Herder's belief" quote); H. Baker, *Modernism and the Harlem Renaissance*, 63 ("a FOLK" quote), 75 ("*radical marronage*" quote); Houston A. Baker Jr., *Afro-American Poetics: Revisions of Harlem and the Black Aesthetic* (Madison: University of Wisconsin Press, 1988), 5 ("national impulse" quote).

3. Henry Louis Gates, "Canon-Formation, Literary History, and the Afro-American Tradition: From the Seen to the Told," in *Afro-American Literary Study in the 1990s*, ed. Houston A. Baker Jr. and Patricia Redmond (Chicago: University of Chicago Press, 1989), 27 ("the black vernacular" and "isolate" quotes), 29 ("know and test" quote); Henry Louis Gates, *The Signifying Monkey: A Theory of Afro-American Literary Criticism* (New York: Oxford University Press, 1988), xii ("informs and becomes" and "repetition" quotes), xi ("revision" and "meta-discourse" quotes). See also Gates and McKay's preface, "Talking Books," to the *The Norton Anthology of African American Literature*, ed. Gates and McKay, xxvii–xli.

4. Huggins, *Harlem Renaissance,* 308–9, 361; Moses, *The Golden Age of Black Nationalism,* 101; Hazel V. Carby, *Reconstructing Womanhood: The Emergence of the Afro-American Woman Novelist* (New York: Oxford University Press, 1987), 164–65.

5. Kenneth Warren, *Black and White Strangers: Race and American Literary Realism* (Chicago: University of Chicago Press, 1993), 99; Favor, *Authentic Blackness,* 7, 8, 4, 9; Nicholls, *Conjuring the Folk,* 4, 7, 11. See also Hazel V. Carby, "Ideologies of Black Folk: The Historical Novel of Slavery," in *Slavery and the Literary Imagination: Selected Papers from the English Institute, 1987,* ed. Deborah E. McDowell and Arnold Rampersad (Baltimore: Johns Hopkins University Press, 1989), 125–43; and Robin D. G. Kelley, "Notes on Deconstructing the 'Folk,'" *American Historical Review* 97 (December 1992): 1400–1408.

6. Huggins, *Harlem Renaissance,* 308–9; Moses, *The Golden Age of Black Nationalism,* 10–11.

7. Warren, *Black and White Strangers,* 101; Favor, *Authentic Blackness,* 7.

8. Nicholls, *Conjuring the Folk,* 133–34.

9. For discussions of Locke's intellectual development, see Leonard Harris, *The Philosophy of Alain Locke: Harlem Renaissance and Beyond* (Philadelphia: Temple University Press, 1989); J. Washington, *Alain Locke and Philosophy;* Akam, "Community and Cultural Crisis"; Stewart, introduction to *Race Contacts and Interracial Relations,* xix–lix; Helbling, *The Harlem Renaissance,* 43–96; G. Hutchinson, *The Harlem Renaissance in Black and White,* 33–61; and Posnock, *Color and Culture.* Posnock argues that Locke and Kallen drew very different emphases from James: Locke developed as a cosmopolitan and "pragmatic pluralist," alert to James's "critique of identity logic," while Kallen became a "rigid pluralist," insisting that Locke organize his life around race. Kallen is, for Posnock, a forerunner of what the neoconservative cultural critic Richard Bernstein (whom Posnock cites approvingly) calls the "dictatorship of virtue" (*Color and Culture,* 191–93). An additional early influence on Locke was the Harvard philosopher Josiah Royce, whose doctrine of "wholesome provincialism," an early version of cultural pluralism, held that the nation was embodied in its regions. In *Race Questions: Provincialism and Other American Problems* (1908; reprint, Freeport, N.Y.: Books for Libraries, 1967), Royce argued that "modern race-problems" were caused "not . . . by anything which is essential to the existence or to the nature of the races of men themselves" but to "antipathies," which, while "instinctive" and "childish," were capable of supersession by reason (47–53).

10. Stewart, introduction to *Race Contacts and Interracial Relations,* xxvii–xlv. For more on Dayal, see Emily C. Brown, *Har Dayal: Hindu Revolutionary and Rationalist* (Tucson: University of Arizona Press, 1975). Locke corresponded extensively with Seme through 1925 (box 164-84, folders 32–38, Alain Locke Papers, Moorland-Spingarn Research Institute, Howard University [hereafter cited as ALP]). For more on Seme, see Moses, *The Golden Age of Black Nationalism,* 212–23. The *Oxford Cosmopolitan* was published in two issues in 1908; listed as coeditors with "A. Le R. Locke" were R. Biske and R. H. Soltau. Gustav Schmoller was a German Social Democrat who opposed left-wing agitation and cautioned against "the old extreme, passionate leaders" who attempt to "inflame the masses for revolution." Schmoller argued, "There is only one choice. We have either to crush the laborers down to the level of slavery, which is impossible, or we must

recognize their equal rights as citizens, we must improve their mental and technical training, we must permit them to organize, we must concede to them the influence which they need in order to protect their interests" ("Schmoller on Class Conflicts in General" (1904), reprinted in *American Journal of Sociology* 20 [January 1915]: 525). Schmoller was an influential figure in early-twentieth-century sociology, being one of the first to grasp the logic of Marxism in order to turn it against Marxists. Locke cited "Schmoller on Class Conflicts in General" in the bibliography to the 1916 lecture series (Locke, *The Critical Temper of Alain Locke*, ed. Stewart, 410). For more on Locke's experiences at Oxford, see Charles Molesworth, "Alain Locke and Walt Whitman: Manifestoes and National Identity," in *The Critical Pragmatism of Alain Locke: A Reader on Value Theory, Aesthetics, Community, Culture, Race, and Education*, ed. Leonard Harris (Lanham, Md.: Rowman and Littlefield, 1999), 175–89.

11. Alain Locke, "The American Temperament," *North American Review* 194 (August 1911): 262–70, reprinted in *The Critical Temper of Alain Locke*, ed. Stewart, 399–406 (quotes on 404, 400, 402). Molesworth thinks that Locke delivered an earlier version of "The American Temperament" at a meeting of the Rationalist Society at Oxford in 1909 ("Alain Locke and Walt Whitman," 177).

12. Locke, "The Great Disillusionment," 108 ("conflict . . . rival each other" quote), 107 ("pretensions . . . with the quarrel" quotes), 106 ("war to the death" quote), 110 ("in each country . . . upon its authors" quotes). Stewart comments that Locke was "the first African American to argue that imperialism caused the war (a position on which W. E. B. Du Bois would elaborate in more detail in his *Atlantic Monthly* article, 'The African Roots of the War,' eight months later") (introduction to *Race Contacts and Interracial Relations*, xl). Locke's Yonkers talk was arranged by his friend John E. Bruce (otherwise known as Bruce Grit), who encouraged Locke's early efforts to aid Arthur Schomburg in setting up his archive of materials on Negro history. Speaking of the resistance that Locke would likely encounter among Washington's blue-veined elite, Bruce noted that Locke might have to "ride roughshod" over "the Washington Negro," who "has not learned how to think black." He concluded, "The masses are hungry for his information and you may depend on them and not the classes for support and encouragement" (Bruce to Locke, 4 May 1915, box 164-17, folder 40, ALP).

13. Locke, "Race Contacts and Interracial Relations" (lecture text), 11–12 ("any true history . . . ethnic fiction" quotes), 32 ("[T]he color-line . . . Russia" quotes), 54 ("instinctive . . . it subsides" quotes), 56 ("Race groups, like class groups . . . class question, after all" quotes), 64 ("Color prejudice" quote); Locke, "Race Contacts and Inter-Racial Relations: A Study in the Theory and Practice of Race" (syllabus notes), 411 ("enigmatic . . . eradicated" quotes).

14. Locke, "Racial Progress and Race Adjustment," 84–85 ("feel that . . . the term" quotes), 86 ("What men mean" quote), 86–87 ("some reactionary nationalism. . . healthy national unity" quotes), 87 ("only kind," "civilization type," and "caste system" quotes), 88 ("We must pin . . . before or after" quote). Stewart asserts that Locke "anticipate[d] Lenin's acknowledgement in the 'Preliminary Draft Theses on the National and Colonial Questions' (1920)" (introduction to *Race Contacts and Interracial Relations*, xxvii). Crucially, the date here is inaccurate: Lenin had been writing about the similarity between African Americans and other oppressed colonial and national minorities since 1913.

15. Locke, "Racial Progress and Race Adjustment," 96 ("counter-theory" and "counter-doctrine" quotes), 97 ("This race pride . . . self-determination" and "free . . . national type" quotes), 99–100 ("The prologue" and "has been . . . reached" quotes), 98 ("the development of social solidarity," "race isolation," and "race integrity" quotes), 99 ("culture-citizenship" quote), 97 ("race types" and "civilization-type" quotes), 100 ("two heterogeneous elements" and "Whatever theory" quotes). Locke appears to have drawn the term *secondary race consciousness* from the sociologist Robert Park, who wrote that "[u]nder conditions of secondary contact, that is to say, conditions of individual liberty and individual competition, characteristic of modern civilization, depressed racial groups tend to assume the form of nationalities. A nationality in this narrower sense, may be defined as the racial group which has attained self-consciousness, no matter whether it has at the same time attained political independence or not." Clearly the word *secondary* modifies *race,* not *consciousness.* That the view of African Americans as a "nation" was not exclusive to the Left is indicated in Park's 1914 remark that "the progress of race adjustment in the Southern states since the emancipation has, on the whole, run parallel with the nationalist movement in Europe." Park noted in particular the likeness of southern Negroes to "Slavic peoples" ("Racial Assimilation in Secondary Groups: With Particular Reference to the Negro," *American Journal of Sociology* 19 [March 1914]: 606–23 [quotes on 620]). All the brackets except the opening ones in the quotations from Locke's text have been supplied by the editor Jeffrey Stewart; evidently Locke's lecture notes were somewhat fragmented.

16. Locke, "Race Contacts and Inter-Racial Relations: A Study in the Theory and Practice of Race" (syllabus notes), 411.

17. Alain Locke, "Steps toward the Negro Theatre," *Crisis* 25 (December 1922): 66–68, reprinted in *The Critical Temper of Alain Locke,* ed. Stewart, 71–73 (quote on 71); Alain Locke, "The Ethics of Culture," *Howard University Record* 17 (January 1923): 178–85, reprinted in *The Critical Temper of Alain Locke,* ed. Stewart, 415–21 (quotes on 416–17, 420).

18. Alain Locke, "The Concept of Race as Applied to Social Culture," *Howard Review* 1 (June 1924): 290–99, reprinted in *The Critical Temper of Alain Locke,* ed. Stewart, 431 ("the methodological foundation . . . *interpretation of race*" quotes), 429 ("evolutionary formula" quote), 527 ("grading of cultures" quote), 425 ("extreme cultural relativism," "denies all," "the genius," and "Nevertheless though there is" quotes), 427 ("instead of regarding culture" and "regarded as itself" quotes), 426 ("redefinition" and "the independent investigation" quotes).

19. Ibid., 428.

20. Alain Locke, review of *Public Opinion in War and Peace,* by Abbot Lawrence Lowell, *Opportunity* 1 (July 1923): 223. Regarding the Harvard scandal, see Raymond Pace Alexander, "Voices from Harvard's Own Negroes," *Opportunity* 1 (March 1923): 29–31.

21. Locke, review of *Public Opinion in War and Peace,* by Abbot Lawrence Lowell, 223. Locke's frequent contributions to *Opportunity* in 1923–24, which dealt with a broad range of issues—from the presence of African American soldiers in the Allied occupying force in the Rhineland to the importance of René Maran's *Batouala*—won him *Opportunity* editor Charles S. Johnson's appreciation as the "virtual dean" of the emerging cultural movement. See Alain Locke,

"Black Watch on the Rhine," *Opportunity* 2 (January 1924): 6–9; Alain Locke, "The Colonial Literature of France," *Opportunity* 1 (November 1923): 331–35; and Anonymous, "The Debut of the Younger School of Negro Writers," *Opportunity* 2 (May 1924): 143. Several of Locke's *Opportunity* essays foreshadowed positions he would elaborate in *The New Negro*. See, for example, "Roland Hayes: An Appreciation," *Opportunity* 1 (December 1923): 356–58; and "A Note on African Art," *Opportunity* 2 (May 1924): 134–38. For more on the political forces at Howard University pushing Locke toward conservatism, see Stewart, introduction to *Race Contacts and Interracial Relations*, xlii; and Logan, *Howard University*, 84–89, 101–9.

22. For more on Du Bois and the notion of folk as "genius," see Moses, *The Golden Age of Black Nationalism*, 50–52; Helbling, *The Harlem Renaissance*, 19–42; Lewis, *W. E. B. Du Bois*, 170–74; and Sundquist, *To Wake the Nations*, 462–83.

23. Alain Locke, "Harlem," *Survey Graphic* 53 (March 1925): 629–30.

24. Alain Locke, foreword to *The New Negro*, ed. Locke, xxv.

25. Ibid., xxvi–xxvii.

26. Alain Locke, "Negro Youth Speaks," in *The New Negro*, ed. Locke, 47.

27. Ibid., 51.

28. Alain Locke, "The Negro Spirituals," in *The New Negro*, ed. Locke, 199–213 (quote on 199). Locke was by no means original in his designation of the spirituals as American folk music. Henry Edward Krehbiel, author of *Afro-American Folksong: A Study in Racial and National Music* (New York: G. Schirmer, 1914), was the most famous among many early-twentieth-century students of the folk making this claim. See also John W. Work, "Negro Folk Song," *Opportunity* 1 (October 1923): 292–94.

29. Alain Locke, "Legacy of the Ancestral Arts," in *The New Negro*, ed. Locke, 254–68 (quotes on 254–55, 267).

30. Outline of "The Survey Graphic *Harlem Issue*," reel 39, part 1, Survey Associates. "The Mirrors of Harlem"—subtitled "Studies in 'Colored' Psycho-Analysis"—was the name of a series of satirical pieces by Floyd J. Calvin that appeared in the *Messenger* in late 1922 and 1923. In January 1924, Walrond published a sketch on Harlem called "The Black City" that may have prompted Locke to think of him as a contributor to the special Harlem issue ("The Black City," *Messenger* 6 [January 1924]: 13–14). Two letters between Locke and Kellogg suggest that Rebecca West's contribution would have been highly valued (Locke to Kellogg, 5 April 1924, and Kellogg to Locke, 7 April 1924, reel 39, part 1, Survey Associates). Although Kellogg purported to be concerned about the length of the third section, he also suggested that the special Harlem issue contain a piece by Mary Austin, hardly a proponent of advanced racial views (Kellogg to Locke, 10 May 1924, reel 39, part 1, Survey Associates). For more on Austin, see chapter 3. The number of words designated for the invited participants' contributions ranged from 2,000 to 3,600. A. Philip Randolph had been invited to participate but had refused. Locke wrote to Kellogg, "I regret this declination of Randolph's," and he would later complain to Langston Hughes that Randolph had "refused to write it for me, and then accused me of being a snob and leaving the proletariat out" (Locke to Kellogg, n.d., reel 39, part 1, Survey Associates; Locke to Hughes, 5 February 1927, box 164-38, folder 3, ALP). Locke's injured stance was disingenuous, because

he had already excluded a statement by one prominent black Socialist. Since Randolph viewed Harrison as a valued mentor, the exclusion of Harrison's piece from the *Survey Graphic* may have influenced Randolph's decision to reject the invitation to contribute to *The New Negro*. It must also be remembered, though, that by the time the special Harlem issue and *The New Negro* appeared, Randolph and the *Messenger* had abandoned much of their earlier radicalism. Although Locke had published a review of Lothrop Stoddard's *New World of Islam* in the *Messenger* in May 1923, relations between Randolph and Locke had probably worn thin by the May 1924 appearance of a "Shafts and Darts" *Messenger* column by George Schuyler and Theophilus Lewis, who awarded the "monthly prize" to Locke, saying, "We experience the great pleasure this month of awarding the elegantly embossed and beautifully lacquered dill pickle to Prof. Altin [*sic*] LeRoy Locke, high priest of the intellectual snobbocracy" for having recently "unburdened his chest of the following gust of flubdubbery": "*Counterassertions against the whites will only generate more prejudice. You must ignore it* and get down to the practical job of working into the American standard of living according to our *separate* capacities. (Italics are ours.) As we go to press it is rumored that the K.K.K. and other patriotic 'Nordics' are considering the presentation of a well-filled purse to the eminent sage because of this 'unconditional surrender' advice" ("The Monthly Prize," "Shafts and Darts," *Messenger* 6 [May 1924]: 183).

31. Kelly Miller, "The Harvest of Race Prejudice," *Survey Graphic* 53 (March 1925): 682–83, 711–12 (quotes on 683); Eunice Hunton, "Breaking Through," *Survey Graphic* 53 (March 1925): 684; Winthrop D. Lane, "Ambushed in the City: The Grim Side of Harlem," *Survey Graphic* 53 (March 1925): 692–94, 713–15; Rudolph Fisher, "The South Lingers On," *Survey Graphic* 53 (March 1925): 644–47 (quote on 646). For further discussion of some of the changes Locke wrought in turning "Harlem: Mecca of the New Negro" into *The New Negro*, see Charles Scruggs, *The Sage in Harlem: H. L. Mencken and the Black Writers of the 1920s* (Baltimore: Johns Hopkins University Press, 1984), 93–94; Sieglinde Lemke, *Primitive Modernism: Black Culture and the Origins of Transatlantic Modernism* (New York: Oxford University Press, 1998), 120–28; and Balshaw, *Looking for Harlem*, 20–23.

32. Jessie Fauset, "The Gift of Laughter," in *The New Negro*, ed. Locke, 161–67 (quotes on 161); Montgomery Gregory, "The Drama of Negro Life," in *The New Negro*, ed. Locke, 153–60 (quotes on 153).

33. Walter White, "Color Lines," *Survey Graphic* 53 (March 1925): 680–82; Walter White, "The Paradox of Color," in *The New Negro*, ed. Locke, 361–68; James Weldon Johnson, "The Making of Harlem," *Survey Graphic* 53 (March 1925): 630–39; James Weldon Johnson, "Harlem: The Culture Capital," in *The New Negro*, ed. Locke, 301–11 (quote on 311); Charles S. Johnson, "Black Workers in the City," *Survey Graphic* 53 (March 1925): 641–43, 718–21 (quote on 721); Charles S. Johnson, "The New Frontage on Negro Life," in *The New Negro*, ed. Locke, 278–98 (quote on 298). As various commentators have noted, the graphics in the two versions of the anthology were quite different. Although the Winold Reiss drawings were featured in both, in the *Survey Graphic* they tended to be clustered together in subject matter (four drawings of Negro women, for example, followed Hunton's essay and preceded Elise J. McDougald's). In addition, the book-length anthology featured many Afrocentric drawings by Aaron Douglas that gave the text

a markedly primitivist cast. Apparently Locke arranged for the models for Reiss's portraits of Negro women to be brought to Reiss's studio; one of the models was McDougald (Locke to Kellogg, n.d., reel 39, part 1, Survey Associates).

34. Elise J. McDougald, "The Double Task: The Struggle of the Negro Woman for Sex and Race Emancipation," *Survey Graphic* 53 (March 1925): 689–91 (quote on 689); Elise J. McDougald, "The Task of Negro Womanhood," in *The New Negro,* ed. Locke, 369–82 (quote on 371–72). McDougald, a vocational guidance counselor in the New York City public schools, had published a piece entitled "The Schools and the Vocational Life of Negroes" two years before (*Opportunity* 1 [June 1923]: 2). Locke probably played a direct role in the revision of McDougald's essay, for Kellogg congratulated him on having "lifted it to an altogether new significance" (Kellogg to Locke, 9 October 1925, reel 39, part 1, Survey Associates).

35. W. A. Domingo, "The Tropics in New York," *Survey Graphic* 53 (March 1925): 648–50 (quote on 648); W. A. Domingo, "Gift of the Black Tropics," in *The New Negro,* ed. Locke, 341–49 (quote on 341); W. A. Domingo, "Restricted West Indian Immigration and the American Negro," *Opportunity* 2 (October 1924): 298–99 (quote on 299).

36. Konrad Bercovici, "The Rhythm of Harlem," *Survey Graphic* 53 (March 1925): 679; Albert C. Barnes, "Negro Art and America," in *The New Negro,* ed. Locke, 19–25 (quotes on 19, 20, 25). For more on Barnes, a wealthy art collector, see Helbling, *The Harlem Renaissance,* 69–96, as well as Hughes's account of Locke's introducing him to Barnes in *The Big Sea,* 184–86. That Barnes's cult of the primitive cannot be attributed solely to his own whiteness is indicated by J. A. Rogers's "Jazz at Home," in which jazz is viewed as "atavistically African," expressive of "Negro rhythm," and "a balm for modern ennui, . . . a safety valve for modern machine-ridden and convention-bound society, . . . a revolt of the emotions against repression" (*The New Negro,* ed. Locke, 220, 217).

37. Melville J. Herskovits, "The Negro's Americanism," in *The New Negro,* ed. Locke, 353–60 (quote on 353–54). Herskovits had adumbrated an earlier version of this piece in "The Racial Hysteria," *Opportunity* 2 (June 1924): 166–68. For more on Herskovits's dramatic reversal of position on African survivals in African American culture, see Walter Jackson, "Melville Herskovits and the Search for Afro-American Culture," in *Malinowski, Rivers, Benedict, and Others: Essays on Culture and Personality,* ed. George W. Stocking Jr. (Madison: University of Wisconsin Press, 1986), 95–126; and Helbling, *The Harlem Renaissance,* 69–96, 159–90. For more on the Locke-Herskovits relationship, see Helbling, *The Harlem Renaissance,* 53–59.

38. Paul U. Kellogg, "Negro Pioneers," in *The New Negro,* ed. Locke, 271–77; Kellogg to Locke, n.d., box 164-88, folder 7, ALP. For more on Kellogg, particularly his advocacy of Woodrow Wilson's brand of self-determination, see Clarke A. Chambers, *Paul U. Kellogg and the "Survey": Voices for Social Welfare and Social Justice* (Minneapolis: University of Minnesota Press, 1971), especially 62–92. The New Negro issue of March 1925 had been preceded by the New Ireland issue of November 1921, the New Russia issue of March 1923, and the New Mexico issue of May 1924.

39. Kellogg, "Negro Pioneers," 271, 273, 277.

40. Locke to Kellogg, 8 October 1925, reel 39, part 1, Survey Associates.

41. Locke to Kellogg, 17 February 1925, ibid; W. E. B. Du Bois, "The Black Man

Brings His Gifts," *Survey Graphic* 53 (March 1925): 655–57, 710; W. E. B. Du Bois, "The Negro Mind Reaches Out," in *The New Negro,* ed. Locke, 385–414; Robert R. Moton, "Hampton-Tuskegee: Missioners of the Masses," in *The New Negro,* ed. Locke, 23–32.

42. Alain Locke, Editorial Comment, *Survey Graphic* 53 (March 1925): 676.

43. Lemke, *Primitive Modernism,* 123–24; Astrid Franke, "Struggling with Stereotypes: The Problems of Representing a Collective Identity," in *The Critical Pragmatism of Alain Locke,* ed. Harris, 23, 24, 34; Christopher M. Mott, "The Art of Self-Promotion; or, Which Self to Sell? The Proliferation and Disintegration of the Harlem Renaissance," in *Marketing Modernisms: Self-Promotion, Canonization, Rereading,* ed. Kevin H. Dettmar and Stephen Watt (Ann Arbor: University of Michigan Press, 1996), 255.

44. Leonard Harris, "Identity: Alain Locke's Atavism," *Transactions of the Charles S. Peirce Society* 24 (Winter 1988): 67–88 (quotes on 67–69); Nancy Fraser, "Another Pragmatism: Alain Locke, Critical 'Race' Theory, and the Politics of Culture," in *The Critical Pragmatism of Alain Locke,* ed. Harris, 14–16, 18.

45. Locke included in the *Survey Graphic* version of the anthology only "The Song of the Son." Although Toomer would subsequently charge that Locke had published parts of *Cane* in *The New Negro* without his permission, a letter from Locke to Kellogg—undated, but apparently written while he was planning the book version of the anthology—would suggest otherwise. "Enclosed reply from Toomer," wrote Locke. "I think we shall have something new yet. If not will be using, with permission Song of the Son from Cane" (Locke to Kellogg, n.d., reel 39, part 1, Survey Associates). A discussion of Toomer's "Georgia Dusk" and "The Song of the Son" will be included in a future volume.

46. Countée Cullen, "Fruit of the Flower," in *The New Negro,* ed. Locke, 132.

47. Countée Cullen, "To a Brown Boy," in *The New Negro,* ed. Locke, 129.

48. Countée Cullen, "In Memory of Colonel Charles Young," in *The New Negro,* ed. Locke, 133; A. Philip Randolph and Chandler Owen, "Colonel Charles Young," *Messenger* 2 (February 1920): 13. Du Bois, eulogizing Young at his funeral, concluded "after reviewing the military career of Col. Young, . . . that he had died of a broken heart" ("Colonel Charles Young, U.S.A.," *Opportunity* 1 [July 1923]: 218–19). Cullen apparently demanded that he be compensated more generously than other poets for his contributions; Locke, writing to Kellogg about the "Cullen incident," complained of the poet's "childishness" (Locke to Kellogg, n.d., reel 39, part 1, Survey Associates).The version of "Heritage" included in both the special Harlem issue and *The New Negro* did not close with the final italicized stanza ending with the highly ironic words, *"Not yet has my heart or head / In the least way realized / They and I are civilized"* (*My Soul's High Song: The Collected Writings of Countée Cullen, Voice of the Harlem Renaissance,* ed. Gerald Early [New York: Anchor Books, 1991], 108).

49. Anne Spencer, "Lady, Lady," in *The New Negro,* ed. Locke, 148. Laura Hapke points out that "[i]nstead of the cry for justice at the heart of Langston Hughes's 'Song of a Negro Wash-Woman,'" Locke chose the pedestrian message of the undistinguished Anne Spencer poem entitled, without irony, "Lady, Lady," in which "very old-fashioned structure and formal diction work against [the poem's] allusion to the work-bleached hands of the black laundress" (*Labor's Text: The Worker in American Fiction* [New Brunswick, N.J.: Rutgers University Press, 2001], 210).

50. Langston Hughes, "An Earth Song," in *The New Negro*, ed. Locke, 142. It appears that, in Locke's original conception, the only Hughes poem to be included in the anthology would have been "Our Land" (Outline, n.d., accompanying Locke to Kellogg, n.d. [1924], reel 39, part 1, Survey Associates).

51. Langston Hughes, "I Too," in *The New Negro*, ed. Locke, 145. For a discussion of Hughes's attachment to Whitman, see Garman, *A Race of Singers*, 67–71. While the leftist poems by Hughes cited here—as well as "Song to a Negro Wash-woman"—all appeared in early 1925 and could not have been included in the *Survey Graphic* version of the anthology, they were all available for inclusion in *The New Negro*. "Song to a Negro Wash-woman" was published in the *Crisis* in January 1925; "Johannesburg Mines" and "Steel Mills" both first appeared in the *Messenger* in February 1925; "God to Hungry Child" and "Rising Waters" appeared, respectively, in the March 1925 and April 1925 issues of the *Workers Monthly*. "Steel Mills," Hughes wrote in *The Big Sea*, had been composed when he was still in high school (29).

52. Claude MacKay, "White Houses," in *The New Negro*, ed. Locke, 134; Claude McKay, "Like a Strong Tree," in *The New Negro*, ed. Locke, 134. McKay was greatly angered by Locke's unilateral decision to change the name of "The White House" to "White Houses," writing to Locke that in so doing he had "destroyed every vestige of intellectual and fraternal understanding" between the two (McKay to Locke, n.d., box 164-67, folder 8, ALP). McKay and Locke also tangled over Locke's reluctance to publish McKay's "Mulatto." As initially conceived, the special Harlem issue would have contained only one poem by McKay, the harshly ironic "America" (Outline, n.d., accompanying Locke to Kellogg, n.d. [1924], reel 39, part 1, Survey Associates).

53. Rampersad, introduction to *The New Negro*, ed. Locke, xix; Du Bois, "The Negro Mind Reaches Out," 407, 408, 412.

54. Du Bois, "The Negro Mind Reaches Out," 385–86.

55. Ibid., 413–14.

56. Yekutiel Gershoni, *Black Colonialism: The Americo-Liberian Scramble for the Hinterland* (Boulder: Westview, 1985), 63, 88. George Hutchinson—to whom I am indebted for this insight regarding Liberia—points out that "the very attempt to reach beyond national boundaries, in what is easily the most radical essay in *The New Negro*, is shadowed—no, absolutely formed—by the very structure of American ideology at its most exceptionalist" (*The Harlem Renaissance in Black and White*, 431).

INDEX

Abramowitz, Howard, 73
Adorno, Theodor, 70, 121, 248
AFL. *See* American Federation of Labor
Africa, 16, 65, 119, 123, 148–49, 238, 246; colonialism and, 126, 245; diaspora and, 15
African American soldiers, 13, 18, 19, 51, 66, 239; lynching of, 24, 26, 41
African American writers. *See* specific writers
African Blood Brotherhood (ABB), 18, 22, 43, 46, 102, 105; black nationalism of, 61–63; communism of, 61–68; *Crusader* as organ of, 18; Du Bois denounced by, 63; internationalism of, 62–63; on race, 102; on working-class unity, 63–64, 66. *See also* Briggs, Cyril V.; *Crusader*; Moore, Richard B.
"African Chief" (Edwards), 47
"African Roots of War, The" (Du Bois), 32, 244
"Aftermath" (Burrill), 41
Against Race (Gilroy) 166, 167
Alaily, H. E., 205
Aldrich, Thomas Bailey, 125
"Alien, The" (Poole), 188
"Alien" (Wood), 192–93
Allen, Theodore, 72–73
"Ambushed in the City" (Lane), 226
America: A Family Matter (Gould), 144
America Comes of Age (Siegfried), 144
American exceptionalism, 108–9,

173, 197, 212, 294n. 56; consensus paradigm and, 71–72
American Federation of Labor (AFL), 10, 14, 40, 60, 73, 90, 110
American Hebrew (journal), 173–74, 175
American Indians. *See* Native Americans
Americanism: Communists and, 113–20; Kallen and, 172–73; *Liberator* radicals and, 187–97; linked with land ownership, 146–47; Locke and, 212, 217–24; metonymic nationalism and, 160–61; New Negro and, 1–2, 18–20; Randolph and Owen and, 52–53, 108–13; Socialist Party and, 106–13; Whitman and, 194–95
—100 percent, 139, 144, 158, 179, 199, 247; anti-Semitism and, 132; "bad" nationalism and, 80; culture and, 148; metonymic nationalism and, 159, 162–63, 168; nativism and eugenics in, 130
Americanism and Social Democracy (Spargo), 106
Americanization, 137–40, 168–70
"Americanization Studies" (Berkson), 169–70
"Americanizing Haiti" (Foley), 188
American Plan, 15, 106, 140, 175, 255n. 14
Americans (Sherman), 136
"American Temperament, The" (Locke), 206
America's Coming-of-Age (Brooks), 176

McKay, Claude, 2, 30, 77, 84, 85,
257n. 22, 260–61n. 44, 261n. 46,
271n. 39, 272n. 44; Baker on, 3;
Call and, 83; on ideology of racism, 102, 103–4; *Liberator* and, 42–
43, 83; Locke and, 241–44; Miller
on, 5; pro-Soviet and anticolonialist poems of, 242; sonnets of, 53,
58; USSR and, 22, 28
Meier, August, 17
Melting-Pot (journal), 10, 119
Melting Pot, The (Zangwill), 140
Melting-pot trope, 133, 136, 140–41,
169, 227, 236. *See also* Cultural
pluralism
Mencken, H. L., 31
Messenger (magazine), 4, 47, 48, 50–
61, 64, 66–67, 86, 101, 227, 264n.
61; on American exceptionalism,
108–9; Bogalusa and, 50–51; on
Bolshevik Revolution, 50; cover art
from, 107, 111, 144; *Crusader* and,
67, 68; Du Bois in, 34, 40; graphics
of, 52–53, 54–58; on internationalism, 49–50; Johnson's essay and,
227–28; labor competition and, 95,
96–98; on lynching and patriotism,
106; McKay and, 242; nationalism
and, 108–12;47; on "Old Crowd"
Negroes, 51, 55; poems in, 53, 58–
59, 237; praise of, 24–25, 30; scientific racism and, 271n. 41; SPA
and, 58–61; on World War I, 51,
105–6, 108–9. *See also* Owen,
Chandler; Randolph, A. Philip
Metonymic nationalism, 160–68,
175, 218, 244, 247–48; "bad" and
"good," 166–67; class-collaborationist character of, 160–61; cultural pluralism and, 161–62, 163;
diaspora and, 166–67; folk in, 235;
Hughes and, 241; identity politics
and, 161–62, 166–67; internationalism and, 163, 167; metaphor and,
161; "Negro Pioneers" and, 232;
New Negro and, 235; 100 percent
Americanism and, 154, 163, 168;
organic trope and, 162, 164–66;
176; self-determinationist, 166;

Whitman and, 194–97. *See also*
Cultural pluralism; Nationalism
Metonymy: and metaphor, 161–62,
281n. 2
Michaels, Walter Benn, 172, 173
Migration north. *See* Great Migration
Miller, Herbert A., 170
Miller, James A., 5, 16, 43, 75
Miller, Kelly, 18, 19, 52, 60, 225–26
Mind of Primitive Man, The (Boas),
148–49, 152
Minor, Robert, 10, 41, 42, 84, 108,
188
"Mob Victim, The" (Williams), 57
Modernism, 73–74, 75, 76, 81, 182
Modernist (magazine), 1, 130
Montgomery, David, 9, 73, 75, 90
Monticello, Ga. *See* "Death farm"
Moore, Richard B., 18, 19, 61–62, 63,
105, 133
Moorland, Jesse, 24
Morgan, Henry Lewis, 87, 173
Moses, Wilson, 15, 200, 202, 203
"Moses That Was to Have Been,
The" (cartoon), 65
Moton, Robert Russa, 18, 26, 110,
134, 256n. 19, 273n. 50, 277n. 16;
Locke and, 233–34
Mott, Christopher, 236
Mulattoes, 32, 123, 124, 133–34, 150,
277–78n. 17
Mulatto in the United States, The
(Reuter), 133–35
Multiculturalism, 161–62, 212, 283n.
14. *See also* Cultural pluralism
Multiracial solidarity, 3, 26, 110–12
Mumford, Lewis, 176, 177
Munson, Gorham, 176, 178, 284n. 18

NAACP. *See* National Association
for the Advancement of Colored
People
Nation, 160, 167, 200, 211, 223;
equated with race, 140–46; as
ideological construct, 117; and organic trope, 180–82; as organic
unit, 120–21, 123, 156; as *patria*,
157, 165
Nation (magazine), 9, 20, 31, 40, 66–